The Reports Of The Magicians And Astrologers Of Nineveh And Babylon In The British Museum

Luzac's

Semitic Text and Translation Series.

Vol. VII.

Luzac's Semitic Text and Translation Series.

VOL. I: THE LAUGHABLE STORIES COLLECTED BY BAR-HEBRÆUS. Syriac Text and Translation. By E. A. Wallis Budge. 21*s.*

VOL. II: THE LETTERS AND INSCRIPTIONS OF HAMMURABI. Vol. I: Introduction and Babylonian Texts. By L. W. King. 21*s.*

VOL. III: THE LETTERS AND INSCRIPTIONS OF HAMMURABI. Vol. II: Babylonian Texts continued. By L. W. King. (*Nearly ready.*)

VOL. IV: THE HISTORY OF THE VIRGIN MARY, AND THE HISTORY OF THE LIKENESS OF CHRIST. Vol. I: Syriac Texts. By E. A. Wallis Budge. 12*s.* 6*d.*

VOL. V: THE HISTORY OF THE VIRGIN MARY, AND THE HISTORY OF THE LIKENESS OF CHRIST. Vol. II: English Translations. By E. A. Wallis Budge. 10*s.* 6*d.*

VOL. VI: THE REPORTS OF THE MAGICIANS AND ASTROLOGERS OF NINEVEH AND BABYLON. Vol. I: Cuneiform Texts. By R. C. Thompson. 12*s.* 6*d.*

VOL. VII: THE REPORTS OF THE MAGICIANS AND ASTROLOGERS OF NINEVEH AND BABYLON. Vol. II: English Translation and Transliteration. By R. C. Thompson. 12*s.* 6*d.*

VOL. VIII: THE LETTERS AND INSCRIPTIONS OF HAMMURABI. Vol. III: Translation and Transliteration. By L. W. King. (*Nearly ready.*)

VOL. IX: THE HISTORY OF RABBAN HORMIZD. Vol. I: Syriac Text. By E. A. Wallis Budge. (*In the Press.*)

VOL. X: THE HISTORY OF RABBAN HORMIZD. Vol. II: English Translation. By E. A. Wallis Budge. (*In the Press.*)

THE REPORTS

OF THE

MAGICIANS AND ASTROLOGERS

OF

NINEVEH AND BABYLON.

THE REPORTS

OF THE

MAGICIANS AND ASTROLOGERS

OF

NINEVEH AND BABYLON

IN THE BRITISH MUSEUM.

THE ORIGINAL TEXTS, PRINTED IN CUNEIFORM CHARACTERS, EDITED WITH TRANSLATIONS, NOTES, VOCABULARY, INDEX, AND AN INTRODUCTION.

BY

R. CAMPBELL THOMPSON, B.A. (CANTAB.),

ASSISTANT IN THE DEPARTMENT OF EGYPTIAN AND ASSYRIAN ANTIQUITIES, BRITISH MUSEUM

VOL. II.

ENGLISH TRANSLATIONS, VOCABULARY, ETC.

London:
LUZAC AND Co.
1900.

HARRISON AND SONS,
PRINTERS IN ORDINARY TO HER MAJESTY,
ST. MARTIN'S LANE, LONDON.

TO

FREDERICK WILLIAM WALKER, M.A.,

HIGH MASTER OF ST. PAUL'S SCHOOL,

A MARK OF GRATITUDE

FOR MUCH ENCOURAGEMENT, HELP,

AND KINDNESS.

Preface.

Since the year 1865, when the late Rev. Edward Hincks, one of the early pioneers of the science of Assyriology, first made known to the world the existence of Assyrian tablets inscribed with texts relating partly to astrology and partly to what we now call astronomy, students have devoted much time to the investigation of this class of documents. Prof. Jules Oppert and the late François Lenormant still further advanced our knowledge of astrological and other cognate texts in a series of learned papers, but it was not until the publication of Prof. Sayce's paper, entitled "The Astronomy and Astrology of the Babylonians," that any very considerable progress was made in this difficult branch of Assyriology. It is true that the cuneiform texts which formed the base of this work had already been published by Sir Henry Rawlinson in the third volume of the "Cuneiform Inscriptions of Western Asia," but Prof. Sayce was the first to show the general drift and meaning of their contents, and to enable us to appreciate the accuracy of the traditions of Greek and Roman writers on Babylonian astrology and astronomy.

With the view of supplementing the labours of the above mentioned scholars, I have printed in the first volume of this work, in cuneiform type, the texts of about two hundred and eighty Astrological Reports, of which only about fifty have hitherto been published. It is hoped that this mass of new material will be useful to Assyriologists, who will now, if we may judge from the descriptions of the tablets of the Kuyunjik Collection given by Dr. Bezold in his "Catalogue," have before them the texts of the complete series of the Reports found at Nineveh. In the second volume I have given transliterations of these texts, and, wherever possible, translations; where translations have been impossible, owing to breaks or the occurrence of words unknown to me, I have made no attempt to render them in English. Of the duplicate texts, about two hundred and twenty in number, the transliterations only have been given. All important variants have been added in the Notes to the translations.

It is unnecessary to insist upon the importance of the texts herein published, but it may be pointed out that the glosses and explanations of difficult phrases, which they frequently give, are of the highest value philologically, and they certainly throw considerable light on the professional methods adopted by the early Mesopotamian astrologers. Moreover, it is probable that a number of the astrological reports were written with the special object of informing the king and his people whether certain months would or would not contain thirty days, and if this be so, we may eventually find it necessary to modify our views concerning the lengths of the various months of the Assyrian year. This point is more fully treated in the Introduction.

In conclusion, my thanks are due to Dr. E. A. Wallis Budge for his valuable help, and to Mr. L. W. King for many useful suggestions.

R. CAMPBELL THOMPSON.

London, March 1st, 1900.

Contents.

Introduction.

For more than two thousand years the records of Babylonian and Assyrian astronomy lay buried and forgotten under the ruins of Assyrian palaces, and all that was known of the subject came from a few passages in the Bible and in the works of Greek and Roman writers. To the Hebrews the sorceries of Babylon were an accursed thing, and the prophet Isaiah[1] scoffs at them in these words: "Stand now with thine enchantments, and with the multitude of thy sorceries, wherein thou hast laboured from thy youth; if so be thou shalt be able to profit, if so be thou mayest prevail. Thou art wearied in the multitude of thy counsels. Let now the astrologers, the stargazers, the monthly prognosticators, stand up, and save thee from these things that shall come upon thee." Among Greek writers Strabo[2] (died A.D. 24) asserted that the Chaldeans were skilled in astronomy and the casting of horoscopes, and Aelian[3] (3rd century A.D.) mentions the fact that both the Babylonians and Chaldeans enjoyed a reputation for possessing a knowledge of astronomy. Achilles Tatius[4] (6th century) reports the

[1] Isaiah xlvii, 12. [2] xvi, 1, 6.
[3] xxii, *ed.* Hercher, Paris.
[4] *Ex Achille Tatio Isagoge, ed.* Petav., 1.

existence of a tradition to the effect that the Egyptians mapped the heavens, and that they inscribed their knowledge on their pillars; the same tradition declared that the Chaldeans claimed the glory of this science, the foundation of which they attributed to the god Bel. For this last belief there seems to be some evidence in a statement of Berosus,[1] to the effect that the god Bel created the stars and sun and moon, and the five planets. Diodorus Siculus,[2] a contemporary of Augustus, tells us that the Babylonian priests observed the position of certain stars in order to cast horoscopes, and that they interpreted dreams and derived omens from the movement of birds and from eclipses and earthquakes. The general evidence of serious writers leads us to believe that astrology formed part of the religious system of the Babylonians, and it certainly exercised considerable influence over the minds of the dwellers between the Tigris and the Euphrates. In any case, the reputation of the Chaldeans, *i.e.*, the Babylonians and Assyrians, for possessing magical powers was so widespread, that the very name Chaldean at a comparatively early date became synonymous with magician. From Mesopotamia, by way of Greece and Rome, a certain amount of Babylonian astrology made its way among the nations of the West, and it is quite probable that many superstitions which we commonly regard as the peculiar product of Western civilisation, took their

[1] *Ancient Fragments, ed.* Cory, *p.* 28.

[2] ii, 29.

origin from those of the early dwellers on the alluvial lands of Mesopotamia.

At the time when the astrological forecasts printed in this book were composed, the district of Babylon, where they were written, was bounded on the north-west by Akkad, on the north-east by Subarti, on the south-east by Elam, and on the south-west by Aḫarrû; in other words, Babylonia was open to invasion on every side. The astrologer or the prophet who could foretell fair things for the nation, or disasters and calamities for their enemies, was a man whose words were regarded with reverence and awe. They were written down as treasures to be preserved for all time and to serve as models for the benefit of his successors in office. The soothsayer was as much a politician as the statesman, and he was not slow in using the indications of political changes to point the moral of his astrological observations. Thus the so-called astrological forecasts contain elements which it will be impossible for the modern student to explain until the complete history of the political relationship of Babylonia with her neighbours is fully known. Nothing was too great or too small to become the subject of an astrological forecast, and every event, from a national calamity such as famine or disaster to the army, down to the appearance of the humblest peasant's last born child, was seriously considered and proved to be the result of causes which had already been duly recognised.

When Assurbanipal, king of Assyria, B.C. 668-

626, added to the royal library at Nineveh, his contribution of tablets included many series of documents which related exclusively to the astrology of the ancient Babylonians, who in turn had borrowed it with modifications from the Sumerian invaders of the country. Among these must be mentioned the Series which was commonly called "The Day of Bel," and which was declared by the learned of the time to have been written in the time of the great Sargon I, king of Agade, *c.* 3800 B.C. With such ancient works as these to guide them, the profession of deducing omens from daily events reached such a pitch of importance in the last Assyrian Empire, that a system of making periodical reports came into being, and by these the king was informed of all occurrences in the heavens and on the earth, and the results of astrological studies in respect to future events. The heads of the astrological profession were men of high rank and position, and their office was hereditary (*see* Diod., II, 29). Under the chief astrologer were a number of officials who on certain occasions together addressed the king; thus Rammânu-šuma-uṣur, Nabû-mušíṣi and Ištar-šuma-iriš write together (*see* K. 5470); Rammânu-šuma-uṣur and Marduk-šakin-šumi write together (*see* KK. 1087, 1197); Rammânu-šuma-uṣur, Arad-Ía, Ištar-šuma-íriš and Akkulanu write together (*see* K. 1428); Ištar-šuma-íriš, Rammânu-šuma-uṣur and Marduk-šakin-šumi write together (*see* K. 527); and Balasî and Nabû-aḫí-íriba write together (*see* KK. 565, 569). Among other duties, it was the duty of the astrologers to write both omen reports and letters, and certain letters mention, incidentally, facts which we should hardly expect to find in this class of document. Thus the writer of K. 167 excuses himself from setting out on a journey because the day is not favourable; the writer of K. 551 tells the story of how a fox made its way into the Royal Park of the city of Assur and took refuge in a lake, but was afterwards caught and killed; and the writer of Rm. 73 tells the king that he believes the twentieth, twenty-second and twenty-fifth days to be lucky for entering into contracts.

The variety of the information contained in these reports is best gathered from the fact that they were sent from cities so far removed from each other as Assur in the north and Erech in the south, and it can only be assumed that they were dispatched by runners or men mounted on swift horses. As reports also come from Dilbat, Kutha, Nippur and Borsippa, all cities of ancient foundation, the king was probably well acquainted with the general course of events in his empire.

Of the documents printed in this book all but three are astrological; they are written on rectangular clay tablets varying in size from $1\frac{1}{2}$ by $\frac{3}{4}$ inch to $3\frac{3}{4}$ by $2\frac{1}{4}$, and they generally bear the sender's name. They contain quotations from ancient astrological works concerning the omens, but it is interesting to note that, although the *ipsissima verba* were preserved, the interpretations were based upon more modern lines. Thus Aḫarrû originally meant the land which lay close to Babylonia on the west, but as the Babylonian power extended the boundaries of the country, Aḫarrû became a name synonymous with Phœnicia and Palestine, and it is in this sense that it is used by the astrologers of the later kingdom. Again, Subartu originally meant a certain district in Northern Babylonia, but in later times it came to mean Assyria proper, and one astrologer, writing in Assyrian, says "We are Subartu." The astronomical reports, which we may subsequently find to have been prepared for use in some way by the astrologers, have been omitted from this volume, because they partake of the nature of letters. We may, however, call attention in passing to those which were sent by Nabûa of the city of Assur to Nineveh, for they concern the movements of the Sun and Moon. Thus in K. 603 he reports that the Sun and Moon were seen together on the fourteenth day of the month, and another report of his states that "we saw the Moon on the twenty-ninth day."

From certain passages in the astrological tablets it is easy to see that the calculation of times and seasons was one of the chief duties of the astrologer in Mesopotamia, and it seems probable that they were acquainted with some kind of machine for reckoning time. In No. 170 (*see* p. lxii) mention is made of an instrument called *abkallu šiḳla*, to which the name *Bêl-riminû-uḳarrad-Marduk* was given. Now the words *abkallu šiḳla* mean "measure-governor," and it is probable that they indicate the existence of a kind of clock. It must not be forgotten too, that Sextus Empiricus (*Adv. Math.* 21) states that the clepsydra was known to the Chaldeans. Herodotus too, (ii, 109), says that the Greeks borrowed certain measures of time from the Babylonians, and from the tablet 83–1–18,247, *etc.*, we learn that the Babylonians actually had a time measure by which they divided the day and the night. This measure was called *Kasbu*, and contained two hours; two *kaṣbu* formed a watch, and three watches made up the night. These facts are proved by the report quoted above, in which we are told that in such and such a day in Nisan the day and night were balanced, there being six *kasbu* of the day and six *kasbu* of the night, the allusion being, of course, to the vernal equinox.

We know from several sources that the Assyrian year consisted of twelve months, each containing usually thirty days, and an intercalary month called the "second Adar" (the Ve'Adar of the Hebrews): the Babylonian year consisted of the same number of months, but two intercalary months, Elul and Adar, were added.

The examination of the texts edited in this volume indicates that the Assyrians, like the Babylonians, had a year composed of lunar months,[1] and it seems that the object of the astrological reports which relate to

[1] On this subject see Oppert, *Zeitschrift für Assyriologie*; *Bd.* XI, p. 310, *Bd.* XII, p. 97; and Lehmann, *ibid. Bd.* XI, p. 432.

the appearance of the Moon and Sun was to help to determine and foretell the length of the lunar month. If this be so, the year in common use throughout Assyria must have been lunar. The calendar assigns to each month thirty full days; the lunar month is, however, little more than twenty-nine and a half days; therefore some of the calendar months must consist of twenty-nine days only. In proof of this statement, I submit the following facts. On No. 171 (*see* p. lxii), which is a report from Balasî, we read, "When the Moon does not wait for the Sun" such and such things will happen. The prediction is followed by the words, which are clearly those of the astrologer, "It appeared on the fifteenth with the Sun." "When the Moon is not seen with the Sun on the fourteenth day of Adar" such and such things will happen. The prediction is followed by the words, which are again clearly those of the astrologer, "The day will complete Nisan." Since the Moon appeared without the Sun on the fourteenth, and with the sun on the fifteenth, the Moon and the Sun will not be in conjunction before the afternoon of the twenty-ninth day; in this case the Moon would not be visible[2] until the first day of the next month. It must be noted that when the

[2] *Cf.* on the period of the Moon's invisibility *Cuneiform Inscriptions of Western Asia*, Vol. III, *pl.* 51, l. 9, "The Moon waned on the twenty-seventh day: we watched for an eclipse of the Sun on the twenty-eight, twenty-ninth, and thirtieth days; the Moon appeared on the first day [of the next month]." In No. 240 (*see* p. lxxvi) it is also stated that the period of the Moon's invisibility may be three days. See also Jensen, *Kosmologie*, p. 30.

astrologer uses the words "this night," he does not refer to the day on which he is writing, but to the *eve* of the day, *i.e.*, last night. The words "The day will complete Nisan" refer to the thirtieth day of the month, and we know from other texts that they indicate that the month will contain thirty full days.[1] A further proof of this is that the omen concerning the appearance of the Moon on the first day is often accompanied by that for "the day in its proper length," *i.e.*, the ordinary full length day in the calendar month. Not infrequently a note is added to the effect that the day completes the month. Here we must notice in passing the use of the words *ûmu utarra*, *i.e.*, "the day turns back." The astrologer uses these words in cases where the Moon has been seen with the Sun on the fourteenth day, to indicate that the Moon will appear on the thirtieth day of the month, and therefore there will be only twenty-nine days in the next month (*see* No. 53, obv. 2, p. xliii). In certain cases where the phrase *ûmu utarra* occurs, *e.g.*, Nos. 62 and 70, the omens on the tablets relate to the moon on the thirtieth day.

An examination of No. 171 shows that this tablet was written at the end of the year in the month Adar, and that the calendar month corresponded with the lunar month, and further, since Nisan (which began the year) is the only other month mentioned, it is

[1] *Cf.* the passages :—No. 36, obv. 3 *minat arḫi . . . ûmu XXX* [kám] *ušal*[*lam*], No. 42, obv. 4, *ša ina* [arhu] *Tašrîti ûmu ušallamma*, No. 52, obv. 1, [ilu] *Sin ina* [arhu] *Nisanni ûmu ušaliam.*

clear that no second Adar was used in this year. If all the months had contained thirty days each, and to these an intercalary Adar had been added every six years to make up the solar year, as we should naturally expect would have been done, it would hardly be possible for the calendar month and the lunar month to correspond so exactly at the end of a year in which an intercalary month was not added. We are therefore probably right in assuming that each month did not necessarily contain thirty days, and there is evidence to show that the intercalary month was added at a period less than six years.[1] From the above it is clear that the length of the month was foretold from the appearance of the Moon and Sun on or about the fourteenth day of the month. In No. 119 the astrologer reports that the Moon was seen on the twelfth day with the Sun, and he makes use of the phrase "The Moon appears out of its time." It is interesting to note that Maimonides, in speaking of the Moon, says "When the Moon is seen on the thirtieth day, she is called the Moon seen in its time,"[2] and the same writer seems to refer to the variation in the length of the month, *i.e.*, whether it contains twenty-nine or thirty days, when he states that Marcheswan and Kislew may be either "full" or "hollow."[3]

[1] On the months containing twenty-nine and thirty days in use at Babylon in the era of the Seleucidæ, *see* Epping and Strassmaier, *Astronomiches aus Babylon*, p. 179.

[2] Kiddush Haḫodesh, *ed.* Witter, Jena, 1703, I, 4.

[3] *Op. cit.*, VIII, 5.

From various indications derived from the astrological reports, it is clear that the class of magicians who calculated the length of the months and published information concerning them formed a very important section of the Babylonian and Assyrian priesthood, and it is evident from the denunciations hurled against them by Isaiah, in whose book they are described as *môdî'îm leḥŏdašim* (Isaiah, xlvii, 13), that they occupied one of the most prominent places in the hierarchy of Babylon.

The Assyrians called the seven planets by the same names by which they were known in Babylonia, *i.e.*, *Sin* (the Moon), *Šamaš* (the Sun), *Umunpauddu* (Jupiter), *Dilbat* (Venus), *Kaimânu* (Saturn), *Gudud* (Mercury), *Muštabarrû-mûtânu* (Mars). The twelve signs of the Zodiac, which were also known to the Babylonians, are thus called :—

	Late Babylonian.[1]	Assyrian.
Aries	*Ku (sarikku)*	*Ínmîsara.*[2]
Taurus	*Te-te*	*Gud-Anna.*[3]
Gemini	*Tuâmu*	*Tuâmu.*
Cancer	*Pulukku*	*Allul.*[4]
Leo	*Arû*	*Urgula,*[5] *Urmaḫ.*[6]
Virgo	*Širû*	*Širû, Dilgan.*[7]
Libra	*Zibanitu*	*Zibanitu.*
Scorpio	*Aḳrabu*	*Aḳrabu.*
Sagittarius	*Pa*	*Pabilsag.*[8]

[1] *See* Epping and Strassmaier, *Astronomiches aus Babylon*, p. 149; Jensen, *Kosmologie*, p. 497.

[2] *Kosm.*, p. 61 f.

[3] *Kosm.*, p. 62.

[4] *See* p. xxxv.

[5] *Kosm.*, p. 66.

[6] *See* p. lxxii.

[7] *See* p. xl.

[8] *Kosm*, p. 496.

	Late Babylonian.[1]	Assyrian.
Capricornus	*Enzu*	[2]
Aquarius	*Gu*	*Gu-Anna.*[3]
Pisces	*Nunu*	*Nun-šamî* (?)[4]

The reports of the Mesopotamian astrologers prove that their writers deduced omens from all the celestial bodies known to them, but it is clear that the Moon was the chief source from which omens were derived.

The shape of the Moon's horns was examined with great care, and it was noted whether they were pointed, "equal," or "unequal." Thus we are told that "If the horns are pointed, the king will overcome whatever he goreth"; the action of the king is here likened to the use to which horns are put by animals. And again we read, "When the Moon rideth in a chariot,[5] the yoke of the king of Akkad will prosper." And again, "When the Moon is low at its appearance, the submission [of the people] of a far country will come to the king."

Halos, both of the Moon and of the Sun, were fruitful sources from which omens were derived. Two halos were known:—One of 22°, called *tarbaṣu*, and the other of 46°, called *supuru*. Each of these words mean "sheepfold," and it is understood that the Moon is the shepherd of the stars or the celestial

[1] *See* Epping and Strassmaier, *Astronomiches aus Babylon*, p. 149; Jensen, *Kosmologie*, p. 497.

[2] *Kosm.*, p. 73. [3] *Kosm.*, p. 497. [4] *See* p. lv.

[5] Compare the idea of the Greek goddess Selene.

"sheep" which are within the halo. The influence of the Moon on sheep and cattle upon earth is thus described: "Thy word, O Moongod, maketh sheep-fold and cattle-pen to flourish." When a *tarbaṣu*, *i.e.*, smaller halo, was seen to surround the Sun with the gate, *i.e.*, interruption, opposite the south, it was thought that a south wind would blow; but this has been the experience of all observers of the weather, for the direction of the interruption indicates that wind and rain will come from that quarter.[1] It is well known that Sun-halos are usually seen in the west or south-west when the Sun is low on the horizon, and the lower portion of the halo is cut off by the gloom of the horizon. In European countries[2] storms usually come from those quarters of the sky, and this is also true for Mesopotamia. It is interesting to note that a tablet (K. 200) is inscribed with omens which are derived from the interruptions of a halo which correspond to the four cardinal points. From the presence of planets or constellations within the halo of the Moon, numerous omens are derived. The words, "When the Sun stands within the halo of the Moon." would at first sight appear to prove that the word *tarbaṣu* does not mean "halo," but we learn from the notes written by the astrologers (*see* No. 176) that by the word "Sun" we must understand the "Star of the Sun," *i.e.*, Saturn, and we now know that the omen for the Sun in such a case would be given just as if the

[1] *Cf.* Theophrastus, *ed.* Wood, p. 64.

[2] Abercromby, *Weather*, p. 36.

Sun were occupying the place of Saturn. From Eratosthenes, too, we learn that Saturn was called Sol.[1]

There are no omens for Venus or Mercury standing in the halo of the Moon, for neither planet can appear near the full Moon. When a star, standing in the halo of the Moon, is described in the omen as *Lubad*, a common name for Mercury, it must, of course, be understood to mean simply "planet."

Dark halos round the Moon were regarded by the Assyrians, as well as by other nations, as indications of rain, and it is noteworthy that a Greek writer like Theophrastus[2] says, "Dark halos are a sign of rain, particularly those seen in the afternoon." Aratus, the Cilician, informs us that dark solar halos indicate rough weather.[3]

The appearance of the Sun with the Moon about the fourteenth day was noted with great care, and for the express purpose of calculating whether the month would contain twenty-nine or thirty days.

The astrologers noted:—(1) whether the Sun and Moon were seen together above the horizon; (2) whether they were balanced (*šitḳulu*), that is to say, both on the horizon, one setting and the other rising; (3) whether one had set and the other had not yet risen, both celestial bodies being, in consequence, below the horizon, that is to say, invisible (*šutatû*). The word "invisible" represents as nearly as possible

[1] *Ed.* Bernhardy, *Hygin.*, II, 42.
[2] *Ed.* Wood, 22, p. 60.
[3] *Diosemeia, ed.* Prince, p. 43.

the meaning of *šutatû*, as we may see by the phrase *miḫissu šutatû*, *i.e.*, "whose wound (or sickness) is invisible," which occurs in the hymn to Nírgal.[1] The same view of the meaning of this word is also held by Dr. Jastrow.[2] The word *šutatû* had probably another shade of meaning also, for the word *ittintu*, which means the gradual disappearance of the Moon as it draws near the Sun at the end of the month, is once used as its equivalent (*see* No. 124, obv. 4).

In several places in astrological reports we meet with the words *nidu nadi*, which seem to mean "casting a shadow, or image, or reflection." The "image" appears at the sun's zenith, to the right or left of the Sun; in one case four such "images" are mentioned. I cannot help thinking that these "images" refer to mock suns.

A number of omens were derived from the entrances of planets into the signs of the Zodiac, and the influence of the stars in the various sections of it was thought to be very considerable. The places where the gods stood in the Zodiac were called *manzalti*, a word which means literally "stations," and we are probably right in assuming that it is the equivalent of the *mazzâlôth* mentioned in II Kings, xxiii, 5.[3] The use of the word in late Hebrew is, however, somewhat more vague, for *mazzal*, though literally meaning a constellation of the Zodiac, is also

[1] Rawlinson, *Cuneiform Inscriptions*, IV, 24, 1, 36,37.

[2] See *Religion of Babylonia*, p. 359.

[3] See Jensen, *Kosm.*, p. 348.

applied to any and every star, and in *Berêshîth Rabbâ*, *c.* x, it is said, "One *mazzal* completeth its circuit in thirty days, another completeth it in thirty years."

From certain texts we learn that the star *Aḳrabu* was sometimes seen within the halo of the Moon. Now according to Jensen,[1] *Aḳrabu* may mean either the Scorpion or Venus; but in the case of the star within the halo of the Moon, Scorpio, and Scorpio only, is referred to by the astrologer.

It is not always easy to follow the train of reasoning which guided the derivation of omens; on the other hand, others are based on common everyday experience. Thus, dark clouds heralded wind; thunder on the last day of the Moon was followed by steady markets; thunder on a cloudless day indicated the advent of darkness, storm, and famine; storms were the heralds of favourable events; earthquakes portended destruction, the invasion of enemies, insurrections and the fall of buildings; eclipses typified disturbance, and their evil effects could only be averted by prayers. In the series of prayers entitled the "Lifting of the Hand,"[2] we find a number of formulæ which are to be recited with the object of securing the protection of the gods during and after eclipses, and it is certain that they formed no unimportant section of the devotional literature of the Assyrians. For the purpose of accurately recording partial eclipses, the face of the Moon was divided into four parts, and each part was identified with a certain country (*see* p. lxxxv);

[1] *Kosmologie*, p. 71. [2] King, *Babylonian Magic and Sorcery*.

the portion to the right was Akkad, that to the left was Elam, the upper part was Aḫarrû, and the lower part Subartu. A total eclipse of the Moon was called *atal mâtâti, i.e.*, a "darkness of the countries."

The greatest possible care was taken by the astrologers to observe and to record the duration and extent of partial eclipses.

Some of the portents from births recorded in the Reports are remarkable, and among these may be mentioned one in which we are told that the writer augured an increase of power to the king, because a sow brought forth a pig which had eight legs and two tails (*see* p. xci). This curious object was, we are told, afterwards preserved in brine.

A perusal of the Astrological Reports will convince the reader that the style and language in which they are written are not only somewhat obscure and difficult grammatically, but that their writers took pains to make their forecasts and portents as unintelligible to the uninitiated as possible. Whenever they were able they added an alternative portent. It is possible, indeed probable, that many of the difficulties which encompass the study of Babylonian magic, astrology and sorcery, will be removed by the publication of abundant material, and that at length we may obtain to a knowledge of the general principles which guided the astrologer in formulating the decisions as to the future, which exercised such a great and lasting influence over the minds of the dwellers in Mesopotamia.

TRANSLATIONS.

TRANSLATIONS.

I. When the Moon Appears on the First Day of the Month.

No. 1. When the Moon appears[1] on the first day, there will be silence, the land will be satisfied. When the day is long according to its calculation, there will be a long reign. From Bulluṭu.

Obv. 1. The appearance of the Moon on the first day indicated that the calendar month began coincident with the lunar month, and that the day was its proper length.[2]

Obv. 2. KA.GI.NA = *sanâḳu ša pî* (Brunnow, *List*, No. 618). It is glossed *pu-u i-kan* in No. 42, Obv. 5.

Obv. 4. The day is calculated to last as long as the Sun remains above the horizon. *Cf.* 81-2-4, 63, Obv. 15, 'the day is the Sun,' and No. 173, Obv. 2, 'the Suns are days.' The use of *minâti* is closely paralleled by the Syriac *menyâna* in *hânôn d'menyâna d' sahra m'nên*, 'those who measure the duration of the moon.' (*S. Ephraemi Syri*, *Opera Selecta*, *Ed. Overbeck*, *Oxonii*, 1865, 72, 3.) Nos. 2–6 are very similar. No. 5, Obv. 3, contains the note *minat arḫi ûmu XXX ušallam*, *i.e.*, in consequence of the Moon's appearance on the first day, the thirtieth day of the month will be completed. See Introduction, p. xxi.

[1] K. 960, a large tablet beginning this way, has been omitted, the remainder being almost illegible. Of other so-called astrological reports, K 115, consisting of quotations from prayers similar to those of the Raising of the Hand, and sent by Ištar-šuma-ìriš, and such tablets as 83-1-18, 206, Bu. 91-5-9, 156 ('lucky days'), *etc.*, and the large unsigned tablets, which probably are not included in this Series, have been omitted.

[2] It will be noticed that the preterite is rarely used by the astrologers to express past time (except in the protases of omens) when speaking of astrological phenomena; the present with *-ma* attached is far more common. The general rules for the tenses in these texts are:—Omen-protasis, preterite; Omen-apodosis, present. Outside the omens, the present does duty for the future or present, while past time is expressed by the present with *-ma* appended.

No. 7. When the Moon appears on the first day, there will be silence, the land will be satisfied. When the day is long according to its calculation, there will be a long reign. When the Moon is full, the king will go to pre-eminence. From Ištar-šuma-íríš.

Obv. 5. *Agû Apir*, literally 'puts on a royal head-dress.' See Jensen, *Kosm.* p. 103 ff.

No. 9. When the Moon appears on the first day, there will be silence, the land will be satisfied. This is for Nisan and Tisri (?). When the Moon is regularly full, the crops of the land will prosper, the king will go to pre-eminence.

Obv. 4. *Agû Apir kaimânu ma*, *i.e.*, the Moon is full on the same day in each month. This will happen if the astrologers are careful in regulating the length of the calendar month. The omen differs slightly in No. 10, obv. 5, 'The crops of the land will prosper, the land will dwell in security, the king will go to pre-eminence.' No. 11, rev. 2, has the writer's comment, 'It is a lucky omen for the king, my lord.' No. 11A, rev. 2, differs slightly in the omen for the length of the day, 'there will be a long reign, the years of the king (will be numerous).' Nos. 12–14 are very similar.

No. 15 (*Obv.* 5 *ff.*). In Tammuz the Moon and Sun were seen with one another on the fourteenth. From Bíl . . . . May Bel and Nebo give greeting, happiness, health, long days, long years, and the establishing of the foundation of the throne of the king, my lord.

No. 16 (*Obv. ff.*). Adar and Elul, the beginning of a year, are like Nisan and Tisri. At the beginning of the year the Moon sends a lucky sign for the long reign of the king, my lord. From Aššur-šarani.

No. 17 (*Obv.* 6 *ff.*). When the Moon appears on the first day, it is lucky for Akkad, evil for Elam and Aḫarrû. The month Ab is Akkad. It is lucky for the king, my lord. From Nabû-šumâ-iškun.

No. 18 (Rev. 3 ff.) contains a communication from Bíl-naṣir. 'Bíl-ípuš, the Babylonian magician, is very ill: let the king command that a physician come and see him.' Rev. 5, *lillik-limur* are the equivalents of the Hebrew jussive. *Cf.* I Sam. xviii, 21, *etc.*

No. 19 (*Rev.* 1 *ff.*). May Assur, Samas, Nebo and Merodach day after day, month after month, year after year, grant happiness, health, joy and exultation, a secure throne for ever, for long days and many years to the king my lord. From Nabû-iḳbi.

No. 20 is similar to No. 19, except obv. 5 ff. 'When hail comes in Sebat, there will be abundance for men and the market will be high.' The word *abnu*, properly 'stone,' is used for hail in No. 261, obv. 4.

No. 21 (*Obv.* 5 *ff.*). Two or three times during these days we have looked for Mars, but could not see it. If the king, my lord, should say 'Is it an omen that it is invisible?' it is not. From Ištar-šuma-íriš.

Obv. 5. The idiom for 'two or three' is the same in Assyrian as in Hebrew. *Cf.* II Kings, ix, 32. On *Muštabarrû-mutânu* see Epping and Strassmaier, *Astronomiches aus Babylon*, p. 110.

Obv. 8. *irtibi* Jensen, *Kosm.* pp. 15, 226A.

Rev. 2. For this use of *mimini* after an interrogative *-u*, *cf.* K. 522, 9, 14 (quoted Delitzsch, *Handwörterbuch*, under *izirtu*, p. 38a).

No. 21A (*Obv.* 3–4). Mars went forth from Cancer (*Allul*) last night.

Obv. 4. *Allul.* That this is a constellation and not a single star is apparent from K. 4292, obv. 17, ff. (Craig. *Astrol. Astron. Texts*, Leipzig, 1899) *Ana* ^{mul} *LUL . LA ana tibut*(*ut*) *šâri* ^{mul} *LUL . LA*[1] ^{mul} *AL . LUL. Ana kakkabâni* ^{pl} ŠI ^{pl} ša ^{mul} *AL . LUL . DIR* ^{pl} *la tibut šâri,* etc.). In the reports, the appearance of Allul within the Moon's halo is recorded about twelve times; once within the halo about the same time as Gemini (No. 114), and once about the same time as Regulus (No. 114A). Further we are told that Venus passes from

[1] ^{mul} LUL . LA is explained by *sa-ar-rum* (W.A.I. II, 49, 3, 35), probably by mistake for LUL . A (*i.e.*, Mars).

Allul to the tropic of Cancer in five or six days (No. 207), *i.e.*, 8–9 degrees. Cancer is the only constellation which agrees with these conditions.

The later name of Cancer was Pulukku (Jensen, *Kosm.* p. 311), but this does not occur in these texts.

No. 22 (*Obv.* 4—*Rev.* 3). Assur, Samas, Nebo and Merodach have delivered Kush and Egypt into the hands of the king, my lord. In the army of the king, my lord, . . . they have carried off their spoil (and) . . . have made all their forces enter thy royal seat Nineveh, and have enslaved their captives. In the same way may Samas and Merodach deliver the Cimmerians and Mannaî . . . all that are opposed to the king into the hands of the king, my lord. May the king, my lord, capture all the silver, gold, . . . (and) their forces.

Obv. 4. Since the writer states that Kush and Egypt have been overcome, and prays that the Cimmerians and Mannaî may meet wiih the same fate, it may be inferred that the letter was written about the time of Assurbanipal's third expedition. Egypt was not finally subdued until his second campaign, and it was shortly after this that the Assyrians came into contact with the Lydian king, Gyges. Gyges, finding the Cimmerians too strong for him, followed the advice which had been given him in a dream, and sent to ask help from Assyria. His request was granted, and the Cimmerians submitted for a time; but the Lydian king forgot the benefits of Assurbanipal, and sent his army to aid Psametik, king of Egypt, who was chafing under the Assyrian yoke. The Assyrians naturally resented this breach of faith and withdrew their help, thereby allowing the Cimmerians to rise against Lydia for a second time. Gyges was slain, and his son, who made peace with Assyria, ruled in his stead. Then followed the fourth expedition, directed against the Mannaî with a successful issue, and it is probably to these events that our tablet refers. We may therefore assume that it was written about 660 B.C.

II. Omens from the Horns of the Moon.

No. 25. When the Moon appears on the thirtieth of the month . . . . . . will devour. When at the Moon's appearance its horns point away from one another, there will be an overthrowing of fortresses and downfall of garrisons. There will be obedience and goodwill in the land. (GI = *taraki* . GI = *šalamu* . GI = *kânu* 'its horns are *kunna*.') It is evil for Aḫarrû, but good for the king, my lord. From Zakir.

Obv. 3. *turruka*: *tarâku* is to 'rend asunder,' and probably here is the opposite of *mitḫara*, No. 26, Obv. 6. We find on K. 7192 a description of the various shapes of the Moon's horns (Obv. 3 *ff.*), 'When the Moon's horns are *UR.BI.MI*[pl] (equally dark), UR.BI *nam-ra* (equally bright), KI.LA.DAN *mit-ḫa-ra*, KI.LA.DAN NU *mit-ḫa-ra*, *kima* GIŠ.BAN (like a bow), *kima* GIŠ.MA.(TU) (like a boat).'

Obv. 4, 5. *paṭar*, *arad*, infinitives used as nouns. For *arâdu* in this sense, *cf.* Deut. xx, 20.

No. 26. When the Moon's horns face equally, there will be a secure dwelling for the land. When at the Moon's appearance (its horns) are pointed, the king wherever his face is set will rule the land, (or) wherever he presses on will overcome. From Iraššiilu, the king's servant, the greater.

Obv. 6. *mitḫara* I, 2 of *maḫâru* = 'to be equal.' *Cf.* Aratus (*Diosemeia*, *ed. Prince*, p. 41), 'If on the third day the two horns do not undergo any change, and (the Moon) does not shine, lying upon her back, but the points of her horns incline equally . . . .'

Rev. 1. *udduda* II 1, of *îdîdu* = 'to sharpen.'

Rev. 6. *maḫrû* is used also in this way of Ašaridu. The converse is *ḳaṭnu*, i.e., Ašaridu *maḫrû* and Ašaridu *ḳaṭnu*, which seems to point to two different people.

No. 28 (*Obv.* 3–5). When the Moon at its appearance a bright day (?) . . . . *kurusissu* will come and devour the sesame. (*Rev.* 2 *ff.*) When a star shines forth and like a knot (?) from sunset to sunrise disappears, in Elam . . . the enemy will capture . . . : the forces of Elam . . . . . From Zakir.

Obv. 4. *kurusissu*, perhaps a worm or insect.

Rev. 2. SUR, *i.e.* *iṣrur*, is the usual word for a star rising.

Rev. 3. The character *lib* (?) may be *ḳi* (?).

No. 29 (*Obv. 2 ff.*). When at the Moon's appearance its horns are pointed, the king of Akkad wherever he goes will rule the land, (or) the king of Akkad wherever his face is set will ravage the land. When at the Moon's appearance its face is turned to the left . . . . dates and . . . (?) . . . When at its appearance a north wind blows (in that month a flood will come). Jupiter passed to the place of sunset: there will be a secure dwelling, welfare lucky for the land. When the Sun reaches its zenith with a parhelion (?), the king will be angry and there will be war. (Jupiter has remained in the heavens many days.) From Ašaridu, the greater, the king's servant.

Obv. 2. *idda;* see No. 26.

Rev. 4. *nidu*; see Introduction, p. xxvii. For the character translated *izziz*, *cf.* No. 181, obv. 4, and Amiaud et Méchinaux, *Tableau Comparé*, No. 226. A variant is given in No. 183, obv. 3, *iz-ziz.*

No. 30. When at the Moon's appearance its right horn is long and its left horn is short, the king's hand will conquer a land other than this. When the Moon at its appearance is very large, an eclipse will take place. When the Moon at its appearance is very bright, the crops of the land will prosper. When the day is long according to its calculation, there will be a long reign. The thirtieth day completed the month. In Elul an eclipse of Elam. From Nírgal-íṭir.

Obv. 6. *ikru:* Syriac *k'ra.*

Rev. 1 *ibta'il* is the opposite of *unnut; cf.* No. 167, rev. 7, *ba'il u šaruru naši*, contrasted with l. 10, *unnut u šarurušu maḳtu;* and No. 232, rev. 3 where *utanat* is contrasted with *ib'il.* Both *ba'il* and *unnut* seem to indicate a gradual change into *šaruru naši* (becoming bright) and *šaruru maḳtu* (brilliance smitten) respectively. Another form of the root *a-n-t* seems to be *ittintu* (IV, 2), used constantly for the Moon's approach to the Sun and gradual disappearance or fading away; see No. 124, obv. 1, *etc.* It is once used, presumably by mistake, for *šutatû* (No. 124, obv. 4), but the similarity of the two words may have occasioned a scribe's blunder. Further instances of *ba'il* are:—No. 183, 5, *ina ba'il zimušu adir:* 89–4–26, 160, obv. 8–10 ^{mul}*Muštabarrû-mûtânu ba'il* ^{mul}*Muš tabarrû-mûtânu adu'lib* ^{arhu} *Airi ba'il šaruri naši*, *i.e.* 'Mars is bright: since the middle of Iyyar it has gradually grown bright and has assumed a brilliance.' W.A.I. III, 53, 1, 5, *etc.*: K. 2894, pub. P.S.B.A. 1893, p. 317, l. 17 *kakkabâni* ^{pl} *-šu ba-'-lu.* *Unnut* from No. 167, rev. 10, appears to mean 'grows dim': *cf.* also K. 7661, obv., Col. I, 1 [*Ana sin ina tamarti*] *-su un-nu-ut u SI* ^{pl} *-šu AN . DI . RI . A*, *etc.*, and No. 274 P. obv. 1, *unut ša atali* . . . 'The gradual darkening caused by the eclipse.' *Cf.* also the omen on No. 60, obv. 1. On the other hand, *ittintu* may be a quadriliteral root like *ikkilmi*.

Rev. 5–6. On these see Introduction, pp. xxi, xxviii.

No. 31 (*Obv.* 3–5). When the Moon at its appearance is bright, the heart of Akkad will live, will be bright, the people will see plenty.

No. 32 (*Rev.* 1 *ff.*). When the Moon appears on the thirtieth of Tammuz, there will be a wasting of countries. (Let not the king be anxious (?) about the evil: the Moon has been darkly full and its horns have . . . which is lucky for the king). From Ašaridu the greater, the king's servant.

Rev. 4. The Moon's crown is dark and its horns visible, *i.e.*, the dark portion of the Moon's circle is to be seen.

No. 33 (*Obv.* 3 *ff.*). Mars which has stood in Scorpio to go forth . . . turns. Until the twenty-fifth day of the month . . . (it stays), it then goes forth, its brilliance being diminished. Let the king, my lord, be satisfied, let the king rejoice greatly; until it goes forth let the king take care of himself. From Iraššì-ilu, the king's servant, the greater.

No. 35 (*Obv.* 8 *ff.*). When at the Moon's appearance its horns are sharp and bright, the king of Akkad, wherever his face is set, will rule the lands. When the Moon at its appearance is bright, ... its heart will live, the people will see plenty. When at the Moon's appearance its horns are equally bright, hostile kings will fare well. When the day according to its calculation is long, there will be a reign of long days. The thirtieth day completed Nisan and Tammuz. From Nirgal-iṭir.

No. 37 (*Obv.* 1–3). When at the Moon's appearance in the intercalary month Adar its horns are pointed and dark, the prince will grow strong and the land will have abundance. (*Rev.* 3 *ff.*) When the Moon stands in a fixed position, there will be want of rain. In the intercalary Adar, the Moon was seen with the Sun on the fourteenth day. From Nírgal-íṭir.

No. 38 (*Obv.* 6 *ff.*). When Regulus (*Šarru*) assumes a brilliance, the king of Akkad will effect a completion. From Munnabitu.

Obv. 6. On *Šarru* = Regulus, see Epping and Strassmaier, *Astronomiches*, p. 127.

No. 39 (*Rev.* 1 *ff.*). Happy welfare to the land, the Moon will smite the foe. The Moon has occulted Mercury. From Nírgal-íṭir.

No. 43. When the Moon at its appearance is full, the king will go to pre-eminence, the land will dwell in security. (At its appearance the Moon was full.) When at the Moon's appearance its right horn is dark in the heavens, there will be a steady market in the land, a revolt will take place in Aḫarrû. ('Its right horn dark in the heavens,' which they explain by 'in heaven is obscured and is not visible.'). At the Moon's appearance its right horn is Aḫarrû. When the Moon appears on the first day it is lucky for Akkad, unlucky for Elam and Aḫarrû. The Moon will be seen without the Sun on the fourteenth day From Nabû-aḫî-íriba.

Obv. 7. ḪI . GAR glossed *bar-ti* here and *bar-tu* in No. 237.
Rev. 4. The scribe evidently explains *dirat* as the perm. fem. from a root of which he thinks DIR (= *ḫalâpu*) a part.

No. 44 (*Rev.* 3 *ff.*). (When) in Nisan on the first day (the Moon) appears and a north wind blows, the king of Akkad will be happy. Mercury at sunset has stood (?) within Kumal; it is lucky for the king my lord; the king of Aḫarrû will be slain with the sword. (The forces of) the king, my lord, in Egypt .... will conquer.

Rev. 6. Kumal is explained in No. 101, rev. 2 ff. [mul] *muš-tabarrû—mûtânu kakkab Aḫarrî* [ki] | [mul] *Dilgan-ša-arki-šu-MUL.MUL* [mul am] *KU . MAL* | [mul] *KU . MAL kakkab*

Aḫarri, *i.e.*, Mars = star of Aḫarrû : Dilgan-whose-back-part-is-Mulmul = Kumal : therefore Kumal = star of Aḫarrû.

Dilgan is variously explained by GUD . UD (Mercury), Muštabarrû-mûtânu (Mars), and ŠU . GI, in Brunnow's *List*, No. 51. But it cannot be either Mercury or Mars, for from Rm. 95 (Craig, *Astr. Texts*, 84, 12) 'When its stars *elita ninmudu*,' it is obvious that it is a constellation. (*Cf.* also l. 13 and K. 2329, 91, obv. 5). On ŠÚ . GI, see No. 49.

The true explanation of Dilgan is given on No. 88, rev. 8, *Dilgan* = *Absin*, *i.e.*, 'Crops,' 'growth' (Virgo); moreover, it is remarkable that the omen for Dilgan in the Moon's halo forebodes 'no growth of corn.'

Now, as has been shown above, Kumal is Dilgan-whose-back-part-is-Mulmul (two stars or Mars), *i.e.*, probably part of Virgo, while the astrologer is perhaps playing on the double meaning of Mulmul to deduce an omen hostile to the king of Aḫarrû. Kumal, like Dilgan, relates to crops (Craig, *Astr. Texts*, No. 36, obv. 22).

Rev. 9. From this remark we may perhaps put the date of the tablet at 670–660 B.C.

No. 45 (*Obv.* 3–5). When the Moon at its appearance stands in a fixed position, the gods intend the counsel of the land for happiness. (It appeared on the first day.)

Obv. 4. *milku* is the only word given for the simple ideograph (No. 5525 in Brunnow's *List*).

No. 48. When the Moon appears on the first of Kislew, the king of Akkad wherever he goes will ravage the land (or) the king of Akkad wherever his face is set will rule the land. (On the fourteenth day the Moon was seen with the Sun.) There will be an overthrowing of fortresses and downfall of garrisons; there will be obedience and good will in the land. As for the rest, the king (will see?) their good luck. May the king soon hear a happy report and greeting. From Ašaridu.

No. 49. When the Moon rides in a chariot in the month Sililiti, the rule of the king of Akkad will prosper and his hand will overcome the enemy. (The month Sililiti is Sebat.) In Sebat a halo surrounded (the Moon) in the Pleiades (Šugi). When a halo surrounds the Moon and Aldebaran (*Anna-mir*) stands within it, the king will fare well: there will be truth and justice in the land. From Nabû-ikiši of Borsippa.

Obv. 1. For *Si-li-pu-ut-ti* in the text, read *Si-li-li-ti.*

Obv. 5–6 give an explanation of the phrase 'rides in a chariot,' for Šugi has been explained to mean 'chariot-yoke' (see Brown, *Proc. Soc. Bibl. Arch.*, XV, p. 329). Šugi occurs in the following passages:—(*a*) No. 49, where the Moon may be surrounded by a halo in Šugi, (*b*) No. 206, where Šugi may stand in the Moon's halo, (*c*) No. 184, where Mercury is as low down (?) in Taurus as Šugi, (*d*) No. 226, where Mercury rises to the midst of Šugi from the place of Sunset in Nisan (*i.e.*, Aries-Taurus), (*e*) No. 244A, where its 'circle' may be bright, (*f*) Nos. 244 and 246, where it may grow dim (?) over the Moon and enter the Moon. From (*c*) and (*d*) it is evidently near Taurus, from (*a*) (*d*) and (*e*) it is evidently a group, and from (*f*) it is evidently a small group. Now it has been suggested to me that, as Mercury cannot be in Orion (one identification of Šugi), and further that the Moon does not deviate from the ecliptic more than a little over 5°, Šugi is probably the Pleiades. This identification agrees with the facts above. The Pleiades are a small group, 4° from the ecliptic, and the rare word *kurkurru* (No. 244A) might very well be applied to them.

Anu-agû, from the three cases where it occurs, may very well be a single star, and from No. 106 it would appear to be in Taurus, in which case it will be Aldebaran, for which no suitable identification has been suggested.

No. 51. The Moon will complete the day in Nisan. From Nabû-aḫi-íriba.

Obv. 1. On the meaning of this text, see Introduction, p. xxi.

No. 52. The Moon will complete the day in Iyyar. The . . day the Moon and Sun will be seen together. The night (?) of the thirteenth, the night of the fourteenth a watch was kept but no eclipse occurred. Seven times I have been raised . . but no eclipse occurred. I send a sure report to the king, my lord. From Ṭabû-ṣil-Marduk, the nephew of Bîl-naṣir.

Obv. 2. The lacuna is better supplied by 'the fifteenth day' than by 'the thirteenth' as in the transliterations.

No. 53 (*Obv.* 1–4). The Moon completed the day in Adar: on the fourteenth the Moon will be seen with the Sun: the Moon will 'draw back' the day in Nisan and Iyyar.

No. 54. The Moon will complete the day in Sebat. From Nabû-aḫî-íriba.

No. 55 (*Obv.* 4 *ff.*) Concerning Mercury, of which the king, my lord, sent me, yesterday Ištar-šuma-írîš in the palace proclaimed its going forth to Nabû-aḫî-íriba. The omens in the festival day came, they have all been observed and seen, they have passed off. From Balasi.

Obv. 8. *igdiri* I, 2 of *ḳarû* 'to call.' The 'going forth' indicates the exit of Mercury from some constellation.
Rev. 3. *iptušu*, *cf.* Syr. *pâš.*

III. When the Moon appears on the Twenty-eighth Day.

No. 57. Of that which to the king, my lord, I sent, the gods shall straightway (?) open his ears .... When the Moon appears on the twenty-eighth day, it is lucky for Akkad, unlucky for Elam. On the twenty-eighth day the Moon .... from the adverse (?) omen ....

Rev. 4. It is doubtful whether the gloss should be read [*ul*]-*tú mi-ḫi-ir* or [*it*]-*tam-mi-ḫi-ir.*

No. 58. When the Moon at its appearance appears on the twenty-eighth day as the first day, it is evil for Aḫarrû. When the Moon appears on the twenty-eighth day, it is lucky for Akkad, unlucky for Aḫarrû. From the Chief Physician.

The scribe first wrote the sender's name the wrong way up on the reverse, and afterwards corrected his mistake, writing it again the right way and partly erasing the former.

IV. When the Moon appears on the Thirtieh Day.

No. 59. When the Moon appears on the thirtieth day, there will be cold (or) there will be the clamour of the enemy in the land. When at the Moon's appearance it appears high, the enemy will seize upon the land. When the Moon at its appearance is fiercely bright, the month will bring harm. When at the Moon's appearance its horns look at . . . . a flood will come. From Iraššî-ilu, the king's servant (the greater).

> *Obv.* 2. *Šurubbû* is always explained by *kuṣṣu* in these texts.

No. 60. When the Moon at its appearance is dim and one cannot define (?) it, rain will fall. When the Moon appears on the thirtieth day, there will be cold (or) there will be the clamour of the enemy in the land. When the Moon at its appearance appears low, the submission of a distant land will come to the all-powerful king. From Iraššî-ilu, the king's servant (the greater).

> *Obv.* 1. On *unnut*, see No. 30, note on *ibta'il.*
> *Obv.* 2. *Umandi lit.* 'make great.'

No. 62. When the Moon appears on the thirtieth of Nisan, Subartu Aḫlamû will devour: a foreign tongue will gain the ascendency in Aḫarrû. (We are Subartu.) When the Moon appears on the thirtieth day, there will be cold in the land. (*Šurubbû* = *kuṣṣu*).

The Moon appeared without the Sun on the fourteenth of Tebet: the Moon completes the day in Sebat. On the fourteenth it appears without the Sun; the Moon completes the day in Adar. On the fourteenth it appears without the Sun; the Moon will complete the day in Nisan. From Nabû-aḫi-íriba.

No. 63. When the Moon appears on the thirtieth of Iyyar, Aḫarrû Subartu will slay with the sword. From Munnabitu.

No. 64. When the Moon appears on the thirtieth of Iyyar, the abundance of Aḫarrû Aḫlamû will devour. From Nabû-ikiša, of Borsippa.

No. 64B contains a mention of the Itu' tribe (Obv. 4), and of Mugallu (Obv. 5). Expeditions were undertaken against the Itu' in the years 791, 783, 782, 777, and 769 B.C., but they were evidently loyal and faithful vassals in the seventh century (see Harper, *Assyrian Letters*, No. 388). Mugallu was king of Tabal and, according to Assurbanipal, was a source of trouble to Esarhaddon and Sennacherib. From the mention of this king in a letter about omens, it is obvious that he was regarded as a dangerous enemy by the Assyrians. (See K. 1263, rev. 5–10, and *cf.* Knudtzon, *Gebete an den Sonnengott, sub voce.*)

No. 66. When the Moon appears on the thirtieth of Siwân, the abundance of Aḫarrû Aḫlamû will devour. When the Moon appears on the thirtieth day, there will be cold, (or) there will be the clamour of the enemy in the land. When the Moon at its appearance appears low, the enemy will seize on the land. When the Moon at its appearance appears low, the submission of a far country will come to the king, (or) a messenger will come. From Irašši-ilu, the king's servant.

Obv. 6. It will be observed that the omen of No. 60, rev. 1 ff., does not correspond to this line, but with *ušappil* of rev. 2–4.

No. 67. When the Moon appears on the thirtieth of Siwan, the abundance of Aḫarrû Aḫlamû will devour. (The Month Siwan =Aḫarrû: it is evil for Aḫarrû). Saturn has not once approached Venus; it has no omen. From Šum-idina.

No. 68 (*Obv.* 5 *ff.*). When at the Moon's appearance a north wind blows, during that month a flood will come. When at the Sun's zenith a parhelion (?) stands on its right, Ramman will inundate. Mars advanced (*i.e.*, proceeded to its own front) and stood away from Scorpio. To-morrow I will inform the king, my lord. From Balasî.

Rev. 2. *Ana panatuššu illak* is the explanation of the unusual word *uttamiš*. Delitzsch, 92 b, explains inf. *itmušu* as a synonym of *alâku*. See No. 70, rev. 3.

No. 69 (*Obv.* 3–7). When the Moon at its appearance is dark, the land will see plenty; the land will eat plentiful . . . (?). When the Moon at its appearance is dark and its left horn is bent, its right horn being straight, thou wilt overcome (?) the land of the enemy. Ramman will inundate.

Obv. 4. GAN . BA: see also Nos. 34, obv. 3, and 88, obv. 5, and W.A.I. III, 54, 3, 15. *Nap-ša* may be a gloss.
Obv. 5. *kipat*, Syriac *kâph.*
Obv. 7. *tazaḳip.* See Delitzsch, *sub voce.*

No. 69A (*Obv.* 4–6). When at the Moon's appearance a west wind blows, during that month there will be sickness . . . it is evil for Aḫarrû.

No. 70 (*Obv.* 5 *ff.*). When the Moon is fiercely bright, the month will bring harm. Two consecutive months, Iyyar and Siwan, the day has 'turned back.' When a parhelion (?) stands on the right of the Sun, Ramman will inundate, (or) rains and floods will come.

Mars has turned and proceeded (gone straight forward) into Scorpio. It is evil. Later on they shall finish the first part of the matter; I will finish what is going forth to the king; we shall yet see the decisions which will come and remain. From Nabû-aḫî-îriba.

No. 72 (*Obv.* 1–2). When the Moon appears on the thirtieth of Ab, there will be a devastation of Akkad.

No. 73. When the Moon appears on the thirtieth of Ab, there will be a devastation of Akkad. Let not the all-powerful king leave me: it is I who daily beg of the king for my hunger; and now to brickwork he has set me, saying, 'make bricks.' Let not the king, my lord, leave me and I shall not die. From Ṭâbia.

No. 74 (*Obv.* 4–6). When the Moon appears on the thirtieth of Kislew, the king of Aḫarrû will be slain by the sword.

No. 76 (*Obv.* 1—*rev.* 3). When the Moon appears on the thirtieth of Ṭebet, Subartu Aḫlamû will devour; a strange tongue will gain the ascendancy in Aḫarrû. (Ṭebet = Elam.) From

Bulluṭu. On the twenty-ninth day we kept watch, but there was much cloud and we could not see the Moon: on the thirtieth we kept watch and saw the Moon.

Rev. 4. For *matiḫ*, see Delitzsch, *sub voce.*

No. 81 (*Obv.* 3 *ff.*). When the Moon appears on the thirtieth of Sebat, a total eclipse will happen. From the chief scribe.

Obv. 4. On *atal mâtâti*, see Introduction, p. xxix.

V. Various Omens from the Moon.

No. 82 (*Obv.* 1–10). When the Moon out of its calculation delays and does not appear, there will be the invasion of a powerful city. (On the sixteenth (?) it appeared.) When the Moon does not appear, the gods intend the counsel of the land for happiness. (On the fourteenth and fifteenth god was not seen with god.) When the Moon is not seen with the Sun on the fourteenth or fifteenth of Elul, lions (?) will die and traffic will be hindered. When the light of the Moon and Sun is dark, the king with his land and people will repel the angry. The Moon and Sun will be eclipsed, (or) for some months god will not be seen with god.

Obv. 1. On *iḫḫiramma*, see Jensen, *Kosm.*, p. 76.

Rev. 6 *ff.* Contain a suggestion to the king that he should not despise the omens afforded by these phenomena, but should avert the evil by making a *nam-bul-bi* ceremony or prayer. L. 7, *išaṭu* probably = Syriac *šâṭ*, 'despise.' NAM . BUL . BI is the heading of a series of incantations (King, *Bab. Magic*, p. 129), and in K. 602 (Harper, *Assyrian Letters*, No. 23) it is put on a par with ŠÚ . IL . LA . KAN . MIŠ and *šiptu*, *i.e.*, 'the prayers of the lifting of the hand' and 'incantations.' As to its more exact meaning, the following passages are instructive: W.A.I. IV, 17, rev. 14, 15, *ilu Šamšu attama mudî riksišunu | muḫalliḳ raggi mupaššir NAM . BUL . BI-i.* BUL = *pašaru* and is used so in S. 1513, obv. 1 *ff.* [*NAM*] . *BUL . BI ḪUL ṢIR . . . . ḪUL-šu BUL-ma ana šarri u bîti-šu NU . TI . .*, *i.e.*, 'The NAM . BUL . BI of the evil of a snake . . . dissipate its evil that it affect not the king nor his house.' *Cf.* also 80–7–19, 36, obv. 3 *ff.* *m Akkullanu šû issapra mâ* [uu] *Šamšu ina napâḫi-šu mâ ibašši Aki II ŠÚ . SI atalî išakan mâ NAM . BUL . BI laššu, i.e.*, an eclipse of the Sun took place at its zenith extending over two ŠÚ . SI of its surface, but no prayer to avert the evil was made. 81–2–4, 49 (Harper, No. 370), rev. 1 *ff.*, *Ina VII ûmi ŠÚ . IL . LA-i-ni ša ina pân ilâni* [pl] *mušiti ù NAM . BUL . BI . ḪUL kalâmi issiniš innipaš.* 83–1–18, 37 (Harper, No. 355), rev. 12 *ff.*, *NAM . BUL . BI itapaš mâ ar* (?)-*ni-šu ana ili lultima NAM . BUL . BI lipušu mâ lu-itiḳ.*

No. 83. When the Moon . . . in its course, Bel will speak to the land. (It has not been explained.) On the thirteenth day it was seen with the Sun. From Bíl-li', son of Ígibi, the magician.

No. 85. When the Moon disappears, evil will befall the land. When the Moon disappears out of its reckoning, an eclipse will take place. (The Moon disappeared on the twenty-fourth day.) When a halo surrounds the Sun on the day of the Moon's disappearance, an eclipse of the left side of the Moon will take place.

In Kislew a watch was kept for the eclipse, the halo surrounding the Sun and the disappearance of the Moon (being the causes of the watch for an eclipse in Kislew) having been observed. May the king, my lord, know, and may he rest happy. From Iraššî-ilu, the king's servant (the greater).

Obv. 6. On an eclipse of Elam = the left side of the Moon, see Introduction.

No. 86 (*Obv.* 1–5). When the Moon is invisible, but two crescents are seen, there will be hostility in the land. (The Moon has appeared in brightness with the Sun. Alone before the Sun it was brilliant.) The face of the town of Assur the king . . . . (*rev.* 2–10). When Venus goes to the front of Sibzianna, country to country, brother (to) brother will be hostile; there will be a slaughter of men and cattle. When the stars of Sibzianna are brilliant, heaviness will weigh down and evil will be done. From Nírgal íṭir.

Obv. 4. *parig.* *Cf.* Syr. *aphreg* splenduit.

Rev. 3. Sibzianna. It has been suggested that this is Arcturus, Bootes, or Regulus. From No. 86, written for the month Ab, we are told that 'Venus stands before Sibzianna,' and, 'the stars of Sibzianna are brilliant,' which show that it is a constellation (not a single star), near the Ecliptic, and, consequently, cannot be Arcturus or Regulus. Further, we are told in No. 203 that Sibzianna stands within the halo of 22°. As Arcturus is 30° from the Ecliptic, and the Moon cannot vary more than 5° 8′ from the Ecliptic, Sibzianna cannot be Arcturus; and since out of the large constellation of Bootes, only two small stars at most could stand within the halo, it would be assuming too much to say that these stood for the whole of Bootes.

From No. 86, as no planet known to the Assyrians could diverge more than 8° from the Ecliptic, if we give a logical meaning to the words *ina pân*, we may fairly consider that Sibzianna is within 8° of the Ecliptic. Further, from No. 244 B, we learn that (1) Libra, and (2) Sibzianna went before (*ana pân*) the Moon: consequently that which holds good for Libra, which is an Ecliptic constellation, will also hold good for Sibzianna. Again, No. 203, written for Nisan, says that Sibzianna stood within the Moon's halo. Full Moon being then approximately in Libra, we may fairly assume that this took place at some point near the Ecliptic between Leo and Sagittarius. From No. 244 B, quoted above, it is obvious that Sibzianna is in or near Libra, and the only constellation within 8° of the Ecliptic at this point is Libra itself. It would seem, therefore, that Sibzianna is another name for Libra, and it is quite possible that the meaning of Sibzianna, 'Just shepherd of Heaven,' is connected in some way with the 'Balance.'

It is true that in the list of 'Pair-stars' (W.A.I. III, 57, 6), we find Libra mentioned among them as well as the 'Twins-*ina-šid*-Sibzina,' but it may be either because the scribe, in his wish to make a list of seven twins, just as he has made lists of seven *mâšu*, *etc.*, has repeated the same stars under a different name, or more probably 'the pair' of Sibzianna refer to some pair outside Libra altogether—such as Arcturus and Spica.

Rev. 7. *Kabtu ukdappašamma.* *Cf.* Heb. *kâphâš* in Lam. iii, 16: but the meaning of the phrase is doubtful.

No. 87 (*Obv.* 3–5). When the Moon is full on a cloudy day, the Moon will smite the foe.

No. 88. When the Moon out of its calculated time tarries and is not seen, there will be an invasion of a mighty city. (It was invisible on the fifteenth; on the sixteenth it was seen with the Sun.) When Mars stands opposite a planet, corn will be valuable. When a comet reaches the path of the Sun, *Gan-ba* will be diminished; an uproar will happen twice. These words concern Akkad. (Mars left an interval of four degrees (?) away from Saturn, it did not approach: to . . . it reached. (So) I determine. Without fail (?) let him make a *nam-bul-bi* ceremony for it.) When the Moon appears on the sixteenth, the king of Subarti will grow powerful and will have no rival.

Obv. 9. *pâti* is the *perm.* of *patû*, the root of *upatti* in No. 112, obv. 6, where an elaborate explanation of *patû*, *ṭiḫû* and *ḳarâbu* is given. *upatti* is explained by *itti iḳrib* or la *iṭaḫḫi*. *Cf.* Syr. *p'tha* se dilatavit.

attasḫa. See vocabulary and *cf.* K. 1049, rev. 9, and S. 1368, obv. 12 (Harper, Nos. 38 and 357). The meaning is doubtful.

10. *mînu ḫiṭṭu*. See vocabulary and *cf.* Harper, No. 356, rev. 3 *ff.*, *ina ḳapsi ikalli ina pân šarri irrab mînu ḫiṭṭu Šumma etc.:* No. 390, rev. 7 *ff.*, *ultu rîši ša šarru iṣbatannini mînu ḫiṭaî ina pân šarri šá šarru bêli išpuranni-mâ*, etc. *Cf.* the use of the Heb. *ḥâṭâ* to miss.

Rev. 4. The latter part of this line is an unusual addition to this omen. It appears to read *ÍDIN. NA gur-ru uṣaḫḫar*, but is uncertain. *Gurru* is the measure for corn, *etc.*, and the whole phrase would seem to imply the diminution of the crops. *Cf.* No. 185, 11, *etc.*

Rev. 10. These three lines are evidently a later addition and show the phenomena which occurred after Balasî had signed his name. L. 12 indicates that the tablet was written at the end of a year.

No. 89, rev. 7, contains the important explanation NIGIN = *la-mu-u*. The mention of Šamaš-šum-ukin (*l.* 11) will fix the approximate date of the tablet. *Mâr šatti*, 'son of a year,' is perhaps to be compared to the Hebrew idiom. Edge 3, 'oil, honey and spices,' seems to refer to some offerings.

VI. Omens from Halos.

No. 90. To the king of countries, my lord, thy servant Bíl-ušízib (?) May Bel, Nebo and Samas bless the king, my lord. When the Sun stands within the halo of the Moon, in all lands they will speak the truth, the son will speak the truth with his father. (Saturn has stood within the Moon's halo.) When a halo surrounds the Moon and Allul stands within it, the king of Akkad will prolong his life. When a 'river' surrounds the Moon, there will be great inundations and rains. (Allul has stood within the Moon's halo.) (*Obv.* 10–*Rev* .5 *mutilated, Rev* 6 *ff.*). Arad-Gula . . . Bíl-ikiša (?) in my presence I heard . . . this . . . which Mardia heard . . . . the chief: Yadi', the chief, and the chieftainess of all the land of Yaki-manu before the general in Van they appointed, and now they say 'the murderer of our lord shall not grow great before us.' Let the lord of kings ask the general (that he may hear the health of the king), how it troubles (?) me (and) Mardia, who is chief of the servants of the household of the general, his lord, when I had left, entered under Nérgal-ašarid: the interpreter (?) and the chief officers he brought before Nírgal-ašarid. They entered into agreements and carried away to their homes a talent of silver with them . . . . .

Obv. 3. On the Sun in the Moon's halo = Saturn, and on *tarbaṣu* = halo, see Introduction, p. xxiv.

Obv. 8. *nâru* is probably the corona.

Rev. 13. *igganni*, possibly from *igû*, 'be weary,' but doubtful.

No. 91. When a halo surrounds the Moon and Jupiter (*Umun-pauddu*) stands within it, there will be an invasion of the forces of Aḫarru (or) there will be corn and there will be no blasting; the king of Akkad will see siege. When a 'river' surrounds the Moon, there will be verdure and vegetables (?) in the land. Rain will fall. (A halo surrounded the star . . . .) When Jupiter (*Marduk*) grows very bright, that land will eat abundance. (The star Marduk has taken Mercury to its position and has risen high.) After it on the fourteenth . . . . From Balasí.

No. 92. When a halo surrounds the Moon and Jupiter (*Sagmígar*) stands within it, the king of Akkad will be besieged. From Nírgal-ítir.

No. 94. Last night a halo surrounded the Moon, and Jupiter (*Sagmígar*) and Scorpio stood within it. When a halo surrounds the Moon and Jupiter (*Sagmígar*) stands within it, the king of Akkad will be besieged. When a halo surrounds the Moon and Jupiter (*Nibíru*) stands within it, there will be a slaughter of cattle and beasts of the field. (Marduk is Umunpauddu at its appearance ; when it has risen for two (or four?) hours it becomes Sagmígar ; when it stands in the meridian it becomes Nibiru.) When a halo surrounds the Moon and Scorpio stands in it, it will cause men to marry princesses (or) lions will die and the traffic of the land will be hindered. (These are from the series 'When a halo surrounds the Moon and Jupiter stands within it, the king of Aḫarru will exercise might and accomplish the defeat of the land of his foe.' This is unpropitious.) From Nabu-mušísi.

> *Obv.* 8. It is uncertain whether one or two *kasbu* is meant.
> *Rev.* 1. *uštâḫḫâ* III[II], 1 (like *ušmalli*) from *ṭìḫu*. For this use of the word *cf.* K. 848, obv. 1–5, *Ana ûmu XV* [Mim] *Sin u Šamšu . . . . . un-ni-ni-ia li-ka-a [i]-ḳab-bi ina ûmu(mu) šú-a-tu ûmu(mu) a-na* [ilu] *Šamši i-ḳar-rab a-na SAL . BI TÍ-ḫi (i.e. iṭaḫḫi) SAL . BI UŠ ir-ri*, 'When the Moon and Sun . . . . on the fifteenth day, "Receive my prayer," he shall say : on that day let him approach the Sun by day ; let him draw near his wife, his wife shall conceive a man-child.' Boissier, *Documents* I, 2, p. 93, K. 1994, obv. 16, *Ana NA Ana SAL TÍ.*

No. 95. (*Obv.* 1–4). When a halo surrounds the Moon and Jupiter stands within it, the king will be besieged. (Its halo was not joined (*i.e.* was interrupted) : it does not point to evil.)

(*Rev.* 1 *ff.*). The omen is adverse but will be in heaven for good luck. When Sar-ur and Sargaz, of the Scorpion's sting, are brilliant, the weapons of Akkad will come. From Nabu-šuma-iškun.

> *Obv.* 5. A . ÍDIN. W.A.I. V, 46 1, 46 = *banat riḫutum.* From No. 153 it would appear to be a star of Virgo.
> *Rev.* 3. *Sar-ur and Sar-gaz* are therefore *lambda* and *upsilon* of the Scorpion. See also Brown, P.S.B.A, 1890, p. 201.

No. 96. The night of the . . . day Jupiter (*Sagmigar*) stood within the halo of the Moon. Let them make a *nambulbi* ceremony. The halo was open on one side. From Nabû-aḫî-íriba.

Obv. 1. Further examination of the text showed that what had first been read "I" was an unintentional mark on the tablet. There are two deep scratches or indentations at this point in the line, which have obliterated the original character. "I" would, of course, be an impossibility.

No. 97. When a halo surrounds the Moon and Regulus stands within it, women will bear male children. From Nírgal-íṭir.

No. 98 (*Obv.* 1–8). When a dark halo surrounds the Moon, the month will bring rain (or) will gather clouds. (Saturn stood within the Moon's halo.) When a halo surrounds the Moon and Mars stands within it, there will be a destruction of cattle; Aḫarrû will be diminished. (It is evil for Aḫarrû.)

No. 99 (*Obv.* 10 *ff.*). When a halo surrounds the Moon and Mars stands within it, there will be a destruction of cattle in all lands; the planting of dates will not prosper (or) Aḫarrû will be diminished. When a halo surrounds the Moon and two stars stand within it, there will be a long reign. When Mars and a planet stand facing one another, there will be an invasion of Elam. When Mars . . . . goes forth, the king of Elam will die. From Bamâi (?).

Rev. 1. Variants (*e.g.*, No. 101, obv. 1) give 'planting and dates.'

No. 100 (*Obv.* 1–4). When a halo surrounds the Moon and Saturn stands within it, they will speak the truth in the land: the son will speak the truth with his father. Welfare of multitudes.

Obv. 1. See No. 90 on Saturn.

No. 101 (*Obv.* 5 *ff.*). When a halo surrounds the Moon and a planet stands within it, the king his troops will be besieged. When a halo surrounds the Moon and Dilgan-after-which-is-Mulmul stands within it, the herds of the land will prosper. (Mars is the star of

Aḫarrû, Dilgan-after-which-is-Mulmul is Kumal: Kumal is the star of Aḫarrû). From Iraššî-ilu.

Rev. 2. On this see No. 44.

No. 103 (*Obv.* 6 *ff.*). When a halo surrounds the Moon and a planet stands within it, robbers will rage. (Saturn stood within the halo of the Moon.) When Jupiter (*Sagmigar*) draws near to Taurus, the good fortune of the land passes away (or) the generation of cattle and sheep is not prosperous. (Jupiter has entered Taurus: let the king, my lord, keep himself from the storm-wind.) When Mars (*Apin*) reaches the path of the Sun, there will be a famine of cattle, there will be want. (Mars reached Saturn.) When a planet and Mars stand facing one another, there will be an invasion of the enemy. When Mars (*Lul-a*), its rising is dark . . . its light like . . .

Rev. 4. Saturn being the star of the Sun, Mercury is said to have reached the path of the Sun when it draws near Saturn. In the three cases in these texts where *Apin* occurs, it is followed by an explanatory note which shows that *Apin* = *Muštabarrû-mûtânu* (No. 239, 1, 6: No. 272, *r* 1, 3). *Cf.* W.A.I., V, 46, 1, 1, mul APIN = ilu Anu = Mars (Epping and Strassmaier, *Astron.*, p. 173), and the list K 4195, Col. III, IV, where among the names for Mars Apin occurs.

No. 106. When a halo surrounds the Moon and *Anu-agû* stands within it, there will be . . . in the land. (Taurus stood within the halo of the Moon: for two days, an omen of evil, it has stood within the halo of the Moon.) From Nabû-ahî-íriba.

No. 107 (*Rev.* 1 *ff.*). When a halo surrounds the Moon and Mars (*Sudun*) stands within it, a king will die and his land be diminished; the king of Elam will die. (*Sudun* = Mars; Mars is the star of Aḫarrû; it is evil for Aḫarrû and Elam; Saturn is the star of Akkad (?); it is lucky for the king, my lord.) On the fourteenth the Moon was seen with the Sun: let the king, my lord, rest happy. From Iraššî-ilu, the king's servant.

No. 108 (*Obv.* 6 *ff.*). The omen changes not. Now I send the royal observation to the king, my lord. From Zakir.

No. 110. When a halo surrounds the Moon and Cancer (Allul) stands within it, the king of Akkad will prolong life: showers will fall. May Assur, Samas, Nebo, and Merodach, life to life (?) for long days to the king, my lord, give. From Nabû-iḳbi.

No. 111 (*Obv.* 5 *ff.*). When a halo surrounds the Moon and a north wind blows, the exalted gods . . . bring (?) . . . When a halo surrounds the Moon and it is thin, there will be a giving of years to the king.

Obv. 8. *idlul*, Heb. *dâlâl, dal.*

No. 112 (*Obv.* 3–*Rev.* 11). Last night a halo surrounded the Moon: it was interrupted. When a *usurtu* surrounds the Moon, there will be an eclipse. (An eclipse is a disturbance.) Last night a *usurtu* surrounded the Moon; it was interrupted.

When Venus draws near Scorpio, evil winds will come to the land; Ramman will give his rains, Ea his channels to Gutî. When 'it draws near' (*ṭiḫû*) to the 'Breast of Scorpio' (so it has been determined) it does not 'approach' (*ḳarâbu*). *ipatti* = *itti iḳrib.*

The planets are those whose stars pass on their own road over themselves.

When *A-idin* reaches Mars, Ramman will inundate. Mars has drawn near (?) to *Nun-šamí.* Rain has not come yet (?).

No. 114 (*Obv.* 1–3). Last night a halo surrounded the Moon and Gemini stood within it.

No. 117. When the greater halo surrounds the Moon, that land will be enlarged, destructions will surround men. When it surrounds and Cancer (*Allul*) stands within it, the king of Akkad will prolong life. When Regulus stands within it, women will bear male children. When the greater halo surrounds the Moon and is thin, there will be a giving of years to the king. (A great halo has surrounded it and has remained for many nights and is uninterrupted.) From Šapiku, of Borsippa.

Obv. 1. On *supuru* see Introduction.

VII. When the Moon and Sun are seen with one another.

(A) *On the Twelfth Day.*

No. 119 (*Obv.* 1–7). When the Moon appears out of its expected time, the market will be low. (It was seen with the Sun on the twelfth.) When the Moon and Sun are seen with one another out of their expected time, a strong enemy will overcome the land: the king of Akkad will accomplish the defeat of his foe.

(B) *On the Thirteenth Day.*

No. 120. When the Moon and Sun are seen with one another on the thirteenth day, there will not be silence: there will be unsuccessful traffic in the land: the enemy will seize on the land. From Aplâ.

No. 123 (*Obv.* 4 *ff.*). When a north wind prevails and blows, prosperity will come to all fruit trees. The Igigi gods will be at peace with the land: the land will see abundance. (*Iṣi rikipti* = garden fruit of all kinds.) This year dates and grapes (?) will prosper. The Moon appeared on the thirtieth of Tisri: from to-day as far back as Elul, which has passed, on the thirteenth day the Moon has not been seen with the Sun. When the Sun reaches the zenith and the sky is dark, years of prosperity, the king will grow strong. From Nírgal-íṭir, son of Gašuzu (?)-Tutu.

> *Obv.* 4. *sadrat.* This word is used twice of the wind, several times of storms (*imbaru*) and also in connection with earthquakes.
>
> *Rev.* 2. *balat.* Heb. *bâlâ.*
>
> *Rev.* 4. *isimu.* Probably the verb from which *sâmu* 'dark comes.

(C) *On the Fourteenth Day.*

No. 124. When the Moon reaches the Sun and with it fades out of sight, its horns being dim, there will be truth in the land, and the son will speak the truth with his father. (On the fourteenth the Moon was seen with the Sun.) When the Moon and the Sun are invisible, the king will increase wisdom; the king of the land, the foundation of his throne will be secure. (On the fourteenth day the Moon was seen with the Sun.) When the Moon and Sun are seen with one another on the fourteenth, there will be silence, the land will be satisfied; the gods intend Akkad for happiness. Joy in the heart of the people. The cattle of Akkad will lie down securely in the pasture-places. When a dark halo surrounds the Moon, it gathers clouds, that month will bring rain. When its horns are dim, a flood will come. (On the fourteenth the Moon was seen with the Sun.)

About the people concerning whom I sent to the king, my lord, the king does not say 'Why?' but has said 'let them bring them hither.' Now the king knows I hold no land in Assyria: I, what is my family to them, or what my life? Who is my god, who is my lord, to whom and how are my eyes turned? Now let my lord king, for whose life I pray Samas, send it unto Aḫišâ, by royal authority, and let his messenger bring the people: let the governor of Babylon cause him to leave. Let Nabu-íṭir-napšâti, my son, the king's servant, come, that with me he may visit (?) the king.

On the explanation of *šutatu*, see Introduction, p. xxvi, and on *ittintu*, see No. 30.

Rev. 5. *Cf.* 1 Sam. xviii, 18, 'who am I, or who my clan' (or 'life').

Rev. 7. *alla:* see Peiser, *Bab. Verträge*, p. 230, and *cf. allu*, Bezold, *Oriental Diplomacy*, p. 72.

Nos. 125–129 are very similar. No. 130, obv. 3, contains an unusual addition to the omen for the invisibility of the Moon and Sun, 'Mercy and peace will befall the king.' No. 136B is dated in the eponymy of Labasi, the fourteenth of Tisri (B.C. 655).

No. 137 (*Rev.* 1–4). When at the Moon's appearance a south wind blows, there will be a slaughter of Aḫarrû. When a parhelion (?) stands on the left of the Sun and .... (?), anarchy the king of Aḫarrû to ... will take him.

No. 139 (*Obv.* 5 *ff.*). The rest of the matter is lucky for the king, my lord. The Moon went into clouds so that we could not see it. When the Moon at its appearance goes into clouds, a flood will come (*Nikilpû = alaku*). When at the Moon's appearance heaven pours down, rain will rain. In rain-clouds it appeared. From Nabu-aḫî-íriba.

Obv. 5. *riḫti dibbi.* See Delitzsch, p. 618B, and *cf.* Harper, Nos. 342, edge 21, and 57, obv. 10.

No. 140. When the Moon does not wait for the Sun and disappears, there will be a raging of lions and wolves. It was seen with the Sun on the (fifteenth). When the Moon appears out of its time, there will be an overwhelming of (cities ?). On the fifteenth it was seen with the Sun: afterwards in Tisri the Moon will complete the day. From Balasî.

No. 141 (*Rev.* 5–6). When at the Moon's appearance a south wind blows, in that month a south wind will prevail.

No. 144 (*Obv.* 1–3). On the fourteenth the Moon and Sun were seen with one anothet.. Last night a halo surrounded the Moon, Saturn stood within it near the Moon.

Obv. 3. *Cf.* the omen in rev. 1–2, 'When the Sun stands within the Moon's halo,' and for an explanation see Introduction.

No. 145 (*Rev.* 1 *ff.*). When Jupiter becomes bright, the weapons of the king of Akkad will prevail over those of his foe. Regulus stands either on the right or left of Jupiter. Now it has stood three . . . . on the left of Jupiter. From Rimutu.

No. 146 (*Rev.* 1–6). When Mercury disappears at sunset it will rain as it disappears. Mars has assumed a brilliance: Lubad-dir is for prosperity of people: Lubad-dir (means) that corpses are angry (?): Lubad-dir is Mars. From Nírgal-íṭir.

No. 147 (*Rev.* 4 *ff.*), *and* **No. 148** (*Rev.* 1 *ff.*). When (the omen) portends a reign of long days for the well-being of the all-powerful king and his people, the Moon at its proper time is invisible with the Sun, rivalling its position.

Compare the omens for the Moon's appearance on the first day together with the day in its proper length, which are so frequently found on the same tablet. *Uštatâ* is the pres. III, 2 of *atû*, whence also *šutatû*.

No. 151 (*Obv.* 3–6). On the fourteenth for some months, god has appeared with god, namely Tisri, Marcheswan, and Kislew, three consecutive months (for happiness and long life to the king, my lord) they have been seen. (*Rev.* 2 *ff.*) When Scorpio is dark in the centre, then will be obedience. (This is when a 'covering (?)' reaches the Moon and Mercury.) In Kislew, the fifteenth day a man should consecrate to Nírgal, he should raise a willow (?)-branch in his hand; he will be safe in his journeys or travels: the sixteenth day, the seventeenth day he should sacrifice an ox before Nebo, an ox should be smitten in the presence of Nebo; the eighteenth day the god (?) should be apparelled, the night of the nineteenth a censer. From Nabû-šuma-iškun.

Rev. 4. The last two characters u-da should be *liš-kin*: I did not find a variant to correct my text by until too late.

No. 152 (*Rev.* 1 *ff.*). They shall bring in that tablet of the Day of Bel which we have written, for the king, my lord, to see, and they shall give us the Akkadian tablet of the king. They shall enclose three "stars" therein on the front, and shall direct the officer that whoever opens the document shall close it in his presence.

Rev. 2. A particular scribe was appointed for the day of Bel: *cf.* No. 160, rev. 5, and 81–2–4, 98, obv. 11 *ff.*, *ultu* *am A . BA ûm ilu ÍN . LIL gabbu imaḫḫaru uširrubu.*

Rev. 4. On the 'Akkadian tablet,' *cf.* King, *First Steps in Assyrian*, p. xxv, note.

No. 153 (*Obv.* 7 *ff.*). When the Moon stops in its course, the market will be low. On the fifteenth it was seen with the Sun. Last night a halo surrounded the Moon and Virgo (*Absin*) and Spica (*A-idin*) stood within it. When a halo surrounds the Moon and Spica (Pan) stands within it, brigands will be rampant and there will be much robbery in the land. When a 'river' surrounds the Moon, there will be great rains and showers. A-ídin stood within the halo of the Moon. From Nabû-ikiša, of Borsippa.

Rev. 2. A-ídin, from the above would appear to be a single star of Virgo. It is therefore probably Spica, which is the most conspicuous star of the group. Pan here evidently explains A-ídin, as also in No. 118, where there is no other star for it to refer to, and it is probably another name for Spica.

No. 154 (*Obv.* 1–2). On the first day I sent to the king thus: 'On the fourteenth the Moon will be seen with the Sun.' (*Rev.* 6.) On the fourteenth the Moon was seen with the Sun.

No. 155 (*Rev.* 1 *ff.*). The king, my lord, has not asked 'How did the clouds appear?' Last night its going forth which I saw during the day—half came forth; it went as far as the 'ground' in the middle. There is an omen from the sight for the . . . when the king sees a clear day, for two-thirds of a *kasbu* (80 minutes) of the day it will stand with the Sun. From Nabû-ikiša, of Borsippa.

Rev. 4. *iṣu*. Cf. *iṣi iriḫi* 'half the diameter' (Oppert, JA. xvi, 513, quoted Muss. Arnolt, *Dict.*, 86, a), and *iṣu* 'small.'
Rev. 7. The characters destroyed may be *um kì*.
Rev. 8. Probably read *šarru im-ru sinip kasbu ûmu*.

(D) *On the Fifteenth Day.*

No. 156 (*Obv.* 1–3). When the Moon and Sun are seen with one another on the fifteenth day, a powerful enemy will raise his weapons against the land. The enemy will destroy the gate of my city.

Obv. 3. *Âli-ia* 'my city' occurs elsewhere. (*Cf.* Nos. 162, 163, *ia*, No. 158, MU.) The magicians are at variance as to the precise formula, for we find 'the enemy will destroy the shrines of the great gods' (No. 157), or 'the city gates' (No. 159).

No. 158. The reverse is too mutilated to make connected sense, but it seems that the writer is apologising for not having sent the usual despatch, 'for that he has been sick and there was no interpreter of omens.' He concludes with the conventional 'let not the king leave me, and I shall not die.'

No. 162 (*Rev.* 2 *ff.*). When Jupiter goes with Venus, the prayer of the land will reach the heart of the gods. Merodach and Ṣarpanitum will hear the prayer of thy people and will have mercy on thy people.

Let them send me an ass that it may ease my feet. From Nírgal-íṭir.

> *Rev.* 7. The character which I read *šipâ*^II is written *lam* in the text. If LAM (= *išipu*) be translated 'sorcery' it gives no sense.

No. 163 (*Obv.* 4 *ff.*). When Mercury (or a planet) . . . appears, there will be corpses. When Cancer (*Allul*) is dark, a destructive demon will seize on the land and there will be corpses. From Nabû-aḫî-iddina.

No. 164 (*Rev.* 1–8). When the brilliance of a star shines from east to west, want (?) will overcome the foe, ... will seize upon the land. Iyyar, Siwan, Tammuz, Ab, Elul—these five months on the fourteenth day the Moon has not been seen with the Sun. May the king, my lord, know and give heed.

No. 165 (*Obv.* 5–6). When Anna becomes bright, the foe will make havoc.

> *Obv.* 5. Brunnow's *List*, No. 145, gives ^mul AN . NA = ^ilu Sin, *i.e.*, the Moon. But AN . NA also = Anu, and therefore probably Mars: see No. 103.
>
> *Obv.* 6. *nami-A iḫammiš*, *lit.* 'dash (to) ruins.'

(E) *On the Sixteenth Day.*

No. 166. When the Moon and Sun are seen with one another on the sixteenth day, king to king will send hostility. The king will be besieged in his palace for the space of a month. The feet of the

enemy will be against the land; the enemy will march triumphantly
in his land. When the Moon on the fourteenth or fifteenth of
Tammuz is not seen with the Sun, the king will be besieged in his
palace. When it is seen on the sixteenth day, it is lucky for
Subartu, evil for Akkad and Aḫarrû. From Akkullanu.

No. 167 (*Rev.* 7 *ff.*). When Mars, (the star of ?) Subartu grows
bright and assumes a brilliance, it is lucky for Subartu. And when
Saturn, the star of Aḫarrû, grows dim and its brilliance is smitten, it
is evil for Aḫarrû: there will be a hostile attack on Aḫarrû. From
Šapiku, of Borsippa.

No. 168 (*Obv.* 1–5). When the Moon on the fourteenth or
fifteenth of Nisan is not seen with the Sun, the troops the expedition
of the foe . . . . . it will be plundered and the land . . . . : there will
be a revolt in the land.

No. 170 (*Obv.* 1—*Rev.* 6). When the Moon on the fourteenth
or fifteenth of Sebat is not seen with the Sun, a copious flood will
come and the crops will be diminished. The *Abḳallu šiḳla 'Bíl-riminû-uḳarrad-Marduk'* stopped last night: in the morning it shall
be explained. O King! thou art the image of Marduk, when thou
art angry, to thy servants! When we draw near the king, our lord,
we shall see his peace!

    Obv. 4. What *Abḳallu Šiḳla* means it is difficult to say.
Abḳallu = 'ruler, mighty one,' while *šiḳla* might be referred to
the root *š-ḳ-l* 'to weigh, balance.' It appears to be some
instrument called 'Bíl-riminû-uḳarrad-Marduk' (*cf.* the wall of
Babylon 'Imgur-Bíl'), which stopped in the night. It may
have been some kind of clock.

No. 171 (*Obv.* 4–5). When the Moon on the fourteenth
of Adar is not seen with the Sun, there will be a devastation of Ur.

No. 172 (*Rev.* 3-6). When a planet changes the stars of
heaven, the king of countries will make an end. (Mercury has
grown bright and (thereby) changed the stars.)

VIII.—Omens from the Sun.

No. 173. When a halo surrounds the Sun, rain will fall. (The Suns are days.) From Iraššî-ilu.

Obv. 2. See note on No. 1, obv. 4.

No. 174 (*Obv.* 5–6). When a halo surrounds the Moon and the Sun in the East stands in it, the troops will fight a strange land.

No. 175. When the Sun enters the Moon, all lands (?) will speak the truth. Welfare of all the world. When a planet (?) changes colour opposite the Moon and enters the Moon, lions will die and the traffic of the land (will be hindered) (or) cattle will be slain. (Saturn has entered the Moon.) From Aššur-šarani.

Obv. 4. The changing colour probably refers to the apparent dimming of a star near the Moon.

No. 176. When the Sun stands in the place of the Moon, the king of the land will be secure on his throne. When the Sun stands above or below the Moon, the foundation of the throne will be secure; the king will stand in his justice. When the Sun and Moon are invisible, the king of the land will increase wisdom. (Last night Saturn drew near to the Moon. Saturn is the star of the Sun. This is its interpretation; it is lucky for the king. The Sun is the king's star.)

No. 177. When the Sun stands above the Moon (or) below the Moon, the foundation of the king's throne will be secure. When the Sun stands in the place of the Moon, there will be justice in the land. From Nabû-iḳbi.

No. 178. When the Sun reaches its zenith and goes forward, the reign of the All-powerful king will be long. When a halo surrounds the Sun in the morning in Adar, in that month a flood will come, (or) heaven will rain. (It is connected with the omen for Jupiter: the rest of the matter is that its omen is for rain and flood.)

Obv. 1. On *napâḫu*, see Oppert, *Zeits.*, I, 1886, p. 218.

No. 179 (*Obv.* 1–5). When a halo surrounds the Sun, and its opening points to the south, a south wind will blow. When a south wind blows on the day of the Moon's disappearance, heaven will rain (?).

No. 180 (*Obv.* 5 *ff*). Saturn stood within the halo of the Moon, and was opposite. This is the omen for the thirteenth day instead of 'the Moon was seen on the thirteenth day.' (Put) instead of this 'Saturn stood within the halo of the Moon.' When a dark halo surrounds the Moon, the month will bring rain (or) will collect clouds. When Regulus is dark, the king will grow angry and his rule .... he will turn and will not slay, he will have ... (Saturn before Regulus ....). From Nabû ...

No. 181. When the Sun reaches its zenith and is dark, the unrighteousness of that land will come to nought. When the Sun reaches its zenith and is dark, prosperity of people (or) there will be war in the land, (or) revolt (or) disasters to the king of all lands. When the Sun is dark with a dark light at its zenith, an eclipse happens and Ramman will inundate. (During the morning watch for Elam at the Sun's zenith this happened.) When it thunders in Iyyar, wheat and vegetables will not be prosperous. (The star of which I told the king, my lord, is very dim; it does not remain constant (?), it does not clear.) From Zakir.

Obv. 3. *uddâti* perhaps Heb. *êd* 'calamity.'

Rev. 5. *atinnu* doubtful. Perhaps we may compare the Heb. *êthân*.

Rev. 6. *umassi; masû*, II, 1 = 'purify.'

No. 182. When a parhelion (?) stands in the path of the Sun, the gods will take counsel for the good of the land. When four parhelia (?) stand, there will be destruction of oxen and wild beasts. When a parhelion (?) goes forth at the Sun's zenith, rain and flood will come. When the Sun reaches its zenith, in its path a parhelion (?) stands, the willow trees of the land will be thrown down (?). From Iraššî-ilu, the king's servant, the greater.

No. 183. When a bright star appears in the ecliptic (?), there will be a slaughter of Elam with the sword. When the Sun reaches its zenith in a parhelion (?), the king will grow angry and raise the sword. (*Explanation of ideograph.*) Jupiter has stood for a month over its reckoned time. When Jupiter passes to sunset, the land will dwell peacefully. Jupiter has stood for a month over its reckoned time. Marcheswan is the month of the king, my lord.

(*Rev.* 5 *ff.*). The handmaiden of the king, my lord, has gone (?) to Akkad; I cannot tarry, [for] she has run away; let the king, my lord, [send and] fetch her and give her to me. From Bîl-li', son of Ígibi, the magician.

Rev. 6. There are slight traces of characters at the end of this line.

IX.—OMENS FROM STARS.

No. 184 (*Obv.* 1—*Rev.* 3). When Jupiter appears at the beginning of the year, in that year its corn will be prosperous. (Mercury has appeared in Nisan.) When a planet (or Mercury) approaches Lî, the king of Elam will die. When Mars (*Šanumma*) approaches Aries, the people will be widespreading, the land will be satisfied. Mercury appeared in Taurus; it had come down (?) as far as the Pleiades (*Šugi*).

Obv. 6. On ÍN . MÍ . SAR . RA = Aries, see Jensen. *Kosm.*, p. 61.

No. 185. When Jupiter stands fast in the morning, hostile kings will be fortunate . . . in Siwan, brought near, where the Sun shone, it stood; in the brightening of its brilliance it was darkened; its zenith was complete as the zenith of the Sun; angry gods will be favourable with Akkad, there will be copious rains, plentiful floods in Akkad; corn and sesame will be plentiful and the price of one *ḳa*-measure of corn will be given for one *gur*. The gods in heaven will stand in their places, their shrines will be overflowing. (When) *Gam* assumes a brilliance, the foundation of the throne will be secure. When Regulus assumes a brilliance, the king of Akkad will effect completion. When Jupiter appears in the ecliptic, there will be a flood and the crops of the land will prosper. From Bamaî.

Obv. 1. *Širti.* *Cf.* Delitzsch, p. 635, b., under *ši'âru.*

Obv. 11.   1 GUR=300 ĶA. Meissner, *Altbabylonische Privatrecht,* p. 101.

Rev. 1. ᵐᵘˡ GAM. W.A.I. V, 46, 1, 3, ᵐᵘˡ *GAM* = *kakku ša ķatâ* ⁱˡᵘ *Marduk.* There is an interesting astrological letter (K. 7655) which mentions this omen (obv. 13).

No. 186 (*Obv.* 5 *ff.*). When Jupiter grows bright, the king of Akkad will go to pre-eminence. When Jupiter (*Íngišgalanna*) grows bright, there will be floods and rains. (*Íngišgalanna = Sagmígar.*) When Jupiter appears in Iyyar, the land . . . . When Jupiter (*Nibiru*) culminates, the gods will give peace, troubles will be cleared up, and complications will be unravelled. Rains and floods will come ; the amount of crops, with regard to the cold, will be out of all proportions to the amount of cold on the crcps. The lands will dwell securely. Hostile kings will be at peace, the gods will receive prayers and hear supplications ; the omens of the magician shall be made apparent. From Nírgal-íṭir.

Rev. 3. *išâtum—dalḫâtum,* Delitzsch, p. 143, b.

Rev. 9–10. See Delitzsch, *apâlu,* 113, a.

No. 187 (*Obv.* 1–6). When Jupiter (*Sagmígar*) passes to the place of sunset, there will be a dwelling securely, kindly peace will descend on the land. (It appeared in front of Allul.) When Jupiter (*Sagmígar*) assumes a brilliance in the tropic of Cancer and (becomes?) *Nibiru,* Akkad will overflow with plenty, the king of Akkad will grow powerful. (*Rev.* 5 *ff.*) When a great star like fire rises from sunrise and disappears at sunset, the troops of the enemy in battle (or) the troops of the enemy in slaughter will be slain. At the beginning of thy reign Jupiter was seen in its right position ; may the lord of gods make thee happy and lengthen thy days ! From Ašaridu, the son of Damķa.

No. 188 (*Obv.* 9 *ff.*). Now what I have seen I send to the king, my lord. The omens such as . . . to Allul it drew near. A second report I have determined, to the king my lord, I have sent.

No. 189 (*Obv.* 1–2). When Jupiter (*Sagmígar*) appears in Elul the land will eat good food.

No. 190. When Jupiter (*Sagmigar*) appears in Marcheswan, king to king will send hostility. When Jupiter (*Sagmigar*) stands in the 'Brilliance of Pabilsag,' there will be destructions in the land. When the same star approaches *Indubanna*, the market will go up. (*Indubanna* is the 'Brilliance of Pabilsag.') From Nabû-Šuma-iškun.

Obv. 3. On 'Pabilsag' = the sting of Scorpio, see No. 236 G, and Sagittarius, Jensen, *Kosm.*, p. 496.

No. 192. When the Moon occults Jupiter (*Sagmigar*), that year a king will die (or) an eclipse of the Moon and Sun will take place. A great king will die. When Jupiter enters the midst of the Moon, there will be want in Aḫarrû. The king of Elam will be slain with the sword: in Subarti . . (?) will revolt. When Jupiter enters the midst of the Moon, the market of the land will be low. When Jupiter goes out from behind the Moon, there will be hostility in the land.

Obv. 7. ḪI . GAR . , No. 193, gives the variant *i-ba-ru* (obv. 3).

No. 193 (*Obv.* 4–5). When the Moon darkens Jupiter, the king of kings, his hand will overpower his enemies.

No. 194 (*Obv.* 1–3). When Jupiter passes to the right of Venus, a strong one will conquer Gutî with the sword.

No. 195. When Jupiter stands in front of Mars, there will be corn and men will be slain, (or) a great army will be slain. When Jupiter and Mars . . . the god will devour (or) rains will be given upon the land. (*Uštaddanu šutadunu* resolved ?) When Mars approaches Jupiter, there will be a great devastation in the land. When Jupiter and a planet, their stars face, evil will befall the land. When Mars (*Lubad-dir*) and Jupiter (*Rabû*) approach, there will be a slaughter of cattle. (*Lubad-dir* is Mars, *Rabû* is Jupiter.) Mars has approached Jupiter. When Mars (*Šanamma*) approaches Jupiter, in that year the king of Akkad will die and the crops of that land will be prosperous.

This omen is evil for the lands; let the king, my lord, make a *Nambulbi*-ceremony to avert the evil. From Nabû-ikiša of Borsippa.

Obv. 3. On *Sarri*, see III R. 57, 62a.

Obv. 5. *mitluk*, perm. I, 2 of *malâku*. The Ethpe'el of the corresponding Syriac root has the meaning of *deliberavit;* the Assyrian word is perhaps used as a grammatical term.

No. 197. When Regulus approaches in front of the Moon and stands, the king will live many days; the land will not be prosperous. From Aplâ.

No. 199 (*Obv.* 1–2). The omen which is unlucky for the king is good for the land: the omen which is good for the land is unlucky for the king.

No. 200. When a star shines and its brilliance is as bright as the light of day, in its shining it takes a tail like a scorpion, it is a fortunate omen, not for the master of the house, but for the whole land. When there is *binnu* in all lands, violence will pass away, there will be justice, abundance will be plentifully produced; ruin for the master of that house (or) that king will stand in his justice. There will be obedience and good-will in the land. (This is from ....) When a great star (Jupiter?) shines from north to south, and its brilliance [it takes a tail like a scorpion?] ..... This is according to the tablet (that tells) that Nebuchadnezzar brought Elam to ruin. When Mercury appears in Tammuz, there will be corpses. When *intina-maššig mulluḫ* at its rising, prosperity of crops, the market will be steady. This concerns Mercury. From Nabû-mušíṣi.

Obv. 4. *binnu*, see Delitzsch, 180, b.

Rev. 5. For this campaign of Nebuchadnezzar I, *c.* 1140 B.C., see KT. III 1, 164, and *cf.* obv. 3 with col. I, l. 25, *Ritti-Marduk bîl bîti ša Bît-Karziyabku.*

7. *Intinamaššig*, see Jensen, *Kosm.*, p. 54.

No. 201. After two hours of the night had passed, a great star shone from north to south. Its omens are propitious for the king's desire. The king of Akkad will accomplish his mission. From Ašaridu (the greater), the king's servant.

No. 202. When a great star shines from east to west and disappears and dulls (?) its brilliance, the army of the enemy will be destroyed in battle. When a star like a light (or) like a torch shine, from east to west and disappears, the army of the enemy will be slain in its onslaught. Two great stars were observed one after the other in the middle watch. From Ašaridu (the greater).

No. 203. When Venus disappears at sunrise in Nisan from the first to the thirtieth day, there will be desolation. When a halo surrounds the Moon and Sibzianna stands within it, the king of Subarti will work mightily, his land will have abundance. (Sibzianna stood within the Moon's halo . . .) From Aḫiša of Erech.

Obv. 3. *urubati*, according to 205, r 1 = *bikâti* 'weepings.' *cf.* also K 4166. *Obv.* 3, *ú-ru-ba-tú* | *bi-ka-tú*.

No. 204 (*Obv.* 4–6). When Venus changes . . . . (There will be) a hostile expedition : insurrection (or) treason.

Obv. 6. *ḳašrâti*, Heb. *ḳešer*.

No. 205 (*Obv.* 1–4). Venus is now disappearing at sunrise. When Venus is brilliant, it is not good for those days which are no the full length and which are too long.

Obv. 3. On *umi ša la ušallimu*, see Introduction.

No. 205A (*Obv.* 3). When Spica (*A-idin*) reaches Mars (*Mulmul*), it will rain.

No. 206 (*Obv.* 5–8). When Venus fixes its position, the days of the prince will be long, there will be justice in the land. Venus in the Tropic of Capricorn . . . (*Rev.* 4–6.) When a halo surrounds the Moon and the Pleiades (Sugi) stand within it, in that year there will be a slaughter of men : sheep will not approach oxen.

No. 207. Venus is appearing at sunset in the Tropic of Cancer: this is its interpretation. When Venus appears in Siwan, there will be a slaughter of the enemy. When Venus appears in the Tropic of Cancer, the king of Akkad will have no rival. Five or six days ago it reached Allul. This is its interpretation. When Venus (*Uza*) approaches Allul, there will be obedience and welfare in the land: the gods will have mercy on the land. Empty . . (?) will be full and the crops of the land will prosper; the sick in the land will recover. Pregnant women will perfect their offspring. The great gods will show favour to the sanctuaries of the land, the houses of the great gods will be renewed. (*Uza* = Venus.) From Šumaï.

Rev. 3. *iššikku.* See Muss-Arnolt, *Dict.*, *sub voce.*

No. 208. Venus is now disappearing at sunset. When Venus grows dim and disappears in Ab, there will be a slaughter of Elam. When Venus appears in Ab from the first to the thirtieth day, there will be rains, the crops of the land will be prosperous. (In the middle of this month Venus appeared in Leo at sunrise.) From Nírgal-ítir.

Obv. 3. *uštaktit* perhaps = become frightened. See Del., 363 b.

No. 209 (*Obv.* 1–5). When Sarur and Sargaz of the tail of Scorpio are brilliant, the weapons of Akkad will make an onslaught. (Venus has appeared in Pabilsag.) When Venus (Ištar) puts on the diadem of the Moon divided, there will be desolations.

Obv. 4. *muniksisa* $\sqrt{}$*kasâsu.* Rev. 1 '(when) Venus (puts on) a dark crown' perhaps indicates that the New Moon occults her.

No. 210. When Venus in Kislew from the first to the thirtieth day disappears at sunrise, there will be famine of corn and straw in the land. The lord of kings has spoken thus, 'Why hast thou not [observed?] the month, and sent the lucky and unlucky?' The prince of the kingdom has been neglected, has not been obeyed. May the lord of kings when his face is favourable lift up my head that I may make my decisions and tell the king, my lord. From Ašaridu.

Obv. 7. *inațiš* perhaps Heb. *națaš*, but by no means certain.

No. 211 (*Obv.* 1—*Rev.* 2). When Venus appears in Sebat, the crops of the land will prosper: . . . will be prosperous: mercy and welfare will be in the land. Venus stood in the midst of Anunitum. When Venus appears in Virgo, rains in heaven, floods on (earth), the crops of Aḫarrû will prosper; fallen ruins will be inhabited.

No. 213 (*Obv.* 1–5). When Scorpio approaches the front of the Moon and stands, the reign of the king will be long; the enemy will come, but his defeat will be accomplished.

No. 215 (*Obv.* 4, *ff*). The Breast of Scorpio which stood on the right horn of the Moon has not approached the Sun (?): nothing changes. When Scorpio stands within the Moon's halo, it is for rains and floods. (The king shall see its omen; it will rain.) When in Iyyar the fifteenth day to Ía . . . , in the evening watch he will turn his peace into glory. From Nabû-šuma-iškun.

No. 216. Saturn has appeared in Leo. When Leo is obscured, for three years lions and jackals . . . and kill men. The traffic of the land (Aḫarrû) will be hindered. When a planet culminates in Ab, the bed of warriors will be wide. From Ašaridu.

Rev. 3. 'The bed of warriors wide' refers to plague. See No. 232, Obv. 3.

No. 216c. Mercury has appeared. When Mercury appears for a month, floods and rain. Mars (*Lubad-dir*) for prosperity of people. From Nírgal-iṭir.

No. 217. Mercury is visible at sunrise. When Mercury appears for a month, rain and floods. When Mercury appears either in Iyyar or Siwan, a flood will come and benefit the fields and meadow lands. When Mercury stands in the east, there will be an invasion of Subarti and Kašši against the land.

This is the fact (?) of the matter: I have not come to Nineveh (because) the magicians to write in the palace (? began ?) . . Whatever . . . on the front of it 'Nineveh' I will make: unless they have begun I shall not come in; let them give me a sealed letter. From Nabu-mušiṣi.

The latter part apparently refers to the writing of some inscriptions, but the text is too mutilated to make certain.

No. 218. When Mercury is seen in Iyyar, a flood will come and benefit the fields and meadow lands. When Jupiter reaches Mars (*Mulmul*), it will rain. On the fourteenth the Moon and Sun were not seen with one another: on the fifteenth god was seen with god. The king of Subarti will have no rival. (I have heard from my father.) From Bíl-aḫî-íriba.

No. 219. When Mercury culminates in Tammuz, there will be corpses. When Leo is dark, the heart of the land will not be happy. Long live the lord of kings! From Ašaridu.

No. 220. When Mercury culminates in Elul, there will be a heightening of the market, an increase of cereals. Long live the lord of kings! From Ašaridu (the less).

No. 221. Mercury is visible at sunrise in the precincts of Virgo. This is its interpretation. When Mercury (*Nunu*) approaches Spica (*Pan*), the crops of the land will prosper, the cattle will be numerous in the fields, the king will grow strong and will overcome (?) his enemies. Sesame and dates will prosper. When Mercury culminates in Elul, there will be a heightening (of the market), an increase of cereals. When *Daḫ* is visible in Elul . . . will prosper. (*Daḫ* = Mercury.) From Ašaridu, the son of Damḳa, the king's servant.

> *Obv.* 2. AB . SIN = *širû* (Brunnow, *List* No. 3832) = Virgo (Epping and Strassmaier, *Zeits.*, VII, 220).

No. 222. When Mercury appears in Elul, there will be a heightening of the market, an increase of cereals. When Leo (*Ur-maḫ*) makes its stars to shine, let the king wherever he goes (guard himself?). When Leo (*Urgula*) is dark, lions and jackals will rage and the traffic of Aḫarru will be hindered. From Ṭabia.

> *Obv.* 2. The fourth sign ÁŠ may perhaps be read *ina* here, *i.e. ina napaš nissabu*; but Brunnow, *List*, No. 23 = *mitḫaru*, and it is possible that *maḫiru* may be intended here.

No. 223. When Mercury culminates in Marcheswan, the crops of the land will prosper. When Scorpio is dim in the centre, there will be obedience in the land. (Mercury stands within Scorpio.) When in the flaming light of Scorpio (*-Išḫara*) its breast is bright, its tail is dark, its horns are brilliant, rains and floods will be dry in the land: locusts will come and devour the land; devastation of oxen and men: (the weapon is raised and the land of the foe) is captured. . . Scorpio . . .

Obv. 5. No. 223A gives several variants. *Rev.* 5–6, 'its horns *ningula* (or) *ninbuṭa*.' 7–8, 'Its tail *iṭati*, rains and floods NIM [pl] -ni (i.e., *išakku* 'will be high').

No. 224. [Mercury] is visible. When Mercury is visible in Kislew, there will be robbers in the land. From Nírgal-íṭir.

No. 225 (*Obv.* 3, *ff.*) Mercury stands within Simmaḫ. When Mercury approaches the 'Star of the Tigris' there will be rains and floods. (Mercury is visible at Sunrise.)

Obv. 4. [mul] MAS . TIG . GAR = *Anunitu* (Brunnow, *List*, No. 1878).

No. 226. Mercury is visible with Mars (*Mulmul*) at sunset; it is ascending to Šugi. There will be rains and floods. When Jupiter appears at the beginning of the year, in that year its crops will prosper. From Nadinu.

No. 228. Mercury stands in Leo. When Leo is dim, the heart of the land will not be happy. When Regulus is dim, the director of the palace will die. From Nabu-mušíṣi.

Obv. 1. *Cf.* No. 199A, *Obv.* 1–2.

No. 230 (*Obv.* 1—*Rev.* 1). When Spica (*Pan*) stands within the Moon's halo, lawless men will rage and there will be robbery in the land. It will not change to evil. The halo of Virgo is for rain and flood; it is turning cold.

No. 231 (*Obv.* 1–6). When Mars is visible in Tammuz, the bed of warriors will be wide. When Mercury stands in the north, there will be corpses, there will be an invasion of the king of Akkad against a foreign land. When Mars approaches Gemini, a king will die and there will be hostility.

Obv. 2. No. 232, *Obv.* 3, explains the omen 'bed of warriors' as referring to plague.

No. 232. Mars is visible in Tammuz: it is dim. When Mars is visible in Tammuz, the bed of warriors will be wide: (it refers to plague.) When Mars stands in the east, there will be an invasion of Subarti and Kašši against the land. When Mars culminates indistinctly (?) and becomes brilliant, the king of Elam will die. When Nírgal in its disappearing grows smaller, like the stars of heaven is very indistinct, he will have mercy on Akkad. The forces of my troops will go and slay the army of the enemy, an audacious land they will overcome. The troops of the foe will not be able to stand against my troops. The cattle of Akkad will lie down securely in the fields: sesame and dates will prosper. When Mercury approaches Mars (Nabû), horses will die. (*La isniḳ* = *la ḳurbu.*) When Mars is dim, it is lucky; when bright, unlucky. When Mars follows Jupiter, that year will be lucky. From Bulluṭu.

Obv. 6. *ummuliš* and cf. *ummul*, see Delitzsch, p. 83, b.
Obv. 12. *ṣarramu*, cf. Syr. *ṣ'rama* audacia.
Rev. 4. For *nin* in the text, read *dam.*

No. 233. When Mars is visible in Elul, the crops of the land will prosper, the land will be satisfied. Mars (*Lubad-dir*) is for abundance of people. Mars at its disappearance became brilliant. From Nabû-iḳbi.

No. 234. When Mars approaches the Moon and stands, the Moon will cause evil to inhabit the land. When a planet stands at the left horn of the Moon, the king will act mightily. When a star stands at the left front of the Moon, the king will act mightily. When a star stands at the left rear of the Moon, the king of Akkad will work mightily. When Virgo (*Dilgan*) stands at its left horn, in that year the vegetables of Akkad will prosper. When Virgo (*Dilgan*) stands above it, in that year the crops of the land will prosper. When a star stands at the left horn of the Moon, a hostile land will see evil. When a star stands at its left horn, there will be an eclipse of the king of Aḫarru. The *Gan-ba* of that land will be diminished; it will rain. When a star stands at its left horn, an eclipse of the king of Aḫarrû will take place. When at its left horn a star (stands) Rammânu will devour in a hostile land (or) an eclipse will take place, (or) an eclipse of the king of Aḫarrû: his land will be diminished. From Zakir.

No. 235. Mars had reached Cancer (*Allul*), it has entered it: I kept watch, it did not stay, it did not remain but came out below it. A breeze (sprang up) as it went forth; its interpretation to the king my lord I send. If ever (one) sends to the king, my lord, thus: 'When Mars approaches Allul, the prince (will die?),' when it stands and waits . . . it is evil for Akkad. If ever one sends to the king, my lord, thus: 'When a planet (appears?) in a blast of wind, the king of Subarti . . . .' (This word implies 'weakness'; let not the king lay it to heart.) Last night it thundered. When it thunders in Ab, the day is dark, the heaven rains, lightning lightens, floods will be poured in the channels. When it thunders on a cloudless day, there will be darkness (or) there will be famine in the land. From Akkullanu.

Rev. 1. The king of Subarti = the king of Assyria, from No. 62, Obv. 4, 'We are Subarti.'

No. 236. Mars has entered the precincts of Cancer (*Allul*). It is not counted as an omen. It did not stay, it did not wait, it did not rest; speedily it went forth. From Bíl-naṣir.

Obv. 6. *ikaši*, *cf.* Syriac *kâš* destitit, quievit.

No. 236G (*Obv.* 4). Mars stands in Pabilsag (the sting of Scorpio means Pabilsag). Mars stands and waits in Pabilsag.

Obv. 6. For ana . . ḳabi = 'means,' *cf.* No. 232, 3, and on Pabilsag = Ziḳit Aḳrabi, *cf.* No. 272, obv. 9.

No. 237. When Urbarra Urmaḫ . . . distant days . . to the land . . . Urbarra = [Mars], Urmaḫ = [Leo], Mars stood in . . . When a star shines and enters . . . there will be a revolt. From Nabû-aḫî-íriba.

Obv. 1. *Urbarra.* According to K 4195, Col. III–IV, it = Mars.

No. 239 (*Obv.* 1–5). When Mars (*Apin*) approaches Scorpio, the prince will die by a scorpion's sting, and his son after him will take the throne; the dwelling of the land . . the land another lord . . the boundary line of the land will not be secure.

No. 240. When Mars (*Mulmul*) is darkened over the Moon and stands, the king will act mightily, his land will be enlarged. From Nabû-ikiša of Borsippa. May Bel and Nebo give long days and happiness to the king of countries, my lord. With the king we have acted innocently. Now among my brothers in the palace an attack on the treasury was made and they slew the scribe whom the king had caused me to take with them, and my magician; and to me they said 'It was an edict with us.' I went with my brothers and peace shall be made and I will keep the watch of the king, my lord. Why . . . . may Bel and Nebo be gracious (?); O king, judge thou . . .

Obv. 1. DAR = *barâmu* (Brunnow, *List*, No. 3482). See Jensen, *Kosm.*, p. 7.

Obv. 9. *masartu*, perhaps from *asâru* besiege.

No. 241 (*Obv.* 4, *ff.*). When at the Moon's appearance Mars (*Mulmul*) stands at its side, the king will act mightily, his land . . . When Mars enters the Moon and goes forth northward, the heart of the land will be happy: the king of Akkad will grow powerful and will have no rival. From Bíl-aḫî-íriba, son of Labaši-ili.

Obv. 4. On this plural verb, *cf.* No. 243A, obv. 1–2.

No. 243 (*Obv.* 3). On Ištar (Venus) wearing a crown, see No. 209.

No. 243A (*Obv.* 1–2). Mulmul is used with a plural verb.

No. 243B (*Rev.* 1, *ff.*). When at the beginning of the year Mars stands in the *našu* of Venus, the enemy or a flood will spoil the crops. From Nírgal-iṭir.

Rev. 3. The vertical stroke in the last sign may be a fracture, and the whole word will therefore read *umarrum*.

No. 244. When the Pleiades (Šugi) over the Moon are darkened and stand, (and) enter the Moon, the king will stand in his might, will dwell, and will enlarge his land, and to his land will be good: there will be justice and truth in the land. From Ištar-šuma-íriš.

No. 244A (*Obv.* 1–2). When the Pleiades, their circle is bright . . . the house (against) its master will revolt.

Obv. 1. *kurkurru*, Heb. *kârâr* revolve. See No. 49.

No. 244B (*Obv.* 2–3). When Libra . . . before the Moon, the reign of the king will be long.

No. 245. When the Moon occults *Kilba*, there will be an eclipse of Subarti. When Spica (*Pan*) is darkened over the Moon and enters the Moon, the days of the prince will be long. The Moon for one year is long. Let the king give heed, let him not pass it by, let him guard himself, let not the king go into the street on an evil day until the time of the omen has passed. (The omen of a star lasts for a full month.) From Iraššî-ilu, the king's servant.

No. 246B (*Obv.* 1–3). When *Simmaḫ* grows bright, an invasion of an army . . . .

No. 246F. When a star stands in front of the Moon . . . the king will act mightily. When Mars approaches the Moon and waits, the Moon will cause evil to dwell in the land. When a star stands on the left of the Moon, the land of the foe will see evil. From Nabû-íriba.

No. 247. What is this favour which Ištar has granted the king, my lord? . . . . (*Rev.* 3 *ff.*) When a star (?) turns back and appears, the king will prolong life. From Ištar-šuma-íriš.

X. Omens from Clouds.

No. 248. When a cloud grows dark in heaven, a wind will blow. From Nabû-aḫî-íriba.

XI. Omens from the Moon's Disappearance.

No. 249 (*Obv.* 3 *ff.*). On the twenty-seventh the Moon disappeared. When the day of the Moon's disappearance in one month three times (occurs), an eclipse will take place, and the gods for three days in heaven will . . . . When the Moon appears on the thirtieth of Elul, there will be a devastation of the land. . . . This thirtieth day (it should appear). The lord of kings has spoken thus, 'Does the omen change?' The Moon waned on the twenty-seventh: the twenty-eighth and twenty-ninth in heaven (are) the intervening space, and on the thirtieth the Moon reappears. Unless it appears there will be an uncovered interval of four days in heaven: otherwise the interval will not be four days. Long live the king! From Ašaridu.

Obv. 4. *ûm bubbuli.* Jensen, *Kosm.*, p. 91.

Rev. 3. *bûtu* ($\sqrt{\text{b-'-d}}$) 'originally perhaps dividing point or space' (Muss-Arnolt, *Dict.*, 147, b). The root idea is 'separation.'

Rev. 5. *immatima* with precatives: *cf.* the use of double jussives in Hebrew (Ps. cix, 20, *etc.*).

Rev. 6. *babti* in contracts 'unpaid, uncovered' (Muss-Arnolt, *Dict.*, 146a). *Libid, ibid,* same root as *bûtu* above.

XII. Omens from Storms.

No. 250. When a storm comes upon the land, the crops will be increased, the market will be steady. When a storm prevails in the land, the 'reign' of the land will rule great power. When a storm bursts in Sebat, an eclipse of Kašši will take place. From Ašaridu, the king's servant.

Obv. 3. *sadir*, see No. 123, obv. 4.

Obv. 6. For the explanation of an eclipse of Kašši, see Introduction.

No. 251 (*Obv.* 3 *ff.*). When there is a storm in the land, prosperity of people. When a storm prevails in the land, the 'reign' of the land will rule great power. When a storm bursts on the day of Zu (?) (it has not been recorded: a storm is lucky and does not bring to evil. Last night a star 'the head of Scorpio' stood in front of the Moon. Its omen changes not, there is none, it has not been determined).

If *Ṣurru* the Moon (?) . . . (7) it is a constant omen.

Let them lay the month under a ban; every star of heaven has gone (?) and in the evil of the month Kislew, unless it pass, let them ban it.

Rev. 8 *ff.* We may find a parallel to this in Job iii, 8, 'Let them ban it that ban the day.' *Litruru* is the I, 2 conj. of *arâru*, the same word as used in the Hebrew.

No. 252. When a storm bursts in Adar, blight will come upon the land. The Uruk-god divides from Nebo (PA) to Nebo (ÚR), it will not rain. When the Uruk-god divides over a city, the city, the king and its princes will be happy. From Aḫišâ of Erech.

Obv. 3. ilu TIR.AN.NA=*Uruk*, Brunnow, *List*, No. 7665. Esarhaddon (KT. ii, 138, VI, 6) explains how he adorned the arches of his palace with a glaze, so that both in shape and colour they looked like *ilu Tiranna*, *i.e.*, the rainbow. It occurs elsewhere in the storm texts, 'When it thunders, the day is dark, heaven rains, Uruk divides, lightning lightens,' *etc.* (No. 258, obv. 1–3). *Cf.* K. 200, rev. 21, 'When a halo surrounds the Moon and *Tiranna* in its midst.... (and l. 23) when a halo surrounds the Moon and the halo like *Tiranna* II ú....' Perhaps there is some connection between the word *Uruk* and the Syr. *ûrâgâ* 'versicolor.'

No. 252E (*Obv.* 13). Of that which the king, our lord, sent us, saying, 'Have ye had rain?' We have had much (?) rain.

XIII. Omens from Thunder.

No. 253. When it thunders on the day of the Moon's disappearance, the crops will prosper and the market will be steady. When it rains on the day of the Moon's disappearance, it will bring on the crops and the market will be steady. Long live the lord of kings! From Ašaridu.

No. 254 (*Obv.* 5 *ff.*). If Rammânu should thunder in the midst of the Sun, there will be mercy upon the land. ('In the midst of the Sun' which they say when, the Sun being at its zenith,

Rammânu speaks in the morning from the direction of the Sun's zenith.) From Balasî.

Rev. 2. The character *ik* may be *ri.*

No. 256. Of the work of which the king, my lord, spoke, this night of the twenty-second, with regard to Venus and *Kaksidi* we ourselves will do it, the magicians shall do it. When Rammânu thunders in the midst of the star Lî, the king's hand will overcome a land other than this.

Obv. 5. *kaksidi.* See Jensen, *Kosm.*, p. 49 *ff.*

No. 256A (*Obv.* 5 *ff.*). When Rammânu thunders in the great gate of the Moon, there will be a slaying of Elamite troops with the sword: the goods of that land will be gathered into another land. (This is what is when the Moon appears and it thunders.) From Buluṭu.

No. 256D (*Obv.* 1—*Rev.* 2). When it thunders in Ab, the day is dark, the heaven rains (?) the crops of the land will prosper. When it thunders on a cloudless day, there will be famine. When lightning lightens on a cloudless day, Rammânu will inundate. ('A cloudless day' = Ab. 'Rammânu will inundate,' which they say when . . . .) When a storm wind blows from the south, there will be a devastation of Aḫarrû.

Obv. 2. *irub* or *irup.* SU . SU . RU is explained as *irpi* (see No. 87, obv. 3, 5, 6).

No. 257. When it thunders in Ab, the day is dark, heaven rains, lightning lightens, waters will be poured forth in the channels. When it thunders on a cloudless day, there will be darkness (or) famine in the land.

Concerning this sickness the king has not spoken from his heart. The sickness lasts a year: people that are ill recover. Do thou grant, O king my lord, that they pursue the worship of the gods and pray the gods day and night. Does truth ever reach the king and his family? A man should kill a calf (?) without blemish, he should cut it in pieces; he himself should say as follows, 'A man that is in full health, his days are short (?): he is sick, his days are long.' From Ištar-šuma-íris.

Rev. 3. *iluttu*, perhaps from √*alâdu*, *aširtu* √*ašaru*, 'prosper, thrive.'

Rev. 4. *ibatti*, uncertain. *Cf.* however numerous Semitic words beginning with the root letters *b-t-* meaning 'to cut.' *Cf.* also the ceremony in Gen. xv, 10.

No. 258 (*Obv.* 7 *ff.*). When it rains in Ab there will be a slaughter of men. When a storm wind comes from the west, there will be a destruction of Aḫarrû. When it thunders twice, the land which sent thee hostility will send thee peace. From Nabû-aḫi-iriba.

No. 259. When it thunders in Tisri, the day is dark, heaven rains, the rainbow is divided, lightning lightens, the gods will have mercy on the land. From the Chief Scribe.

No. 260. When it thunders in Tisri, there will be hostility in the land. When it rains in Tisri, death to sick people and oxen (or) slaughter of the enemy. From Ṭabia.

No. 261. When it thunders in Sebat, there will be an invasion of locusts. When it thunders in Sebat, heaven will rain with stones.

No. 262 (*Obv.* 5, *ff.*). When it thunders in Adar, the day is dark, heaven rains, lightning lightens, a great flood will come, and the crops (will prosper). From . . .

XIV. Omens from Earthquakes.

No. 263. When the earth quakes through the whole day, there will be a destruction of the land. When it quakes continually, there will be an invasion of the enemy. From Nabû-iḳbi, of Kutha.

Obv. 2. *Nâšu* is used for heaven and earth quaking at the approach of a god. When Ninib marches, the heaven and earth quake (*inuššu* Rm. 126, Rev. 3–4 Delitzsch, p. 454, b). We can finally settle the meaning of *rîbu* from a comparison of these texts. No. 266, *Obv.* 5. *ff.* reports 'Last night *rîbu irtubu*.' Then follow three prognostics, the protases of which are (1) *Ana ina* [arḫu] *Ṭibiti ri-i-bu ŠU-ub* (2) *Ana ina* [arḫu] *Ṭibiti*

KI (= *irṣitu*) *ŠU-ub* (3) *Ana ina muši KI i-ru-ub.* From the first two it is obvious that *rîbu ŠU-ub* and *KI ŠU-ub* are closely analogous in meaning, or they would not have both been used to explain *rîbi irtubu.* It needs little further demonstration that *ŠU-ub* = *irûb;* but this can be directly proved from W.A.I. III, 61, rev. I, 3, where the protasis *inuma ri-i-bu i-ru-ub* is followed by the apodosis *šarru ina âl nakri uš-ba*, which is practically the same as that for *rîbu ŠU-ub* in our present text, both being omens for Tebet. Again, a comparison of W.A.I. III, 61, *obv.* III, 27, and No. 265, *obv*, 1–2 (both omens for Nisan), will show that *rîbu irûb* = *KI irûb.* The former has ínuma *ri-i-bu i-ru-ub šarru mât-su BAL-su nap-paḫ-tum in-nap-paḫ*, and the latter *Ana ina* arḫu *Nisanni KI i-ru-ub šarru mât-su BAL-su* . . . Further, No. 264, though beginning 'of the *rîbi* of which the king, my lord, sent me, this is its interpretation,' yet in all three explanations given below it uses *KI-tim* or *KI*. We have now to settle the meaning of *rîbu.* No. 266, rev. 3–4, gives *Ana ina muši KI i-ru-ub na-zak mâti* . . . *šumkutí* (*i*) *mâti*, but No. 267, rev. 1–2, gives as a variant *Ana KI ina muši i-nu-uš na-zak mâti* . . . . . . , and No. 265, Obv. 3–4, *Ana KI-tim ina muši i-nu* . . *na-zak mâti šumkutí* (*i*) *mâti.* From this it is plain that *irûb* = *inuš*, and the meaning of *inuš* 'shakes, quakes' is certain (Delitzsch, p. 454, b). We may therefore consider that *rîbu irûb* = *irṣitu irub* = *irṣitu inuš* = 'the earth quakes.'

Obv. 4. *Sadir* appears to have the meaning of 'prevailing.' It is used of the wind and storms. See Note to No. 123, Obv. 4.

No. 264. Concerning the earthquake of which the king, my lord, sent me, this is its interpretation. When the earth quakes continually there will be an invasion of the enemy. When the earth quakes in the night, harm will come to the land (or) devastation to the land . . . .

Of the remainder we can guess approximately at the sense. Apparently Ištar-šuma-íriš himself felt an earthquake in the night, and he reports on it in *ll.* 7–8, as well as giving the explanation above in *l.* 5. He is evidently writing his report in answer to the king's question in the beginning of Nisan 655 B.C. (*cf.* Edge 1, 'Eponym Labasi'), but he does not seem certain whether the earthquake which the king felt happened in Nisan or the last month of the preceding year, for he sends the omen for an earthquake in Nisan, and then says 'unless it began in Adar.'

No. 265. When the earth quakes in Nisan, the king's land will revolt from him. When the earth quakes during the night, harm will come to the land, or devastation to the land. From Aplâ.

No. 265A (*Rev.* 3 *ff.*). The ends of the lines are mutilated, but I think we may read 'When the earth quakes in Tammuz, the prince will be magnified in the land of his foe.'

No. 265C (*Obv.* 1–2). The hiatus may be supplied from W.A.I. III, 61, III, 51, 'When the earth quakes in Tisri, the crops will prosper, there will be hostility in the land.'

No. 266 (*Obv.* 5, *ff.*). Last night there was an earthquake. When the earth quakes in Tebet, the king will sit in the city of his foe. When the earth quakes in Tebet, the palace of the prince will be smitten and go to ruins. When the earth quakes in the night, there will be harm to the land (or) devastation to the land. From the Chief Astrologer.

No. 267 (*Obv.* 12–15). When the earth quakes in Sebat, the corn its weight will weigh; there will be expeditions of the enemy. When the earth quakes in Sebat, another prince will sit in the palace.

Obv. 8. *Šamû issu* 'heaven speaks' = thunder.

Obv. 3. i.e. *kibrat irbitti*, Brunnow, *List*, No. 5782.

Obv. 10–11. *Íriškigal ikkilla-ša kima ur . . . . irṣitim mâtu inadi(di)*. Íriškigal is known to us through the Tell-el-Amarna tablets. (See Bezold-Budge, *Tell-el Amarna Tablets*, LXXXV.) She was invited to a feast of the gods and apparently entered the fourteen gates of their abode; but she and Nirgal quarrelled and he 'began to beat her head from the seat to the floor,' whereat she besought him not to kill her. Staying his hand he listened to her: he was to be husband, she the wife, and they were to rule the wide earth: and so he took her, kissed her, and dried her tears, and whatever she desired was done for her.

The explanation of the 'mourning of Íriškigal' is evidently to be sought here, but what it means is difficult to say. The writer of the Tell-El-Amarna tablet perhaps intended an explanation of the word Íriškigal, when he finished his story with *minamma tirišinni*, 'whatever thou askest me.'

No. 267A. When the heavens are darkly smitten (?), there will be plenty in the land.

Ṣillâ has sent by the hand of Šakin-šumi thus, 'I will put thee to death, for why dost thou say "Sillâ has taken away my property;" now Munnabitu is the witness of thee, and Bíl . . . is my judge.' What witness is there in regard to such of my property as he has taken? If he learns all that I have told the king (and there is still some which I have not told the king) he will take it all. I have prayed in my father's house, but he has always acted craftily; he is always plotting against the men of my family (?). Let not the king, my lord, leave me. From Zakir.

Obv. 1. This text has been published by Pinches, *Texts in the Babylonian Wedge-writing*, p. 10, and again by Harper, *Assyrian Letters*, No. 416. The text of the first line may be read *Ana šamí adir-ma ḪI-iṣ*. .

Rev. 1. *iššû, lamidû;* verbs in dependent sentences and therefore with final *-u*.

Rev. 4. *Ḳatâ ultíli.* To 'lift the hands' is often an expression for prayer. *Cf.* the Series 'the Lifting of the Hand' (King, *Babylonian Magic*).

Rev. 6. *amša-ti-iá.* Possibly this may be *amíl ša balâṭi-iá;* for this use of *balâṭu*, *cf.* No. 124, rev. 5.

XI. Omens from Eclipses.

No. 268. I have not informed the king, my lord, of the account of the eclipse with my own mouth, I have not yet written, so I send to the king. Of the eclipse, its evil up to the very month, day, watch, point of light where it began and where the Moon pulled and drew off its eclipse—these concern its evil.

Siwan = Aḫarrû, and a decision to Ur is given: it is evil for the fourteenth day, (which they explain 'the fourteenth day = Elam.') The exact point where it began we do not know; the Moon drew off part of its eclipse in a south-westerly direction. It is evil for Elam and Aḫarrû. From the east and north, when bright, it is lucky for Subarti and Akkad; it says that they will have favour (?) The omen of all lands:—the right of the Moon is Akkad, the left Elam, the top Aḫarrû, the bottom Subartu . . . .

(*Rev.* 3 *ff.*) The omen is favourable and the king, my lord, may be content. Jupiter stood in the eclipse; it portends peace for the king, his name will be honourable, unique . . . Of that name, let the king be bountiful towards anyone who shall greet the king; if the king be humble, the king of the gods of heaven and earth will send peace to the king, my lord. The king may say something thus: 'The king of the gods (thou sayest) will send peace; why then hast thou sent this about Sirrapu and Arubî?' I thus in my turn, 'Let the king go on in his work, let him continue upon his work, and may the king, my lord, be happy. May Bel and Nebo give all lands to the king, my lord.'

The king, my lord, gave me a command saying, 'keep my watch and tell me what happens.' Now all that has taken place before me with a propitious greeting to the king, my lord, unto the king I send. Twice, thrice . . in the presence of the king his hands (?) . . . and may the king enter into the despatches (?) . . . . that I have sent true words to the king. From Munnabitu.

Obv. 2. *kûmu* 'instead,' 'on the other hand.'

Obv. 3. *urrîtu*, evidently of the same root as *urru* 'daylight,' 'light.'

Rm. 193, from Zakir has not been inserted. The obv. is much broken; the rev. gives the omens for an eclipse from the 1st to the 30th of Siwan, for an eclipse on the 14th of Siwan (as in No. 270, rev. 1), for Pabilsag (as No 271, obv. 8). Rev. 13 *ff.* explains 'The evening watch is for corpses, the evening watch for three months and days . . . the . . is Akkad, Siwan is Aḫarrû, the fourteenth day is Elam.'

No. 269. When ḪU . BI . A is dark in the west, there will be a famine for the king of Aḫarrû . . . . When . . is dark and a south wind 'rises,' locusts will come. When there is an eclipse of the Sun on the twenty-eighth of Iyyar, the king's days will be long, . . the land will eat an abundant market. (In Iyyar the Sun was eclipsed; it will eat plenty, the king's days will be long.) When the Sun at its zenith is like a crescent and becomes full like the Moon, the king will conquer the land of his enemy, the land will overcome (?) its evil and see happiness. When the Sun is eclipsed on the twenty-ninth of Iyyar, the shadow beginning in the north and remaining on the south, its left horn being pointed and its right horn long, the gods of the four regions will be troubled, a great . . will speak by the mouth of the god; the invasion of a . . king will come, the throne until the fifth year he will hold (?): there will be a revolt in Akkad: son will slay his father, brother will slay his brother, sick princes . . . days in Akkad, that king a dog will destroy: the enemy will capture a fenced (?) city, that king will die and there will be fighting in the temple of Bel. There will be corpses on the first day, the king of Aḫarrû . . . . (remainder multilated).

Obv. 4. *kupuru*, evidently connected with the Heb. *kâphâr* 'cover,' is the shadow of the eclipse. The ideograph = an enclosed shadow.

Obv. 7 refers to the Sun's appearance during an eclipse.

Obv. 8. *kaṭ lim* = ? Heb. *ḳâṭâl.*

Obv. 12. The first sign is probably not *lu*.

No. 270 (*Obv.* 4 *ff.*). When an eclipse happens and a north wind blows, the gods will have mercy on the land. When the Moon rises darkly, there will be a darkening of . . . (?) When the Moon rises darkly . . . . , destruction of all lands. When the Moon rises darkly and becomes like . . . (?), the king will devastate countries in defeat, (or) the gods will devastate countries in defeat. When the Moon is dark in Siwan, Rammânu after a year will inundate the crops of the land. When an eclipse happens in Siwan in the evening watch, inrush of fish and locusts. When an eclipse happens on the fourteenth of Siwan, the king has the completing of the year, dies, and his son, who has no title to the kingdom, seizes the throne and there will be hostilities. When from the first to the thirtieth of Siwan an eclipse happens, an eclipse of the king of Akkad, . . . of might will be, and Rammânu will inundate the crops of the land.

A great army (or) an army will be slain. Though for prosperity the king, city, and people work mightily and they are successful, there will be no springing up of produce in that year. When on the . . day an eclipse happens, and the god in his shadow . . . . until the middle watch, the end, and the north part of the Moon comes into thy hand, to Ur and the king of Ur a decision will be given; the land of Ur will see famine: corpses will be numerous. The king of Ur, his son injures him, and the son who injures his father Šamaš overcomes him, and in the pain of his father he will die: the son who has no title to the kingdom takes the throne. An eclipse of the evening watch is for corpses. When the day is fine in the evening watch, it is for three months and ten days. Siwan = Aḫarru : the fourteenth day = Elam: the evening watch = Akkad . . . to the king happiness . . .

Obv. 16. *bubulti: biblu, bibiltu* = produce.

No. 271 (*Obv.* 1–3). When an eclipse happens on the fourteenth of Siwan, and of the god in his shadow, the third side above is in shadow and the fourth side below is clear, it comes over the second side in the evening watch, and in the middle watch the end of its shadow appears and the second side comes into thy hand . . . (*The remainder to line 7 is similar to the preceding.*)

(*Obv.* 8 *ff.*) [When] . . below Pabilsag is dark, a decision is given to Muttabal and Babylon. An eclipse of the morning watch is for sickness, and a bright day in the morning watch is for three months and ten days. (The morning watch = Elam, the fourteenth day = Elam, Siwan = Aḫarru, the second side = Akkad) . . . . .

(*Rev.* 2 *ff.*) When an eclipse happens in the morning watch and it completes the watch, a north wind blowing, the sick in Akkad will recover. When an eclipse begins on the first side and stands on the second, there will be a slaughter of Elam: Guti will not approach Akkad. When an eclipse happens and stands on the second side, the gods will have mercy on the land. When the Moon is dark in Siwan, after a year Rammânu will inundate. When the Moon is eclipsed in Siwan, there will be flood and the product of the waters of the land will be abundant. When in Siwan an eclipse of the morning watch happens, the temples of the land will be smitten, Samas will be hostile. (*Rev.* 14.) When an eclipse happens in Siwan out of its time, an all-powerful king will die, and Ramman will inundate; a flood will come and Ramman will diminish the crops of the land; he that goes before the army will be slain.

No. 271 A. The Moon appeared on the 15th of Elul (with) the Sun; the eclipse failed. . . .

No. 272 (*Obv.* 7 *ff.*). When Sarur and Sargaz of the sting of Scorpio are bright, the weapons of Akkad will come. (The sting of Scorpio is the great lord Pabilsag). Venus is standing in Pabilsag. When Nirgal stands in Pabilsag, a strong enemy will raise (his weapons in) the land, Bel will give his weapons to the enemy; the wide forces of the enemy will slay troops. When Scorpio is dark, the kings of all lands will cause hostility (?) (or) the kings of all lands will rival (?). When Scorpio assumes a darkness, the food of men will be evil. (Mars stood within it.) When Libra is dark, the third year locusts will come and devour the crops of the land (or) locusts will devour the land . . . will devour the standing crops. The third year . . . Mars has stood within Scorpio: this is its interpretation. When Mars approaches Scorpio, the prince will die by a scorpion's sting (or) will be captured in his palace. . . . .

When Jupiter has culminated and passed Regulus and brightened it, the back part of Regulus (which Jupiter had passed and brightened) reaches and passes Jupiter, and it (Jupiter) then goes to its disappearance, there will be war, and the enemy will come and seize the throne, the land will be ravaged twice.

All the omens that have come to me concern Akkad and its princes; none of their evil concerns the king my lord: the eclipse of the Moon and Sun which happened in Siwan—these omens which are evil for Akkad and the kings of Aḫarrû are for Akkad; and yet in this month Marcheswan an eclipse happened . . . and Jupiter stood within the eclipse—it is well for the king, my lord. This is all which Bîl-ušîzib has sent to the king. Let the king so act that I may raise myself before the king, my lord. The princes of Akkad whom the king, thy father, had appointed have ravaged Babylon and carried off the goods of Babylon: in consequence of these omens of evil which have come to me, let the army of the king go and in the palace . . . capture them and appoint others in their stead. Unless the king acts speedily, the foe . . . . : he shall come and change them. I am clear. . .

Obv. 11. Nírgal is Mars: Jensen, *Kosm.*, p. 135.

Obv. 12. *mattu* is evidently a gloss to *miṣu* from the root *maṣû* to be broad.

Rev. 4. Evidently here we have a description of an apparent retrogression of Jupiter which appears to have formed a 'loop' near Regulus. Such a case happened to Mars and Regulus in 1868. In cases where a phenomenon repeats its action, the result of such an omen will also have a double effect —the land will be ravaged twice. *Cf.* also 'when it thunders twice, the land which sent thee hostility will send thee peace' (No. 258, rev. 3).

Rev. 13. *našaka, i.e.*, I may no longer prostrate myself.

No. 272c. An eclipse of the Moon will take place on the fourteenth of Adar. When on the fourteenth of Adar an eclipse of the evening watch happens to the Moon, a decision will be given to the all-powerful king, the king of Ur and Aḫarrû. Jupiter and Venus . . . in the eclipse of the Moon. When in Adar an eclipse of the Moon takes place, the king of Elam . . . When in Adar an eclipse of the evening watch . . . When in Adar from the first to the thirtieth day an eclipse happens, the reign of the king will be long, hostility . . . When for peace the king, the city and its people work and are at peace . . . (?) a flood will come and the great waters will burst forth. When the eclipse happens, let the king, my lord, send and for the king the great waters in Akkad . . . and burst forth, someone shall hear of it. From Nírgal-ițir.

Rev. 4. *ina* ŠI . MU. The text is slightly doubtful; it might possibly be translated 'within a year.'

No. 273. On the fourteenth an eclipse will take place; it is evil for Elam and Aḫarrû, lucky for the king, my lord; let the king, my lord, rest happy. It will be seen without Venus; to the king, my lord, I say 'there will be an eclipse.' From Iraššì-ilu, the servant of the king (the greater).

No. 274. To the king of countries, my lord, thy servant Bíl-usur (?) May Bel, Nebo and Šamaš be gracious to the king my lord. An eclipse has happened but it was not visible in Aššur; this eclipse passed the city Aššur, wherein the king is dwelling; now there are clouds everywhere so that whether it did or did not happen we do not know. Let the lord of kings send to Assur, to all cities, to Babylon, Nippur, Erech and Borsippa; whatever has been seen in those cities the king will hear for certain. The omens (?) . . the omen for an eclipse happened in Adar and Nisan; I send all to the king, my lord, and they shall make a *nambulbi*-ceremony for the eclipse. Without fail (?) let not the king omit (?) to act rightly. The great gods in the city wherein the king dwells have obscured the heavens and will not show the eclipse; so let the king know that this eclipse is not directed against the king, my lord, or his country. Let the king rejoice.

(When) it thunders in Nisan, corn (?) will be diminished.

No. 274A. The eclipse will pass, it will not take place. If the king should say 'What omens hast thou seen?'—the gods have not been seen with one another . . . . . the eclipse will pass, the Moon will be seen with (?) the Sun. From Munnabiṭu.

No. 274B (*Rev.* 1, *ff.*). The messenger who went to Marduk . . . returned, saying 'We have not been able to see the Sun, it is clouded over.' They have not seen it, nor have we, so we cannot return its report (?).

No. 274F (*Obv.* 1–8). To the king, my lord, I sent 'An eclipse will take place.' Now it has not passed, it has taken place. In the happening of this eclipse it portends peace for the king, my lord. Iyyar is Elam, the fourteenth day is Elam, the morning watch is . . . .

XVI. Omens from Akulutum.

No. 275. *Akulutum.* Though evidently connected with the root *akâlu* 'to eat,' the meaning is quite doubtful. It might perhaps be 'rust' or 'mildew.'

XVII. Omens from Births.

No. 276 (*Obv.* 1). IZ. BU UŠ u SAL. LA *i.e.* a hermaphrodite.

Obv. 'When a hermaphrodite is born which has no . . the son of the palace will rule the land (or) the king will capture.'

No. 277. When a fœtus has eight legs and two tails, the prince of the kingdom will seize power.

A certain butcher whose name is Uddanu has said 'When my sow littered, (a fœtus) had eight legs and two tails, so I preserved it in brine, and put it in the house.' From Nirgal-iṭir.

Obv. 5. [am] *maḫiṣu*, i.e. 'the smiter,' but doubtful.

Rev. 2. *ṭâbtu-andidil*: *cf. ina ṭabti ušnil* of Nabû-bil-šumi, W.A.I. V, 7, 40 (Delitzsch, 439a). *Andidil* would appear to be a form like *uktataṣar*, Delitzsch, 591, a.

Rev. 3. It is possible that *bîtu* has the meaning of 'box' as *bêth* has sometimes in Hebrew.

TRANSLITERATIONS.

TRANSLITERATIONS.

I. Omens from the Moon's appearance on the first day, and from full Moon.

No. 1. *Obv.* (1) Ana Sin ûmu I ^{kám} innamir (2) sanâḳu ša pî (3) lib-bi mâti iṭâb (ab) (4) Ana ûmu ana minâti ^{pl}-šu írik (5) pâl ûmí ^{pl} arkûti ^{pl} (6) šá ^{m} Bu-ul-lu-ṭu. [81–2–4, 133.]

No. 2. *Obv.* (1) [Ana Sin] ûmu I ^{kám} innamir(ir) (2) sanâḳu ša pî lib mâti iṭâb (ab) (3) Ana ûmu a-na minâti ^{pl}-šu írik (4) ûmí ^{pl} pal-í arkûti ^{pl} *Rev.* (1) ša ^{m} Ša-pi-ku mâr [Bar-sib ^{ki}]. [81–2–4, 134.]

No. 3. *Obv.* (1) [Ana Sin ûmu I ^{kam}] innamir(ir) (2) sanâḳu ša pî lib mâti iṭâb (3) Ana ûmu a-na minâti ^{pl}-šu írik (4) pâl ûmí ^{pl} arkûti ^{pl} (5) šá ^{m} Bu-ul-lu-ṭi. [83–1–18, 185.]

No. 4. *Obv.* (1) Ana Sin ûmu I ^{kám} innamir sanâḳu ša pî [lib mâti iṭâb] (2) Ana ûmu a-na minati ^{pl}šu [írik] (3) pâl ûmí ^{pl} arkûti $^{\text{[pl]}}$ (4) šá ^{m} Bu-ul-[lu-ṭu]. [82–5–22, 83.]

No. 5. *Obv.* (1) [Ana ûmu ana] minâti-šu írik (2) pâl ûmí^{pl} arkûti ^{pl} (3) mi-na-at arḫi ûmu XXX ^{kám} ú-[šal-lam] (4) Ana Sin ûmu I ^{kám} innamir(ir) sanâḳu ša pî (5) lib mati iṭâb (6) [ša ^{m}]^{ilu} Nabû-ikiša(ša) mâr [Bar-sib ^{ki}]. [K. 900.]

No. 6. *Obv.* (1) Ana Sin ûmu I ^{kam} [innamir] (2) sanâḳu ša pî [lib mâti iṭâb] (3) Ana ûmu (mu) ana minâti [^{pl} írik] (4) pâl ûmí [^{pl}arkûti] (5) šá $^{\text{m ilu}}$ . . . . [K. 1388.]

No. 6a. *Obv.* (1) Ana Sin ûmu I ^{kám} [innamir] (2) sanâḳu ša pî . . . (3) lib mâti iṭâb . . . (4) Ana ûmu ana minâti ^{pl}-šu [írik] (5) pâl ûmí ^{pl} arkuti $^{\text{[pl]}}$ (6) šá $^{\text{m ilu}}$ Nabû-mu-ší-ṣi. [S. 1664.]

No. 7. *Obv.* (1) Ana Sin ina ûmi I ^{kám} innamir (2) sanâḳu ša pî lib mâti iṭâb (3) Ana ûmu a-na mi-na-ti-šu í-ri-ik (4) pâl ûmí ^{pl} arkûti ^{pl} (5) Ana Sin ina tamarti-šu agû a-pìr (6) Šarru a-ša-ri-tam (*sic*) illak (ak) (7) šá ^{m} Ištar-šuma-íríš (íš). [K. 696].

No. 8. *Obv.* (1) [Ana] Sin ûmu I ^{kám} [innamir] (2) sanâḳu ša pî lib [mâti iṭâb] (3) Ana ûmu ana mi-na-ti-šu [irik] (4) pâl ûmí ^{pl} arkûti $^{[pl]}$ (5) . . . . . ûmu XXX ^{kám} míš tum . . . . (6) ú-šal-[lam] *Rev.* (1) ûmu I ^{kám} . . . . (2) Damḳu . . (3) limutti Îlama (ma) ^{ki} . . . . (4) ûmu XIV ^{kám} itti ^{ilu} Šamši [innammar] (5) šá ^{m} Ba-la-si-i. [K. 784.]

No. 9. *Obv.* (1) Ana Sin ûmu I ^{kám} innamir (2) sanâḳu ša pî lib mâti iṭâb (ab) (3) šá ^{arhu} Nisanni ^{arhu} Tašrîti (?) (4) Ana agû a-pìr kâimânu-ma (5) íbûr mâti iššir šarru a-ša-ri-du-tam illak (ak). [82-5-22, 60.]

No. 10. *Obv.* (1) Ana Sin ûmu I ^{kám} [innamir] (2) Sanâḳu ša pî lib [mâti iṭâb] (3) Ana ûmu (mu) ana minâti ^{pl}-šu írik(ik) (4) pâl ûmi ^{pl} arkûti ^{pl} (5) [Ana Sin] ina tamarti-šu agû a-pìr (6) kaîmânu-ma íbur mâti iššir *Rev.* (1) . . a-bur-riš uššab (ab) (2) šurru ašaridu-tam illak (ak) (3) ša $^{m\ ilu}$ Nabu-iḳ-bi (4) mâr Kûtî ^{ki}. [K. 744.]

No. 11. *Obv.* (1) Ana ûmu ana minâti ^{pl}-šu írik (2) pâl ûmí ^{pl} arkûti ^{pl} (3) mi-na-at arḫi ûmu I ^{kám} ú-šal-lam . . (4) Ana Sin ûmu I ^{kám} innamir (ir) (5) sanâḳu ša pî [lib mâti] iṭâb(ab) (6) Ana Sin ina tamarti-šu . . . ka-a-a . . . ma (7) íbur mâti iššir . . *Rev.* (1) šarru a-ša-ri-du-tam [illak] (ak) (2) damiḳti ša šarri bíl-ia šú-ú (3) ša $^{m\ ilu}$ Nabû-ikiša (ša) mâr Bar-sib^{ki}. [K. 756.]

No. 11A. *Obv.* (1) Ana Sin ina ûmi I ^{kám} innamir [sanâḳu ša pî] (2) lib mâti [iṭâb] (3) Ana Sin ina tamarti-šu [agû apir] (4) kaîmânu-ma [íbûr mâti iššir] (5) mâtu a-bur-riš [uššab] (6) šarru ašaridu-[tam illak] (7) Ana ûmu ana minâti ^{pl}-[šu írik] *Rev.* (1) pâl ûmí ^{pl} [arkuti ^{pl}] (2) šanât ^{pl} šarri [maʿ dâti ?] (3) ša ^{m} Ṭâbu-[ṣil ^{ilu} Marduk]. [K. 1308.]

No. 12. *Obv.* (1) Ana Sin ûmu I kám innamir (ir) [sanâḳu ša]pî (2) lib-bi mâti i-ṭa-ab (3) Ana ûmu ana minâti pl-šu írik(ik) (4) pâl ûmí pl arkûti pl (5) Ana Sin ina tamarti-šu agû a-pìr kaîmânu-ma (6) íbûr mâti iššir mâtu a-bur-riš uššab (ab) (7) šarru a-ša-ri-du-tam illak (ak) (8) ša m Ṭa-bi-ia. [81–2–4, 85.]

No. 13. *Obv.* (1) Ana Sin ûmu I kám innamir sanâḳu ša pî lib mâti iṭâb (ab) (2) Ana Sin ina tamarti-šu agû [apir kaîmânu-ma] (3) íbûr mâti iššir [mâtu aburriš uššab] (4) šarru ašaridu-[tam illak] (5) ša m Aḫî pl-ša-a am [Urukai]. [K. 840].

No. 14. *Obv.* (1) Ana Sin ûmu I kám innamir (ir) (2) sanâḳu ša pî (3) lib mâti iṭâb (4) Ana Sin ina tamarti-šu agû a-pìr (5) šarru ašaridu-tam (6) illak (ak) *Rev.* (1) m ilu Nírgal-íṭir(ir). [K. 701.]

No. 15. *Obv.* (1) Ana Sin ûmu I kám innamir (ir) sanâḳu ša pî (2) lib mâti iṭâb (ab) (3) Ana ûmu(mu) a-na minâti pl-šu írik (4) pâl ûmí (mí) arkûti pl (5) Ana ina arḫu Du 'ûzi ûmu XIV kám Sin u Šamšu (6) itti a-ḫa-miš innammaru pl *Rev.* (1) A-na šarri bíl-ia ardu-ka (2) m Ṭâbu-ṣil-ilu Marduk mâr-šu (3) ša m ilu Bíl . . . . (4) ilu Bíl u ilu Nabû šú-lum ṭu-ub lib-bi (5) ṭu-ub šîri a-ra-ku úmí pl (6) ur-ru-ku pa-li-í (7) u ku-un-nu išid iṣu kussi (8) [ša] šarri bíl-ia a-na da-ri-iš (9) liḳ-bu-ú. [K. 754.]

No. 16. *Obv.* (1) Ana Sin ûmu I kám innamir sanâḳu sâ pî (2) lib mâti iṭab (ab) (3) Ana ûmu ana minâti pl-šu írik (4) pâl ûmí pl arkûti pl (5) arḫu Addaru arḫu Ululu rîš šatti (6) ki-i šá arḫu Nisannu arḫu Tašrîtu *Rev.* (1) ina rîš šatti (2) ilu Sin itti damiḳtim (tim) (3) šá arak ûmi(mí) palî (4) a-na šarri bí-ili-ia (5) i-sa-ap-ra (6) šá m ilu Aššur-šar-a-[ni]. [K. 775.]

No. 17. *Obv.* (1) Ana Sin ina tamarti-šu agû a-pìr (2) Šarru ašaridu-tam illak (ak) (3) ûmu I kám innammar-ma (4) Ana ûmu ana minâti pl-šu írik (5) pâl ûmí(mí)- šu arkûti pl (6) mi-na-at arḫi (7) ûmu XXX kám ú-šal-lam-ma *Rev.* (1) Ana Sin ûmu I kám innamir-ma (2) damiḳti mâtu Akkadi ki (3) limutti mâtu Ílama u Aḫarrî (4) arḫu Abu mâtu Akkadu ki (5) damiḳti ša šarri bí-ili-iá (6) ša m ilu Nabû-šuma-iškun (un). [K. 803.]

No. 18. *Obv.* (1) Ana Sin ûmu I ^{kám} innamir (ir) (2) Sanâḳu ša pî lib mâti iṭâb (ab) (3) [Ana] ûmu ana minâti ^{pl}-šu írik (ik) (4) pâl umí ^{pl} arkûti ^{pl} (5) [Ana] Sin ina tamarti-šu agû a-pir *Rev.* (1) šarru a-ša-ri-du-tam illak (ak) (2) ša $^{\text{m ilu}}$ Bíl-naṣir (ir) (3) $^{\text{m ilu}}$ Bíl-ípuš (uš) mâr Bâbili $^{\text{ki am}}$ ḪAL (4) ma-a-du ma-ru-uṣ (5) šarru liḳ-bi-ma ^{am} asu (6) lil-lik-ma li-mur-šu. [83–1–18, 195.]

No. 19. *Obv.* (1) Ana Sin ûmu I ^{kám} innamir (ir) sanâḳu ša pî (2) lib-bi mâti i-ṭa-bi (3) Ana ûmu (mu) ana minati ^{pl}-šu írik (ik) (4) [pâl ûmí] ^{pl} arkûti ^{pl} (5) . . . . na . . šamí(í?) (6) . . . . . šarri bí-ili-ia (7) . . . . . il-tap-ra *Rev.* (1) ^{ilu} Aššur ^{ilu} Šamšu ^{ilu} Nabû u ^{ilu} Marduk (2) ûmu (mu) a-na ûmu (mu) arḫu a-na arḫi (3) šattu a-na šatti ṭu-ub lib-bi (4) ṭu-ub šíri ḫi-du-ti u ri-ša-a-ti (5) ^{iṣu} kussi ša ki-na-a-ti (6) a-na da-riš a-na ûmí ^{pl} arkûti ^{pl} (7) ù šanâti ^{pl} ma-ʿ-da-a-ti (8) a-na šarri bí-ili-ia lid-di-nu (9) ša $^{\text{m ilu}}$ Nabû-iḳ-bi.

[Rm. 198.]

No. 19A. *Obv.* [Ana Sin ûmu] I ^{kám} innamir (ir) (2) [sanâḳu ša pî] lib-bi mâti iṭâb (ab) (3) [Ana ûmu ana minâti] ^{pl}-šu írik (ik) (4) [pâl ûmí ^{pl}] arkûti (*Remainder lost.*) *Rev.* (*Top wanting.*) (1) . . . . (2) [ûmu a-na ûmi arḫu] a-na arḫi (3) [šattu] a-na šatti (4) [ṭu-ub] lib-bi ṭu-ub šíri (5) [ḫi-du]-ti ri-ša-a-ti ^{iṣu} kussi (6) [ša ki-na]-a-ti a-na da-riš (7) [a-na umí] ^{pl} arkûti ^{pl} šanâti ^{pl} (8) [ma-ʿ]-da-a-ti a-na šarri (9) [bí-]ili-iá lid-di-nu.

[80–7–19, 154.]

No. 20. *Obv.* (1) [Ana Sin] ûmu I ^{kám} innamir (ir) (2) sanâḳu ša pî lib mâti iṭâb (ab) (3) Ana ûmu ana minâti ^{pl}-šu írik (ik) (4) pal-í ûmí ^{pl} arkûti ^{pl} (5) Ana ina ^{arḫu} Šabâṭi abnu illik(ik) (6) nu ḫu-uš niši ^{pl} . . . . *Rev.* (1) [Ša]-ḳi-í maḫiri (2) $^{\text{[ilu]}}$ Aššur ^{ilu} Šamšu ^{ilu} Nabû u ^{ilu} Marduk (3) $^{\text{[iṣu]}}$ kussi ša ki-na-a-ti (4) [a]-na da-riš a-na ûmí ^{pl} (5) [arkûti] ^{pl} a-na šarri (6) [bí-ili]-ia id-dan-nu (7) [ša ^{m}] ^{ilu} Nabû-iḳ-bi. [83–1–18, 219.]

No. 21. *Obv.* (1) Ana Sin ûmu I ^{kám} innamir (2) sanâḳu ša pî lib mâti iṭâb (3) Ana ûmu (mu) a-na mi-na-ti-šu í-ri-ik (4) pâl ûmí ^{pl} arkûti ^{pl} (5) ^{ilu} Muštabarrû-mûtânu . . . II-ú III-šu (6) ina ûmí (mí) an-ni-i ní-ta-ṣar (7) la ni-í-mur (8) ir-tí-bi *Rev.* (1) is-su-ri šarru bí-li i-ḳab-bi (2) ma-a ittu-šu-ú mí-mí-ni í-ba-ši (3) šá ir-bu-u-ni (4) la-aš-šu (5) šá m Ištar-šuma-íriš. [Bu. 91–5–9, 14.]

No. 21A. *Obv.* (1) [Ana ûmu ana mi-na]-ti-šu í-ri-ik (2) [pâl] ûmí pl arkûti pl (3) [ilu Muštabarrû-mûtânu] (a-nu) mu-šu an-ni-u (4) .... ilu AL-LUL ú-ṣa (5) [šam] Ištar-šuma-íriš (iš).

[83–1–18, 224.]

No. 22. *Obv.* (1) [Ana] Sin ûmu I kám innamir [sanâḳu ša pî] lib-bi mâti iṭâb (ab) (2) Ana ûmu (mu) ana minâti pl-[šu írik] pâl ûmí pl arkûti [pl] (3) Ana Sin ina tamarti-šu agû [apir šarru] ašaridu-tam illak (ak) (4) ilu Aššur ilu Šamšu ilu[Nâbû ilu] Marduk mâtu Ku-ú-ši u mâtu Mi-ṣir (5) a-na ḳatâ II šarri [bí-ili-ia] i-im-nu-ú ina í-mu-ḳu (6) ša šarri bí-ili-i[a . . .] ḫu-bu-us-su-nu (7) iḫ-tab-tu-nu ..... ši ú (?) ka (?) i-da-šu-nu (8) ma-la ba-šú-[u alu Ni]-na-a ki šú-bat šarru-ú-ti-ka (9) ul-tí-ri-bu [u] ḫu-bu-us-su-nu (10) a-na ardâni pl [ípušu ?] ki-i pi-i an-nim-ma (11) ilu Šamšu u ilu Marduk [mâtu Gi] -mir-ra-a (12) am Man-[na-a-a . .] pl ma-la la-pa-an *Rev.* (1) Šarri ..... [ana] ḳatâ šarri bí-ili-ia (2) lim-nu-ú [šarru bí]-ili-a li-iḫ-bu-ti (3) kaspa ḫuraṣa .... i-da-šu-nu (4) ma-la [ba-šu-u . . .] šu-nú la tal-la-ka (5) . . . aš ..... ri .... ka ti (6) a-na ni ...... [šarri] bí-ili ...., bi (7) ḫi-[du-ti] lib-bi [ṭub šíri iṣu kussi] (8) ša ki-na-a-ti [ana da]-riš [ana ûmí] pl (9) ù šanâti pl arkâti [pl] . . . pl (10) [a]-na šarri bí-ili-ia . . . šu lid-di-[nu] (11) ša m ilu Nabû-[iḳ]-bi.

[83–1–18, 202 + 305.]

No. 22A. *Obv.* (1) [Ana Sin ûmu I kam in]-na-mir (2) [pû] i-ka-nu (3) [lib] ma-a-ti i-ṭa-bi (4) . . išid ta-mar-ti ilu Sin (5) . . . it-tab-ši (6) . . . is (?) . . (?) za ní ḫa (7) pâl-šu i-ka-nu *Rev.* (1) . . ma-'-du (2) . . . ma-'-ar (3) .... GUD UD (4) . . . ta-mar-ti ilu Sin (5) . . . tam-mar-ma (6) [ša m ilu] Nírgal-íṭir (ir).

[K. 856.]

No. 22B. *Obv.* (1) Ana Sin ûmu I kam innamir (ir) sanâḳu ša pî (2) lib-bi mâti iṭâb (ab) (3) [Ana ûmu ana minâti-šu] írik (4) [pal ûmí pl] arkûti pl (5) .... [in]-nam-ru (6) . . . i in-nam-ma-ru (7) . . na ki (?) it (?) ul iš-šim-mi *Rev.* (1) . . . ia a-na bíl šarrâni pl (2) ...... uḳ-bi (3) .... [lu]-da-ri (4) ša m A-ša-ri-du.

[K. 753.]

No. 23. *Obv.* (1) Ana Sin ina ^{arhu} Du 'ûzi (?) ûmu I ^{kám} innamir (2) sanâḳu ša pî lib mâti iṭâb (3) Ana Sin ina tamarti-šu agû a-pìr (4) šarru ašaridu-[tam] il-lak (5) Ana Sin agû a (?)-da (?)-ru a-pìr (6) ^{ilu} Sin [nakra] i (?)-maḫ-ḫa-aṣ (7) ûmu adaru a (?) pìr .... ší-ir-ti (?) *Rev.* (1) ...... (2) Ana Sin ina ... (3) Šarru .... (4) mâtu .... (*Remainder, some three lines, obliterated.*)

[80–7–19, 65.]

No. 23A. *Obv.* (1) Ana Sin NU ŠI (?) .... (2) Ana Sin la innamir ilâni ^{pl} (?) ..... (3) milku (?) ..... (4) Ana agû IM DIR a-pìr Zi ..... (5) ^{iáru} Šûtu itbi-ma ..... (6) : UK-ma ḪA . A : ınbu ..... (7) Sin ina tamarti ..... *Rev.* (1) maṣṣartu ša .... (2) IM .... (*Remainder lost.*) [K. 12283.]

No. 24. *Obv.* (1) ..... ^{kám} innamir ^{ilu} Rammânu iraḫiṣ (iṣ) (2) ..... (3) ..... ti ra ûmu XXIX ^{kám} ^{ilu} Sin innammar (4) ..... pâl ûmu(mu) arkûti ^{pl} (5) ..... pû la ki-nı a-lak-ti (6) [la ṭab]-ti ina mâti iraššì(ši) (7) ..... ^{kám} adi ûmi XXX ^{kám} adi arḫi (8) ... araḫ ^{mâtu} Í lama (ma) ^{ki} (9) [ša ^{m} ^{ilu} Bíl-li'] mar ^{m} Í-gi-bi ^{am} mašmašu. [K. 1399.]

No. 24A. *Obv.* (1) Ana Sin ina tamarti-šu agû apìr kai-mânu-[ma] (2) mâtu a-bur-riš uššab (ab) šarru [ašaridutam illak] (3) Ana ḳarnâti ^{pl} šu ..... (4) mir-ra ..... (5) mir (*Remainder broken off.*) *Rev.* (1) [ša ^{m}] ^{ilu} Bíl-šuma-iškun(un).

[K. 12367 + 13175.]

II. Omens from the Horns of the Moon.

No. 25. *Obv.* (1) [Ana] Sin ina ^{arhu} ? ûmu XXX ^{kám} innamir (2) ..... ^{ki} ikkal (3) [Ana Sin ina] tamarti-šu ḳarnâti ^{pl}-šu tur-ru-ka (4) [paṭar bi-ra]-a-ti (5) [a-rad maṣṣarâti taš-mu-ú (6) [u sa-li]-mu ina mâti ibašši [ši] *Rev.* (1) GI : ta-ra-ki (2) GI : ša-la-mu (3) GI : ka-a-nu (4) ḳarnâti^{pl}-šu kun-na (5) limutti ša ^{mâtu} Aḫarrî ^{ki} ù damiḳti (6) ša šarri bíl-ia (7) ša ^{m} Za-kir. [K. 770.]

No. 26. *Obv.* (1) Ana Sin ûmu I kám innamir (ir) (2) sanâḳu ša pî lib mâti iṭâb(ab) (3) Ana Sin ina tamarti-šu agû a-pìr (4) íbûr mâti iššir [šarru] ašaridu-tam (5) [illak] ak (6) Ana Sin karnâti pl -šu . . . . mit-ḫa-ra (7) Ana mâti šubtu ní-iḫ-tum *Rev.* (1) Ana Sin ina tamarti-šu ud-du-da (2) šarru a-šar pa-nu-šu šaknu (nu) (3) mâta i-bí-íl (4) : a-(*sic*) ú-sa-na-ḳu ú-na-kap (5) ša m Iraššì(ši) ilu ardu ša šarri (6) maḫru(u). [83–1–18, 242.]

No. 27. *Obv.* (1) Ana Sin ûmu I kám innamir sanâḳu ša pî lib mâti iṭâb (2) Ana Sin ina tamarti-[šu]ḳarnâti . . . . . (*Two (?) lines broken out*) (5) . . . du si (7) . . . . . da (6) dan . . . . . . ru ša kar . . . . . *Rev.* (1) Ana ḳarnâti pl-su tur-ru-ka (2) paṭar alu bi-ra-a-ti (3) a-rad maṣṣarâti pl taš-mu-ú (4) u sa-li-mu ina mâti ibašši(ši) (5) GI | ta-ra-ku | GI. | ka-a-nu (6) man-za-za ki-i-ni izzaz(az)-ma (7) ša m A-ša-ri-du maḫru(û). [K. 874.]

No. 28. *Obv.* (1) Ana Sin ina ûmu I kám innamir sanâḳu ša pî [lib mâti iṭâb] (2) Ana umî(mî) ana minâti pl-šu írik [pâl ûmi pl arkûti pl] (3) Ana Sin ina tamarti-šu ûmu namru í-di . ⁖ . (4) ku-ru-sis-su tibû-ma (5) šamaššammâ ikkal (6) ki . . . . ši-ma (7) Ana agû a-pìr šarru a-ša-ri-du-tam *Rev.* (1) illak(ak) (2) [Ana] kakkabu iṣrur-ma ki-ma ḳi (?)-iṣ-ri (3) [ultu] írib šamši ana ṣît šamši irbi ma mâtu Í lama ki (4) . . . . zag-mu nakri ikašad-dim . . . (5) ummâni(ni) ša mâtu Í lama ki . . . . . . (6) ša m Za-kir.

[80–7–19, 59.]

No. 29. *Obv.* (1) [Ana Sin] ûmu I kám innamir sanâḳu ša pî lib mâti iṭab (2) [Ana Sin] ina tamarti-šu karnâti pl-šu id-da (3) šar Akkadi ki í-ma illaku(ku) mâta ibíl(íl) (4): Šar Akkadi ki í-ma pani pl-šu šaknu(nu) (5) mâta un-na-áš (6) [Ana Sin ina] tamarti-šu ana šumíli-šu pani pl šu šaknu(nu) (7) . . . . -ni saluppu u . . . . pl (8) [ina] tamarti-šu iltanu illak ma (*Remainder of obv. and top of rev. broken off.*) *Rev.* (1) . . . šamí(í) izzizi(zi) (2) mul SAG . MÍ . GAR a-na írib šamši ittiḳ(iḳ) (3) šubtu ni-iḫ-ti šalmu(mu) damiḳ-tim(tim) ana mâti (4) [Ana ilu Šamšu] ina ni-du ippuha(ha) šarru izziz-ma işu kakku ibašši(ši) (5) mul SAG. MÍ. GAR umí pl dannûti pl ina šamí(í) (6) izzaz(az)-ma (7) [sam] A-ša-ri-du maḫrû(ú) ardu ša šarri. [S. 86.]

No. 30. *Obv.* (1) Ana Sin ûmu I kâm innamir(ir) sanâḳu ša pî (2) lib mâti iṭâb (3) Ana Sin ina tamarti-šu agû a-pìr (4) šarru a-ša-ri-du-ti il-lak (5) Ana Sin ina tamarti-šu ḳarnu imitti-šu írik-ma (6) ḳarni šumíli-šu ik-ru (7) šarru mâtu la šú-a-tum ḳat-su i-kaš-šad (8) Ana Sin ina tamarti-šu rabiš irbi (9) Atalû išakkan(an) *Rev.* (1) Ana Sin ina tamarti-šu rabiš ib-ta-il (2) íbûr mâti iššir. (3) Ûmu(mu) a-na mi-na-ti-šu írik (4) pal-í ûmí pl arkûti pl (5) Ûmu XXX kâm ú-šal-lam-ma (6) Ana ina arḫu Ululi atal Ílama(ma) ki (7) ilu Sin išakkan (an) (8) ša m ilu Nírgal-íṭir(ir). [K. 741.]

No. 31. *Obv.* (1) Ana Sin ûmu I kâm [innamir] (2) sanâḳu ša pî lib mâti iṭâb (3) Ana Sin ina tamarti-šu immir(ir) (4) mâtu Akkadu libbu-ša ibaluṭ(uṭ) inamir(ir) (5) ummâni(ni) nuḫša immar(mar) (6) Ana Sin ina tamarti-šu karnâti pl-šu ú-du-[da] (7) Šar Akkadi ki í-ma pani pl-šu [šaknu] (8) mâtu i bi-[il] *Rev.* (1) Ana ûmu(mu) a-na mi-na-ti-[šu írik] (2) pali pl ûmi pl [arkuti pl] (3) Ana ûmí pl a-na mi-na-ti-[šu-nu íriku] (4) šanât pl šarri ina . . . . (5) ši-i-ma . . . . . (6) Šanâti pl an-nu-ti ú-ma . . . (7) a-dan-niš a-na . . . . (8) ina íli šá í-da-at . . . (9) is-dir-u-ni ûmu I kâm pl-ni . . (10) Šá m Ištar-šuma-íríš. [K. 788.]

No. 32. (1) [Ana Sin ina tamarti]-šu agû a-pìr (2) [íbûr mâti] iššir matu a-bur-riš uššab (3) šarru ašaridu-tam illak (4) Ana Sin ina tamarti-su karnâti pl-šu id-da (5) Šarru mât nakri-šu ú-nak-[kap] *Rev.* (1) Ana Sin ina arḫu Du 'ûzi ûmu XXX kâm [innamir] (2) sapaḫ(aḫ) mâtâti . . (3) šarru a-na limutti la ú-ga-ri (?) (4) . . Agû a-pìr adâru u karnâti pl šu (5) . . . . ra damiḳti ša šarri (6) [ša m A-ša]-ri-du maḫrû(ú) (7) [ardu ša] šarri. [K. 12388 + 13101.]

No. 33. *Obv.* (1) Ana Sin ina ûmu I kâm innamir(ir) (2) sanâḳu ša pî lib mâti iṭâb(ab) (3) mulMuštabarrû-mûtânu (a-nu) (4) ša ina lib mul Aḳrabi u-zu . . . . (5) a-na a-ṣi-í . . . (6) il-ta-pat (7) a-di ûmi XXV kâm ša arḫu . . . . *Rev.* (1) ù ša-ru-ru-šu ma-aḳ-[tu] (2) lib ša šarri bí-ili-iâ lu-ṭa-a-[bi] (3) šarru ma-'-diš lu-ḫa-[di] (4) a-di uṣ-ṣu-ú (5) ma-ṣar-ti ša ram-ni-šu (6) šarru li-iṣ-ṣur (7) ša m I rašši (ši)-ilu ardu ša šarri maḫru(u). [83-1-18, 243.]

No. 34. *Obv.* (1) [Ana Sin ina tamarti-šu] agû a-pìr íbûr mâti iššir [mâtu] (2) [Aburriš] uššab(ab) šarru asaridu-tam [illak] (3) [Ana Sin ina tamarti-šu] ḳarnâti pl-šu id-da GAN . BA iṣ (?) . . . (4) ina mâti ibašši(ši) (5) [Ana Sin ina tamarti]-šu SI pl-šu ud-du-da šar Akkadi ki í-[ma] (6) [illaku mâta] un-na-aš : í-ma pa-nu-šu šak-nu. (7) [mâta ibíl . .] pi ma damiḳti mâtu Akkadi ki limutti mâtu í-lama (ma) ki (8) [i-di]-du ṣa-pa-ru šá [ḳarni] (9) [ina íli ṭí]-í-mí am-mi-i šá ana íli . . . (10) . . . uṣur (?) iš-pu-[ra] (11) šarri bíl-iá a . . . *Rev.* (1) . . . la aḫ ḫi . . (2) . . a-ki na (?) mut . . . (3) ma-'-du-ti a-bu . . . . (4) . . . . pl-ni í-pu-šu šarru bí-ili . . . (5) . . '-í šá a-na šarru bíl-iá a . . . . (6) . . lab (?)-ba ka-a-a-ma-nu ú . . . . (7) . . muḫ-ḫi-ia ú-ṣa . . (8) šarri pa-al-ḫa-ku ma-a . . (9) . . ni i-ḳab-bi-ma aš . (10) . . lu ší-bi-[la] (11) šá m A-kul-la-[nu]. [83–1–18, 205.]

No. 35. *Obv.* (1) [Ana Sin ûmu I kam innamir] sanâḳu ša [pî] lib mâti iṭâb (2) . . . da íbûr mâti iššir (3) . . . ibašši(ši) (4) . . . . . ma adrûti pl (5) . . . . ḫu (?) . . . su lis-su (6) [Ana Sin ina] tamarti-šu karnâti pl-šu ud-du-da šar Akkadi ki (7) í-ma illaku(ku) mât nakri un-na-aš (8) [Ana] Sin ina tamarti-šu karnâti pl-šu id-da-ma namra pl (9) šar Akkadi ki í-ma pa-nu-šu šak-nu *Rev.* (1) mâtâti ibíl(íl) (2) Ana Sin ina tamarti-šu immir(ir) [Akkadu] ki libbu-šu ibaluṭ(uṭ) (3) ummâni(ni) nuḫša immar(mar) (4) Ana Sin ina tamarti-šu ḳarnâti pl mitḫariš namra pl (5) Šarrâni pl nakrûti pl išal-limu pl (6) [Ana] ûmu ana mi-na-ti-šu írik (7) pâl-í ûmí pl arkûti pl (8) arḫu Nisannu u arḫu Du 'ûzu ûmu XXX kám ú-šal-lam-ma (9) [ša] m ilu Nírgal-íṭir(ir). [81–2–4, 103.]

No. 36. *Obv.* (1) Ana ûmu(mu) ana [minâti pl-šu írik] (2) pâl [ûmí pl arḳûti pl] (3) mi-na-at arḫi ûmu XXX kám ú-šal-[lam] (4) [Ana Sin] ina tamarti-šu ḳarnâti pl-šu ud-du-da (5) [Šar Akkadi ki] í-ma pani pl-šu šak-nu (6) [mâta] un-na-aš : í-ma pa-nu-šu šak-nu (7) [mâti] i-bí-íl *Rev.* (1) í-di-du : ṣa-pa-ru ša ḳar-ni (2) arḫu Du 'ûzu mâtu Subartu ki (3) šá m Ak-kul-la-ni. [Bu. 89–4–26, 159.]

No. 36A. *Obv.* (*Top broken.*) (1) . . iṣ ina . . . (2) í-di-du ṣa-[pa-ru ša ḳar-ni] (3) ina iš-di ta-mar-[ti] . . (4) šarru palî-šú . . . (5) ma-ḫi-ru ma a . . . *Rev.* (1) mul LU . BAD GUD (?) [UD ?]

(2) Ana Sin ina tamarti-šú . . . (3) Ana Sin ina ûmi I kám innamir . . (4) . . . bubbuli (?) (*Remainder lost.*) [K. 12469.]

No. 37. *Obv.* (1) Ana Sin ina arḫu DIR . ŠÍ . KIN . TAR ina tamarti-šu (2) karnâti pl-šu ud-du-da-ma pi-il (3) rubû idannin-ma mâtu(ú) inaḫaš(aš) (4) . . . : pi-lu . . . : sa-a-mu (5) Ana Sin ina tamarti-su agû a-pir (6) Šarru ašaridu-tam illak(ak) *Rev.* (1) Ana Sin ûmu I kám innamir sanâḳu ša pî (2) lib mâti iṭâb(ab) (3) Ana Sin manzas-su kînu izziz(iz) (4) uk-ku-u ša zunni (5) ina arḫu DIR . ŠÍ . KIN . TAR ûmu XIV kám (6) Sin itti ilu Šamši in-nam-mar (7) ša m ilu Nírgal-íṭir(ir). [K. 729.]

No. 38. *Obv.* (1) Ana ilu Sin ûmu I kám innamir pu-ú kînu (2) lib-bi mâti iṭâb (3) Ana ilu Sin ina tamarti-šu ḳarnâti pl-šu id-da (4) šar Akkadi ki a-šar pa-nu-šu šak-nu (5) ma-a-ti i-bi-íl (6) Ana mul šarru ša-ru-ru na-ši (7) Šar Akkadi ki ga-mí-ru-tum (8) ípuš(uš) *Rev.* (1) *Rev.* (1) ša m Mun-na-bi-tu. [K. 1398.]

No. 39. *Obv.* (1) Ana Sin ûmu I kám innamir sanâḳu ša pî (2) lib mâti iṭab (3) Ana Sin ina tamarti pl šu agû a-pir šarru ašaridu-[tam] illak (4) Ana ḳarnâti pl-šu mitḫariš namra pl (5) šarrâni pl nakrûti pl išallimu [pl] (6) it-ti ilu Šamši innammar(mar) (?) . . (7) . . bît ta-mar-ti . . . (8) . . ilu (?) it-ta (?) [mar ?] Rev. (1) Šul-mu damḳu ana mâti ur-ra . . (2) ilu Sin nakri i-maḫ-ḫa-[aṣ] (3) mul LU . BAD . GUD . UDina lib (?) ilu (?) Sin (4) iz-za-az . . . (5) ša m ilu Nírgal-íṭir(ir). [S. 1062.]

No. 40. *Obv.* (1) [Ana] Sin ûmu I kám innamir(ir) sanâḳu ša pî (2) lib-bi mâti iṭâb (3) [Ana ûm] bubbuli a-na mi-na-tí-šu (4) îrik ûmí pl palî (?) arkûti pl. [K. 804.]

No. 41. *Obv.* (1) Ana Sin ina tamarti-šu agû a-pir (2) kaîmânu-ma íbûr mâti iššir (3) mâtu a bur-riš uššab(ab) (4) Šarru ašaridu-tam illak(ak) (5) Ana Sin ina tamarti-šu ḳarnu imitti-šu írik (6) ḳarnu šumili-šu ik-ri (7) šar mâti la šú-a-ti *Rev.* (1) ḳat-su ikašad(ád) (2) Ana . . [ûmu XXX] kám ú-šal-lam-ma (3) Ana ûmu ana minâti pl-šu írik (4) pâl ûmí pl arkûti pl (5) Ana Sin ûmu I kám innamir-ma (6) damiḳti mâtu Akkadi ki (7) limutti mâtu Í-lama u Aḫarrî (8) ša m ilu Nabû-Šuma-iškun(un). [K. 791.]

No. 42. *Obv.* (1) [Ana Sin ina] tamarti-šu [agû apìr kaîmânu-ma] (2) [šarru] a-ša-ri-du-[tam illak] (3) mâtu a-bur-riš uš-[šab] (4) šá ina ^{arḫu} Tašrîti ûmu(mu) ú-šal-la-ma (5) Ana Sin ûmu I ^{kám} innamir [1] sanâḳu ša pî (6) lib mâti i-ṭa-ab (7) Ana Sin ûmu I ^{kám} innamir-ma damiḳti ^{mâtu} akkadi ^{ki} (8) limutti ílama(ma) ^{ki} [u] A-ḫar-ri-í *Rev.* (1) Ana Sin ina tamarti-šu . . . (*Remainder, five lines, illegible except for a few characters.*) [S. 1073.]

No. 43. *Obv.* (1) [Ana Sin] ina tamarti-šu [2] agû a-pi-ir (2) [šarru] a-ša-ri-du-tam illak(ak) [mâtu] a-bur-riš uš-sab (4) [ina] na-mu-ri-šu a-gu-u ip-pi-ir-ma (5) Ana Sin ina tamarti-šu [3] ḳarnu imitti-šu šamu(ú) di-rat (6) maḫiru ki-í-nu ina mâti ibašši(ši) (7) na-aš-kun [4] barti ina ^{matu} Aḫarrî ^{ki} ibašši(ši) *Rev.* (1) ḳar-nu imitti-šu šamu(ú) di-rat (2) Šá iḳ-bu-u-ni (3) ina ša-mí-í i-ḫal-lu-up-ma la in-na-mir (?) (4) [5] DIR ḫa-la-pu | šá ḳar-ni (5) ^{ilu} Sin ina tamarti-šu ḳarnu imitti-šu ^{mâtu} Aḫarrû ^{ki} (6) Ana Sin ûmu I ^{kám} innamir-ma damiḳti Akkadi ^{ki} (7) lum-nu ^{mâtu} Í lama(ma) ^{ki} Aḫar-ri-í (8) ^{ilu} Sin ûmu XIV ^{kám} ultu ^{ilu} Ša-maš (9) in-na-mar (10) [šá] $^{m\ ilu}$ Nabû-aḫî ^{pl}-íriba. [K. 705.]

No. 44. *Obv.* (1) [Ana Sin ûmu I ^{kám}] innamir(ir) (2) [sanâḳu ša pî] lib mâti iṭab(ab) (3) [Ana ûmu ana] mi-na-ti-šu írik (4) [pâl] ûmí ^{pl} arkûti ^{pl} (5) [Ana Sin ina] tamarti-šu ḳarnâti ^{pl}-šu ud-du-da (6) šarru a-šar ú-sa-na-ḳu ú-nak-kap (7) [Ana Sin] ina tamarti-šu ḳarnâti ^{pl}-šu mit-ḫa-ra (8) [a]-na mâti šú-ub-tum ní-iḫ-tum *Rev.* (1) [Ana Sin ina] tamarti-šu agû a-pìr íbur mâti iššir (2) [šarru] ašaridu-tam illak(ak) (3) [Ana . . . . . ^{arḫu}] Nisanni ina ûmi I ^{kám} innamir(ir) (4) $^{[sâru]}$ iltanu illik lib šar Akkadi ^{ki} (5) . . . . . šu iṭâb(ab) (6) [^{mul} LU.BAD] GUD.UD ina írib Šamši ina lib ^{mul} KU.MAL (7) . . . damiḳti ša šarri bí-ili-ia (8) . . . šar Aḫarrí ^{ki} ina ^{isu} kakki šumḳut(ut) (9) . . . [šarri bí]-ili-ia ša ina ^{mâtu} Mi-ṣi-ir (10) . . . . i-kaš-ša-du. [80-7-19, 63.]

No. 45. *Obv.* (1) [Ana] Sin ina ûmi I ^{kám} [innamir] (2) sanâḳu ša pî lib [mâti iṭâb] (3) Ana Sin ina tamarti-šu manzas-su (?)

[1] KA . GI . NA., *glossed* pu-u i-kan. [2] AGA, *glossed* a-gu-u.
[3] SI ZAG. -su Ana -ú, *glossed* ḳar-nu i-mit-ti-šu ša-mu-u.
[4] ḪI . GAR, *glossed* bar-ti. [5] DIR, *glossed* di-ir.

kînu [izziz] (4) ilâni ^{pl} milik mâti ana ^{sal} damiḳti imalliku $^{[pl]}$ (5) ša ina ûmi I ^{kám} in-nam-ma-ru (6) Ana ûmu ana mi-na-ti-šu írik (7) pâl ûmí . . [arkûti ^{pl}] (8) . . . du (?) . . . *Rev.* (1) . . umu XXX ^{kám} ú-sal-lam-[ma] (2) . . in-nam-mar-[ma] (3) ^{arḫu} Ululu (?) ^{arḫu} . . . . (4) IV arḫâni ^{pl} . . . . . (5) u ûmu I ^{kám} innammar . . (6) ša šarru bí-[ili] (7) . . . (*Remainder lost.*) [83–1–18, 203.]

No. 46. *Obv.* (1) Ana Sin ina tamarti-šu (2) ḳarnâti ^{pl}-šu ud-du-da (3) šarru mât nakri-šu ú-na-kap (4) Ana ûmu XIV ^{kám} Sin u ^{ilu} Šamšu (5) itti a-ḫa-miš innamru ^{pl} (6) sanâḳu ša pî lib mâti iṭab(ab) *Rev.* (1) ilâni $^{pl\ mâtu}$ Akkadi ^{ki} (2) a-na damiḳtim(tim) i-ḫas-sa-su (3) ḫu-ud lib-bi niši ^{pl} išakan(an) (4) ša ^{m} Aplâ(a). [K. 172.]

No. 46A. *Obv.* (1) Ana ina ûmi (?) I (?) . . . . . GI (?) *NA (2) lib mâti iṭâb(ab) (3) Ana ûmu . . . . . ilu in-nam-mar (4) damiḳti (?) ša (?) šarri bí-ili-ia (5) . . . . šu (?) a-di . . . iz-za-az (6) . . . KI (?) DU (?) SU (?) ur ḳu (?) (7) . . . rubî arkûti ^{pl} *Rev.* (1) . . $^{mul\ (?)}$ GIR (?) TAB (?) . . ^{ilu} PAN (?) (2) . . . $^{mul\ (?)}$ šarru (?) i(?)-tí-tí-zi (4) ŠI + UM ša šarri bí-ili-ia (5) ina (?) ûmi(mi) ul(?)-li-i (6) . . ki (?) . . . mâtu (?) SIS (?) (7) ^{m} Iraššši(ši)-ilu (8) (*in different hand?*) ^{arḫu} Aîru (?) ûmu I (?) ^{kám}. [K. 904.]

No. 46B. *Obv.* (1) . . nu tar aṣ . . . . . (2) Ana Sin ûmu I ^{kám} innamir [sanâḳu ša] pî [lib mâti iṭâb] (3) Ana Sin ina tamarti-šu ḳarnâti ^{pl} [šu] . . . . (4) šar ^{mâtu} . . . . . (5) Ana Sin ina tamarti-šu ḳarnâti [^{pl}-su] . . (6) ḳarnâti ^{pl} šu . . . . . (7) ḳat-su ikkašad(ád) . . (8) Ana ḳarnu šumíli-šu uk . . . . *Rev.* (1) Ana Sin ûmu XXX ^{kám} innamir . . . . (2) : KA . . . (3) Ana Sin ûmu XXX ^{kám} innamir . . . (4) nim-ma-ḳu . . . (5) Ana Sin ina tamarti-šu . . . (6) Šarru ṣir(muš)-ta . . . (*Remainder wanting.*) [81–2–4, 321.]

No. 47. *Obv.* (1) [Ana] Sin ûmu I ^{kám} innamir (2) sanâku ša pî [lib] mâti iṭab(ab) (3) Ana Sin . . . . . (*ll.* 4 *and* 5 *illegible*) (6) Ana manzazu ki-[i-nu izziz] (7) uk-ku-u ša (zunni] (8) Ana ḳarnâti ^{pl} . . ki innamru ^{pl} (9) mílu illakam(kám) *Rev.* (1) ^{ilu} Bíl u ^{ilu} Nabû lib-bi ša šarri bí-ili-[ia] (2) . . . . bi ana šarri bí-ili-[ia] (3) . . . . . (4) ina lib ^{arḫu} . . . . (5) . . . a . . . an . . . (6) ša ^{m} Šú-ma-a-[a]. [83–1–18, 216.]

No. 47A. *Obv.* (1) . . . . . . (2) . . . . ikkal (3) [Ana Sin ina tamarti-šu] agû a-pìr (4) Šarru [a-ša-ri]-du-ti il-lak (5) . . . . . (6) [Sin nakra i]-maḫ-ḫa-aṣ *Rev.* (1) . . . . ir-pi (2) [Ana Sin ina tamarti-šu] ḳarnu imitti-šu írik (3) [karnu] šumíli-šu ik-ru (4) [Šarru] mâtu la šú-a-tum ḳat-su (5) i-kaš-šad (6) . . . . [K. 1344.]

No. 48. *Obv.* (1) Ana ^{ilu} Sin ûmu I ^{kám} ša ^{arḫu} KAN . ZA ittamar(mar) (2) šar Akkadi ^{ki} í-ma illaku(ku) mâta un-na-áš (3) : Šar Akkadi ^{ki} í-ma pâni ^{pl}-šu šaknu(nu) (4) mâta ibíl(íl) (5) ûmu XIV ^{kám} itti ^{ilu} Šamši it-tan-mar (6) pa-ṭar ^{alu} bi-ra-a-ti (7) a-rad ma-aṣ-ṣa-ra-ti (8) taš-mu u sa-li-mu ina mâti [ibašši] *Rev.* (1) si-it-ti damḳâti ^{pl} šu šarru (2) ḫa-an-ṭiš ṭí-í-mu u šú-lum (3) ša ḫa-di-í šarru i-šim-mu (4) ša ^{m} A-ša-ri-du. [83–1–18, 175.]

No. 49. *Obv.* Ana Sin ina ^{arḫu} Si-li-li-ti ^{išu} Narkabtá ra-kib (2) Šar Akkadi ^{ki} ni-ir-šu iš-šir-ma (3) a-a-bi ḳat-su ikašad (ád) (4) ^{arḫu} Si-li-li-ti ^{arḫu} Šabâṭu (5) [ina] ^{arḫu} Šabâṭi ina lib-bi ^{mul} ŠÚ . GI (6) tarbaṣu ilammi(mi)-ma *Rev.* (1) [Ana] Sin tarbaṣu ilmi-ma ^{mul} AN . NA . MIR (2) ina libbi-šu izziz(iz) šarru ša-lim (3) kit-ti u mi-ša-ri ina mâti ibašši(ši) (4) [ša] $^{m\,ilu}$ Nabû-ikišâ(ša) mâr Bar-sib ^{ki}. [83–1–18, 187].

No. 50. *Obv.* (1) [Ana Sin ina tamarti-šu] ḳarnâti ^{pl} šu zu (?)-ʻ-ú-ma (?) (2) . . . . . . ina ^{išu} kakki šumḳut(ut) (3) [Ana Sin ina tamarti-su] ḳarnâti ^{pl}-šu ša . . di (?) ut (?) ša . . (4) . . šu ḳat-šu ikašad(ád) (5) . . . ŠAG . uš . . . tum (6) . . . . . *Rev.* (1) . . . ni-tum manzas-su kînu [izziz] (2) [taš-mu]-ú u salimu(mu) ina mâti ibašši(ši) (3) . . . . ta-mar-ti (4) [^{mul} LU . BAD .] ŠAG . UŠ a-na šarri (?) (5) . . . tab . . . (6) [. . . lib šarri bí]-ili lu-ṭa-a-[bi] (7) [šarru bí-ili] lu-ḫa-a-[di] (8) . . . . . . [83–1–18, 212.]

No. 51. *Obv.* (1) ^{ilu} Sin ina ^{arḫu} Nisanni (2) ûmu(mu) ú-šal-lam *Rev.* (3) šá $^{m\,ilu}$ Nabû-âḫí ^{pl} íriba. [83–1–18, 190.]

No. 52. *Obv.* [Sin ^{arḫu}] Aîru ûmu(mu) ú-šal-lam (2) [ûmu XIII ?] $^{kám\,ilu}$ Sin u ^{ilu} Šamšu (3) it-ti a-ḫa-miš innammaru ^{pl} (4) [ûmu ?] XIII ^{kám} mu-ši ša ûmu XIV ^{kám} (5) . . . maṣṣartu u atalû la išakan *Rev.* (1) bu . . . ki VII-šu na-ša-ka (2) atalû ul iš-šak-kan (3) a-mat pa-ri-is-tum (4) a-na sarri al-tap-ra (5) ša m Ṭâbu-ṣil-ilu Marduk (6) mâr âḫi-šu ša m ilu Bíl-na-ṣir. [K. 1393.]

No. 52A. *Obv.* (1) .... Sin ... ilu Šamšu (*four lines wanting*) (5) ... V kam ..... (6) arḫu Simânu ûmu XXVIII kám Sin izzaz (?) .. *Rev.* (1) ul (?) i-tap ... (2) ... ilu Sin ûmu(mu) ú-šal-[lam-ma] (3) [mi]-na-a-ti ina ûmu(mu) ... (4) . i-nam- ... (5) .... mâtu Aḫarrû ki (6) [ša m ilu] Nírgal íṭir(ir). [81–2–4, 138.]

No. 53. *Obv.* (*top broken*) (1) ...... [ina arḫu] Addâri ûmu(mu) ú-[šal-lam ?] (2) ûmu XIV kám it-ti in-[nam-mar] (3) ... ina arḫu Nisanni ûmu(mu) ú-tar-ra (4) .... ina arḫu Aíri ûmu(mu) ú-tar-ra (5) .... ina arḫu Simani a-na tur-ra ki inadu(du) (6) .. [ma]-'-du ina pa-ni-iá ul ... (7) ... šarri ša šarrâni pl ..... (*Rev. lost.*) [82–5–22, 66.]

No. 54. *Obv.* (1) ilu Sin ina arḫu Šabâṭi (2) ûmu(mu) ú-šal-lam *Rev.* (1) Šá m ilu Nabû-âḫí pl-íriba. [83–1–18, 189.]

No. 55. *Obv.* (1) ilu [Sin ûmu] ú-šal-lam (2) ša ..... ri-íš šatti (3) damiḳti ša [šarri] bíl-ia (4) ina íli mul LU . BAD . GUD . UD (5) šá šarru bí-ili iš-pur-an-ni (6) it-ti-ma-li m ilu Ištar-šum-íríš(íš) (7) ina lib íkalli ṣa-a-su (8) a-na m ilu Nabû-âḫí pl-íriba ig-di-ri *Rev.* (1) i-da-a-ti ina NU . BAD-ti (2) it-ta-al-ku gab-bi-šu-nu it-ta-aṣ-ru (3) í-ta-am-ru ip-tu-šú (4) šá m Ba-la-si-i. [K. 1335 + 80–7–19, 335.]

No. 56. *Obv.* (1) [Ana Sin ûmu I kam innamir] sanâḳu ši pî lib mati iṭâb(ab) (2) .... ni-du-šú (?) u šubat-su niḫ(iḫ) (3) .... ana di-mi-iḳ-ina (4) .... i-ta-mi (5) ... šar Aḫarri kiššutam(tam) ibíl(íl) (6) .... kakkabâni pl it-tab-ši (7) .... DU DU . Sin nakri iští'í (?) (8) ..... ga-a .. *Rev.* (1) mul ilu IMIN . BI ilâni pl rabûti pl (2) ... dan-ni-šu-nu mâtâti pl ni .. (3) .. pl i ḫi (?) .... ma (4) ... damiḳtim(tim) .... ku (5) .. ší ..... a (6) .. at ..... ma (7) ..... ḫa. [K. 1341.]

No. 56A. *Obv.* (1) Ana Sin ûmu I kám .... (2) pa-li-[í] ... (3) šípâ II ša ... (4) ina ... (*Remainder broken off.*) [K. 5723.]

III. Omens from the Moon's appearance on the twenty-eighth day.

No. 57. *Obv.* (1) šá a-na šarri bíl-ia aš-pur . . . (2) mu-uk [1]uzni ^{pl} šá šarri [bíl-ia] (3) ilâni ^{pl}-ni ú-pat-tu (?) . . . (4) šúm-ma mí-mí-ni a-na . . . (5) ultu libbi-šu i-da-bu-ub ina . . . (6) i-ḫar-ru-bu | [2]ittu | ultu . . . (7) [i]-šap-par-u-ni ma-a . . . (8) . . . u a . . . *Rev.* (1) . . . [ûmu] XXVIII ^{kám} innamir (?) . . . [damiḳti] ša (?) ^{mâtu} Akkadi ^{ki} limutti ^{mâtu} Ílama $^{\text{[ki]}}$ (3) ûmu XXVIII $^{\text{kám ilu}}$ Sin is . . . (4) . . . [3]ultu mí-ḫir itti šá . . . (5) . . . ú (*Left-hand edge*) (1) šarru bí-ili . . . (2) . . . . . [K. 8432.]

No. 58. *Obv.* (1) Ana Sin ina tamarti-šu kima ûmu I ^{kám} ûmu XXVIII ^{kám} innamir . . . (2) limuttim(tim) Aḫarrî ^{ki} (3) Ana Sin ûmu XXVIII ^{kám} innamir (4) damiḳti ^{mâtu} Akkadi ^{ki} limutti ^{mâtu} Aḫarri ^{ki} *Rev.* (1) ša ^{am} Rab-asû. [K. 693.]

IV. Omens from the Moon's appearance on the thirtieth day.

No. 59. *Obv.* (1) Ana Sin ina ûmi XXX ^{kám} innamir(ir) (2) šú-ru-ub-bu-ú : rigmu(mu) nakri ibašši(ši) (3) Ana Sin ina tamarti-šu ša-ḳu-ma innamir(ir) (4) nakru ina mâti i-liḳ-ḳi (5) Ana Sin ina tamarti-su ḫar-bi-iš na-an-mur (6) arḫu ni-zik-tum ub-ba-lu *Rev.* (1) Ana Sin ina tamarti-šu ḳarnati ^{pl}-[šu] . . ḳa (?) ru (2) i-na-aṭ-ṭa-lu (3) mílu illakam(kám) (4) ša ^{m} Iraššì(ši) ilu ardu ša šarri (5) maḫrû(u). [K. 1395.]

No. 60. *Obv.* (1) Ana Sin ina tamarti-šu un-nu-ut-ma (2) ma-am-ma la ú-ma-an-di-šu (3) zunnu izanun(nun) (4) Ana Sin ûmu XXX ^{kám} innamir(ir) (5) šú-ru-ub-bu-ú : rigmu(mu) nakri (6) ina mâti ibašši(ši) *Rev.* (1) Ana Sin ina tamarti uš-tap-pil-ma inna-mir(ir) (2) šú-púl-ti mâti ru-uḳ-ti (3) ana šar kiššuti illakam(am) (4) ša ^{m} Irašši(ši)-ilu ardu ša šarri makrû(u). [82–5–22, 53.]

[1] PI . MIŠ, *glossed* uz-ni. [2] ŠI + UM, *glossed* it-tú
[3] TA mí-ḫir ŠI + UM, *glossed* [ul]-tú mí-ḫi-ir it-ti.

No. 61. *Obv.* (1) Ana Sin ûmu XXX ^{kám} innamir (2) Šú-ru-ub-bu-ú (3) . . . rigmu(mu) ^{am} nakri ibašši(ši) (4) šá $^{\text{m ilu}}$ Nabû-mu-ší-ṣi. [80–7–19, 54.]

No. 62. *Obv.* (1) [Ana Sin ^{ina}] ^{arḫu} Nisanni umu XXX ^{kám} [innamir] (2) [Su]-bar-tum At-ḫa-ma-a [ikkal] (3) [1]lišânu aḫitum (tum) ^{mâtu} Aharrû ^{ki} [2]i-bí-íl (4) a-ni-nu Subartu ^{ki} (5) Ana Sin ûmu XXX ^{kám} innamir (6) šú-ru-ub-bu-u ina mâti ibašši(ši) (7) šú-ru-ub-bu-u ku-uṣ-ṣu *Rev.* (1) ^{ilu} Sin ina ^{arḫu} Ṭábiti ûmu XIV [^{kám}] (2) ultu ^{ilu} Ša-maš in-na-mar[ma] (3) ^{ilu} Sin ina ^{arḫu} Šabâṭi ûmu(mu) ú-šal-lam (4) ûmu XIV ^{kám} ultu ^{ilu} Ša-maš in-na-mar (5) [^{ilu} Sin ina] $^{\text{ar u}}$ Addâri ûmu(mu) ú-tir-ra (?) (6) . . . . . . ^{ilu} Ša-maš in-na-mar . . . (7) [^{ilu} Sin ina] ^{arḫu} Nisanni ûmu(mu) ú-šal-lam [šá $^{\text{m ilu}}$ Nabû]-aḫí ^{pl} í-riba. [S. 1974.]

No. 63. *Obv.* (1) Ana Sin ina ^{arḫu} Âiri umu XXX ^{kám} innamir (2) Aḫarrû ^{ki}-ú subarti ^{ki} (3) ina ^{isu} kakki idâk . . . (4) [Ša] ^{m}Mun-na-bi-tu. [K. 776.]

No. 64. *Obv.* (1) Ana Sin ina ^{arḫu} Âiri ûmu XXX ^{kám} innamir (2) duḫ-da Aḫarrî ^{ki} (3) ^{am} Aḫ-la-mu-ú [ikkal] (4) ša $^{\text{m ilu}}$ Nabû-ikiša(ša) mâr [Bar-sib ^{ki}]. [83–1–18, 299.]

No. 64A. *Obv.* (1) [Ana Sin ina] ^{arḫu} Âiri ûmu XXX innamir (ir) (2) [duḫ-da ^{mâtu}] Aḫarrî Aḫ-la-mu-ú ikkal (3) . . . . du ru ù u šaḫlukta (4) . . . . . . Aḫarrî ibašši (5) . . . . du kima . . . . . dar . . *Rev.* (1) . . . . da (2) . . . . itti Šamši innamar(mar) (3) . . . . ú-ší-it-tí-iḳ (4) [Ša ^{m} A-ša]-ri-du. [K. 1340.]

No. 64B. *Obv.* (*top wanting*) (1) [Ana Sin ina] ^{arḫu} Âiri ûmu XXX ^{kám} [innamir] (2) [duḫ-da] Aharrî ^{ki} (3) [Aḫ]-la-mu-ú ikkal (4) [^{am}] I-tu-ú-a-a ša šarri [bíl-ia ?] (5) [Ana] muḫ-ḫi ^{m} Mu-gal [lu . . .] (6) . . . íli-šú-nu *Rev.* (1) . . [. . Aḫ ?]-la-mu-u . . . . (2) . . . lib-bi il-li-[ku ?] (3) . . . . . at (?). (*Remainder wanting.*) [K. 1927.]

[1] ÍMÍ BAR-tum, *glossed* li-ša-a-nu a-ḫi-tum.
[2] i-bí-íl, *glossed* [i]-bi-il.

No. 65. *Obv.* (1) Ana Sin ina ûmi XXX ^{kám} innamir(ir) (2) šú-ru-bu-ú (3) : rigmu nakri ibašši(ši) (4) Ana Sin ina ^{arḫu} Simâni ûmu XXX ^{kám} innamir(ir) (5) duḫ-du Aḫarrî ^{ki} (6) Aḫ-[la]-mu-ú ikkal *Rev.* Ša ^{m} Irašši(ši)-ilu ardu ša šarri (2) maḫru(u).

[82–5–22, 50.]

No. 66. *Obv.* (1) Ana Sin ina ^{arḫu} Simâni ûmu XXX ^{kám} innamir (2) duḫ-du Aḫarri ^{ki} Ah-la-mu-[u ikkal] (3) Ana Sin ina ûmi XXX^{kám} innamir (4) Šú-ru-ub-bu-ú : rigmu(mu) [nakri] (5) ina mâti ibašši(ši) (6) Ana Sin ina tamarti-šu uš-tap-pil-ma [innamir] *Rev.* (1) .. mâtu i-liḳ-ḳi (2) [Ana Sin ina] tamarti-šu ú-šap-pil-ma innamir(ir) (3) [šu]-pil-ti mâti ruḳti(ti) (4) [Ana] sarri kiššuti illak(ak) : ^{am} mâr-šipri (5) . . . il-la-ka (6) ša ^{m} Iraššì-ilu ardu ša šarri maḫrû(u).

[K. 809.]

No. 67. *Obv.* (1) Ana Sin ina ^{arḫu} Simâni ûmu XXX ^{kám} innamir (2) duḫ-da Aḫarrî ^{ki} Aḫ-la-mu-ú ikkal (3) ^{arḫu} Simânu ^{mâtu} Aḫarrû limutti ^{mâtu} Aḫarrî (4) ^{mul} LU . BAD . SAG . UŠ (5) ídi-šam a-na muḫ-ḫi ^{mul} Dil-bat (6) ul iḳ-ru-ub *Rev.* (1) ittu-šu ia-a-nu (2) Ša ^{m} Šuma-idina(na).

[83–1–18, 194.]

No. 68. *Obv.* (1) [Ana Sin ina] ^{arḫu} Simâni ûmu XXX ^{kám} innamir (2) [duḫ-da] A-ḫar-ri-i | Aḫ-la-mu-u ikkal (3) [Ana Sin] ûmu XXX ^{kám} innamir šú-ru-ub-bu-u (4) ri-gim nakri ibašši(ší) (5) [Ana Sin] ina tamarti-šu iltanu illik (6) Arḫu šuâtu mílu illakam(kám) (7) [Ana Šamšu] ina napaḫi-šu ina imitti-šu ni-du . . . (8) ^{ilu} Rammânu iraḫiṣ(iṣ) *Rev.* (1) ^{mul} muštabarrû-mûtânu(a-nu) ut-ta-mí-iš (2) a-na pa-na-tu-uš-šu il-lak (3) ultu ^{mul} Aḳrabi in-ni-mí-da (4) ši-i-a-ri a-na šarri bíl-ia (5) ú-šaḫ-ka-am (6) [ša] ^{m} Ba-[la-si]-i.

[K. 774.]

No. 69. *Obv.* (1) Ana Sin ina ^{arḫu} Simâni ûmu XXX ^{kám} innàmir(ir) (2) duḫ-du Aḫarri ^{ki} Aḫ-la-mu-ú ikkal (3) Ana Sin ina tamarti-šu adir mâtu nuḫša immar (4) GAN . BA . nap-ša mâti ikkal (5) Ana Sin ina tamarti-šu adir-ma ḳarnu šumili-šu ki-pat (6) ḳarnu imitti-šu id-di-it (7) mâtu nakri ta-za-ḳip ^{ilu} Rammânu iraḫiṣ *Rev.* (1) Ana Sin ina tamarti-šu rabiš ib-ta-'-il (4) ibûr mâti iššir (5) Ana ina ^{arḫu} Simâni ûmu XIV ^{kám} Sin itti šamši (6) in-nam-mar (7) ša $^{\text{m ilu}}$ Nírgal-íṭir(ir).

[82-5-22, 49.]

No. 69A. *Obv.* (1) [Ana Sin] ina arḫu Simâni ûmu XXX kám innamir (2) da-aḫ-du Aḫarri [ki] (3) Aḫ-la-mu-ú ik (?)-[kal] (4) [Ana] Sin ina tamarti-ši išru Aḫarrû [illak] (5) ina arḫi šuâti mur-ṣu us (?) . . . (6) [lu]-um-nu ša mâtu MAR[TU] (7) . . . na ak . . . . *Rev.* (1) . . . mâr . . . . (*Remainder lost.*)

[80–7–19 176.]

No 70. *Obv.* (1) Ana Sin ina arḫu Simâni ûmu XXX kám innamir (2) duḫ-du Aḫarrî ki Aḫ-la-ma-a ikkal (3) Ana Sin ûmu XXX kám innamir šú-ru-ub-bu-u (4) . . . ri-gim am nakri ibašši(ši) (5) Ana Sin ina tamarti-šu ḫar-biš na-an-mur (6) arḫu ni-zik-tú ub-ba-la (7) II arḫâni da-rat a-ḫi-í-iš (8) ûmu(mu) ut-tir-ir-ra arḫu Aîru arḫu Simânû (9) ina [1] imitti Šamši ni-du na-di (10) ilu Rammânu iraḫiṣ(iṣ) . . . zunni pl mîli pl *Rev.* (1) il-lak-u-ni (2) mul mušta-barrû-mûtânu (a-nu) is-su-uḫ-ur (3) ut-ta-mí-iš ina pa-na-tu-uš-su | ina lib Akrabi (4) il-lak lum-nu šú-ú (5) ma-ḫir-tú, ár-ḫi-iš lu-gam-mí-ru (6) uṣ-ṣu-ú šá šarri bíl-ia lu-u-šam-gur (7) a-du ni-mar-u-ni a-di-í šá il-lak-u-ni (8) iz-za-zu-u-ni (9) šá m ilu Nábû-âḫî-íriba.

[81–2–4, 79.]

No. 70A. *Obv.* (1) Ana ina arḫu Âbi ûmu XXX kám innamir (2) sapaḫ(aḫ) [mâtu Akkad ki] (3) Ana ina arḫu Abi . . . . (4) ti . . . .

[K. 1320.]

No. 71. *Obv.* (1) Ana Sin ina arḫu Âbi ûmu XXX kám innamir (ir) (2) Sapaḫ(aḫ) mâtu Akkadi ki (3) Ana Sin ûmu XXX kám innamir(ir) (4) šú-ru-ub-bu-ú (5) [: rigim] am nakri ibašši(ši) *Rev.* (1) Ša m Ṭa-bi-ia.

[83–1–18, 182.]

No. 72. *Obv.* (1) Ana Sin ina arḫu Âbi unu [XXX] kám innamir (2) sapaḫ mâtu akkadi ki (3) Ana Sin ûmu XXX kám innamir (4) Šú-ru-ub-bu-ú (5) . . . rigmu (mu ?) am nakri ibašši(ši) (5a) [ša (?) m] Arad-ilu Í-a (5a. *The name of the sender has been written in a small hand diagonally.*)

[K. 1383.]

No. 73. *Obv.* (1) Ana Sin ina arḫu Âbi ûmu XXX kám innamir (ir) (2) sapaḫ(aḫ) mâtu Akkadi ki (3) Šar Kiš-ša-ti bí-ili-a (4) la

[1] *glossed* i-mit-ti ilu Ša-maš.

ú-maš-šír-an-ni a-na-ku *Rev.* (1) ûmu (mu)-us-su a-na íli (2) bu-bu-ti-ia šarri i-maḫ-ḫar (3) u ín-na a-na libitti it-ta-az-ki-in-ni (4) um-ma li-bit-ti li-bi-in (5) Šarri bí-ili-ia la ú-maš-šir-an-ni-ma (6) la a-ma-ti (7) Ša ^{m} Ṭa-bi-ia. [Bu. 89–4–26, 11.]

No. 74. *Obv.* (1) Ana Sin ûmu XXX ^{kám} innamir (2) šú-ru-ub-bu-[u] (3) . . . rigim nakri ibašši(ši) (4) Ana ina ^{arḫu} kisilimi ûmu XXX ^{kám} innamir (5) Šar Aharrî ^{ki} (6) ina ^{isu} kakki šumķut . . *Rev.* (1) ^{mâtu} Aḫarrû ^{ki} í (?) . . . (2) it-tu iš-ša- . . . (3) lu-u-ša . . zi (?) (4) ina muḫ-ḫi-ni i . . . (5) ša ^{am} Rab-A . BA. [Rm. 203.]

No. 75. *Obv.* (1) Ana Sin ina ^{arḫu} kisilimi ûmu XXX ^{kám} innamir (2) Šar Aḫarrî ^{ki} (3) ina ^{isu} kakki šumķut(ut) *Rev.* Šá $^{m\ ilu}$ Nabû-aḫî ^{pl}-íriba. [K. 692.]

No. 76. *Obv.* (1) Ana Sin ina ^{arḫu} Ṭíbiti ûmu XXX ^{kám} innamir (2) Subarta ^{ki} Aḫ-la-mu-u ikkal (3) lišânu aḫitum(tum) ^{mâtu} Aharrî ibíl [il] (4) ^{arḫu} Ṭíbita ^{mâtu} í lama(ma) ^{ki} (5) Šá ^{m} Bu-ul-lu-ṭu *Rev.* (1) ûmu XXIX ^{kám} ni-ta-ṣar urpâtu dan-[nat?] (2) ^{ilu} Sin la ni-mur (3) ûmu XXX ^{kám} ni-ta-ṣar ^{ilu} Sin ni-ta-[mar] (4) ma-ti-iḫ a-dan-niš . . (5) šá ûmu XXIX ^{kám} šú-ú . . . . (6) ina muḫ-ḫi ķur-bu mí-i-nu . . (7) šá šarru bí-ili i-ķa-bu-u . . . . [83–1–18, 183.]

No. 77. *Obv.* (1) Ana ina ^{arḫu} Ṭíbiti Sin ûmu XXX ^{kám} innamir (2) Subarta ^{ki} Aḫ-la-mu-u ikkal (3) lišânu a-ḫi-tú ^{mâtu} Aḫarrí ^{ki} ibíl(íl) (4) Ana Sin ina tamarti-šu ša-pi-il (5) Šú-pu-ul-ti mâti ruķti(ti) (6) a-na šar kissûti illakam(kam) (7) Šá ^{m} Bu-ul-lu-ṭi. [83–1–18, 184.]

No. 78. *Obv.* (1) Ana Sin ina ^{arḫu} Ṭíbiti ûmu ^{kám} innamir (2) Subarta ^{ki} Aḫ-la-mu-ú ikkal (3) lišânu a-ḫi-tum ^{mâtu} Aḫarrî ^{ki} (4) ibíl(íl) *Rev.* (1) ša $^{m\ ilu}$ Nírgal-íṭir(ir). [K. 722.]

No. 79. (1) [Ana Sin] ina ^{arḫu} Ṭíbiti ûmu XXX ^{kám} (2) Subarta ^{ki} Aḫ-la-mu-ú ikkal (3) lišânu a-ḫi-tum (4) Aḫarrî ibíl(íl) (5) [Ana] Sin ina tamarti-šu ķarnâti ^{pl}-šu (6) [mir?]-ra-a ù la . . . pa (7) a (?) mat (?) damiķtim(tim) ina mâti ibašši(ši) (8) $^{m\ ilu}$ Nírgal-íṭir(ir). [83–1–18, 173.]

No. 79A. *Obv.* (1) Sin ina arḫu Ṭíbiti ûmu [XXX kám innamir] (2) Subarti ki Aḫ-[la-mu-u ikkal] (3) lišânu a-ḫi-tum [mâtu Aḫarri] (4) ibíl [il] (5) [ša] m Aplâ-a mâr Bar-sib ki. [K. 1407.]

No. 80. *Obv.* (1) Ana Sin ina arḫu Ṭíbiti ûmu XXX kám innamir(ir) (2) Subarti ki Aḫ-la-mu-u ikkal (3) lišânu aḫitum(tum) mâtu Aḫarri ki (4) i-bí-íl *Rev.* (1) šá m Šú-ma-a-a. [K. 713.]

No. 80A. *Obv.* (1) [Ana Sin ina arḫu] Ṭíbiti ûmu XXX kám innamir(ir) (2) [Subarti] am Aḫ-la-mu-[u ikkal] (3) [lišânu] a-ḫi-[tum mâtu Aḫarrî ki ibíl] (*Remainder broken off.*) *Rev.* (1) ša m ilu Nabû-iḳ-[bi] (2) mâr kûtî . . . [82–5–22, 72.]

No. 81. *Obv.* (1) Ana Sin ûmu XXX kám [innamir] (2) šú-ru-ub-bu-ú . . . rigim nakri ibašši(ši) (3) Ana Sin ina arḫu Šabâṭi ûmu XXX kám innamir (4) atal mâtâti išakan(an) *Rev.* (1) šá am Rab-dup-šar. [80–7–19, 56.]

Miscellaneous fragments concerning the Moon's appearance on the thirtieth day.

No. 81A. *Obv.* (1) . . . . ši (2) . . . . I i (?) (3) . . . . XXX kám innamir (4) . . . . tu ki (5) . . . . ikkal. (*Remainder wanting.*) [Bu. 91–5–9, 38.]

No. 81B. *Obv.* (*Top wanting.*) (1) . . . . . mâti su . . (2) . . . . [ûmu] XXX kám innamir . . . (3) [. Šú]-ru-ub-bu-u : rigim nakri . . . . (4) šá m Ba-ma-a-[a]. [Bu. 89–4–26, 37.]

No. 81C. *Obv.* (1) . . . . ûmu XXX kám innamir (2) . . . . tu ki (3) . . . . ú ikkal (4) [ša m ilu Nabu]-šuma-iškun(un). [80–7–19, 66.]

No. 81D. *Obv.* (1) . . . . XXX kám innamir (2) . . . . Aḫarru ki (3) . . . . la-mu-ú . . . . (4) [ša m] ilu Nabu-âḫî pl [íriba]. [80–7–19, 197.]

No. 81E. *Obv.* (1) Ana Sin . . . . . (2) šú . . . . . (3) . . . rigim . . (4) ša m ilu Nabû . . . . . [D.T. 249.]

No. 81F. *Obv.* (1) .... itti Šamši innamir (2).... Subarti ^{ki} (3).... Subarti ^{ki} (4) ... (5)... tar-ru (6) .... Sin innamir *Rev.* (1).... Aḫarru ^{ki} (2).... ikkal (3)..... du. [80–7–19, 62.]

No. 81G. *Obv.* (1) ..... innamir (2) ..... rigim nakri ibašši(ši) (3)..... mu-ur-ṣu (4)..... | [1] šumili. (*Remainder lost.*) *Rev.* (1)..... (2).... íriba. [83–1–18, 314].

No. 81H. *Obv.* (1) Ana Sin ina ..... (2) itti ..... (3) a ..... (4) Ana Sin ina la ..... (5) maḫiru .... (6) limutti ... (*Remainder broken.*) *Rev.* (*Top wanting.*) (1) ^{am} nakru ina .... (2) Ana Sin ina la .... (3) ti ...... [K. 1307.]

No. 81I. *Obv.* (1) Ana ^{ilu} Sin .... (2) Šarru .... (3) Ana ^{ilu} Sin ..... (4) Šarru .... (5) ^{iṣu} ..... (*Remainder wanting: slight traces on reverse.*) [81–3–18, 885.]

No. 81K. *Obv.* (1) ..... ^{kám} in-na-mir (2) ..... Aḫarrî ^{ki} (3)..... ú ikkal (4) [Ana Sin manza]-as su kînu izziz(iz) (5)... pat (?) zunni (6).... is-sit-tí ípuš(uš)-ma (7).... mur-ṣa-at *Rev.* (1).... ta-mu-ú (2)..... ut (*Remainder of reverse broken, except the writer's name.*) (3) [Ša $^{m\ ilu}$ Nírgal]-íṭir(ir). [K. 901.]

V. Various Omens from the Moon.

No. 82. *Obv.* (1) Ana ^{ilu} Sin ina la si-ma-ni iḫ-iḫ-ram-ma la innamir (2) tí-bi-í âl kiš-ša-tú ûmu XIII ^{kám} innammar-ma (3) Ana ^{ilu} Sin la innamir ilâni ^{pl} milik mâti ana damiḳtim(tim) imaliku ^{pl} (4) ša ûmu XIV ^{kám} ûmu XV ^{kám} ilu itti ili la innammaru(ru) (5) Ana ^{ilu} Sin ina ^{arhu} Ululi lu-ú ûmu XIV ^{kám} lu-ú ûmu XV ^{kám} (6) itti ^{ilu} Šamši la innamir UR . A ^{pl} imâtu ^{pl} alkâti ipparrasu ^{pl} (7) Ana ^{ilu} Sin u ^{ilu} Šamšu ud-da-su-nu du-'-ú-mat (8) Šarru itti mâti-šu u nîši ^{pl} zi-ni i-na-kap(kip) (9) ^{ilu} Sin u ^{ilu} Šamšu atalû išakanu ^{pl}-ma: ša ûmu XIV ^{kám} (10) arḫu-us-su ilu itti ili la innammaru(ru) *Rev.* (1) Ana ûmu XVI ^{kám} ^{ilu} Sin u ^{ilu} Šamšu itti a-ḫa-miš innamru ^{pl} (2) Šarru ana Šarri ^{sal} nukurti išappar šarru ina îkalli-šu ana minati [arḫi]

[1] KAB-šu, *glossed* šú-mí-li-šu.

(3) ú-ta-sar šíp nakri ana máti-su išakan(an) nakru ina mati-[šu] (4) šal-ṭa-nišillaku pl (5) . . . šar Subarti ki i-dan-nin-ma mâḫiri la iraššì(ši) (6) A-na íli ta-ma-ra-a-ti ·a-gan-na-a-ti (7) ša ilu [Šamši ?] šarru la i-ša-ṭu lu-ú NAM . BUL . BI (8) lu-ú . . . . madul-lu ša a-na íli kir-bu (9) sarru li-pu-uš (10) ša m Mun-na-bi-tu.

[K. 769.]

No. 83. Obv. (1) Ana ilu Sin ina ša-da-ḫi-šu *ú-*ší . . . . (2) ilu ÍN . LIL ana mâti i-tam-ma-am-ma (3) ul ip-pa-aš-šir (4) ûmu XIII kám itti ilu Šamš innammar-ma Rev. (1) Ša m ilu Bíl-li' mâr m Í-gi-bi (2) am mašmašu. [K. 1734.]

No. 84. *Obv.* (1) Ana Sin ina a-la-ki-šu . . . (2) lum-nu . . . . (3) ûmu XIII kám in [nam-mar-ma] (4) IV arḫâni pl i-da-at a . . . . (5) ûmu (mu)-us-sa innammar ina lib-bi . . . (6) it-tan-ta-ḫa ûmu XIII kám it . . . . (7) Šarru bí-ili a-na lum-ni lu la . . . (8) Ana ilu Sin ina tamarti-šu [1]Šamu(ú) ša . . . (9) [1] Šamu(ú) i-za-nun . . . milu [illak] *Rev.* (1) ina [2]urpâti . . . . . (2) Ana [3]mul ilu . . . . (3) [4]ba-il šúm-ma (4) šúm-ma kuṣṣu . . . (5) mul ilu Imbaru (?) . . . . (6) šú-ru-bu-u [ku-uṣ-ṣu] (7) Ana mul Šanamma(ma) mul MAS-TAB-BA . . . (8) rubû imât šá iḳ-bu-u-ni-a. (*Left-hand edge.*) Ša m ilu Nabû-âḫí pl íriba. [K. 877.]

No. 85. *Obv.* (1) Ana Sin it-bal limuttim(tim) mâta išakan(an) (2) Ana Sin ina la mi-na-ti-šu bi-ib-lum ú-bil (3) Atalû išakan(an) (4) ûmu XXIV kám Sin i-tab-bal-ma (5) Ana ilu Šamšu ina ûm bubbuli tarbaṣu ilmi (6) Atal ílama(ma) ki išakan(an) (7) ina arḫu kisilimi ma-ṣar-t iša atalî *Rev.* (1) tarbaṣu ša ilu Šamši il-mu-ú (2) u Sin ša it-ba-lu (3) a-na ma-ṣar-ti ša atalî (4) ša arḫu kisilimi in-nam-mar (5) Sarru lu-i-di (6) lib-bi šarru bí-ili-ia (7) lu-ṭa-a-bi (8) ša m Iraššì(ši)-ilu ardu ša šarri maḫrû(u). [K. 752.]

No. 85A. *Obv.* (1) Ana Sin ina la mi-na-ti . . . . . (2) ûmu XIII kám ilu itti [ili innammar] (3) ûmu XIII kám Sin u Šamsu itti

[1] ANA-ú, *glossed* ša-mu-u.
[2] IM[DIR], *glossed* ur-[pa-ati].
[3] MULDINGIR . . . , *glossed* mu-ul-ilu . . . . .
[4] ba-il, *glossed* ba-il.

[Ahamiš innammaru] (4) pû la kînu A. DU.. (5) A-[na Šar] mâtâti bí-ili-i.... (6) ilu.... [ilu] Marduk a-na šarru [bí-ili] (7) ba-[la]-ṭi ûmí pl ru-ḳu-[u-ti]... (8) Kiš-šú-ut bí-lu-ti.... (9) ṭu-ub lib-bi u.... (10) Šar mâtâti bí-la-a... *Rev.* (1) Ša ina bilat ḫurâṣi i (?)..... (2 pa-ni ša šarri bí-ili-ia..... (3) ín-na a-na-ku am..... (4) ina ſkalli-šu..... (5) ma-am-mu NIN ul.... (6) ina bu-bu-ti ša a ka.... (7) ſḳli bîti u mim(sal)-mu ma la.... (8) ma-am-mu ul it.... (9)'u am ḳa-al lu ša a..... (10) ia-a-nu la-a ma.... (11) li..... [K. 1606.]

No. 86. *Obv.* (1) Ana Sin la innamir-ma II azkari innamru pl (2) nu-kúr-ti ina mâtâti iš-šak-kan (3) Sin ina ni-ib-ṭi-í it-ti ilu Šamši innammar-ma (4) í-du-ú ina pa-an ilu Šamsi pa-ri-ig (5) pa-anša BAL. BAT. ki šarru súh.... (6) [Ana] ina arḫu Abi ûmu XXX kám ilu Sin in-na-mar (7) [Ana] ina arḫu Âbu ûmu XXX kám innamir sapah(aḫ) mâti Akkadi ki *Rev.* (1) Ana ina arḫu Abi ûmu XVI kám Sin itti Šamši in-na-mar (2) Ana mul Dil-bat ana mi-iḫ-ri-ti.... (3) mul SIB. ZI. AN. NA izziz mâtu ana mâtu (4) Aḫu aḫî inakir(ir) šumḳutim(tim) amſlûti (5) ù bûli ibašši(ší) (6) Ana mul SIB. ZI. AN. NA kakkabâni pl šu it-ta-na-an-bi-ṭu (7) kab-tu uḳ-da-ap-pa-ša-am-ma (8) li. mut-ti ip-pu-uš (9) mul Dil-bat ina pa-an mul SIB. ZI. AN. NA izzaz-ma (10) Ša m ilu Nírgal-íṭir(ir).
[Rm. 194.]

No. 86A. *Obv.* (1) [Ana Sin] la innamir[ma] (2) [II UD.] SAR pl innamru [pl] (3) [sal] nukurti ina matâti iššakkan (4).... ûmu I [kám] (5).... u ilu..... *Rev.* (1)... ma.... (2) [ša m] Apla-a.... [83-1-18, 312.]

No. 87. *Obv.* (1) Ana Sin ina tamarti-su man-za-za kînu izziz(iz) (2) uk-ku-u ša zunni (3) Ana agû ûmu irpi a-pìr (4) Sin am nakri i-maḫ-ḫa-aṣ (5) UD ŠU. ŠU. RU ûmu (mu) ir-pi (6) UD ŠU. ŠU. RU ûmu(mu)... (7) ina lib-bi (?) (8) Ana Sin....... (*Remainder, perhaps one or two lines, lost.*) *Rev.* (1) Ana ina mâti..... (2) pâl mâti šu..... (3) Ša m A-ša-ri-du maḫrû(ú) (4) ardu ša šarri. [83-1-18, 177.]

No. 87A. *Obv.* (1).. Sin šá in-na-mir-u-ni (2) [man za]-su ki-í-ni ina lib urpati ṣalimti it-ta-mar (3) [Ana] sin ina arhu Simâni ûmu XXX ^{kám} innamir (4) duḫ-da] Aḫarri ^{ki} Aḫ-la-mu-u ikkal (5) .... ša-ni-í sapaḫ(aḫ) matâti (6) [Ana Sin ina tamarti-šu] ḳarnati ^{pl} šu tur-ru-ka (7) [paṭar bi-ra]-a-ti (8) [arad maṣṣarâti taš]-mu-u (9) [salimu ina mâti] ibašši(ši) *Rev.* (1) ..... ta-ra-ku (2) [ša]-la-mu : | man-za-su ki-í-nu (3) [izzaz] (az)-ma . . . ina urpati ṣalimti innammar-ma (4) šá ^{m} Ak-kul-la-ni. [K. 1007.]

No. 88. *Obv.* (1) [Ana Sin ina] la si-ma-ni-šu iḫ-ḫi-ra ma la innamir (2) [tí]-bi-í âl kiš-ša-ti (3) .... ûmu XV ^{kám} i-rab-bi-ma ûmu XVI ^{kám} itti ^{ilu} Šamši innammar-ma (4) Ana ^{mul} muštabarrû-mûtânu(a-nu) ^{mul} LU . BAD [1]is-sa-na-aḫ-ḫar ší-im iḳ.ḳir (5) Ana ^{mul} Ú . NAG . GA ^{šu} ḫarran ^{ilu} Šamši ikšud(ud) GAN . BA iṣaḫir (6) ša-ni-iš ri-ig-mu išakan(an) (7) An-nu-ti di-ib-bi a-na ^{mâtu} Akkadi ^{k} (8) ^{mul} muštabarrû-mûtânu(a-nu) | ir-bi | ú-ba-ni ultu pan ^{mul} LU . BAD . SAG . UŠ (9) pa-a-tí la iṭ-ḫi ina íli . . . ik-šú-ud at-ta-as-ḫa (10) mí-i-nu ḫi-iṭ-ṭu NAM . BUL . BI-šu lu-í-pi-iš (11) Ana Sin ûmu XVI ^{kám} innamir Šar Subarti ^{ki} i-dan-nin-ma (12) ma-ḫi-ra la i-ra-aš-ši *Rev.* (1) Ana Sin tarbaṣu ilmi-ma ^{mul} LU . BAD . ina libbi-šu izziz(iz) (2) ḫab-ba-a-tum in-na-an-da-ru (3) Ana Sin tarbaṣu ilmi-ma ^{mul} Muštabarrû-mûtânu(a-nu) ina libbi-šu izziz(iz) (4) ṣaḫlukti bûli kittu ibašši . . . ? (5) mí-ri-šu saluppu la išširu ^{pl} : ^{mâtu} Aḫarrû ^{ki} iṣaḫir (6) Ana Sin tarbaṣu ilmi-ma ^{mul} DIL . GAN ina libbi-šu izziz(iz) (7) la šur-ru-u ší-im (8) ^{mul} DIL . GAN ^{mul} AB . SIN. (9) šá ^{m} Ba-la-si-i (10) $^{[mul]}$ Muštabarrû-mutânu(a-nu) ultu lib an-ni-i-í i-pat-ti il-lak (11) . . . mí (?) ^{mul} LU . BAD . ŠAG . UŠ (12) . . . ina ^{arḫu} Nisanni ûmu(mu) ú-šal-lam. [K. 712.]

No. 89. *Obv.* (1) Ta-mar-ti ^{ilu} Sin šá ûmu XVI ^{kám} it-ti .... (2) ûmu XVI ^{kám} ^{mâtu} Subartu . . í ..... (3) û kit-tum lum-nu šá ^{mâtu} Akkadí .... (4) Ana Sin ina la si-ma-ni-šu iḫ ..... (5) Ana Sin ina ^{arḫu} Addâri lu ûmu XIV ^{kám} lu ûmu [XV ^{kám} innamir] (6) Uru ^{ki} [2]ri ..... (7) ûmu XVI ^{kám} ^{ilu} Sin u ^{ilu} Šamšu [itti aḫamis innạmru] (8). . . [šarru] ina íkalli-šu ana mi-na-[ti arḫi ú-ta-sar] (9) . . . [nakru] ina mâti-šu šal-ṭa-nis [illak] (10) ...... innammar-ma .... (11) .... mí-mí-í-ni ..... (12) . . . da (?)-bu-u-ni la ..... (13) .... la il .... (14) .... ma (?) pur-ru-us .... *Rev.* (1)

[1] issanaḫḫar, *glossed* ma-ḫi-ru. [2] *Erasure of* ú ?

. . . sadurri . . . . . (2) . . . Sin ru-di . . . . (3) Ana . . . . . šu ru-di . . . . (4) ina íli ^{ilu} muštabarrû-mûtâni (a-ni) šá ina íli . . . . (5) la aš-šu la i-ṭa-aḫ-ḫi . . . (6) ^{ilu} LU . BAD iṣ-ru-ur-ma ^{ilu} Šam-šu ilmi . . (7) [1]NIGIN : la-mu-u : . . . . . (8) ina íli šá ina pu-ti-i-šu ik . . . (9) pi-šir-šu a-na šarri bíl-iá as-sap-[ra] (10) ina íli ^{isu} ḳa-lu-a-tí bi-it šarri . . . (11) ap-tí-tí ina íli šarri mâr šarri $^{m\,ilu}$ Šamaš [šuma-ukin] (12) ú-sa-ri-ir . . . . (*Left-hand edge*) (1) Sin a-dan-niš da-an-ḳu (2) . . . i-ri-ṣi-ṣi mâr Šatti (3) . . . ni ù šamni ^{pl} dišpi riḳḳi (4) . . . ka-na ša šarri liš-al (5) I [ša] ^{m} Ak-kul-la-ni. [K. 1304.]

VI. Omens from the Moon's halo.

No. 90. *Obv.* (1) Ana šarri mâtâti bí-ili-ia ardu-ka $^{m\,ilu}$ Bíl-ú-[ší-zib ?] (2) ^{ilu} Bíl ^{ilu} Nabû u ^{ilu} Šamšu a-na Šarri bí-ili-ia lik-ru-ú-[bu] (3) Ana Šamšu ina lib tarbaṣi Sin izziz ina mâti kalâmi kit-ti i-ta-mu-ú ^{mul} (4) mâru itti abî-su kit-ti i-ta-mi (5) ^{mul} LU . BAD . ŠAG . UŠ ina lib tarbaṣ Sin izzaz-ma (6) Ana Sin tarbaṣu ilmi-ma ^{mul} AL . LUL ina libbi šu izziz(iz) (7) Šar Akkadi ^{ki} balaṭa ur-rak (8) Ana Sin nâru ilmi(mi) ri-iḫ-ṣu u ra-a-du rabûti ^{pl} ibaššu $^{[pl]}$ (9) ^{mul} AL . LUL ina tarbaṣ sin izzaz-ma (10) Šarru dan-nu ki-i-nu . . . . (11) [i]-na tar-ṣi šarri abî-[ka] . . . . (12) . . ma a-na šarri bí-ili . . . . (13) . . ṭa-a-bi zu . . . (14) . . pi-ḳit-ti *Rev.* (1) . . . na-da-nu . . . (2) . . [man]-di-í-ma . . . . (3) . . šu i . . . . . (4) . . . kit . . . (5) . . i . . . (6) . . . ^{m} Arad ^{ilu} gu-la (7) . . . BA -ša ina muḫ-ḫi ší-ma-ku . . . . a-ga-a . . . (8) ša ^{m} Mar-di-ia il-tí-mí . . . . ^{am} Na-si ku (9) ^{m} I a-di-' ^{am} [na]-si ku ù ^{am} na-si-ka-tu (10) ša ^{mâtu} Ia-ki-ma-nu gab-bi ina pân ^{am} rab-šakí ina ^{mâtu} Man-na-a-a (11) uk-tin-nu-šu u ín-na i-ḳab-bu-ú um-ma bíl da-mí ša bíl-i-nu ina íli-i-nu (12) ul i-rab-bi bíl šarrâni ^{pl} ^{am} rab-šakí ^{p} liš-al ša-lam šarri liš-mí (13) a-ki ig-ga-an-nim-ma ^{m} Mar-di-ia ^{am} ša pan ki-na-tu (14) ša bît ^{am} rab-šakí bíl-šu ki-i ú-maš-ši-ru ina šú-pa-la (15) $^{m\,ilu}$ Nírgal-Ašaridu i-tí-ru-ub ^{am} UR . li-ša-nu (16) ù ^{am} rab-ki-ṣir ^{pl} a-na pa-an $^{m\,ilu}$ Nírgal-Ašaridu (17) ib-ba-ka a-di-í i-iṣ-ba-tu-ú (18) ù I bilat $^{a-an}$ kaspi it-ti-šu-nu (19) a-na bîtâti ^{pl}-šu-nu i-na-aš-šu . . *Left-hand edge* (1) . . . mu-ru-šu GAR ma'du ŠÍ BI (2) . . . . iṣ ṣab-tan-ni šarru lu-u- (3) i-di. [83-1-18, 47.]

[1] NIGIN, *glossed* ni-gi-in.

No. 91. *Obv.* (1) Ana Sin tarbaṣu ilmi-ma mul UMUN . PA . UD . DU ina libbi-[šu izziz] (2) tibut(ut) ummân mâtu A-ḫar-[ri-i] (3) : ší-im ibašši-ma ub-bu-tu la ibašši . . (4) : šar Akkadi ki ú-sur-tú immar(mar) (5) Ana Sin nâru ilmi ur-ḳi-tú ŠÍ . TAR . NU (6) ina mâti ibašši(ši) (7) : zunni izanun(nun) (8) tarbaṣu mul . . . . . ilammi-ma *Rev.* (1) Ana mul ilu Marduk mí-iš-ḫu im-šu-uḫ (2) mâtu-ša nap-ša ik-kal (3) . . . . mul ilu Marduk mul LU . BAD . GUD . UD . (4) a-na man-za-zi-šu ú-ša-ḫaz-ma (5) i-ša-ḳa-am-ma (6) arki-šu ûmu XIV kam . . . ilu (?) (7) šá m Ba-la-[si i]. [K. 86.]

No. 92. *Obv.* (1) [Ana Sin] tarbaṣu ilmi-ma (2) ilu SAG . MÍ . GAR ina libbi-šu izziz (3) šar Akkadi ki û-ta-sar (4) ša m ilu Nírgal-íṭir(ir). [83–1–18, 221.]

No. 93. *Obv.* (1) Ana Sin tarbaṣu ilmi-ma (2) ilu SAG . MÍ . GAR ina libbi-šu izziz (3) Šar Akkadi ki ú-tas-sar (4) Ana Sin tarbaṣu ilmi-ma (5) mul AL . LUL . ina libbi-šu izziz (6) šar Akkadi ki balaṭa ur-[rak] *Rev.* (1) šá m Istar-šuma-írîš(íš).

[80–7–19, 57.]

No. 94. *Obv.* (1) Mušu an-ni-ú ilu Sin tarbaṣu ilammi-[ma] (2) ilu SAG . MÍ . GAR mul Aḳrabu ina libbi-[šu izzazu] (3) Ana Sin tarbaṣu ilmi-ma ilu SAG . MÍ GAR ina libbi-šu izziz(iz) (4) Šar Akkadi ki ú-ta-sa-ar (5) Ana Sin tarbaṣu ilmi-ma ilu Ni-bi-ru ina libbi-šu izziz(iz) (6) šumḳutim(tim) bûli na-maš-ší-í ša ṣíri (7) mul ilu Marduk ina tamarti-šu ilu UMUN . PA . UD . DU . (8) (I. II. ?) kas-bu i-šaḳ-ḳa-ma ilu SAG . MÍ . GAR *Rev.* (1) ina ḳabal šamí(í) izzaz-ma ilu Ni-bi-ru (2) Ana Sin tarbaṣu ilmi-ma mul Akrabu ina libbi-šu izziz (3) ínâti pl uš-taḫ-ha-a (4) zakkari pl . . . níši pl imâtu pl-ma alkât mâti ipparrasu pl (5) an-nu-ti ša TUS . KAR (6) Ana Sin tarbaṣu ilmi-ma UMUN . PA . UD . DU ina libbi-šu izziz(iz) (7) Šarru Aḫarrî kiššûtam(tam) ípuš-ma a-bi-ik-ti mât nakri-šu išakan(an) (8) an-ni-ú a-ḫi-ú (9) šá m ilu Nabû-mu-ší-ṣi.

[K. 120A.]

No. 95. *Obv.* (1) Ana Sin ṭarbaṣu ilmi-ma ilu SAG . MI . GAR (2) ina libbi-šu izziz šarru ú-ta-sar (3) tarbas-su ul ka-ṣir (4) ana limutti ul i-la-pat (5) Ana mul A . ÍDIN ki mu (?) . . . . (6) ú-šu-uz ana a . . . *Rev.* (1) ittu | mi-ḫir ù ana damiḳti (2) ina šamí(í) i-ba-aš-ši (3) Ana ^{ilu} SÁR . UR u ^{ilu} SÁR . GAZ (4) ša-zi-ḳit ^{ilu} Aḳrabi (5) it-ta-na-an-bi-ṭu (6) ^{isu} kakki ^{mâtu} Akkadi ^{ki} (7) [it]-bu-ú (8) ša $^{m\ ilu}$ Nabû-šuma-iškun(un). [K. 785.]

No. 96. *Obv.* (1) Mu-šú šá umi I ^{kám} (2) ^{mul} SAG . MÍ . GAR ina [1]tarbaṣ ^{ilu} Sin (3) it-ti-it-zi (4) NAM . BUL . BI li-pu-u-šú (5) tar-ba-ṣu la ka-aṣ-ru (6) šú-u *Rev.* (1) Sa $^{m\ ilu}$ Nabû-aḫi ^{pl}-íriba. [82–5–22, 52.]

No. 96A. *Obv.* (1) Ana Sin tarbaṣu [ilmi-ma] (2) ^{ilu} SAG . MÍ . GAR ina [libbi-su izziz] (3) Sar Akkadi ^{ki} ú-[tas-sar] (4) Ana Sin tarbaṣu ilmi[ma] (5) ^{mul} Sarru ina libbi-[šu izziz] (6) ina šatti šiâti sinnišâti ^{pl} [zakkari ^{pl} ullada ^{pl} (7) . . . .

[82–5–22, 84.]

No. 96B. *Obv.* (1) [Ana Sin tarbaṣu ilmi-ma ^{mul} SAG ?]-MÍ (?) GAR (?) ina libbi-šu izziz (2) [Šar Akkadi ^{ki} ú-ta]-sar (3) [Ana Sin tarbaṣu ilmi ma ^{mul} . . .]-du ina libbi šu izziz (4) . . . . . Aḫarrí ^{ki} (5) . . . . . ma (6) . . . . . ša (7) . . . . . šu (?) *Rev.* (1) . . . . si (2) . . . ^{ki} iliḳki(ḳi) (3) [ša ^{m} Iraššì]-ilu ardu ša šarru maḫrû(u).

[K. 1346.]

No. 96C. *Obv.* (1) Ana ^{mul} SAG . MÍ . GAR . . . (2) ina tarbaṣ ^{ilu} sin [izzaz] (3) tarbaṣu ša ^{arḫu} Simâni . . . . (4) Šarru (?) . . . . (*Remainder lost.*) *Rev.* (*Top wanting.*) (1) Šarru (?) a-na . .

[83–1–18, 311.]

No. 97. *Obv.* (1) Ana Sin tarbaṣu ilmi-ma ^{mul} Šarru (2) ina libbi-šu izziz ina šatti šiâti (3) sinnišâti ^{pl} zakkari ^{pl} (4) ullada $^{[pl]}$ *Rev.* (1) ša $^{m\ ilu}$ Nírgal íṭir(ir). [K. 739.]

No. 98. *Obv.* Ana ^{ilu} Sin tarbaṣu [2]ṣalmu ilmi[mi ?] (2) [3]arḫu [4]zunni [5]ú-kal . . . [6]urpâti $^{[pl]}$ (3) uḳ-ta-ṣa-ra (4) ^{mul} LU . BAD . SAG . UŠ ina Tarbaṣ ^{ilu} Sin i-za-az-ma (5) Ana ^{ilu} Sin tarbaṣu ilmi-ma ^{mul} muštabarrû-mûtânu(a-nu) (6) ina libbi-su izziz(iz) šaḫ-luḳti [7]bûli (7) [8]^{mâtu} Aharrí ^{ki} iṣaḫir(ir) (8) lum-nu ša ^{mâtu} A-ḫar-ri-í

[1] TUR, *glossed* tar-ba-ṣi.
[2] MI ., *glossed* ṣa-al-mu.
[3] ITU, *glossed* ar-ḫu.
[4] A . AN, *glossed* zu-un-nu.
[5] ú-kal, *glossed* ú-ka-la.
[6] IM-DIR [MIŠ .], *glossed* ur-pa-a-ti.
[7] *glossed* bu-u-li.
[8] KUR . MAR . TU ^{ki}, *glossed* $^{ma-at}$ A-ḫar-ri-í.

šú-u *Rev.* (1) Ana ^{ilu} Sin tarbaṣu ilmi-ma ^{mul} Šarru (2) ina libbi-šu izziz(iz) ina šatti šiatî [1] ^{sal} írâti ^{pl} (3) [2]zakkari $^{[pl]}$ [3]ullada ^{pl} (4) ^{mul}. . . . [ina] tarbaṣ Sin izzaz-ma (5) [ša $^{m\,ilu}$ Nabû]-aḫi^{pl}-íriba. [K. 864.]

No. 99. *Obv.* (1) Ana ûmu [XVI ^{kam} Sin u Samšu itti aḫamiš] innamru (2) [šarru ana šarri nukurta] išappar (3) šarru [ina íkalli ana minat arḫi] ú-ta-sar (4) šipâ $^{II\,am}$ [nakri ana mâti]šu iššakan(an) (5) ^{am} nakru [ina mâti-šu šalṭaniš] illak(ak) (6) Ana Sin tarbaṣu ilmi-ma ^{ilu} Šamšu ina lib tarbaṣ Sin izziz(iz) (7) ina mâti kalâmi kit-tú i-ta-mu-u (1) mâru itti abi-šu kit-tú i-ta-ma (9) sa-li-im kiš-ša-ti (10) Ana Sin tarbaṣu ilmi-ma ^{ilu} muštabarrû mûtânu(a-nu) ina libbi šu izziz(iz) (11) saḫlukti bûli ina mâti kalâmi *Rev.* (1) mí-ri-šu saluppu la išširu (2) . . . ^{mâtu} Aḫarru ^{ki} iṣaḫir(ir) (3) Ana Sin tarbaṣu ilmi-ma II kakkabâni ^{pl} ina lib-bi (4) tarbaṣ Sin izzizu ^{pl} pâl ûmí ^{pl} arkûti ^{pl} (5) Ana ^{ilu} mŭstabarrû-mûtânu(a-nu) u ^{ilu} LU . BAD im-daḫ-ḫa-ru-ma izzizu ^{pl} (6) tibut(ut) Í-lama(ma) ^{ki} (7) Ana ^{ilu} Muštabarrû-mûtânu(a-nu) . . . . . mí uṣi (8) Šar Í lama (ma) ^{ki} imât (9) Ša ^{m} Ba (?) -[ma ?]-a-a. [K. 711.]

No. 100. *Obv.* (1) Ana Sin tarbaṣu ilmi-ma ^{ilu} LU . BAD . . . . . . (2) ina libbi-šu izziz(iz) kit-tú ina mâti [itamû] (3) mâru itti Abî-šu kit-tu i-ta-mí (4) sa-lim kiš-ša-ti (5) Ana II ^{mul} Šarru ina libbi-šu izziz(iz) (6) sinnišâti ^{pl} zakkari ^{pl} ullada (7) [Ana II] ^{mul} Muštabarrû-mûtânu (a-nu) ina libbi šu izziz(iz) *Rev.* (1) šaḫlukti bûli ina mâti kalâmi (2) mí-ri-šu saluppa šamaššammu (3) la iššir (4) . . . ^{mâtu} Aḫarrû iṣaḫir(ir) (5) ša ^{m} Arad ^{ilu} Ía. [K. 1405.]

No. 101. *Obv.* (1) Ana Sin tarbaṣu ilmi-ma ^{mul} muštabarrû-mûtânu(a-nu) ina libbi-šu izziz (2) ina mâti kalâmi mí-ri-šum (3) u saluppu la iššir (4) . . . ^{mâtu} Aḫarrû ^{ki} iṣaḫir(ir) (5) Ana Sin tarbaṣu ilmi-ma ^{mul} LU . BAD ina libbi-šu izziz (6) Šarru ummâni-šu ú-taš-šír (7) [Ana Sin tarbaṣu] ilmi-ma ^{mul} DIL . GAN-ša arki-šu *MUL-[MUL] (8) ina libbi-šu izziz utullai (?) ša mâti . . *Rev.* (1) iššir (2) ^{mul} Muštabarrû-mûtânu(a-nu) Kakkab ^{mâtu} Aḫarrî ^{ki} (3) ^{mul} DIL .

[1] SAL · PÍŠ · MÍS, *glossed* í-ra-a-ti.
[2] UŠ . [MÍŠ], *glossed* zak-ka-[ri].
[3] *glossed* [ul]-la-da.

GAN ša arki-šu MUL. MUL. $^{mul\ am}$ KU. MAL (4) $^{mul\ am}$ KU. MAL. kakkab Aḫarrî ^{ki} (5) ša ^{m} Iraššî(si)-ilu. [81-2-4, 83.]

No. 101A. *Obv.* (1) [Ana Sin] tarbaṣu ilmi-ma (2) [^{mul} Muš-tabarrû-mûtânu] a-nu ina libbi-šu izziz (3) . . . tim bu-lum u nam-maš-[ši] (4) [Ana] Sin tarbaṣu ilmi-ma (5) ^{ilu} Šamšu ina libbi-šu izziz(iz) (6) [ina mâti] kit-ti ibašši(ši) (7) [mâru] itti abî-šu kit-[ti] (8) [i]-ta-mu-[u] *Rev.* (1) [^{mul} LU. BAD] SAG. US [ina lib] (2) [tarbaṣ ?] sin izzaz-ma (3) [Ana Sin] tarbaṣu ilmi-ma (4) [II] kak-kabâni ^{pl} ina tarbaṣi itti sin [izzizu] (5) [pâl] ûmí ^{pl} arkûti $^{[pl]}$ (6) [ša] $^{m\ ilu}$ Nabû-iḳ-bi (7) [mâr] kûtî ^{ki}. [83-1-18, 290.]

No. 102. *Obv.* (1) Ana Sin tarbaṣu ilmi-ma ^{ilu} Muštabarrû-mûtânu(a-nu) ina libbi-šu [izziz] (2) šaḫluḳti bu-lim ina mâti kalâmi (3) mí-ri-šu saluppu la iššir (4) . . . ^{mâtu} Aḫarrû ^{ki} iṣaḫir (5) Ana Šamšu ina lib tarbaṣ Sin izziz (6) ina mâti kalâmi kitta i-ta-[mu-u] (7) mâru itti abî šu kit-tú i-ta-[ma] (8) Ana II kakkabâni ^{pl} ina tarbaṣ Sin [izzizu ^{pl}] (9) palí ^{pl} ûmí ^{pl} arkûti $^{[pl]}$ *Rev.* (1) Šá ^{m} Ba-ma-a-a [83-1-18, 246.]

No. 103. *Obv.* (1) . . . XXVIII (?) ^{kám} innamir . . . (2) . . . ni-in-ma . . . . (3) [Ana] Sin tarbaṣu ilmi-ma ^{mul} Muštabarrû-mûtânu (a-nu) [ina libbi-šu izziz] (4) Šaḫluḳti | bûli mâti kalâmi | mí-ri-šu saluppu (5) la iššir . . . ^{mâtu} Aḫarrû ^{ki} iṣaḫir(ir) (6) [Ana] Sin tarbaṣu ilmi-ma ^{mul} LU. BAD ina libbi-šu izziz(iz) (7) [1] ^{am} ḫabbâti in-na-an-da-ru (8) ^{mul} LU. BAD. SAG. UŠ ina tarbaṣ Sin izzaz-ma (9) Ana ^{mul} SAG. MÍ. GAR ana ^{mul} GUD. AN. NA [2] isnik (10) du-un-ḳu mâti i-ḫal-liḳ (11) . . . ta-lit-ti | [3] utullai (?) | [4] ṣíní *Rev.* (1) ul iš-šir (2) ^{mul} SAG. MÍ. GAR ina lib ^{mul} GUD. AN. NA | í-ta-rab (3) Šarru bí-ili ultu pân zi-i-ḳi lu-í-ti-iḳ (4) ^{mul} APIN | [5] ḫarran [6] Šamši | [7] ikšud(ud) ḫušaḫ | [8] bu-u-lim (5) su-un-ḳu ibašši(ši) (6) ^{mul} Muštabarrû-mûtânu-(a-nu) ^{mul} LU. BAD. SAG. UŠ | i-kaš-ša-ad-ma (7) Ana ^{mul} LU. BAD ^{mul} Muštabarrû-mûtânu(a-nu) im-daḫ-ḫar-

[1] MULU. SA. GAZ, *glossed* hab-ba-a-tí.
[2] KÚR. KÚR. *glossed* is-nik.
[3] *glossed* BA. BA. GUD. ḪA. A.
[4] *glossed* UZ. BA. (?) ḪA. A.
[5] KASKAL, *glossed* har-ra-na.
[6] ŠAMAŠ, *glossed* ^{ilu} Ša-maš.
[7] KUR-ud, *glossed* ik-šu-ud.
[8] bu-u-lim, *glossed* bu-u-li.

ú-ma (8) iz-zi-zu * tibut ^{am} nakri (9) Ana [1] ^{mul} LUL. A | [2] nipiḫ-šu | . . [a]-dir | . . . (10) [3] nûri-(?)šu | kima ka . . . . (11) is-sa-na-ḫar . . . . . (12) ^{mul} . . . . *Left-hand edge* (1) Ša ^{m} . . . . . [S. 375.]

No. 104. *Obv.* (1) . . . . . innamir(ir) (2) zunnu u mílu NI. NI. (3) . . . . ^{mul} Muštabarrû-mûtânu(a-nu) ina libbi-šu izziz (4) . . . . ŠA. ZI IK ÍDIN. NA (5). . . [saluppu] la išširu ^{pl} : ^{mâtu} MAR iṣaḫir (6) li-í-ti ma šú (?) . . . . (7) . . . . . šu iššir-ma (8) . . . . kât ^{II} -su ikašad(ád) (9) ^{arhu} šabâti ina tarbaṣ Sin izziz(iz) (10) ^{mul} ^{ilu} A-nim-MIR ina lib . . (11) . . . . u šur (?) -ru (?) ina mâti-šu ibašši (12) . . a [81–2–4, 145.]

No. 105. *Obv.* (1) Ana ina ^{arhu} kisilimi ^{mul} . . . . . (2) gab-su nam-maš . . . . (3) si-mí-šu ni in . . . . (4) zunnu u mílu ana mâti . . . . (5) tibû-ma mâtu ikkal šumḳutim(tim) alpi . . . . (6) ^{iṣu} Kakku in-na-aš-ši-ma . . . . (7) : ik-kaš-ša-ad . . . . (8) ^{ilu} GUD. UD u ^{ilu} . . . . *Rev.* (1) Ana Sin tarbaṣu ilmi-ma [^{mul} Muštabarrû-mûtânu ina libbi-šu izziz] (2) šaḫluḳti bu-lim . . . . (3) Ana . . .-ma kakkabu ina libbi-šu izziz(iz) . . (4) ú-ta-ṣa-ru . . . (5) Ana . . . ma ^{mul} AL. LUL [ina libbi-šu izziz] (6) šar Akkadi ^{ki} ba-la-[ṭa urrak] (7) ^{mul} AL. LUL . . . . . (8) Ana . . . ma kip (?) šu ana . . . . (9) ana mâti na . . . . [82–5–22, 65.]

No. 106. *Obv.* (1) Ana Sin tarbaṣu ilmi-ma (2) ^{mul} Anu [4] agû ina lib-bi šu izziz(iz) (3) . . ša-pi . . ina mati ibašši(ši) (4) . . $^{[mul]}$ GUD. AN. NA ína tarbaṣ Sin (5) iz-za-az-ma (6) II ûmí(mí) i-da-at a-ḫi . . . (7) ina tarbaṣ ^{ilu} Sin it-ti-it-[zi] *Rev.* (1) Šâ ^{m} ^{ilu} Nabû-âḫî ^{pl} -íriba [K. 740.]

(*See also the fragment* 277, I.)

No. 107. *Obv.* (1) Ana Sin tarbaṣu ilmi-ma [II kakkabâni ina lib tarbaṣ Sin izzizu] (2) pâl ûmí [^{pl} arkûti ^{pl}] (3) Ana Šamšu ina tarbaṣ [Sin izziz ina mâti kittu itamû] (4) Mâru it-[ti abî-šu kittu itama] (5) sa-[li-im kiš-ša-ti] (6) Sin tarbaṣu ilammi-ma . . . . (7)

[1] MUL. LUL. A, *glossed* mu-ul KA. A.
[2] KUR-šu, *glossed* ni-pi-iḫ-šu.
[3] MUL . . . . *glossed* nu (?) -ri-šu.
[4] MIR, *glossed* a-gu-u.

Ana Sin tarbaṣu ilmi-ma mul [Muštabarrû-mûtânu ina libbi šu izziz] (8) Šaḫlukti bu-lim ina [mâti KAL. A.] BI, mí-[ri-šu] (9) u saluppu la iššir.. (10)... mâtu Aḫarrû ki iṣaḫir.. *Rev.* (1) Ana Sin tarbaṣu mul SUDUN ina libbi-šu izziz(iz) (2) Šarru imât-ma mât-su iṣaḫir(ir) (3) Šar Í lama(ma) ki imât (4) mul SUDUN mul Muštabarrû-mûtânu(a-nu) (5) mul Muštabarrû-mûtânu(a-nu) kakkab mâtu Aḫarrí [ki] (6) limutti ša mâtu Aḫarrí ki u Í lama(ma) [ki] (7) mul LU. BAD. SAG. UŠ kakkab mâtu Akkadi (?) [ki] (8) damikti ša šarri bí-ili-[ia] (9) ûmu XIV kám ilu itti ili in-[nam-mar] (10) lib-bi sarri bí-ili-ia lu-[ṭib] (11) ša m Iraššî(ši)-ilu ardu ša šarri...

[Bu. 89–4–26, 166.]

No. 108. *Obv.* (1) Ana Sin tarbaṣu ilmi-ma mul Akrabu (2) ina libbi-su izziz ínâti pl (3) ušṭaḫ-ḫa-a zakkari pl (4): níši pl imâtu pl ma (5) alakti illaku pl (6) it-tum ul ta-lap-pat (7) aš-šu ma-aṣ-ṣar-tum ša šarri (8) Ana šarri bíl-iá aš pu-ra (9) Ša m Za-ḳir.

[Bu. 89–4–26, 8.]

No. 109. *Obv.* (1) Sin mušu an-ni-ú ina lib-bi mul Akrabi (2) tarbaṣu-ma ilammi.. a-na[1] ..... míli (3) ilu Dil-bat ilu GUD. UD. a-na ru-ú-bi il-lu-ku (4)..... a-ti i-na lib-bi ú-kal (5)..... dir (6)..... í-mar (7)..... pl (8)..... alu kal-zi *Rev.* (1) ..... tu-ni (2).... nu ša ṭí-mu-ni (3)..... pa-ru-ú-ni (4)..... zi ina am A. BA. ma (5) ina ûmí(mí)-šu il-la-ka (6) m ilu Nabû-mu-ší-ṣi am A. BA íširti (7) šarri bí-li ik-bu-u-ni (8) [i-sa]-ap-ra na-aṣ u pa-ni tú (9)... šá am Rab. A. BA. [82–2–4, 144.]

No. 110. *Obv.* (1) Ana Sin tarbaṣu ilmi-ma (2) mul AL. LUL ina libbi-šu izziz.. (3) šar Akkadi ki balaṭi ur-rak (4) ra-a-du izanun(nun) *Rev.* (1) ilu Aššur ilu Šamšu ilu Nabû u ilu Marduk (2) balaṭi ana (?) ba (?) [la ?]-ṭi a-na ûmí pl (3) Arkûti pl a-na šarri (4) bí-ili-ia id-dan-nu (5) ša m ilu Nabu-iḳ-bi. [Bu. 91–5–9, 9.]

No. 111. *Obv.* (1) [Mušu anniu? Sin tarbaṣu] ilammi(mi) mul AL. LUL ina libbi (2) [izziz] an-ni-ú pi-ší-ir-šú (3) [Ana Sin tarbaṣu] ilmi-ma mul AL. LUL ina lib-bi-šu (4) [iz-zi]-iz šar Akkadi ki ba-la-ṭu ur-ra-ak (5) [Ana Sin tarbaṣu] ilmi-ma iáru iltanu illik(ik)

[1] *Erasure.*

(6) . . . . . ilâni pl šaḳûti pl . . . ilâni pl (7) . . mu (?) uk mâti ú-kal-lu (8) [Ana Sin tarbaṣu] ilmi-ma id-lul na . . (9) . . í a-na . . . *Rev.* (1) . . imbaru ibašši(ši) nu-ḫuš [niši] (2) . . . imbaru sa-dir pa-li-í mâti (3) kiš-šu-tam i-bí-íl (4) . . . imbaru ûmí(mí) ú-sa-dir (5) . . maḫiru ina-pu-uš (6) [ša] m šúma-a-a. [83-1-18, 222.]

No. 112. *Obv.* (1) [Ana Sin tarbaṣu] ilmi-ma mul AL . LUL (2) [ina libbi-šu] izziz(iz) šar Akkadi ki balâṭi ur-rak (3) [mušu] an-ni-ú tarbaṣu ilammi la iḳ-sur (4) [Ana] ilu Sin usurtu ilmi atalû | iša-kan(an) (5) Atalû du-luḫ-ḫu-u (6) mu-šú an-ni-ú usurtu ilammi la iḳ-ṣur (7) Ana mul Dil-bat a-na mul Aḳrabi iṭḫi(ḫi) (8) [1]Šarâni pl | [2]la ṭâbûti pl a-na mâti il-la-ku *Rev.* (1) ilu Rammânu zunni pl-šu ilu í-a naḳ-bi-šu (2) Ana mâtu Gu-ti-í i-nam-din (3) Ki-ma a-na mul Irat-Aḳrabi iṭ-ṭi-ḫi (4) A-ki an-ni í in-na-su-ḫa ú-ma-a (5) ú-di-na ina lib-bi la i-ḳar-rib ki-ma iḳ-di-ri-ib (6) la i-ṭa-aḫ-ḫi i-pa-at-ti | it-ti-iḳ-rib (7) mul LU . BAD pl A-ki ḫa-an-ni-í kakkabâni pl šu-nu (?) (8) [šá] ína pân harrâni-šu-nu ina muḫ-ḫi-šu-nu it-ti-ḳu (9) [Ana mul] A . ÍDIN Ana MULMUL ikšud(ud) ilu Rammânu iraḫis(is) (10) [mul] Muštabarrû-mûtânu(a-nu) ina íli mul Nun-šamí(í) (11) . . . ri-iḫ-ṣi la iḳ-ri-ib (12) . . . lib pa-ni-šu ip-ti-í-ti (*Left-hand edge*) (1) . . . Šì (?) . . . (2) a . . . [83-1-18, 197.]

No. 112A. *Obv.* (1) Ana [Sin] tarbaṣu ilmi-ma mul AL . LUL ina libbi-šu izziz(iz) (2) . . . UD (?) mu (?) ba-la-su (?) . . . a . . . (3) Sin nâru ilmi(mi) A . AN (?) izanun(nun) (4) NUN . . . . . ilammi (mi) . . (5) Sin tarbaṣu . . . . . mul šarru ina libbi šu izziz(iz) (6) šatti šiâti sinnišâti pl zakkari pl ul-la-da (7) [Sin] tarbaṣu ilmi-ma ina lib tarbaṣi *Rev.* (1) II Kakkabâni pl itti ilu sin izzizú pl (2) pâl ûmi [pl arkûti] pl (3) ša ilu nabû-ikiša(ša) mâr Bar-sib ki [83-1-18, 241.]

No. 112B. *Obv.* (1) [Ana Sin] tarbaṣu ilmi[ma] (2) [mul] AL . LUL ina libbi-šu izziz (3) [šar] Akkadi ki balaṭa ur-rak (4) [Ana Sin] tarbaṣu ilmi-ma (5) [ina tarbaṣu] II kakkabâni pl itti Šín [izzizu] (6) [pâl] ûmí pl-šu arkûti [pl] (7) . . . pl ina tarbaṣ . . .

[1] IM . MIS, *glossed* ša-ra-a-ni.
[2] NU . DUG . GA . MIS, *glossed* la ṭa-bu u-ti.

(8) . . . pl ma . . *Rev.* (1) . . . u ilu [Marduk?] . . . (2) [ana] da-riš a-na ûmí pl . . . . (3) a-na šarri bí-ili-iá id-[dan-nu] (4) [ša m] ilu Nabu-iḳ-bi. [81–2–4, 141.]

No. 113. *Obv.* (1) Ana Sin tarbaṣu ilmi-ma II kakkabâni [pl] (2) ina tarbaṣi itti ilu Sin izzizu(zu) pal ûmí pl-šu arkûti pl (4) Ana ilu Sin tarbaṣu ilmi-ma mul AL. LUL. (5) ina libbi-šu izzizu (zu) šar Akkadi ki balaṭà ur-[rak] (6) [Ša m] ilu Nabû-[aḫî] pl-íriba (?) . . . [K. 1921 + 3488.]

No. 114. *Obv.* (1) [Mušu Anniu] Sin tarbaṣu ilammi (2) . . . . mul MAS . TAB . BA . GAL . GAL (3) ina lib-bi izzazu(zu) (4) Ana Sin tarbaṣu ilmi-ma mul AL . LUL ina libbi-[šu izziz] (5) Šar Akkadi ki balaṭà [urrak] (6) Ana Sin tarbaṣu ilmi-ma mul Ú-sur-[tì ina libbi šu izziz] (7) šaḫ-lu-uk-ti . . . . (8) mul Ú-sur-ti mul . . . . *Rev.* (1) Šá m Bu-ul-lu-ṭu [K. 1334.]

No. 114A. *Obv.* (1) [Ana Sin] tarbaṣu ilmi-ma mul AL[LUL] (2) ina libbi šu izziz šar Akkadi ki [balaṭa urrak] (3) Ana Šamšu ina Tarbaṣ Sin izziz mât-su (?) [kittu] (4) i-ta-mu-ú mâru itti abî-šu (5) kit-tú i-ta-mi (6) [Ana] Sin tarbaṣu ilmi-ma mul Šarru ina libbi-šu (7) izziz(iz) sal írâti pl zakkari pl (8) ulladu pl *Rev.* (1) ša m Za-kir [K. 6077.]

No. 115. *Obv.* (1) [Ana Sin tarbaṣu ilmi-ma] II kakkabâni pl (2) [ina lib tarbaṣi itti Sin] izzizu pl (3) [pâl ûmi] pl arkûti (4) . . . . lu tarbaṣu ilmi-ma (5) . . . . . di-du sar ilâni pl na ku (?) šu (6) . . . dam-ḳa-a tu (?) (7) . . . . . ú-ša-aṣ-ba (?) -tu [S. 694.]

No. 115A. *Obv.* (1) Ana Sin tarbaṣu ilmi-ma [itti Sin] (2) MUL . MUL . ina libbi-šu[izzizu] . . . (3) Ana . . . -ma MUL . MUL . [ina libbi šu izziz sinnišâti pl] (4) zakkari pl ullada pl . . . (5) NU šur-ri . . . (6) Ana ina lib tarbaṣi II Kakkabâni [pl itti sin izzizu] (7) pâl ûmí(mi) [arkûti pl] *Rev.* (1) Ana Sin tarbaṣu UD . KIL . UD . . . (2) Ana Sin tarbaṣu ilmi arḫu . . . (3) uḳ-taṣ-ṣa-ra (4) Ša m . . . . . [83–1–18, 214.]

No. 115B. *Obv.* (1) Ana Sin tarbaṣu ilmi-ma [MUL . MUL .

ina libbi šu] (2) izzizu ^{pl} sinnišâti ^{pl} [zakkari ^{pl}] (3) ullada $^{[pl]}$ (4) Ana ina ^{arḫu} kisilimi .... (5) ... na ... (6) ša ^{m} ....
[K. 1311.]

No. 115c. *Obv.* (1) Ana Sin tarbaṣu ilmi-[ma ^{mul} ALLUL ina libbi-šu] (2) izziz(iz) šar Akkadi $^{[ki]}$ ..... (3) Ana Šamšu ina lib tarbaṣ [Sin izziz ina mâti (4) Kit-tú i-ta-[mu-u mâru itti Abî-šu] (5) Kit-tú [i-ta-ma] (6) Ana Sin tarbaṣu ilmi-ma [II Kakkabani ina tarbaṣi] it-ti ^{ilu} [Sin izzizu] (8) pâl-í[ûmí ^{pl} arkûti ^{pl}] *Rev.* (1) Ana Sin tarbaṣu ilmi[ma] ... (2) ina lib-bi-šu izziz(iz) (3) ina mâti kalâmi mí .... (4) la SI . [DI] (5) Ša ^{m} Mun-[na-bi-tu]
[K. 1305.]

No. 115d. *Obv.* (*Two* (?) *lines wanting*) (1) Ka (?) ..... (2) a-du ..... (3) šum ..... (4) $^{am(?)}$ Nakru ..... *Rev.* (1) Ana Sin tarbaṣu ṣalmu ilmi (2) arḫu zunni ú-kal : [urpati ^{pl}] (3) uḳ-ta-aṣ-ṣa-[ra] (4) Ana Sin ina ^{arḫu} Addâri ûmu XXX ^{kám} innammar (5) Ana Sin ina ^{arḫu} Nisanni ûmu XXX ^{kám} innammar (mar) (6) ša $^{m\ ilu}$ Nírgal-íṭir-(ir)
(Bu. 91–5–9, 7.]

No. 115e. *Obv.* (1) [Ana Sin] tarbaṣu ilmi-ma ... (2) [í]-na lib-bi-šu .... (3) id-lu-ti .... (4) ḫu-ub-ti .... *Rev.* (1) úmu(mu) UD (?) ŠÍ (?) .... (2) sapaḫu rabû ... (3) ... ki-i ša ma ..... (4) ... li-pu ... (5) [ša ^{m} Iraššî] ši-ilu (6) mar ^{m} Nu-[ur-za-nu]
[K. 1331.]

No. 115f. *Obv.* (1) Ana ^{ilu} Sin tarbaṣu ilmi [ma ..... (2) ina lib-bi-šu izziz šarru .... (3) li-kun (?) .... (*Remainder lost.*) *Rev.* (1) [sarru-bí]-ili-a lul .... (2) ... di-nu-nu .... (3) ^{am} mar-ik-ka-ru (4) Aḫu-ú-a id-du ... (5) ša šarri bí-ili-ia id .... (6) Ša $^{m\ ilu}$ Bíl-li' i mâr ^{m} [Í-gi-bi ^{am} mašmašu]. [83–1–18, 775.]

No. 116. *Obv.* (*Top wanting*) (1) ... illakam(kám) tarbaṣu nuḫuš tarbaṣi ... (2) ûmu V ^{kám} tarbaṣu ilammi(ma) .. (3) ... ina ṣalam šamši ina ur-ri tarbaṣi ... (4) .. šamû(ú) izanun (nun) ...
[K. 1592.]

No. 116a. *Obv.* (*Top wanting*) (1) : ri-iḫ-ṣu .... (2) tarbaṣ ^{mul} ... (3) u ^{mul} A-nu-ni-[tum] ... (4) ša-nu-ú tarbaṣu ina ... (5)

il (?)-ku (?) ûmu(mu) . . (6) Ša ^{m} A-ša-ri-du . . . *Rev.* ^{m} Za (?)-ad-din i (?)-ši . . (2) mar ^{m} Ḫu-ur (?)-bi-í . . (3) ^{m} Mar (?)-da (?) . . ^{Am} SAG . (4) ša šarru . . . pa-ni-šu . . (5) . . . um . . (*Remainder lost.*) [K. 1338.]

No. 116B. *Obv.* (*Top wanting*) . . . du (?) . . . (2) Ana Sin tarbaṣu ilmi[ma] (3) id-lul . . . . (4) ḫi (?) ma (?) li . . . *Rev.* (1) Sin . . . (*Remainder lost.*) [83-1-18, 881.]

No. 117. *Obv.* (1) Ana Sin supura ilmi mâti šiâtu irappiš(íš) (2) nišî ^{pl} sapḫi (?) ^{pl} ilammu ^{pl} (3) Ana ilmi-ma ^{mul} AL . LUL ina libbi-šu izziz (4) šar Akkadi ^{ki} balaṭâ ur-rak (5) Ana ^{mul} Šarru ina libbi-šu izziz (6) sinnišâti ^{pl} zakkari ^{pl} ullada ^{pl} (7) Ana Sin supuru ilmi-ma id-lul (8) na-da-nu pa-li-í ana Šarri (9) ša tarbašu ra-bu-ú ilmi-ma *Rev.* (1) mu-ši ma-a-du iz-zi-zu-ma (2) la ip-ṭu-ru (3) ša ^{m} ša-pi-ku mâr Bar-sib ^{ki}. [K. 178.]

No. 118. *Obv.* (1) Ana Sin nâru ilmi[mí] (2) ri-iḫ-ṣu u ra-a-du (3) rabûti ^{pl} ibaššu $^{[pl]}$ (4) ^{mul} A . IDIN ina lib-bi i-[zi-iz ?] (5) Ana Sin tarbaṣu ilmi-ma ^{mul} PAN [ina libbi-šu izziz] (6) ašṭûti ^{pl} in-na-[da-ru] (7) ḫu-ub-bu-tu ina mâti [ibašši] *Rev.* (1) šá $^{m\,ilu}$ Nabû-mu-ší-[ṣi]. [K. 801.]

No. 118A. *Obv.* (*Top wanting*) (1) . . . . . an (2) . . . . í-šu-u-ni (3) . . . . . ia (?) (4) . . . . . ra *Rev.* (1) . . . . DUG . GA . BI (2) . . . . ú-šú (3) . . . ^{ilu} TIR . AN . NA a-pìr (4) . . . . [iz]-za-nun (5) . . . . . kan (*Remainder lost.*) [81-2-4, 504.]

VII. Omens from the Moon's appearance with the Sun.

(A) *On the twelfth day.*

No. 119. *Obv.* (1) Ana Sin ina la si-ma-ni-šu innamir (2) maḫiru iṣaḫir (3) umu XII ^{kám} it-ti ^{ilu} Šamšu innammar-ma (4) Ana ina la mí-na-ti-šu-nu ^{ilu} Sin u ^{ilu} Šamšu (5) it-ti a-ḫa-miš innamru ^{pl} (6) ^{am} Nakru dan-nu mâti i-si-' (7) Šar Akkadi ^{ki} Šumḳuta(ta) ^{am} nakri-šu išakan(an) (8) . . . II ^{kám} it ti ^{ilu} Šamši innammar-ma *Rev.* (1) Ana Sin ûmu XII ^{kám} innamir-ma limutti ^{mâtu} Akkadi ^{ki}

(2) damiḳti ílama(ma) ki mâtu Aḫar-ri-i (3) limutti ša mâtu Akkada ki šú-ú (4) šá m ilu Ba-la-si-i. [K. 703.]

(B) *On the thirteenth day.*

No. 120. *Obv.* (1) Ana ûmu XIII kám Sin u ilu Šamšu (2) itti a-ḫa miš innamru pl (3) pû la ikân A-lak-ti la ṭa-ab (?)-ti (4) ina mâti ibašši(si) (5) am nakru ina mâti iliḳḳi(ḳi) *Rev.* (1) ša m Apla-a. [81-2-4, 82.]

No. 121. *Obv.* (1) ûmu XIII kám ilu Sin u ilu [Šamšu] (2) itti a-ḫa-miš innammar(mar?) (3) pû la ikân a-[lak-ti] (4) la mi-šír-ti [ina mâti ibassi] (5) Ana ilu Sin ina a la-ki-[šu] . . . (6) maḫiru i . . . . *Rev.* (1) ûmu XII kam lib ûmu XIII kam [ilu Sin] (2) itti ilu Šamši innammar-ma (3) ša m ilu Nabu-aḫî pl-iddina(na). [K. 794.]

No. 122. *Obv.* (1) Ana ûmu XIII [kam Sin] u Šamšu itti a ḫa-nuš innamru pl (2) pû la ikân alkat mâti la iššir (3) sípâ II nakri ibassi nakru ina mâti iliḳḳi(ḳi) (4) Ana ínuma(ma) Sin ina arḫu . . . [umu] XIV kám lu-ú (5) umu XV kám itti Šamši la innamir ina ši (?) ik (?) . . . (6) ilu ikkal (7) ša m Za-kir [83-1-18, 248.]

No. 123. *Obv.* (1) [Ana umu XIII kam] Sin ù Šamšu itti a-ḫa-miš innamru pl (2) pû [la] ikân alkat mâti la iššir (3) šípâ II am nakri ibašši(ši) am nakru ina mâti iliḳḳi(ḳi) (4) Ana [ina arḫu Ululi?] sâru iltanu sad-rat ma il-lak (5) [a-na ?] iṣí pl ri-kip-ti pl míšaru il-lak (6) ilu IGIGI itti mâti šâl-mu mâtu nuḫša immar(mar) (7) iṣí pl ri-kip pl : inib kiri ka-la-tum (?) (8) Šattu a-ga-a saluppu u karanu išširu pl *Rev.* (1) Ana ina arḫu Tašríti ûmu XXX kám Sin in-nam-mar (2) ul-tu ûmu(mu) an-ni-i a-di arḫu Ululi ša ba-lat (3) umu XIII kám Sin itti Šamši ul in-nam-mar (4) Ana Šamšu ippuḫ-ma šamù(ú) i-si-mu šanâti pl (5) dam-ḳa-a-ti Šarru i-dan-nin (6) ša m ilu Nírgal-íṭir(ir) mâr m Ga (?)-šu (?)-zu-ilu Tu-tu. [K. 763.]

No. 123A. *Obv.* (1) [Ana ûmu XI]II kám ilu Sin [u ilu Šamšu] (2) [it]-ti a-ḫa miš innamru [pl] (3) . . . . . (4) . . . am nakru ina mâti [iliḳḳi] [Bu. 89-4-26, 61.]

(c) *On the fourteenth day.*

No. 124. *Obv.* (1) Ana Sin Šamša ik-šú-dam-ma itti šu it-tin-tu ḳarnu ḳarnu i-dir (2) ina mâti kittu ibašši-ma mâru itti abî-su kit-tú i-ta-mu (3) ûmu XIV kám ilu itti ili innammar(mar)-ma (4) Ana Sin u Šamšu it-tin-tu-ú šar mâti uznâ urappaš(aš) (5) šar mâti išid kussi-šu ikân(an) ûmu XIV kám ilu itti ili innammar(mar)-ma (6) ûmu XIV kám Sin u Šamšu itti a-ḫa-miš innamru pl sanaḳu ša pî (7) lib mâti iṭâb ilâni pl mâtu Akkadi ki a-na damiḳtim(tim) (8) i-ḫas-sa-su ḫu-ud lib-bi ummâni(ni) (9) bu-lim mâtu Akkadi ki par-ga-niš ina ṣíri i-ra-bi-ṣu (10) Ana Sin tarbaṣu ṣalmu ilmi urpâti pl uḳ-ta-ṣa-ra (11) arḫu šuâtu zunni ú-kal (12) Ana ḳarnu ḳarnu i-dir mílu illakam(kám) ûmu XIV kám ilu itti ili innammar-ma *Rev.* (1) Ana íli niší pl ša a-na šarri bí-ili-ia aš-pu-ra (2) Šarru la i-ḳab-bi um-ma mi-nam-ma-ma iḳ-ba-a (3) um-ma niší pl a-na a-gan-na li-bu ku-nu (4) Šarri i-di ki-i íḳla-a ina mâtu Aššuri ia-a-nu (5) a-na ku mi-nu-ú lu zira-a u a-na ša-a-šu-nu mi-nu-u lu (?) balaṭu (6) man-nu ilu-ú-a man-nu bílu-a ína-ia it-ti man-nu ki-i šak-nu (7) Al-la šarru bíl-ia ša ana-ku ilu Šamšu ana balaṭi-ka ú-ṣal-lu-u (8) a-di m Aḫî pl ša-a-a i-na šarri liš-pu-raš-šum-ma (9) am mâr-šipri-su niší pl li-bu-uk rab Babili ki lu-šam-šip (10) m ilu Nabû ítir-napšâti pl mâru-ú-a ardu ša šarri (11) li-bu-kám ma it-ti-ia šarru li-ip . . . . [82-5-22, 89.]

No. 125. *Obv.* (1) Ana ûmu XIV kám Sin u Šamšu itti a-ḫa-miš innamru pl (2) sanâḳu ša pî lib mâti iṭâb(ab) (3) ilâni pl mâtu Akkadi ki ana sal damiḳti (4) i-ḫas-sa-su (5) ša m Aḫî pl ša-a am Uruk ki -a-a [82-5-22, 58.]

No. 126. *Obv.* (1) Ana Sin u ilu Šamšu šú-ta-tu-[u]. (2) Šar mâti uz-nu ú-rap-[pa-aš] (3) Ša ûmu XIV kám ilu it-ti [ili] (4) in-nam-ma-ra *Rev.* (1) ša m Iraššì(ši)-ilu (2) mâr m Nu-ur-za-nu. [K. 698.]

No. 127. *Obv.* (1) Ana Sin u Šamšu iksuda-ma itti-šu it-tin-tú ḳarnu ḳarnu i-dir (2) ina mâti kit-tú ibašši-ma mâru itti abî-šu kit-tú-i-ta-mí (3) šulmu(mu) kiš-ša-ti (4) Ana ûmu XIV kam Sin u Šamšu itti a-ḫa-miš innamru pl (5) sanaḳu ša pî iib-bi iṭâb (*sic*) ilani pl mâtu Akkadi ki (6) A-na damiḳtim(tim) i-ḫa-sa-su ḫu-ud lib-bi ummâni(ni) (7) lib-bi šarri itâb bûl mâtu Akkadi ki (8) par-ga-niš ina ṣíri irabiṣ(iṣ) *Rev.* (1) Ana sin u Šamšu sit-ku-lu mâtu i-kan at-mu-u (2) Ki-í-nu ina pí niší pl išakan(an) šar mâti iṣu kussâ ulabbar(bar) (4) Ana Sin u Šamšu šú-ta-tu-u Šar mâti uz-nu urappaš(aš) (5) Šá m Ba-ma-a-a. [K. 92.]

No. 128. *Obv.* (1) Ana Sin u Šamšu šit-ku-lu mâtu i-ka-na (2) at-mu-ú ki-í-nu ina pî niší pl išakan (3) Šar mâti iṣu Kussaul-abbar(bar) (4) Ana Sin u Samšu šú-ta-tu-ú šar mâti uz-nu (5) ú-rap-pa-aš (6) Ana ûmu XIV kám Sin u Šamšu itti a-ḫa-mis innamru pl (7) sanâḳu ša pî lîb-bi mâti iṭâb(ab) (8) ilâni pl mâtu Akkadi ki (9) a-na da-mí-iḳ-tí (10) i-ḫa- sa-su *Rev.* (1) ḫu-ud lib-bi ummâni(ni) (2) lib-bi, šarri iṭâb(ab) (3) bûl mâtu Akkadi ki (4) ina ṣíri par-ga-niš irabiṣ(iṣ) (5) Šá m Ištar-šuma-íríš(íš). [K. 697.]

No. 129. *Obv.* (1) [Ana ûmu] XIV kám Sin u Šamšu itti a-ḫa-miš innamru pl (2) sanâḳu ša pî lib mâti iṭâb(ab) (3) [ilâni] pl mâtu Akkadi ki ana damiḳtim(tim) i-ḫa-sa-su (4) ḫu-ud lib-bi ummâni(ni) lib šarri iṭâb . . (5) bûli pl mâtu Akkadi ki (6) pár-ga-niš ina ṣíri i-rab-bi-iṣ (7) Ana Sin u Šamšu šit-ḳu-lu (8) [mâtu ikâm] at-mu-ú ki-í-nu (9) ina pî niší pl i-ša-kan (10) šar mâti iṣu kussâ ú-lab-bar. (D.T. 148.]

No. 130. *Obv.* (1) Ana ilu Sin u ilu Šamšu šú-ta-tu-ú (2) Sar mâti uz-nu ú-rap-pa-aš (3) ri-í-mu u šul-mu išakan-šu (4) ša ûmu XIV kám ilu Sin ù ilu Šamšu (5) it-ti a-ḫa-miš in-nam-ma-ru (6) ša m Irašši (ši)-ilu (7) Mâr m Nu-úr-zu-nu. [K. 721.]

No. 130A. *Obv.* (1) Ana ûnu XIV kám Sin u Šamšu itti a-ḫa-miš innamru pl (2) sanâḳu ša pî lib mâti iṭâb(ab) (3) ilâni pl mâtu Akkadi ki ana damiḳtim(tim) i-ḫa-sa-su (4) [bûl] mâtu Akkadi ki pár-ga-niš ina ṣíri irabbiṣ(iṣ) (5) [ḫud libbi ummâni] ni lib šarri iṭab(ab) (6) . . . . . kám (*Remainder of obverse and top of reverse broken off.*) *Rev.* (1) [pa]-ṭar bir-a-ti a-rad IN . [NUN] pl (2) taš-mu-u salimu(mu) ina mâti ibašši(ši). [K. 878.]

No. 131. *Obv.* (1) [Ana Sin u Šamšu] šit-ḳu-lu mâtu i-ka-na (2) [atmu] ki-í-nu (3) [ina pî] niší pl išakan(an) (4) [šar] mâti kussa ulabbar(bar) (5) (Ana Sin u] Šamšu šú-ta-tu-ú (6) Šar mâti uz-nu ú-rap-pa-aš (7) Ana ûmu XIV kám Sin u Šamšu itti a ha-miš innamru pl (8) sanâḳu ša pî lib-bi mâti iṭâb (9) ilâni pl mâtu Akkadi ki (10) a-na damiḳtim(tim) i-ḫa-sa-su (11) ḫu-ud lib-bi ummâni(ni) *Rev.* (1) lib-bi Šarri iṭâb(ab) (2) bûl mâtu Akkadi ki (3) ina ṣíri par-ga-niš irabiṣ(iṣ) (4) šá m Bu-ul-lu-ṭi [Rm. 204.]

No. 132. *Obv.* (1) Ana ûmu XIV kám ilu Sin u ilu Šamšu (2) itti a-ḫa-miš innamru pl (3) sanâḳu ša pî lib mâtí iṭâb(ab) (4) ḫu-ud lib-bi nišî pl išakan(an) (5) ilâni pl mâtu Akkadi ki *Rev.* (1) a-na damiḳtim(tim) i-ḫas-sa-su (2) Ana Sin ù ilu Šamšu Šú-ta tu-ú (3) šar mâti uznâ II ú-rap-pa-aš (4) ša m Apla-a [K. 714.]

No. 133. *Obv.* (1) Ana ûmu XIV kam Sin u Šamšu (2) itti a-ḫa-miš innamru pl sanâḳu ša pi (3) lib-bi mâti iṭab(ab) ilâni pl mâtu Akkadi ki (4) ana damiḳtim(tim) i-ḫa-as-sa-su (5) ḫu-ud lib-bi ummâni(ni) lib-bi šarri iṭâb(ab) (6) bu-lim mâtu Akkadi [ki] pár-ga-niš (7) i-na ṣíri i-rab-bi-iṣ *Rev.* (1) Ana Sin Šamša ikšuda-ma itti-šu it-tí-ni-[tu] (2) ḳarnu ḳarnu i-dir ina mâti kit-tu ibašši . . (3) mâru itti-šu (*sic*) kit-ti i-ta-mi (4) Šarru ilu kussi [ubabbar] bar (5) ûmu XIV kam ud-da-su . . . (6) Šar mâti . . . . (7) Ša m A-[ša-ri-du]
[K. 737.]

No. 134. *Obv.* (1) Ana Sin ilu Šamša ik-šú-dam-ma itti-šu it-tin-tu (2) ina mati kittu ibašši-ma mâru itti abî-šu (3) kit-ti i-ta-mu (4) ûmu XIV kám ilu itti ili innammar (mar)-ma (5) Ana Sin ù Šamšu šú-ta-tu-ú (6) Šar mâti uzna II urappaš(aš) (7) ša umu XIV kám arḫu-us-su (8) ilu itti ili in-nam-ma-ru *Rev.* (1) Ana ûmu XIV kám Sin ù Šamšu itti a-ḫa-miš innamru pl (2) sanaḳu ša pî lib mâti iṭâb (3) ilâni pl mâtu Akkadi ki ana damiḳti(ti) i-has-sa-su (4) ḫu-ud lib-bi nišî pl išakan(an) (5) bu-lim mâtu Akkadi ki par-ga-niš (6) ina ṣíri i-rab bi-ṣu (7) ša m ilu Bíl-šuma-iškun(un) am kalû
[K. 700.]

No. 135. *Obv.* (1) Ana ûmu XIV kám Sin u Šamšu itti a-ḫa-miš (12) innamru pl sanâḳu ša pi lib mâti iṭâb (3) ilâni pl mâtu Akkadi ki ana dimiḳtim(tim) i-[ḫa-sa-su] (4) bu-ul mâtu Akkadi ki par-ga-niš (5) ina ṣíri i-rab-bi-[iṣ] (6) ḫu-ud lib ummâni pl lib šarri iṭâb [ab] *Rev.* (1) [Ana Sin u Šamšu šú]-ta-tu-u ina mâti kittu ibašši-ma (2) mâru itti abî-šu kit-tú i-ta-ma (3) Ana ûmu a-na mi-na-tí-šu írik (4) pâl ûmí pl arkûti pl (5) šá m ilu Rammânu-Šuma-uṣur. [K. 730.]

No. 135A. *Obv.* (1) [Ana ûmu XIV kám Sin u] Šamšu itti [a-ḫa]-miš innamru pl (2) [sanâḳu ša pî] lib [mati] iṭâb(ab) (3) [ilâni pl] Akkada ki a-na damiḳtim(tim) i-ḫa-sa-su (4) [ḫud lib]-bi ummani(ni) lib šarri iṭâb(ab) (5) . . bul mâtu Akkadi ki ina ṣíri par-ga-niš irabbiṣ(iṣ) (6) [Ana Sin] u Šamšu šú-ta-tu-ú Šarru uz-na urrappaš(áš) (7) [Ana Sin u Šamšu] šit-ḳu-lu mâtu ikân at-mu-ú (8) [kînu]ina pî niši pl išakan(an) [Bu. 91-5-9, 161.]

No. 136. *Obv.* (1) [Ana ûmu] XIV kám Sin u Šamšu itti a-ha-miš [innamru pl] (2) sanâḳu ša pî lib mâti iṭab(ab) ilâni pl mâtu Akkada ki ana [damiḳti] (3) i-ḫa-as-sa-su ḫu-ud lib-bi ummâni lib [sarri iṭâb] (4) bu-ul mâtu Akkadi ki par-ga-niš ina ṣíri i-[rab-bi-is] (5) Ana Sin u Šamšu sit-ku (?) lu mâtu i-kan at-mu-u ki-nu ina pî [nišî pl išakan] (6) šar mâti kussa [ulabbar] (7) Ana Sin Šamša ikšuda-ma itti-su it-tin-tú (?) ḳarnu ḳarnu i-dir (8) [ina] mâti kit-tú ibašši-ma mâru itti abî-šu kit-tú i-[ta ma] *Rev.* (1) [Ana Sin u Šamšu sú]-ta-tu-u šar mâti uz-nu urappaš . . (2) . . . kám arḫu . . . . .

[81-2-4, 108.]

No. 136A. *Obv.* (1) [Ana ûmu XIV kam Sin u Šamšu itti] a-ḫa-miš innamru pl (2) [sanâḳu ša pi lib mâti iṭâb] ilâni pl mâtu Akkada ki (3) [ana damiḳti iḫasasu] bu-ul (4) [mâtu Akkadi ki par-ganiš ina ṣíri] i-rab-bi-ṣu (*Remainder lost. Ends of two lines on rev.*) . . . [81-2-4, 483.]

No. 136B. *Obv.* (1) Ana Sin u Šamšu šú-ta-tu-u (2) šar mâti uz-nu ú-rappa-aš (3) ûmu XIV kám it-ti ilu Šamši innammar-ma (4) Ana ûmu XIV kám Sin u Šamšu itti a-ḫa-miš innamru pl (5) sanâḳu ša pî [lib] mâti iṭâb(ab) (6) ilâni pl mâtu Akkadi [ki ana] sal damiḳti (7) [i]-ḫa-sa [su ḫud lib ummâni] bu-lum matu Akkadi ki (8) [parganiš ina ṣíri] i-rab-bi-iṣ *Rev.* (1) . . . . ûmu XIV kám (2) . . . . . . ilu Šamšu (3) it-[ti Aḫamiš it]-tan-ma-ru (4) ki-i . . . . . maš (?) -ša-ar-šu (5) Ana Sin u [Šamšu ši]-it-ḳu-lum (6) at-mu-[u] ki-i-nu (7) ina pi-[i] niši ^{pl} išakan(an) (8) šar kiš-ša-ti ^{iṣu} GU . ZA ú-lab-bar (9) ^{arḫu} Tašrîtu ûmu XIV ^{kám} lim-mí [^{m} La] ba-si. [83–1–18, 286.]

No. 136c. *Obv.* (1) Ana ^{ilu} . . . . . (2) . . . . . (3) . . . . . (4) ûmu XIV [^{kam} ilu itti] ili innammar(mar) . . (5) Ana ^{ilu} Sin u [^{ilu} Šamšu šú]-ta-tu-[u] (6) Šar mâti uz-na ú-rap-pa-aš (7) šarru išid ^{iṣu} GU . ZA . šu i-ka-an *Rev.* (1) Ana ûmu XIV ^{kám} [^{ilu} Sin] u ^{ilu} Šamšu (*Remainder entirely lost.*) [K. 1324.]

No. 136d. *Obv.* (1) [Ana Sin u] Šamšu itti a-ḫa-miš innamru $^{[pl]}$ (2) [sanâḳu ša pî lib] mâti iṭâb(ab) (3) [ilâni Akkada ^{ki} ana damiḳtim] (4) [iḫasasu] ḫu-ud lib ummâni(ni) (5) [lib šarri iṭâb] bu-[ul] ^{mâtu} Akkadi ^{ki} (6) [parganiš ina ṣíri] i-rab-bi-is *Rev.* (1) [Ana Sin Šamšu ikšuda-ma] it-ti-šu it-tin-da (?) (2) [ḳarnu ḳarnu] i-dir mâtu kit-ti ibašši-ma (3) [mâru itti] abî kit-ti i-ta-mu (4) [Sin] u Šamšu[1] a-ḫa-miš innammaru ^{pl}-ma (5) [sar] mâti lu-da-ri (6) [ša ^{m} A-ša]-ri-du ḳa-aṭ-nu. [K. 1312.]

No. 136e. *Obv.* (1) Ana Sin u Šamšu šú-ta-tu-ú (2) šar [mati uzna ú]-rap-pa-aš . (3) Ana Sin [u Šamšu sit-ḳu]-lu (4) mâtu ikân atmû] ki-í-nu (5) [ina pî niši ^{pl} i]-ša-kan (6) [šar mâti ^{iṣu} kussa ú]-lab-bar (7) Ana [sin u Šamšu itti a]-ḫa-miš innamru ^{pl} (8) [sanâḳu ša] pî [lib mâti] itâb (9) ilâni ^{pl} ^{mâtu} Akkada ^{ki} a-na damiḳtim(tim) *Rev.* (1) i-ḫa-sa-a-su (2) ḫud lib ummâni(ni) lib šarri iṭâb (3) bûli ^{pl} ^{mâtu} Akkadi ^{ki} pár-ga-niš (4) ina ṣíri i-rab-bi-iṣ (5) šá ^{m} ^{ilu} Nabû-mu-ší-ṣi. [K. 767.]

No. 136f. *Obv.* (1) [Ana Sin u Šamšu šú]-ta-tu-ú (2) [Šar mâti uzna] ú-rap-pa-aš (3) [ûmu XIV (?) ^{kam} Sin itti] Šamši innam-mar-ma (4) [Ana Sin u Šamšu] šit-ḳul-lu (5) [mâtu i]-ka-nu at-mu-ú ki-i-nu (6) pi-i niší ^{pl} išakan(an) (7) šar mâti ^{iṣu} GU . ZA ú-lab-bar *Rev.* (1) . . . Sin itti Šamši innammar-ma (2) [Ana ûmu XIV ^{kám} Sin ù ^{ilu} Šamšu (3) [itti a-ḫa]-miš innamir sanâḳu ša pî lib mâti iṭâb (4) [ilâni Akkada ^{ki}] ana ^{sal} damikti i-ḫa-as-sa-su (5) [ḫud] niší ^{pl} isakan(an) (6) . . . . KÚR. [S. 1179.]

[1] *The scribe has apparently repeated the sign for* Šamšu.

No. 136G. *Obv.* (1) Ana ûmu XIV kám Sin u Šamšu [itti aḫamiš] (2) innamru pl sanâḳu ša pî [lib mâti iṭab] (3) ilâni pl mâtu Akkada ki ana [damiḳti] (4) i-ḫa-sa-su bu-ul [mâtu Akkadi ki] (5) par-ga-niš ina ṣîri i-rab]-bi-iṣ] (6) ḫu-ud lib-bi niši [pl] (7) lib-bi šarri [iṭâb] *Rev.* (1) Ana Sin u Šamšu šú-ta-tu-[u] (2) šar mâti uz-nu ú-rap-[pa-aš] (3) šarru išid iṣu GU . ZA-šu [ikân] (4) Sin u Samšu šit-ḳul-[lu] (5) at-mu-ú ki-i-[nu] (6) ina pi-i niši pl [išakan] (7) ša m ilu Nabû . . . . [83-1-18, 229.]

No. 136H. *Obv.* (1) [Ana ûmu XIV kam Sin u] Šamšu itti a-ḫa-miš innamru pl (2) [sanâḳu ša pî lib] mâti iṭâb(ab) ilâni pl mâtu Akkadi ki (3) [Ana damiḳti i]-ḫa-sa-su bu-lum mâtu Akkadi ki (4) [ina ṣîri] i-rab-bi-ṣu (5) . . . . . ÍN . TÍ . [NA?] . . (*Remainder of obv. and top of rev. broken.*) *Rev.* (1) [Ana Sin u Šamsu šit-ḳu]-lu at-mu-ú ki-i-nu (2) [ina pî niši pl] išakan(an) šarru išid DIL . TÍ . šu ikân(an) [Ana Sin u Šamšu šú]-ta-tu-ú (4) [šar mâti uz]-nu urappaš(aš) (5) . . . .-ti ibašši(ši) (6) [ša m ilu] Nábû-iḳ-bi. [81-2-4, 273.]

No. 136I. *Obv.* (1) [Ana ûmu XIV kam Sin u Šamšu] it-ti a-ḫa-miš (2) [innamru pl sanâḳu ša pî lib] mâti iṭâb(ab) (3) [ilâni pl mâtu Akkada ki ana damiḳti] i-ḫa-sa-su (4) [ḫud lib] ummâni(ni) (5) [lib sarri iṭâb bûl] mâtu Akkadi ki (6) [ina ṣîri] par-ga-niš (7) [i-rab]-bi-iṣ *Rev.* (1) [Ana Sin u] Šamšu šú-ta tu-u (2) [šar] mâti uz-[na urappaš] aš (3) [ûmu] XIV kám ilu [Sin itti] ilu Šamši inna-mar-ma (4) [Ana] Sin u [Šamšu šit]-ḳu-lim (5) [at]-mu-u ki-[i-nu ina pî] niši pl išakanu(nu) (6) [šar mâti] iṣu [GU .] ZA . ú-lab-bar. [83-1-18, 240.]

No. 136K. *Obv.* (1) . . . . KIL . . . (2) . . mí ki . . . . . (3) ûmu XIV kám . . . . (4) ilu Sín u ilu Šamšu šú-ta-[tu-u] (5) šar mâti uz-na urappaš . . (6) šarru išid iṣu GU . ZA . -šu i-[kan] (7) ûmu XIV kám a-ḫa-miš innamru . . . *Rev.* (1) [. . ûmu] XIV kám innam-mar-ma [damiḳti . . . .] (2) [limutti] ana mâtu [Ílama(ma) ki u MAR [TU ki] (3) . . . . [K. 1339.]

No. 136L. *Obv.* (1) [Ana Sin u Šamšu itti aḫamiš ŠI .]LAL . (2) [sanâḳu ša-pî líb]-bi mâti iṭâb (3) ilâni pl Akkada ki ana damiḳti] i-ḫa-sa-su (4) [ḫud lib ummâni lib]-bi sarri iṭâb (5) [bûl Akkadi ^{ki} ina ṣíri par]-ga-niš i-rab-bi-iṣ (6)..... [ḳarnu] ḳarnu i-dir (7)..... šu kit-tú i-ta-mí (8)..... ka-liš išakan(an) *Rev.* (1) Ana Sin u Šamšu šit-ḳu-lu mâti i-kan (2) at-mu-u ki-í-nu ina pî nišî ^{pl} išakan(an) (3) Šarru ^{isu} GU.[ZA. ulabbar] (4) Ana Sin u [Šamšu] šú-[ta-tu-u] (5) [šar mâti uzna urappaš] (6)...... (7) [sa $^{m\ ilu}$] Nabû-mu-ší-ṣi

[K. 876.]

No. 136M. *Obv.* (1) [Ana]ûmu XIV ^{kâm} Sin u Šamšu itti aḫamiš innamru] (2) sanâḳu ša pî lil mâti iṭâb [ilâni ^{pl} Akkadi ^{ki}] (3) Ana damiḳtim(tim) i-ḫas-sa-su [bûl Akkadi ^{ki}] (4) par-ga-niš ina ṣíri i-rab bi-[iṣ] (5) ḫu-ud lib nišî ^{pl} išakan(an) lib [šarri iṭâb] (6) Ana Sin Šamšu ik-šú-dam-ma [itti-šu ittintu] (7) ḳarnu ḳarnu i-dir ina mâti [kit-tu] (8) ibašši(ši)-ma mâru itti-šu [kit-ti itama] *Rev.* (1) Ana Sin u Šamšu šit-ḳul-lu at-mu-[u kînu] (2) ina pî nišî ^{pl} išakan (an) šarru išid [kussi ikân (3) Ana Sin u Šamšu šú-ta-tu-[u] (4) šar mâti uz-nu urappaš.. (5) kit-ti ibašši... (6) ša $^{m\ ilu}$ Nabû-iḳ-bi....

[K. 789.]

No. 136N. *Obv.* (1) Ana ûmu XIV ^{kâm} Sin u Šamšu [itti a-ḫa]-miš innamru.. (2) sanaku ša pê lib mâti iṭâb(ab) ilâni $^{pl\ mâtu}$ [Akkadi ^{ki}] (3) ana damiktim(tim) i-ḫas-sa-su (4) ḫu-ud lib nišî ^{pl} išakan (an) [lib šarri iṭâb] (5) Ana Sin Šamšu ik-šú-[dam-ma itti-šu ittintu] (6) ḳarnu ḳarnu i-[dir] (7).. la..... *Rev.* (1) Ana Sin u Šamšu [šitḳulu] (2) at-mu-ú ki.. nu ina pî nišî ^{pl} (3) išakan(an) šarru [išid kussi ikan] (4) Ana Sin u [Šamšu šutatû] (5) šar mâti [uzna urappaš] (6) ša $^{m\ ilu}$ Nabu.... [K. 869.]

No. 136O. *Obv.* (1) Ana ûmu XIV $^{kam\ ilu}$ [Sin u ^{ilu} Šamšu (2) it-ti a-ḫa-miš in-[nam-ru] (3) pu-ú i-ka-na lib [mâti iṭâb] (4) ilâni $^{pl\ mâtu}$ (*sic*) a-na da-mí-iḳ-[ti iḫasasu] (5) ḫu-ud lib-bi ummâni (ni) lib-bi [šarri iṭâb] (6) bu-ul ^{mâtu} (*sic*) par-ga-ni-iš ina ṣíri i-rab [bi-iṣ] (7) Ana ^{ilu} Sin u ^{ilu} Šamšu šit-ḳu-lu mâtu i-ka-na (8) at-mu-ú ki-í-nu ina pi-i nišî ^{pl} išakan(an) (9) Šarru ^{isu} GU. ZA ú-la-[bar] *Rev.* (1) Ana ^{ilu} Sin u ^{ilu} Šamšu šú-ta-tu-u (2) Šar mâti [uz]-nu ú-rap-pa-aš (3) Šá ^{m} Ištar-šuma-[íríš]. [K. 773.]

No. 136P. *Obv.* (1) [Ana ûmu XIV ^{kam} Sin u Šamšu] itti a-ḫa-miš innamru ^{pl} (2) [sanâḳu ša pi lib] mâti iṭab(ab) [ilâni ^{pl}

Akkada [ki] ana damiḳtim i-ḫa]-sa-su (4) . . . . . ni *Rev.* (1) [Ana Sin u Šamšu šú]-ta-tu-ú (2) Šar mâti uz-nu [urappaš] aš (3) šá [m] Ištar-šuma-írìš(íš). [Rm. 212].

No. 136Q. *Obv.* (1) [Ana Sin u Šamšu šutatû] šar mâti uz-nu ú-rap-pa-[aš] (2) . . . . . [pl ilu] Sin ûmu XIV [kám] innammar . . (3) . . . . i-dir ina mâti kit-tú ibašši (4) sa-lim kiš-[sa-ti] (*Remainder wanting.*) *Rev.* (1) . . . ka . . (2) [ša [m] Ba]-la-si-i. [K. 11046.]

No. 136R. *Obv.* (*Top wanting*) (1) . . . . . (2) ina ṣíri [irab-biṣ] . . . . (3) Ana Sin u Šamšu šú-ta-tu-[u šar mâti uzna urappaš] (4) Ana Sin u Šamšu šit-ḳu-[lu mâtu ikân] (5) at-mu-[u kînu ina pî nišî išakan] *Rev.* (1) Šarru . DIL . TÍ . . . . . (2) Ana Sin ina tamarti-šu . . . . (3) paṭar bi-ra-a-[ti arad maṣṣarâti] . . . . . . [Bu. 91–5–9, 28.]

No. 136S. *Obv.* (*Top wanting*) (1) [Ana Sin u Šamšu] šú-ta-tu-ú šar [mâti uzna urappaš] (2) . . . ûmu XIV [kám] . . . (3) . . . innammar(mar) . . . (4) . . . íli Sin ki . . . (5) . . . mâti išid DIL . TÍ . . . (6) kit-ti-šu izzaz . . . (7) . . ûmu XIV [kám] itti Sin . . . (8) . . . tarbaṣ Sin izziz . . . (9) mâru itti [abi-šu] *Rev.* (*Top wanting*) (1) . . . ûmu XIV [kám] šattu I [kám] . . (2) šarru kînu šar TIN . TIR [ki] . . . . [Rm. 2, 345.]

No. 136T. *Obv.* (1) [Ana Sin u Šamšu šú]-ta-tu ú (2) [Šar mâti uzna] ú-rap-pa-aš (3) [Ana Sin u Šamšu šit]-ḳu-lu (4) [mâtu ikân at-mu]-u ki-i-nu (5) [ina pî niši [pl]] iš-šak-kan (6) [šarru [isu] GU .] ZA ú-lab-bar (7) [Ana ûmu XIV [kam] Sin u Šamšu] itti a-ḫa-miš innammru [pl] *Rev.* (1) [sanâḳu ša pî lib mâti] iṭâb (2) [ilâni [pl] Akkada [ki] ana damikti] i-ḫa-as-sa-su (3) [ḫud libbi ummâni] iš-šak-kan (4) [i]-na mâti (5) . . . šu inaši(ši) (6) [ša [m ilu] Nírgal]-íṭir(ir). [K. 1322.]

No. 136U. *Obv.* (*Top wanting*) (1) at-mu-ú ki-[í-nu ina pî nišî [pl] išakan] (2) Šar mâti [isu] GU . [ZA] . . . . (3) Ana [1]Šamšu íli-nu Sin šapli tanu . . . . . (5) [Ana Sin u Šamšu] šú-ta-tu-ú (6) kit-ti . . . . (7) [ša [m]] [ilu] Nabû (?) . . . [S. 885.]

[1] Same character as in No. 177, *obv.* 1.

No. 137. *Obv.* (1) Ana ûmu XIV ^{kám} Sin ù Šamšu itti a-ḫa-miš innamru ^{pl} (2) sanâḳu ša pî lib mâti iṭâb ilâni ^{pl} ^{mâtu} Akkada ^{ki} (3) ana damiḳti-i-ḫa-as-sa-su ḫu-ud lib ummâni ^{pl} išakan(an) (4) Ana Sin ù Šamšu šú-ta-tu-ú šar mâti uz-nu [urappaš] aš (5) Ana Sin ù Šamšu šit-ḳul-lu mâtu ikân (6) [at-mu]-ú ki-i-nu ina pi-i nišî ^{pl} išaḳan(an) (7) [šâr] mâti ^{isu} GU . ZA ú-lab-bar *Rev.* (1) Ana [Sin ina] tamarti-šu ^{Sâru} Šûtu itbi (2) Šumḳut Aḫarrî ^{ki} (3) Ana ina šumíli šamši ni-du nadi-ma a (?) du bi tu (4) íš-tú šar Aḫarrî ^{ki} ana a-?-ri-šu [1]iṣbatu-su (5) ša ^{m} ^{ilu} Nírgal-íṭir(ir). [K. 799.]

No. 138. *Obv.* (1) Ana ûmu XIV ^{kám} Sin u Šamšu itti a-ḫa-miš innamru . . (2) [pu]-ú i-ka-na lib mâti iṭâb . . (3) [ilâni] ^{pl} ^{mâtu} Akkada ^{ki} Ana ^{sal} damiḳti i-ḫa-as-sa-su (4) [ḫud] lib-bi ummâni(ni) bu-lum ^{mâtu} Akkadi ^{ki} (5) [ina ṣîri] par-ga-niš i-rab-bi-is (6) [Ana Sin u Šamšu] šú-ta-tu-ú (7) [šar mâti] uznu ú-rap-pa-aš (8) [Ana Sin u] Šamšu šit-ḳu-[lu] (9) [at]-mu-u ki i-nu ina pî [nišî ^{pl} išakan] *Rev.* (1) šar kiššati ^{isu} kussi ú-[lab-bar] (2) Ana ḳar-nu ḳar-nu i-dir mílu illak (?) (3) : zunni ^{pl} ibaššu ^{pl} (4) ^{m} Ba-la-si-i. [K. 795.]

No. 138A. *Obv.* (1) Ana ^{ilu} Sin u ^{ilu} Šamšu šú-ta-tu-u (2) šar mâti uz-na urappaš(aš) (3) [ana] ^{ilu} Sin ^{ilu} Šamša iḳ-šú-dam-ma (4) it-ti-šu it-tin-tum ḳar-nu ḳar-nu i-dir (5) ina mâti kit-tú ibašši(ši) -ma mâru itti abî-šu (6) kit-tum i-ta-am-mí (7) Ana ^{ilu} Sin ina tamarti-šu ḳar-nu ḳar-nu [i-dir] (8) mílu illak . . . . *Rev.* (1) ûmu XIV ^{kám} itti ^{ilu} Šamši innammar . . . (2) Ana ûmu XIV ^{kám} Sin u Šamšu itti a-ḫa-miš innamru . . (3) sanâḳu ša pî lib mâti iṭâb(ab) ilâni ^{pl} Akkadi $^{[ki]}$ (4) ana ^{sal} damiḳti i-ḫa-sa-su ḫu-ud lib nišî ^{pl} (5) išakan(an) lib šarri [iṭâb bu-]ul ^{mâtu} Akkadi ^{ki} (6) par-ga-niš ina ṣéri i-rab-bi-iṣ (7) šá ^{m} Ak-kul-la-ni. [83–1–18, 191.]

No. 139. *Obv.* (1) Ana ^{ilu} Sin ^{ilu} Ša-maš ši-it-ḳu-lu (2) at-mu-u ki-i-nu ina [2]pî [3]nišî ^{pl} išakan(an) (3) šar kiš-ša-ti ^{isu} GU . ZA ú-lab-bar (4) ûmu XIV ^{kám} in-na-mar-ma (5) ri-iḫ-ti di-ib-bi du-un-ḳu (6) ša šarri bíli-ia ina lib [4]urpâti ^{pl} (7) il-lak la ni-mur (8) Ana Sin ina tamarti-šu | ina [4]urpâti ^{pl} [5]iḳilippu(pu) (9) mílu

[1] LU-šu, *glossed* iṣ-ba-tu-uš.
[2] KA, *glossed* pi-i.
[3] UKU . ^{pl}, *glossed* ni-ši.
[4] IM . DIR ^{pl}, *glossed* ur-pa-a-ti.
[5] DIR-pu, *glossed* i-ḳi-lip-pu.

il-la-ak *Rev.* (1) ni-iḳ-il-pu-u a-la-ku (2) Ana Sin ina tamarti šu | [1]Šamû(ú) | [2]šapik(ik) (3) zu-un-nu iz-za-nun (4) ina urpati ša-pi-ik-ti in-nam-mar-ma (5) ša $^{m\ ilu}$ Nabû-aḫî ^{pl}-íriba. [K. 736.]

No. 140. *Obv.* (1) Ana Sin Šamšu la ú-ḳi-ma ir-bi (2) na-an-du-ur níši ^{pl} u âḫî ^{pl} (3) ûmu [XIV] ^{kám} it-ti ^{ilu} Šamši innammar (4) Ana Sin ina la si-ma-šu (*sic*) innamír (5) sa-pa-aḫ . . . . (6) ûmu XV ^{kám} it-ti ^{ilu} Šamši innammar[ma] *Rev.* (1) arki-šu ina ^{arḫu} Tašrîti ^{ilu} [sin] (2) ûmu(mu) ú-šal-lam . . (3) šá ^{m} Ba-la-si-i [K. 706.]

No. 141. *Obv.* (1) Ana Sin u ^{ilu} Ša-maš šit-ḳu-lu (2) at-mu-ú ki-í-nu (3) ina pî nišî ^{pl} iš-ša-kau (4) Šar [mâti] ^{išu} GU . ZA ú-[lab-bar] (*Remainder of obverse and top of reverse lost.*) *Rev.* (1) . . . zi-ḳi-it . . . . . (2) . . . . [3]ilmi-šu mílu illak . . (3) ^{ilu} [Sin mušu au]-ni-ú tarbaṣu il-ti-[mí-ma] (4) ^{mul} GIR . . bi šu ina libbi-šu it-[ti-it-zi] (5) Ana Sin ina tamarti-šu ^{šâru} šûtu illak . . (6) ina arḫi šuâti ^{šâru} šûtu sa-dir (7) ša $^{m\ ilu}$ Nabu-aḫî ^{pl} íriba. [K. 1412 + 1508.]

No. 142. *Obv.* (1) [Ana ûmu XIV ^{kam} Sin u Šamšu it-ti] a-ḫa-miš innamru ^{pl} (2) [sanâḳu ša pî lib] mâti iṭâb(ab) (3) [ilâm ^{pl} Akkada ^{ki} ana] ^{sal} damiḳti i-ḫas-sa-su (4) . . . . illak(ak) (5) bu-lim ^{mâtu} Akkadi ^{ki} pár-ga-niš ina ṣíri [irabbiṣ] (6) Ana Sin ina tamarti šu ḳarnu ḳarnu i-dir (7) mílu illakam(kám) (8) ûmu XIV ^{kám} ud-da su-nu *Rev.* (1) a-ḫa-miš innammaru ^{pl} (2) Ana Sin ina alâki-šu ni-iḫ . . . (3) Ana Sin ina tamarti-šu izziz(iz) . . . . ípuš-ma (4) . . ku-su . . . iḫ-ṣa-at (5) . . . *di-mi-ik-ma (6) . . . kit-ti i-ta-[ma] (7) . . . . na (?)-ši-ma (8) . . . . . ilu (?) [82–5–22, 64.]

No. 143. *Obv.* (1) [Ana] ûmu XIV $^{kám\ ilu}$ Sin u ^{ilu} Šamšu itti a-ḫa-miš [innamru] ^{pl} (2) sanâḳu ša pi lib-bi mâti iṭab(ab) (3) ilâni $^{pl\ mâtu}$ Akkada ^{ki} damiḳtim(tim) i-ḫa-as-sa-su (4) Ana Sin u ^{ilu} Šamšu šú-ta-tu-ú (5) šar mâti uz-nu ú-rap-pa-aš (6) sarru išid ^{išu} GU (*sic*)-

[1] ANA-ú, *glossed* Ša-mu-u. [2] DUB-ik, *glossed* ša-pi-ik.
[3] NIGIN-šu, *glossed* il-mí-šu.

šu i-ka-nu (7) Ana Sin tarbaṣu ilmi-ma mul Aḳrabu ina libbi-šu izziz (8) inâti pl uš-ṭa-ḫa-a (9) am zakkari pl . . . níši pl *Rev.* (1) in-namda-ru-ma alkâti ipparasu pl (2) ša m ilu Nabû-aḫî pl iddina(na)

[K. 1373+83-1-18, 780].

No. 144. *Obv.* (1) ûmu XIV kam ilu Sin ù ilu Šamšu itti a-ḫamiš innammaru pl (2) mu-šu an-ni ilu Sin tarbaṣu iltamí(mí) (3) ilu LU . BAD . SAG . UŠ ina lib tarbaṣi itti ilu Sin izziz(iz) (4) Ana ûmu XIV kám Sin u Šamšu it-ti a-ḫa-miš innamru pl sanâḳu ša pî (5) lib mâti iṭâb ilâni pl mâtu Akkadi ki a-na sal damiḳti i-ḫa-sa-su (6) ḫud lib ummâni pl bu-ul mâtu Akkadi ki par-ga-niš ina ṣíri i-rab-bi-is (7) Ana Sin ina alâki-šu ni-iḫ íbûr mâti iššir : ûmu XIV kám innammar-ma (8) Ana Sin u Šamšu šú-ta-tu-ú šar mâti uz-na urappaš(aš) (9) ša ûmu XIV kám ilu itti ili innammaru pl . . . ilu LU . BAD . SAG . UŠ (10) ûmu XV kám it-ti ilu Sin izzaz(az)-ma *Rev.* (1) Ana ilu Šamšu ina tarbaṣ Sin izziz(iz) ina mâti kalâmi (2) [kit-tu] i-ta-mu-u mâru itti abî-šu kit-[tu itama] (3) . . . ina tarbaṣ Sin izzaz-ma (4) [Ana . . . . ina tarbaṣ] Sin izziz(iz) (5) . . . . . kussi i-ka-na (6) . . . . Sin izzaz(az)-ma (7) [ša m Ak-kul-la ?]-ni. [83-1-18, 228].

No. 144A. *Obv.* (1) Umu XIV kám Sin ù [Šamšu itti aḫamiš innamru] (2) sanâḳu ša pî lib mâti iṭâb(ab) [ilâni pl Akkada ki] (3) Ana damiḳtim(tim) i-ḫa-as-su . . . (4) Ana Sin ù Šamšu šú-ta-[tu-u] (5) šar mâti [uz]-na ú-rap-[pa-aš] (6) umu XIV [kam] it-ti ilu Šamši [innammar-ma] *Rev.* (1) . . . . IV (?) kám tarbaṣu . . . . (2) . . . . . tu-uš . . . . . (3) Ana Sin tarbaṣu [ilmi-ma] MUL . MUL . [ina libbi šu izziz] (4) ina šatti šiâti [sinnišâti pl] zakkari pl [ulada pl] (5) : šar mât-*šu *nakri-šu nu sur . . . . (6) Ana Sin tarbaṣu ilmi-ma id-[lul (7) na-dan pâl [šarri] (8) ša m ilu Nírgal-[íṭir].

[K. 1306+83-1-18, 316.]

No. 144B. *Obv.* (1) Ana ilu Sin ilu Šamša ik-šú-dam-[ma itti šu ittintu] (2) *ḳar-*nu *ḳar-*nu . . . . . (3) mâru itti abî-šu [kittu itama] (4) Ana ilu Sin u ilu Šamšu šit-ḳu-[lu matu ikân atmû kinû] (5) ina pî niší pl išakan(an) . . . . . (6) Ana ilu Šamšu ippuḫa(ḫa)-ma ilu Sin . . . . . (7) iš-di-ḫu šanâti pl . . . . (8) ûmu XIV kám ilu Sin itti ilu [Šamši innammar-ma] (9) Ana ilu Sin ina tamarti-šu ḳarnâti pl [šu . .]

(10) Ana mâti Šubtu ní-[iḫ-tu . . . .] *Rev.* (1) ^{ilu} Sin ûmu(mu) ú-šal-lam-ma UD X . . . . (2) Ana ûmu XIV ^{kám} Sin u Šamšu itti a-ḫa-miš innamru [^{pl} sanâḳu ša pî] (3) lib mâti iṭâb(ab) ilâni $^{pl\ mâtu}$ Akkada ^{ki} [ana damiḳti] (4) i-ḫa-as-sa-su ḫu-ud [lib ummâni] (5) lib šarri iṭab(ab) bûl [Akkadi ^{ki}] (6) par-ga-niš ina ṣíri[irabbiṣ] (7) Ana ûmu XIV ^{kám} innammar-ma damiḳti ^{matu} [Akkadi ^{ki}] . . . . (8) Ša ^{m} Ak-[kul-la-ni]. [Rm. 208.]

No. 144c. *Obv.* (*Top wanting.*) (1) . . . . bûl ^{mâtu} Akkadi $^{[ki]}$ (2) [parganiš ina ṣíri] i-rab-bi-[iṣ] (3) [Ana Sin u Šamšu šit-ḳu]-lu mâtu ikân(an) at-mu-ú (4) [kínu ina] pî nišî ^{pl} išakan(an) (5) [šar mâti) DIL . TÍ ulabbar(bar) *Rev.* (1) . . . ŠI . AN . AŠ A . ŠI ina lib-bi DU (?) . . . (2) . . ina lib tarbaṣ Sin izziz . . . (3) . . . . ^{pl} arkûti $^{[pl]}$ (*Remainder lost.*) [83-1-18, 870.]

No. 144d. *Obv.* (1) ûmu(mu) an-nu-ú ûmu XIV ^{kám} (2) ^{ilu} Sin u ^{ilu} Šamšu a-ḫa-miš i-tam-ru (3) an-nu-ú pi-ši-ir-šu (4) Ana ûmu XIV $^{kám\ ilu}$ Sin u ^{ilu} Šamšu (*Remainder of obverse lost.*) *Rev.* (1) [Ana Sin u Šamšu] *šú-*ta-tu-ú (2) šar mâti ḫa-si-si urappaš (aš) (3) ša ûmu XV ^{kám} it-ti ^{ilu} Šamši in-nam-ru (4) ša ^{m} Na-di-nu. [K. 8393.]

No. 144e. *Obv.* (1) Ana ûmu XIV ^{kám} Sin u Šamšu . . . (2) sanâḳu ša pî lib mâti . . . (3) ana damìḳtim(tim) i-ḫa- . . . (4) lib šarri iṭâb(ab) bu . . . (5) par-ga-niš ina ṣíri . . . (6) Ana Sin Šamša ik-šú-dam . . . (7) ḳarnu ḳarnu i-dir . . . (8) mâru itti abî-šu kit . . . *Rev.* (1) Ana Sin u Šamšu šit-kul-lu mâtu . . . (2) at-mu-ú ki-i-nu ina pî . . . (3) šar mâti $^{i\cdot u}$ GU . ZA ú-lab . . . (4) [Ana] Sin u Šamšu šú-ta-tu-ú šar mâti uz . . . (5) kit-ti ibašši . . (6) Ana [1] Šamšu íli-nu Sin . . . ina šapli-ta-nu *Sin . . . (7) šar mâti ina kit-ti-šu izzaz . . (8) ša $^{m\ ilu}$ Nabû-iḳ-bi . . [K. 1329.]

No. 145. *Obv.* (1) Ana ^{ilu} Sin u ^{ilu} Šamšu šu-ta-tu-ú (2) ina mâti kit-ti ib-ba - aš-ši (3) mâru it-ti Abî-šu kit-ti (4) i-ta-mi (5) Ana Sin u Šamšu šit-ḳul-lu [šar] mâti (6) u-zu-un ú-[rap-pa-as] (7) ûmu XIV $^{kám\ ilu}$ Sin u ^{ilu} Šamšu (8) it-ti a-ḫa-miš in-nam-mar-ma *Rev.* (1) Ana ^{mul} SAG . MÍ . GAR mí-lam-mu šakin(in) (2)

[1] Same character as in No. 177, *obv.*, 4.

Sar Akkadi ^{ki} ^{iṣu} kakki ^{pl}-šu (3) íli ^{iṣu} kakki ^{pl} nakri-šu i-dan-ni-nu (4) ^{mul} šarru lu-ú ina i-mit-ti (5) lu-ú ina šú-mí-lu ^{mul} SAG . MÍ . GAR izzaz-ma (6) ín-na a-du-ú ina šú-mí-lu (7) ^{mul} SAG . MÍ . GAR a-na III-šú ina . . . (8) ú-su-uz (9) ša ^{m} Ri-mu-tu

[83–1–18, 245.]

No. 146. *Obv.* (1) Ana ûmu XIV ^{kám} Sin ù Šamšu itti a-ḫa-miš innamru ^{pl} (2) sanâḳu ša pî lib mâti iṭâb (3) ilâni ^{pl} ^{mâtu} Akkada ^{ki} ana damiḳtim(tim) (4) i ḫa-as-sa-su ḫu-ud lib nísî ^{pl} išakan(an) (5) Ana Sin ù Šamšu šit-ḳu-lu mâtu ikân (6) at-mu-ú ki-i-nu ina pi-i niší ^{pl} išakan(an) (7) Šar kiš-šat ^{iṣu} kussa ú-lab-bar (8) Ana Sin ù Šamšu šú-ta-tu-ú (9) Šar mâti uz-na ù-rap-pa-aš *Rev.* 1 [Ana] ^{mul} LU . BAD . GUD . UD ina írib Šamši zunnu izanun(nun) ma zunnu izanun(nun) (3) ^{mul} Mustabarrû-mûtânu(a-nu) šarura it-tan-ši (4) ^{mul} LU . BAD . DIR nu-ḫuš niše ^{pl} (5) ^{mul} LU . BAD . DIR pagri ^{pl} Šam-ru (6) ^{mul} LU . BAD . DIR ^{ilu} muštabarrû-mûtânu (a-nu) (7) ša ^{m} ^{ilu} Nirgal ítir(ir).

[Rm. 191.]

No. 146A. *Obv.* (1) [Ana Sin] ù Šamšu šú-ta-tu-ú (2) šar mâti uz-na ú-[rap-pa]-aš (3) [Ana] sin ù Šamšu šit-ku-lu (4) mâtu i-kân at-[mu]-ú ki-i-nu ı(5) ina pi-[i nísî ^{pl} i]-šak-kan (6) [šar mâti ^{iṣu} kussa ú]-lab-bar (7) . . . . bi *Rev.* (1) . . . . (2) . . . . [i]-ma-al-li-ku (3) íbûr mâti iššir mâtu nuḫša im-mar (4) ^{arḫu} âiru ûmu XX ^{kám} ṢIR li-duk (5) [Šarru] a-ša-ri-du-ti il-lak (6) ša ^{m} ^{ilu} Nirgal-íṭir(ir).

[K. 842.]

No. 147. *Obv.* (1) [Ana ûmu XIV ^{kám} sin u Šamšu it]-ti a-ḫa-miš innamru ^{pl} (2) [sanâḳu ša pî lib mâti] iṭâb(ab) ilâni ^{pl} ^{mâtu} Akkada ^{ki} (3) [Ana damiḳti] i-ḫas-sa-su lib šarri iṭâb(ab) (4) [ḫud lib] ummâni(ni) bu-lim ^{mâtu} Akkadi ^{ki} (5) [parganiš] ina ṣíri i-rab-bi-iṣ (6) [Ana Sin u Šamšu] šú-ta-tu-ú (7) [Šar mâti] uz-nu urappaš(aš) (8) [Ana Sin ina tamarti]-šu ḳarnâti ^{pl}-šu tur-ru-kám *Rev.* (1) [paṭar] bi-ra-a-[ti] (2) [arad] ma-ṣar-ra-a-[ti] (3) [taš-mu]-u salimu(mu) ina mâti [ibašši] (4) [Ana a-na pâl] ûmí ^{pl} arkûti (5) [ša-lam] šar kiššuti u niší ^{pl} -šu (6) [ina] ûmu(mu) a-dan-ni-šu (7) [it]-ti ^{ilu} Šamši uš-ta-ta-a (8) [Ša]-ni-in man-za-as-su (9) [Ša ^{m} Iraššì]-ši-ilu ardu ša šarri maḫrû(u).

[K. 850.]

No. 148. *Obv.* (1) [Ana] ûmu XIV kâm Sin u Šamšu it-ti [aḫamiš innamru pl] (2) sanâḳu ša pî lil mâti itâb(ab) [ilâni pl Akkada ki] (3) Ana sal damiḳti i-[ḫa-sa]-su ḫu-ud lib [ummâni] (4) šarru ašaridu-tam illak(ak) bu-lim mâtu [Akkadi ki] (5) pár-ga-niš ina ṣíri i-rab-bi-[iṣ] (6) Ana Sin u Šamšu šú-ta-tu-[u] (7) šar mâti uz-nu urappaš . . (8) ša ûmu XIV kâm arḫu . . . . (9) in (?) . . . . *Rev.* (1) Ana a-na pâl ûmí(mí) arkûti [pl] (2) ša-lam (?) šar kiššuti u nišî pl-[šu] (3) ina ûmu(mu) a-dan-ni-šu it-[ti šamši] (4) uš-ta-ta-a ša-ni-in man-[za-as-su] (5) [ša] m Iraššì(ši)-ilu ardu ša šarri (6) maḫ-ru-ú. [K. 807.]

No. 149. *Obv.* (1) [Ana Sin u] ilu Šamšu šú-ta-tu-ú (2) [Šar mâti] uz-na ú-rap-pa-aš (3) [Ana Sin u] ilu Šamšu šit-ḳu-lu mâtu i-ka-nu (4) [atmû ki-i]-nu ina pi-i nišî pl išakan(an) (5) [šar iṣu GU]. ZA ú-lab-bar (*Remainder broken.*) *Rev.* (1) . . . . . ḳi . . . . (2) . . . lib arḫu Ululi arki-i (3) . . . ru-ú ad-ru šu-ú (4) . . . ra-an liš-pur-ma ina lib arḫu Ululi arki-i (5) . . . . li- pu- uš (6) [ša m ilu] Nírgal-íṭir(ir). [83–1–18, 302.]

No. 150. *Obv.* (1) Ana ilu Sin ilu Šamša ik-šú-ud-ma itti-šu (2) it-tin-tu ḳarnu ḳarnu i-dir (3) ina mâti kit-ti ibassi(ši)-ma (4) mâru itti abî-šu kit-ti i-ta-[ma] (5) ûmu XIV kâm ilu Sin u ilu Šamšu (6) it-ti a-ḫa-miš innammaru pl (7) Ana ilu Sin u ilu Šamšu šú-ta-tu-[u] (8) Šar mâti uz-na ú-[rap-pa-aš] *Rev.* (1) šarru išid iṣu kussi-šu i-[kan] (2) ûmu XIV kâm ilu itti ili innammaru . . (3) ri-íš šat-ti ilu Nírgal . . . . (4) na-pir-ti ša ši . . . (5) ûmu XIV kâm itti ilu Šamši it-[tan-mar] (6) damiḳti ša šarri bíl-ia šú-ú (7) ša m ilu Nabû-ikiša(ša) mâr Bar-sib ki. [83–1–18, 186.]

No. 151. *Obv.* (1) Ana Sin u ilu Šamšu šú-ta-tu-ú (2) Šar mâti uz-nu ú-rap-pa-aš (3) ûmu XIV kâm arḫu-us-su ilu itti ili innammar-ma (4) arḫu Tašrîtu arḫu Araḫsamna u arḫu Kisilimu III arḫâni pl (5) arki a-ḫa-miš ana damiḳti u a-rak ûmí(mí) (6) ša šarri bí-ili-iá it-tan-ma-ru (7) Ana Sin ina tamarti-šu karnâte pl šu tur-ru-ka (8) paṭar bi-ra-a-ti a-rad maṣṣarâti pl (9) taš-mu-ú u šalimu(mu) ina mâti ibašši (10) ûmu XIV kâm ilu itti ili innammar-ma (11) Ana Sin ûmu XIV kâm innamir-ma damiḳti mâtu Akkadi ki *Rev.* (1) limutti mâtu Ílama u Aḫarrî (2) Ana mul Aḳrabu ṣalmu ina libbi-šu taš-mu-ú ibašši (3) ša ^{ilu} Sin u ^{ilu} GUD . UD lubûšu (?) ikašad-su-nu (4) Ana ina ^{arhu} Kisilimi ûmu XV ^{kám} ana ^{ilu} Nírgal liš-kin (5) ^{isu} lib-bi GIŠIMMAR ina ķatâ ^{II}-šu liš-ši (6) ina ḫarrani u mí-tí-ķi i-šal-lim (7) ûmu XVI ^{kám} ûmu XVII ^{kám} Alpa ina pân ^{ilu} Nabî i-tar-ra-aṣ (8) Alpu ina pan ^{ilu} Nabî . . . im-maḫ-ḫa-aṣ (9) ûmu XVIII ^{kám} *ilu-*ma il-lab-bi-iš (10) mušu ša ûmi XIX ^{kám} kinûnu (11) ša $^{m\ ilu}$ Nabû-šuma iškun(un). [81–2–4, 102.]

No. 151A. *Obv.* (*Top broken*) (1) [sanâķu ša pî] lib mati iṭâb [ilani ^{pl}] (2) ^{mâtu} Akkada ^{ki} ana ^{sal} damiķti i-[ḫa-sa-su] (3) šarru ga- mí-ru-tam illak[ak] (4) bu-lim ^{mâtu} Akkadi ^{ki} par-ga-niš ina [ṣíri irabbiṣ] (5) Ana Sin ina tamarti-šu ķarnu ķarnu i[dir] (6) mílu illak[ak] (7) ina maḫ-ri-i a-na šarri bí-ili-ia (8) al-tap-ra um-ma ûmu XIV ^{kám} (9) ilu itti ili innammar . . *Rev.* (1) Ana Sin Šamšu ikšud-ma itti-[šu ittintu ina] mâti (2) kit-ti ibašši [maru itti abî-šu kitti] (3) i-ta-mu . . . . . ši . . (4) Ana Sin inat amarti-šu [ķarnâti ^{pl}-šu turruka] (5) paṭar bi-ra-a-ti [arad maṣṣarâti] (6) taš-[mu-u u salimu ina mâti ibašši] (*Remainder broken off*). *Left-hand edge* . . . ra ši-ilu . . . [K. 973.]

No. 152. *Obv.* (1) Ana ûmu XIV ^{kám} Sin u Šamšu itti a ḫa-miš innamru ^{pl} (2) sanâķu ša pî lib mâti iṭâb(ab) ilâni $^{pl\ mâtu}$ Akkada ^{ki} (3) A-na ^{sal} damiķti i-ḫa-sa-su (4) ḫu-ud lib-bi ummâni (ni) lib šarri iṭâb(ab) (5) bûl ^{mâtu} Akkadi ^{ki} par-ga-niš ina ṣíri irabbiṣ (iṣ) (6) Ana Sin u Šamšu šit-ķu-lu mâtu i-ķan (7) at-mu-ú ki-nu ina pî nísî ^{pl} išakan(an) (8) [šar mâti] ^{isu} kussa ulabbar(bar) *Rev.* (1) ^{isu} li'u am-mí-u (2) šá ûm ^{ilu} ÍN . LIL. ša ni-iš ṭur-u-ni (3) lu-ší-ri-bu-u-ni šarru bí-li li-mur (4) ù ^{isu} li' Ak-ka-du-u (5) šá sarri lid-di-nu-na-ši (6) Kakkabâni ^{pl} III $^{ta-a-an}$ ina pu-u-ti (7) ina lib-bi li-ṣi-ru (8) ^{am} SAG . lip-ķi-du ša un-ķu i-pat-tu-ni (9) ina pani-šu í-ṣi-ru-ni [83–1–18, 223.]

No. 153. *Obv.* (1) Ana Sin ^{ilu} Šamša la ú-ķi-[ma irbi] (2) na-an-dur nísî [^{pl} u âḫî ^{pl}] (3) ša ûmu XIV ^{kám} ilu itti ili la in-[nam-mar] (4) Ana Sin ina tamarti-šu ķarnu ķarnu i-[dir] (5) ^{sal} nukurtu išakan(an) . . . (6) ša ûmu XIV ^{kám} ilu itti ili la in-nam-[ma-ru] (7) Ana Sin ina alâki-šu í-zi maḫiru iṣahir(ir) (8) ûmu XV ^{kám} itti ^{ilu} Šamši innammar(mar-ra) *Rev.* (1) mu-ši a-ga-a ^{ilu} Sin tarbaṣu il-ta-mi (2) ^{mul}AB . SIN u ^{mul} A . ÍDIN ina lib-bi ú-šú-us-su (3) Ana Sin tarbaṣu ilmi-ma $^{mul\ ilu}$ PAN ina libbi-šu izziz (4) aštûti ^{pl} (?) in-na-da-ru-ma (5) ḫu-ub-bu-tu ina mâti i-man-du (6) Ana Sin [1] nâru ilmi(mi) ri-iḫ-ṣu u ra-a-[du] (7) rabûti ^{pl} ibašši $^{pl\ mul}$ A . ÍDIN (8) ina tarbaṣ ^{ilu} Sin izzaz(az) -[ma] (9) ša $^{m\ ilu}$ Nabû-ikiša(ša) mâr Bár-[sib ^{ki}]. [K. 793.]

No. 154. *Obv.* (1) ûmu I ^{kám} a-na šarri Al-tap-ra um-ma ûmu XIV ^{kám} (2) ^{ilu} Sin it-ti ^{ilu} Šamšu in-nam-mar (3) ûmu XIV $^{kám\ ilu}$ Sin ù ^{ilu} Šamšu it-ti a-ḫa-miš innamru ^{pl} (4) sanâḳu ša pî lib mâti iṭâb(ab) ilâni $^{pl\ mâtu}$ Akkada ^{ki} (5) Ana ^{sal} damiḳti i-ḫa-as-sa-su ḫu-ud lib nísî ^{pl} išakan(an) (6) bu-lum ^{mâtu} Akkadi ^{ki} par-ga-niš ina ṣíri irabbiṣ(iṣ) (7) Ana ^{ilu} Sin ^{ilu} Šamša ik-šú-dam-ma itti-šu (8) it-tin-ta ḳarnu ḳarnu i-dir *Rev.* (1) ina mâti kitti ibašši(ši)-ma (2) mâru itti abî-šu kit-ti i-ta-mi (3) ûmu XIV $^{kám\ ilu}$ Sin it-ti ^{ilu} Šamši innam-mar-ma (4) Ana ^{ilu} Sin ù ^{ilu} Šamšu šú-ta-tu-ú (5) Šar mâti uz-na urappaš(aš) (6) ûmu XIV $^{kám\ ilu}$ Sin it-ti ^{ilu} Šamši innammar-ma (7) ša $^{m\ ilu}$ Nírgal-íṭir(ir). [83-1-18, 171.]

No. 155. *Obv.* (1) [Ana] Sin ù ^{ilu} Šamšu šú-ta-tu-ú (2) [Šar] mâti uz-[na] urappaš(aš) šarru išid ^{iṣu} kussi-šu ikân (3) Ana ûmu XIV $^{kám\ ilu}$ Sin u ^{ilu} Šamšu itti a-ḫamis innamru ^{pl} (4) pû mâti ikân lib mâti iṭâb(ab) lib šarri iṭâb(ab) (5) ilâní $^{pl\ mâtu}$ Akkada ^{ki} ana damiḳtim(tim) i-ḫas-sa su (6) ḫu-ud lib-bi niši ^{pl} išakan(an) (7) bu-lum ^{mâtu} Akkadi ^{ki} par-ga-niš ina ṣíri irabbiṣ(is) (8) Ana Sin ûmu XIV $^{[kam]}$ innamir-ma damiḳti ^{mâtu} Akkadi ^{ki} (9) limutti ^{mâtu} Ílama (ma) ^{ki} u Aḫarrî ^{ki} *Rev.* (1) Šarru bí-la-a la i-ḳab-bi um-ma (2) urpatu ak-ka-' i-ta-mur (3) mu-ši a-ga-a a-ṣu-ú-šu ša a-mur (4) ina lib-bi ûmu(mu) i-ṣu it-ta-ṣa-a (5) ḳaḳ-ḳar-šu ša ina lib-bi in-nam-ma-ru (6) ik-ta-šad i-da-at ša a-ma-ru ši-i (7) ša ší-í-[ri] . . i ûmu(mu) pi-tu-ú (8) šarru IM . . . . kas-bu ûmu(mu) (9) it-ti ^{ilu} Šamši iz-za-az (10) ša $^{m\ ilu}$ Nabû-ikiša(ša) mâr Bár-sib ^{ki}. [83-1-18, 48.]

No. 155A. *Obv.* (1) [Ana ûmu XIV ^{kám} Sin u] Šamšu itti a-ḫa-[miš innamru] (2) [sanâḳu ša pî] lib-bi mâti [ṭâb] (3) [ilâni ^{pl}] ^{mâtu} Akkadi $^{[ki]}$ (4) [Ana] damiḳti i-ḫa-sa-su (5) [ḫud] lib-bi um-mâni(ni) lib-bi šarri iṭâb(ab) (6) bûl ^{mâtu} Akkadi ^{ki} (7) ina ṣíri par-

1 Erasure.

ga-niš irabbiṣ(iṣ) (8) Ana ilu Sin u ilu Šamšu šit-ḳu-lu (9) mâtu i-ka-na at-mu-u ki-[i-nu]. (10) ina pî nišî pl išaḳan(an) (11) šar mâti ilu DIL. TÍ ulabbar(bar) *Rev.* (1) Ana Sin u Šamšu šú-ta-tu-ú (2) šar mâti IZ. KU. PI *urappaš(aš) (3) ultu lib-bi ûmí (mí).... (4) ûmu(mu).... (5) mu-šú.... (6) UD mu (?).... (7).... [K. 6078.]

No. 155B. *Obv.* (1) Ana ûmu XIV kám ilu Sin u ilu...... (2) taš-mu-ú u sa-li-[mu ina mâti ibašši]. (3) ša m ilu Bíl-na-ṣir... (4) ki-ma ša a-na šarri bí-[ili-ia ašpur] (5) [um]-ma a-dir ší ûmu(mu).... (6) maṣṣarti ša ilu Sin ia-[a-nu].... (7).. UD ḫu (?).... (8) a-mat.... (9).... (10) ni. (?)... *Rev.* (1) ilu Sin.... (2) šarru ša ḳa-as-[su].... (3) ni-iš ḳa-ti.... (4) ilu Sin u ilu [Šamšu].... (5) ul-tu arḫu Nisanni.... (6) ú-ma-a ša šarri bí-ili.... (7) it-ti ni-iš ḳa-ti.... (8) ûmu XIV kám ilu....

[83–1–18, 296.]

(D) *On the Fifteenth Day.*

No. 156. *Obv.* (1) Ana ûmu XV kám Sin u Šamšu itti a-ḫa-miš [innamru] (2) am nakru dan-nu ișu kakki pl-šu ana mâti inaša (3) abul ali-ia am nakru ina-ḳar (4) Ana Sin Šamša la û-ḳi-ma ir-bi (5) na-an-dur níšî pl u âḫî pl *Rev.* (1) arḫu Simânu mâtu Aḫarrû (2) ûmu XV kám mâtu Aḫarrû (3) šá [m Ba]-ma-a-a.

[Bu. 91–5–9, 8.]

No. 157. *Obv.* (1) Ana ûmu [XV] kám Sin u Šamšu (2) itti a-ḫa-miš innamru pl (3) am nakru dan-nu (4) ișu kakki pl-šu ina mâti inaša(a) (5) parrakki pl ilâni pl rabûti pl ina-ḳar (6) Ana Sin u Šamšu la ú-ḳi-ma ir-bi (7) na-an-dur níšî pl (8) ù âḫî pl *Rev.* (1) šá [m] ilu Nabû-mu-ší-ṣi. [K. 866.]

No. 157A. *Obv.* (1) Ana [ûmu XV kam Sin u Šamšu itti aḫamiš innamru] (2) am [nakru dannu ișu kakki pl-šu ana mâti inaša] (3) abul [ali nakru inaḳar] (4) Ana Sín u Šamšu [la uḳi-ma irbi] (5) na-an-dur UR. [MAḪ u âḫî] (6) ša m ilu...

[83–1–18, 292.]

No. 157B. *Obv.* (1) [Ana ûmu XV kam] Sin ù Samšu (2) [itti a-ḫa]-miš innamru pl (3) [nakru dan]-nu išu kakki pl-šu (4) [inaša]-a (5) [abul ali] am nakru ina-ḳar (6) . . . . : mâtu Aḫarrû ki (7) [ša m] ilu Nírgal-íṭir(ir). [K. 1369.]

No. 157C. *Obv.* (1) Ana Sin ûmu XV kám it-[ti Šamši] (2) in-na-mir . . . . (3) du . . . . (4) mâtu . . . . *Rev.* (1) ša i-ga (?) . . . . (2) um-ma ûmu XV (?) . . . . (3) ilâni pl-ka ki . . . . (4) ša m ilu Bíl-na-[ṣir]. [K. 12017.]

No. 157D. *Obv.* (1) Ana ûmu XV [kám] ilu Sin [u ilu Šamšu] (2) it-ti a-ḫa-mí-iš innamir (3) am nakru dan-nu išu kakki pl-šu (4) a-na mâti i-na-ša-a (5) abulli pl am nakru i-na-ḳar (6) Ana ilu Sin u ilu Šamšu la ú-ḳi-ma ir-bi (7) na-an-dur níši u aḫi *Rev.* (1) šá m Ištar-šuma-ìríš(íš). [Rm. 195.]

No. 158. *Obv.* (*Top broken.*) (1) [irbi? na-an]-dur . . (2) [níši pl] u UR . BAR . [RA . MIŠ] (3) Ana ûma XV [kám Sin u Šamšu] itti a-ḫa-miš [innamru] (4) am nakru dan-nu [išu] kakki pl-šu ana mâti [inašâ] (5) pân abulli-MU am nakru iṣabbat(bat?) *Rev.* (1) m Ṭâbu-šar-Bílti (?) am (?) SAG (?) am Rab-pi-[šir?] (2) ša am šú-ša-nu lubušu (?) . . . aḫi (?) . . am . . (3) nišî pl ša šarru bí-la-a id-*di-na-[an-ni] (4) ul-taḫ-ṭu-ni lik-kas-*si *i . . . . (5) it-ta-šú-ú mar-ṣa-ku u am Rab-pi-[šir?] (6) ia-a-nu šarru la ú-maš-šir-an-ni-[ma] (7) la a-ma-ti (8) . . . . [83–1–18, 225.]

No. 158A. *Obv.* (1) [Ana ûmu] XV kám Sin u ilu Šamšu itti a-ḫa-[miš innamru] (2) nakru dan-nu išu kakki pl-šu ana mâti inašâ(a) (3) abul ali nakru ina-ḳar (4) Ana Sin ilu Šamšu la ú-ḳi-ma ir-bi (5) na-an-dur níši u âḫi (6) ša m ilu Nabû-aḫî pl-iddina(na) (7) . . . . Dil-bat ki [K. 755.]

No. 159. *Obv.* (1) Ana ûmu XV kám Sin u Šamšu itti a-ḫa-miš [innamru] (2) nakru dan-nu išu kakki pl (3) a-na mâti i-na-aš-ša-[a] (4) Abulli pl am nakru i-na-[ḳar] (5) Ana Sin u Šamšu la ú-ḳi-ma ir-[bi] (6) na-an-dur níši u UR . [BAR . RA] (7) Ana Sin ina tamarti-šu ḳarnu ḳarnu i-[dir] (8) šarrâni pl ša mâti kalâmi imâtu [pl] *Rev.* (1) Ana ina arḫu Simâni ûmu XVI [kám] . . . . (2) aš-la ša išu ílippi (?) . . . (3) a-na ma-ḫi-ir-ti li . . . . (4) šídu mu-šal-li-im (5) it-ta-na-ar . . . . (6) šá ^{m} Ištar-šuma-íriš. [Km. 200.]

No. 160. *Obv.* (1) Ana Sin Šamšu la ú-ḳi-ma ir-bi (2) na-an-dur níši u âḫi (3) ûmu XV ^{kám} itti Šamši innammar-ma (4) ina ^{arḫu} Nisanni ûmu(mu) ú-šal-lam (5) ûmu XV ^{kám} Sin itti Šamši in-nam-mar (6) a-na íli ^{išu} li-'-a-nu (7) . . . . duppâni ^{pl} . . . . (8) . . . . kit . . . . (9) . . . . ni . . . . *Rev.* (1) . . . . ina Uri $^{\text{[ki]}}$ . . . . (2) . . a-na šarri aḳ-bu-ú-[ma] (3) . . šarru lu-ú-ḫa-si-is (4) ša ^{m} Šú-ma-a (5) ^{am} Dup-šar ûm ^{ilu} ÍN . LIL (6) pân (?) ki-is-ri-íš-šu.

[80–7–19, 61.]

No. 160A. *Obv.* (1) Ana ^{ilu} Sin ^{ilu} Ša-maš [šitḳulu] (2) at-mu-ú ki-[i-nu ina pî nišî] (3) iš-šak-kan šar [mâti] (4) ^{išu} GU . ZA [ulabbar] (5) ûmu XV ^{kám} ultu [Šamši] (6) in-na-[mar-ma] (7) Ana ^{ilu} Sin ^{ilu} Ša-maš [šutatu] (8) šar mâti uz-[na urappaš] (9) ûmu XIV ^{kám} in-[nam-mar-ma]. (*Reverse broken off.*) [K. 994.]

No. 160B. *Obv.* (1) Ana ûmu XV ^{kám} Sin u [Šamšu itti] (2) a-ḫa-miš innamru [nakru dannu] (3) ^{išu} kakki ^{pl}-šu ana mâti i-na-[aš-ša-a] (4) abul ali-ia [nakru inaḳar] *Rev.* (1) ^{arḫu} Šabâṭi ^{mâtu} MAR ^{mâtu} . . . . (2) ûmu XV $^{\text{kám mâtu}}$ MAR . . . . (3) limutti ša ^{mâtu} MAR . . . . (4) ú-il-tum ara . . . . [83–1–18, 220.]

No. 161. *Obv.* (1) Ana ûmu XV ^{kám} Sin u Šamšu itti a-ḫa-miš innamru ^{pl} (2) ^{am} nakru dan-nu ^{išu} kakki ^{pl}-šu (3) a-na mâti inaši(ši) (4) abul ali [1] nakru ina-ḳar (5) Ana Sin ina la si-ma-ni-šu iḫ-ḫi-ram-ma innamir (*sic*) (6) ti-bi-í âl kiš-šu-ti (7) Ana Sin ina alâki-šu í-zi (8) maḫiru iṣaḫir(ir) (9) Ana Sin u Šamšu la ú-ḳi-ma irbi(bi) (10) na-an-dur níši ^{pl} (11) ù âḫi ^{pl} *Rev.* (1) šá ^{m} Ba-ma-a-a.

[K. 718.]

No. 162. *Obv.* (1) Ûmu XV ^{kám} Sin ù Šamšu itti a-ḫa-miš innamru ^{pl} (2) nakru dan-nu ^{išu} kakki ^{pl}-šu ana mâti inašâ(a) (3) abul ali-ia nakru i-na-ḳar (4) Ana Sin ina ^{arḫu} Âiri ûmu XXX ^{kám} in-na-mar (5) Ana Sin ina ^{arḫu} Âiri ûmu XXX ^{kám} innamir duḫ-du

[1] *Erasure.*

Aḫarri ki (6) Aḫ-mu-ú (*sic*) ikkal (7) Ana Sin ina arḫu Âiri ûmu XVI kám it-ti ilu Šamši *Rev.* (1) in-na-mar (2) Ana mul SAG. MÍ. GAR it-ti mul Dil-bat il-lak (3) un-nin mâti ana lib ilâni pl ib-ba-aš-šu-ú (4) ilu Marduk u ilu Ṣar-pa-ni-tum ṣu-li-í (5) ša ummâni(ni)-ka i-šim-mu-ma (6) ri-í-mu a-na ummâni(ni)-ka i-ra-aš-šu-ú (7) ístín(ín) imíru lid-di-nu-nim-ma šíp-ia (8) ina muḫ-ḫi lu-šap-ši-iḫ (9) ša m ilu Nírgal-íṭir(ir). [Rm. 196.]

No. 163. *Obv.* (1) [Ana] ûmu XV kám Sin ù ilu Šamšu itti a-ḫa-miš innamru pl (2) am nakru dan-nu iṣu kakki pl-šu ana mâti inašâ(a) (3) abul ali-ia am nakru i-na-ḳar (4) Ana mul LU. BAD *ina arḫu Du'uzi innamir(ir) (5) pagrâni pl ibaššû pl (6) Ana mul AL. LUL a-dir (7) utukku ḫab-lim mâta iṣabbat(bat)-ma *Rev.* (1) pagrâni pl ina mâti ibaššû pl (2) ša m ilu Nabû-aḫî pl-iddina(na).

[83–1–18, 244.]

No. 164. *Obv.* (1) Ana ûmu XV kám Sin u Šamšu it-ti a-ḫa-miš innamru . . (2) am nakru dan-nu iṣu kakkî pl-šu (3) ana mâti i-na-aš-ša-a (4) abul ali nakru i-naḳ-ḳar (5) Ana Sin iḫ-ḫi-ram-ma la inna-mir(ir) (6) tí-bi-í al kiš-ša-ti (7) ûmu XV kám itti ilu Šamšu innammar-ma *Rev.* (1) Ana mi-ši-iḫ kakkabi ultu šáru šadi (2) a-na šáru Aḫarrî im-šu-uḫ (3) kar-ti nakri abikta a-a . . . (4) mâta iliḳḳi(ḳi) (5) arḫu Aíru arḫu Simânu arḫu Du'ûzu arḫu Abu arḫu Ululu (6) V arḫâni pl an-nu-ti (7) ûmu XIV kám ilu itti ili la innammar . . (8) šarru lu-ú-i-di u lu-ḫa-si-[iš] (9) ša m Iraššî(ši)-ilu ardu ša šarri maḫrû(u).

[K. 805.]

No. 165. *Obv.* (1) Ana ûmu XV kám Sin u Šamšu itti a-ḫa-[miš] (2) innamir am nakru dan-nu (3) iṣu kakki pl-šu ana mâti i-na-aš-ša-a (4) abul ali am nakru i-na-kar (5) Ana mul AN. NA míš-ḫa im-šuḫ (6) am nakru na-mí-í-A i-kam-miš. [K. 727.]

No. 165A. *Obv.* (1) Ana ûmu XV kám Sin u [šamšu] (2) it-ti a-ḫa-miš innamru [pl] (3) am nakru dan-nu iṣu [kakki pl] (4) ana mâti DIL DIL . . . . (5) [parakki] pl ilâni [pl inaḳar] (*Remainder lost.*) *Rev.* (*Top broken.*) (1) tí-bi-í âl kiš-ša-ti (2) ûmu XV kám ilu itti ili innammar-ma (3) ša m Iraššî(ši)-ilu ardu ša šarri maḫrû[u].

[K. 843.]

(E) *On the Sixteenth Day.*

No. 166. *Obv.* (1) Ana ûmu XVI kám Sin n Šamšu itti a-ḫa-miš innamru pl (2) šarru ana šarri sal nukurta išappar(ár) (3) šarru ina íkalli-šu a-na mi-na-at ar-ḫi (4) ú-ta-sar šíp nakri a-na mâti-šu (5) am nakru ina mâti-šu šal-ṭa-niš illaku pl (6) Ana Sin ina arḫu Du'ûzi lu-u ûmu XIV kám lu-u ûmu XV kám (7) itti ilu Šamši la innamir(ir) *Rev.* (1) šarru ina íkalli-šu ú-ta-sar (2) ûmu XVI kám innamir-ma damiḳti mâtu Subarti ki (3) limutti mâtu Akkadi ki u mâtu Aḫarrî ki (4) šá m Ak-kul-la-ni. [K. 694.]

No. 167. *Obv.* (1) Ana ûmu XVI kám Sin u Šamšu itti a-ḫa-miš innamru pl (2) šarru ana šarri limuttim(tim) išappar(ár) šarru ina íkalli-šu (3) a-na minât pl arḫi ú-ta-sar (4) šíp nakri ana mâti-šu išakan(an) nakru šal-ṭa-niš illaku pl (5) Ana Sin tarbaṣu ilmi-ma mul Muštabarrû-mûtânu(a-nu) ina libbi-šu izziz (6) šaḫluḳti [bûli mí]-ri-šu u saluppu la išširu (7) [: mâtu MAR .] TU ki iṣaḫír (8) . . . . . du ina mâti kit-ti ibašši-ma (9) [mâru itti abí-šu kit]-ti i-ta-mi *Rev.* (1) . . . [LU] . BAD ikšuda-ma i-ti-iḳ (2) . . . dan-nu ina mâti ibašši(ši) (3) . . . . mus ni akalí (?) ikšud(ud) (4) . [NI .] BAT-a-nu ilu SAG . UŠ ikšuda-ma (5) . . . ša . lim šu NIGIN (?) zi-nu (6) . . . Aḫarri ki in-nam-din (7) ilu muštabarrû-mûtânu(a-nu) . . mâtu Subartu ki ba-'-il (8) ù ša-ru-[ru] na-ši damiḳti ša mâtu Subarti ki šú-ú (9) ù mul LU . BAD . SAG . UŠ kakkabu ša mâtu Aḫarrî (10) un-nu-ut ù ša-ru-ru-šu ma-aḳ-tu (11) limutti ša mâtu Aḫarri ki ti-ib mât nakri (12) i-na mâtu Aḫarrî ki ib-ba-aš-ši (13) ša m Ša-pi-ku mâr Bár-sib ki. [80-7-19, 371 + S. 366.]

No. 167A. *Obv.* (1) [Ana Sin u Šamšu šú ta]-tu-ú (2) [šar mâti uzna ú]-rap-pa-aš (3) . . . . Akkadi ki (4) . . . . dir (?) ši (*Remainder lost.*) *Rev.* (*Top wanting.*) (1) [šarru ana minat arḫi] ú-ta-sar (2) . . . . šu-ú (3) . . . . u ša u damiḳti (4) . . . . iá (5) [ša m ilu Bíl-šuma ?]-iškun(un). [K. 14150.]

VIII. Omens from the Moon's Appearance without the Sun.

No. 168. *Obv.* (1) Ana Sin ina arḫu Nisanni lu ûmu XIV kám lu [ûmu XV kám] (2) itti ilu Šamši la innamir . . (3) ummâni(ni) ḫarran am nakri a-na .... (4) iḫ-ḫab-ba-ta-nim-ma mâtu .... (5) bartu ina mâti ibašši .. (6) Ana ûmu XVI kam Sin u Šamšu itti a-ḫa-[miš innamru] (7) šarru ana šarri [nukurta išappar] (8) šarru ina îkalli-šu [ana minat arḫi utasar] (9) [šíp] am nakri [ina mâti-šu išakan] (10) am nakru šal-ṭa-[niš ina mâti illaku] *Rev.* (1) Ana ûmu XVIII kam Sin u Šamšu itti [aḫamiš innamru] (2) šar Subarti [ki] (3) maḫira [ul iraššî] (4) šá m Ištar-šuma-íríš(íš).

[K. 733.]

No. 169. *Obv.* (1) Ana Sin ina arḫu Du'ûzi lu ûmu XV kám lu ûmu XV kám (2) it-ti ilu Šamši la innamir(ir) (3) šarru ina íkalli-šu ú-ta-sar (4) Ana ûmu XVI kám Sin u Šamsu it-ti a-ḫa-[miš] (5) in-nam-ru šarru ana šarri (6) nu-kúr-tum i-šap-par šarru ina ina [íkalli-šu] (7) [ana mi]-na-at arḫi ú-ta-[sar] *Rev.* (1) [šíp nakri] ana mâti-šu iš-[šak-kan] (2) [nakru] ina mâti-šú šal-ṭa-niš it-ta-[lak] (3) [Ana] Sin ûmu XVI kám innamir-ma limutti mâtu Akkadi [ki] (4) damiḳti mâtu Subarti ki (5) šá m Šú-ma-a-a. [K. 695.]

No. 170. *Obv.* (*Top broken*) (1) Ana Sin ina arḫu Šabâṭi *ûmu *XIV kám *lu *ûmu *XV kám (2) itti Šamšu la innamir mílu gab-šu illak-ma (3) íbûru iṣaḫar(ár) (4) ab-ḳal-lu ši-iḳ-la (5) ilu Bíl ri-mi-nu ú-ḳar-rad ilu Marduk (6) ina muši i-zu-uz-ma *Rev.* (1) ina ší-í-ri it-tap-šar (2) šar kiššûti ṣa-lam ilu Marduk at-ta (3) a-na lib-bi ardâni pl ni-i-ka (4) ki-i tar-'-ú-bu ru-'-ub-ti (5) ša šarri bíl-ni ni-il-ta-da-ad (6) u su-lum-mu-ú ša šarru ni-ta-mar (7) am-mí-ni am ki-na-at-ú-a (*Remainder broken off*) (*Left-hand edge*) (1) ša m A-ša-ri-[du] (2) maḫrû(û) .... [82-5-22, 63.]

No. 171. *Obv.* (1) [Ana Sin] u Šamšu la ú-ḳi-ma ir-bi (2) na-an-dur níši pl u âḫi pl (3) ûmu XV kám it-ti ilu Šamši innammar-ma (4) Ana Sin ina arḫu Addâri ûmu XIV kám it-ti ilu Šamši la innamir (5) [ŠA. ḪA] LAM. MA Uri ki (6) [Sin ina arḫu] Nisanni ûmu (mu) ú-šal-lam *Rev.* (1) šá m Ba-la-si-i. [S. 1027.]

No. 172. *Obv.* (1) Ana Sin ina arḫu Addâri ûmu XIV kám lu ûmu XV kám itti Šamši la innamir (2) šaḫluḳti Uri ki (3) Ana Sin ina la si-ma-ni-šu iḫ-ḫi-ram-ma la innamir (4) tibí(í) al kiššut(ut) | šanâti pl ša .... (5) Ana ûmu XVI kám Sin u Šamšu itti a-ḫa-

[miš innamru] (6) šar Subarti ki GAB. [RI la iraššî] (7) ša lib-bi dup-pi.... (8) Ana Sin tarbaṣu ilmi-ma mul [muštabarrû-mûtânu ina libbi-šu izziz] (9) šaḫlukti bûli ina mâti kalâmi [mîrišu] (10) [u] saluppu la SI-[DI: Aḫarrû ki iṣaḫir] (11).... du.... (12).... (*Remainder of obv. and top of rev. broken off.*) *Rev.* (1).... a-na mul LU. BAD. itḫi ḫa (?) a (?).... (2) [mul Muštabarrû]-mûtânu (a-nu) a-na mul LU. BAD. SAG. UŠ iṭaḫḫi-ma (3) [Ana mul] LU. BAD kakkabâni pl šamî(î) ú-lap-pat (4) šar mâtâti ú-ḳat-ti (5) ilu Muštabarrû-mûtânu(a-nu) i-ba-il-ma (6) kakkabâni pl ú-lap-pat-ma (7) ša m A-ša-ri-du maḫrû(ú) ardu ša šarri. [79-7-8, 100.]

IX. Omens from the Sun.

No. 173. *Obv.* (1) Ana Šamša tarbaṣu ilmi zunnu izanun(nun) (2) Šamší(í) ûmi(mi) *Rev.* (1) ša m Iraššî(ši)-ilu. [81-2-4, 106.]

No. 174. *Obv.* (1) Ana ilu Šamšu ina tarbaṣ Sin izziz(iz) (2) kit-tu ina mâti ibašši-ma (3) mâru itti abî-šu kit-tu i-ta-mí (4) sa-lim kiš-ša-ti (5) Ana Sin tarbaṣu ilmi-ma ilu NIN. IB ina libbi-šu izziz (iz) (6) itti nakri ummâni(ni) i-ḳab-ba-al (7) šá m ilu Nabû-mu-ší-ṣi. [K. 719.]

No. 174a. *Obv.* (1) Ana Sin tarbaṣu ilmi-ma [Šamšu] (2) i-na lib-bi-šu izziz [kittu ina mâti ibašši] (3) mâru it-ti abî-šu [kittu itama salim kiššati] (4) ilu Dil-bat.... (5) arḫu u ûmu (mu).... (6) un-ḳi-ma.. (7) Ana mul Dil-bat ina arḫu Nisanni [ultu ûmi I kám] (8) adi ûmi XXX kám ina [ṣit Šamši itbal] (9) ú-ru-ba-a-ti [ibaššu] *Rev.* (1) Ana mul Dil-bat ina nipiḫ-ša ki.... (2) lib mâti i-[ṭâb?].... (3) i-na ṣit Šamši limuttu.... (4) ša m Iraššî(ši)-ilu mâr m Nu-[ur-za-nu]. [K. 1330.]

No. 175. *Obv.* (1) Ana ilu Šamšu ana lib Sin írub mâtu.... (2) kit-ta i-ta-[mu-u] (3) sa-li-im kiš-ša-ti (4) [Ana] mul LU. BAD ana íli Sin ibrum-ma (5) ana lib Sin írub níšî pl imâtu pl-ma (6) alkat mâti... bûl dîku pl (7) ilu LU. BAD. SAG. UŠ ina lib Sin í-ta-rab (8) ša m ilu Aššur-šar-a-ni. [Rm. 207.]

No. 176. *Obv.* (1) Ana ^{ilu} Šamšu ina man-za-zi ^{ilu} Sin izziz(iz) (2) šar mâti ina ^{isu} kussi i-ka-na (3) [Ana] Šamšu (?) íli-ta-nu Sin šapli-ta-nu Sin izziz(iz) (4) . . išid ^{isu} kussi i-ka-na (5) šar mâti ina kit-ti-šu izzaz(az) (6) Ana Šamšu (?) u Sin šú-ta-tu-u (7) šar mâti uz-nu ú-rap-pa-aš *Rev.* (1) [1]mušu an-ni-i-ú (2) ^{mul} LU . BAD . SAG . UŠ a-na ^{ilu} Sin (3) iḳ-di-ri-ib ^{mul} LU . BAD . SAG . UŠ (4) kakkab: ^{ilu} Šamši šú-ú (5) ki-i an-ni-i-í (6) pi-ší-ir-šu damiḳti ša šarri šú-u (7) ^{ilu} Šamšu kakkab šarri šú-u. [81–2–4, 80.]

No. 177. *Obv.* (1) Ana Šamšu (?) íli-nu ^{ilu} Sin (2) . . . šapli-ta-nu Sin izziz (3) šarru išid kussi-šu ikan(an) (4) Ana Šamšu (?) ina manzaz Sin izzaz (5) Kit-ti ina mâti ibašši(ši) *Rev.* (1) ša $^{m\,ilu}$ Nabû-iḳ-bi. [K. 745.]

No. 178. *Obv.* (1) [Ana] ^{ilu} Ša-maš [2] ippuḫa-ma ana [3] pani-šu [illak ?] (2) šar kiš-ša-ti palî-šu írik (3) Ana ina ^{arḫu} A-da-ri ^{ilu} Ša-maš ina ší-rim (4) tarbaṣu ilmi ina arḫi šuâti (5) mílu illakam(kam) . . . šamû(ú) izanun(nun) (6) ina lib it-ti šá ^{mul} SAG . MÍ . GAR (7) šú-ú *Rev.* (1) ri-iḫ-ti di-ib-bi (2) ki-i it-ti šú-ma (3) a-na zu-un-ni a-na mí-li. [K. 780.]

No. 179. *Obv.* (1) Ana ^{ilu} Ša-maš tarbaṣu ilmi-ma (2) bâb-šu ana ^{šâru} šûti [4]iprus (3) ^{šâru} šûtu i-za-az (4) Ana ina [5]ûm bubbuli ^{šâru} šûtu [íllak] (5) [6]šamû(ú) . . . . . . (6) ûm bubbuli . . . . *Rev.* (1) ^{ilu} Sin ina . . . . (2) ûmu(mu) . . . . (3) ša $^{m\,ilu}$ Nabû-aḫî ^{pl}-íriba. [83–1–18, 227.]

No. 180. *Obv.* (*Top wanting.*) (1) [ûmu] XIII ^{kám} šarru . . . . (2) Ana ^{ilu} ša-maš ina tarbaṣ Sin izziz(iz) ina mâti kalâmi (3) ki-it-tú i-ta-mu-u mâru it-ti abî-šu kit-tum i-ta-mí (4) sa-lim kiš-ša-ti (5) ^{mul} LU . BAD . SAG . UŠ ina tarbaṣ Sin izzaz-ma (6) it-tam-mí-ḫi-ir it-ti šá ûmi XIII ^{kám} šú-u (7) ina íli šá ^{ilu} Sin ûmu XIII ^{kám} in-na mir-u-ni (8) ana íli šú-u ^{mul} LU . BAD . SAG . UŠ ina tarbaṣ ^{ilu} Sin it-ti-it-zi *Rev.* (1) Ana ^{ilu} Sin tarbaṣu [7]ṣalmu ilmi

[1] MI, *glossed* mu šu. [2] KUR-ma, *glossed* ip-pu-ḫa-ma.
[3] ŠI-šu, *glossed* pa-ni-šu. [4] TAR, *glossed* ip-ru-[us].
[5] UD . NÁ . A . AN, *glossed* ûm bu-ub-bu-li.
[6] ANA-ú, *glossed* ša-mu-u. [7] MI, *glossed* ṣa-al-mu.

arḫu zunna ú-kal (2) . . . urpâti ^{pl} uk-ta-ṣa-ra (3) Ana ^{mul} Šarru [1] a-dir šarru [2] íziz-ma [3] íntûti ^{pl}-šu (4) . . . . ma [4] utir-ma [5] la idâk(ak) (5) . . . . [6] ú [7] iraššši(ši) (6) . . . . [^{mul} LU . BAD] SAG . UŠ ina pân ^{mul} šarru (*Remainder wanting.*) (*Left-hand edge.*) (1) šá $^{m\ ilu}$ Nabu . . . . [K. 781.]

No. 181. (1) Ana Šamšu ippuḫa-ma adir za-lap mâti šiâtî iḫallik (2) Ana Šamšu ippuḫa-ma adir nu-ḫus nišî ^{pl} : taḫaṣu ina mâti išakan (3) : bartu : ud-da-a-ti ana šar mâti kalâmi (4) Ana Šamšu ina nipih-šu šaruru adru adir (?) atalû išakan-ma (5) ^{ilu} Rammânu iraḫiṣ(iṣ) (6) maṣṣarti ša ší-í-ri ša ^{mâtu} Ílama(ma) ^{ki} (7) ina ni-pi-iḫ ^{ilu} Šamši it-tum an-ni-tú (?) . . *Rev.* (1) ta-at-tal-ka (2) Ana ina ^{arḫu} Âiri ^{ilu} Rammânu pí-šu iddi AŠ . A . AN (3) u ḳû-ú (?) la išširu ^{pl} (4) kakkabu ša ana šarri bíl-iá aḳ-bu ma-'-diš (5) un-nu-ut a-tin-nu ul i-šak-kam-ma (6) ul ú-mas si (7) ša ^{m} Za-kir.

[Rm. 201.]

No. 181A. *Obv.* (1) Ana Šamšu ippuḫa-ma ša-ru-ru . . . . (2) ^{işu} kakku . . . . (3) Ana Šamšu ippuḫa-ma šumíli-šu . . . . (4) ul . . . . (*Remainder of obv. and top of rev. broken off.*) *Rev.* (1) Ana šarri šulmu(mu) ana . . . . (2) atal ÍŠ . BAR ša . . . . (3) ina ^{işu} li'i . . . . . (4) ša $^{m\ ilu}$ Nírgal-[íṭir]. [K. 1309.]

No. 181B. *Obv.* (1) . . zal-lum-mu . . . . (2) . . ^{*ilu} *A-*nim . . . . (3) nišî ^{pl} . . . . (4) marṣuti ^{pl} (5) alu itti ali . . . . (6) aḫu aḫi . . . . *Rev.* (1) šar Ílama(ma) . . . . (2) ûmí ^{pl}-šu kir . . . . (3) Ana Šamšu ina ni-du ippuḫa(ḫa) šarru . . . . (4) ^{işu} kakki inašši(ši) . . . . (5) $^{[mul]}$ SAG . MÍ . GAR ^{arḫu} UD . . . . (6) . . . . í ik tu . . . . (7) [šar] mâtâti lu-da-[ri] . . . . (*Possibly the name of the writer.*) [K. 1316.]

No. 182. *Obv.* (1) Ana ni-du ina ḫarran Šamši nadû ^{pl} ilâni ^{pl} milik mâti (2) Ana ^{sal} damiḳti imalliku ^{pl} (3) Ana IV ni-du nadû ^{pl} (4) šaḫluḳti alpi ^{pl} u ú-ma-am (5) Ana ina nipiḫ Šamši ni-du a-ṣi

[1] a-dir, *glossed* . . . di (?)-ir. [2] ḪUŠ-ma, *glossed* í-zi-iz-ma.
[3] TIL (?) MIŠ-šu, *glossed* ín-tu-ti-šu. [4] GUR-ma, *glossed* ú-*tar-a-ma.
[5] NU GÁZ-ak, *glossed* la i-da-ak. [6] . . ú, *glossed* . . šú-u.
[7] DUK-ši, *glossed* i-ra-aš-ši.

(6) zunnu u mílu illaku ^{pl} *Rev.* (1) Ana Šamšu íppuḫ ina ḫarrâni-šu ni-du nadû ^{pl} (2) šurinni mâti inadu ^{pl} (3) ša ^{m} Iraššì(ši)-ilu (4) ardu ša šarri maḫ-ru-u. [K. 119.]

No. 183. *Obv.* (1) Ana kakkabu zal-lum-mu-ú ^{pl} ina šú-uṭ ^{ilu} A (?)-nu (?) innamir (2) šumḳutim(tim) Ílama(ma) ^{ki} ina ^{iṣu} kakki ibašši(ši) (3) Ana ^{ilu} Šamšu ina ni-di ippuḫa(ha) šarru iz-ziz-ma ^{iṣu} kakka (4) inašši(ši) : (*ideograph*) = šar-ri (5) ^{mul} SAG . MÍ . GAR ana muḫ-ḫi a-dan-ni-šu arḫi izzaz-ma (6) Ana ^{mul} SAG . MÍ . GAR ana írib Šamsi ítiḳ(iḳ) *mâtu [šubti] (7) ni-iḫ-ti uššab(ab) (8) ^{mul} SAG . MÍ . GAR ana muḫ-ḫi a-dan-ni-šu arḫi izzaz-ma *Rev.* (1) Ana ^{arḫu} Araḫšamma arḫu ša šarri bí-ili-ia šú-ú (2) Ana ^{ilu} Sin ûmu I ^{kám} innamir sanâḳu ša pî lib-bi mâti iṭâb(ab) (3) Ana ûmu(mu) ana minâti ^{pl}-šu írik pâl ûmu(mu) írik (4) ûmu I ^{kám} ^{ilu} Sin innam-mar-ma (5) am-ti ša šarri bí-ili-ia ana ^{mâtu} Akkadi ^{ki} ul-ṭi (?)-ra-a (6) la aš-ba-ku taḫ-tí-liḳ šarru bí-ili-a . . . . ? (7) li-bu-uk-niš-šum-ma lid-di-nu-nu (8) ša $^{m\ ilu}$ Bíl-li' mâr ^{m} Í-gi-bi ^{am} mašmašu.

[K. 188.]

No. 183A. *Obv.* (*Top wanting.*) (1) Ana ^{ilu} Šamšu ippuḫa-ma a-na . . . . (2) šar kiš-ša-tú (3) pa-lu-ú . . . . (4) ina ^{arḫu} Nisanni ina riš [šatti] (5) ^{ilu} šamšu a-ra-ak [ûmí] (6) šá šarri bíl-ia iḳ-di-bi . .

[Rm. 209.]

No. 183B. *Obv.* (1) Ana ina ^{arḫu} Addâri Šamšu ina ḳabal ^{ilu} BIL (2) izziz(iz) mâtu ú-ṣur-tum (3) ma-na-ah-tum immar(mar) (4) ínuma(ma) ÍN . TÍ . NA ÍN . TÍ . NA (5) dan-nu ibašši(ši)-ma *Rev.* (1) ša ^{m} Za-kir. [83–1–18, 196.]

X. Omens from Stars.

No. 184. *Obv.* (1) Ana $^{mul\ ilu}$ Marduk ina riš šatti innamir(ir) (2) šattu šiâtu šašurri-šu iššir (3) ^{mul} LU . BAD . GUD . UD ina ^{arḫu} Nisanni innammar-ma (4) Ana ^{mul} Bi-ib-bu ana $^{mul\ iṣu}$ Li-í iṭḫi (5) šar Ílama(ma) ^{ki} imât (6) Ana ^{mul} šanumma(ma) ana ^{mul} ÍN . MÍ . SAR . RA iṭḫi (7) nišî ^{pl} irappašu ^{pl} lib mâti iṭâb(ab) *Rev.* (1) ^{mul} LU . BAD . GUD . UD ina lib-bi ^{mul} GUD . AN . NA (2)

[it]-tan-mar a-di mul ŠÚ . GI (3) [ú ?]-ri-du (4) Ana . . . . arḫu in-na-mar (5) [zunni] pl u míli pl (6) ša m . . . . [K. 759.]

No. 185. *Obv.* (1) [Ana mul SAG . MÍ . GAR ina] ší-ir-ti ik-tu-un (2) [šarrâni pl] nakrûti pl išallimu pl (3) . . . . arḫu Simâni ú-ḳar-rib-ma (4) [A-šar] ilu Šamšu ul-ta-pa-a izziz(iz) (5) [ina ba-]'-il zi-mu-šu adir (6) [ni]-pi-iḫ-šu ki-ma ni-pi-iḫ ilu Šamši ga-mir (7) ilâni pl zi-nu-ti itti mâtu Akkadi ki išallimu pl (8) zunni daḫ-du-ti míli si-id-ru-ti (9) ina mâtu Akkadi ki ibaššu pl (10) ší'u u šamaššammu i-ma-id-ma (11) maḫiru I ḲA a-an a-na I GUR innadin(in) (12) [ilâni] pl ina šamí(í) ana man-zal-ti-šu-nu izzazu pl (13) [parakki] pl-šu-nu duḫ-du immaru pl *Rev.* (1) [Ana ilu] *GAM šarura na-ši (2) išid kussi ikân(an) (3) Ana mul Šarru šarura na-ši (4) šar Akkadi ki ga-mí-ru-tam ípuš(uš) (5) Ana mul SAG . MÍ . GAR ina ḫarran šu-uṭ ilu A-nu innamir (6) mílu ibašši-ma íbûr mâti iššir (7) [ša] m Ba-ma-a-a. [K. 871.]

No. 186. (1) [Ana mul SAG .] MÍ . GAR ina ší-ir-ti ik-tu-[un] (2) [šarrâni pl] nakrûti pl išallimu pl (3) [Ana mul SAG . MÍ .] GAR ša-ru-ru na-ši šarru ša-[lim] (4) [lib mâti] iṭâb mâtu nuḫša immar(mar) (5) [Ana mul] SAG . MÍ . GAR ba-'-il šar Akkadi ki (6) [a]-ša-ri-du-tam il-[lak] (7) [Ana mul] ÍN . GIŠGAL . AN . NA i-ba-'-il (8) míli pl u zunni pl [ibaššû] (9) mul ÍN . GIŠGAL . AN . NA : mul SAG . MÍ . [GAR .] *Rev.* (1) Ana mul SAG . MÍ . GAR ina arḫu Aîri innamir mâtu sa . . . . (2) [Ana] mul ni-bi-ru ippuḫa(ḫa)-ma ilâni pl šulma(ma) [iraššu ?] (3) í-ša-a-tum inammiru pl dal-ḫa-a-tum i-zak-[ka-a] (4) zunni pl ù míli pl illaku pl-ni (5) di-iš íbûri ana ÍN . TÍ . NA di-iš ÍN . TÍ . NA (6) [ana íbûri] uš-ta-bar-ru mâtâti šub-ti . . (7) [niḫ]-tum uššabu pl šarrâni pl nakrûti pl išallimu [pl] (8) [ilâni pl] ikribi i-maḫ-ḫa-[ru] (9) [taš-li]-tum i-šim-mu-ú tí-rit am [ḪAL] (10) [i]-nap-pa-lu (11) [ša m ilu] Nírgal-íṭir(ir). [82-5-22, 57.]

No. 187. *Obv.* (1) [Ana mul] SAG . MÍ . GAR a-na írib Šamši i-ti-iḳ (2) [šubti] ni-iḫ-ti šu-lum sal damiḳti ana mâti ur-ra-da (3) i-na pa (?)-an mul AL . LUL in-nam-mar-ma (4) Ana mul SAG . MÍ . GAR ina ḫarran-šú-uṭ ilu Bíli (5) šarura naši-ma ilu Ni-bi-ru . . lib (?) . . . . (6) mâtu Akkada ki ina-ḫi-iš šar Akkadi ki i-dan-[nin] (7) Ana mul ni-bi-ru ippuḫa-ma ilâni pl šulma(ma) iraššì pl (8) [i ?]-šir-tu ibašši(ši) í-ša-a-ti i-nam-mi-ra (9) dal-ḫa-a-ti i-zak-ka-a zunnu u mílu (10) [illaku] ^{pl}-ni di-iš íbûri a-na ÍN. TÍ. NA *Rev.* (1) *di-iš ÍN. TÍ. NA a-na íbûri uš-ta-har-ri (2) mâtâti šubti ni-iḫ-ti uššabu ^{pl} ilâni ^{pl} iḳribi (3) maḫ-ru taš-li-ti ší-mu-ú tírit $^{pl\ am}$ HAL (4) i-ta-nap-pal (5) Ana kakkabu Rabû ša ki-ma išati ša ultu ṣit Šamší iṣrur-ma (6) ina írib Šamši irbi(bi) ummâni(ni) $^{[am]}$ nakri ina taḫaṣi (7) : (?) ummâni(ni) $^{[am]}$ nakri ina miḳti-ša šumḳut(ut) (8) ri-íš šarru-ti-ka ^{mul} SAG. MÍ. GAR ina man-za-zi-šu (9) ki-i-ni it-tan-mar bíl ilâni ^{pl} lib-ba-ka (10) lu-ṭi-ib-ka ûmí(mí)-ka lu-ur-rik(?) (11) ša ^{m} A-ša-ri-du mâr ^{m} Dam-[ḳa]. [K. 806.]

No. 187A. *Obv.* (1) . . . SAG. MÍ. GAR ina ^{arhu} Aîri * innamir (2) . . . . *ḫia . . . . ilammi (?) (3) . . . SAG. MÍ. GAR ina . . . . innamir (4) . . . DU-ma *ibûr mâti iššir (5) . . . SAG. MÍ. GAR ina tamarti-šu DIR (6) . . . ina ^{mâtu} Akkadi ^{ki} ibašši(ši) (7) . . . Marduk *MUL. MUL ikšud(ud) (8) . . . SI-šu ibašši(ši) *Rev.* (1) [ša ^{m} A]-ša-ri-du maḫrû(ú) (2) [ardu] ša šarri.

[K. 1394.]

No. 188. *Obv.* (1) [Ana ^{mul}] SAG. MÍ. GAR ina ^{arhu} Du'ûzi . . (2) šú-ub-tum ni-iḫ-[tum] . . . . (3) . . ^{mul} SAG. MÍ. GAR ina ḫarran [šut Bíli ?] (4) šar Akkadi ^{ki} i-dan-nin-ma (5) Ana ^{mul} SAG. MÍ. GAR ana arki . . . (6) ina ^{mâtu} Í lama(ma) $^{ki\ ilu}$ . . . . (7) i-na-an-ḍu-ma ^{ilu} Nírgal . . . (8) ^{mul} SAG. MÍ. GAR . . . (9) ú-ma-a a-du-u . . . . (10) a-mu-ru-u-ni a-na šarri bíl-*a *Rev.* (1) . . . as-sa-ap-ra (2) i-da-a-ti ki-ma . . it-ta-an-ta-ḫa (3) a-na ^{mul} AL. LUL iḳ-di-ri-ib (4) ú-il-tú ša-ni-tú a-na-as-sa-ḫa (5) a-na šarri bíl-ia ú-ša-kan-ma.

[K. 870.]

No. 189. *Obv.* (1) Ana ^{mul} SAG. MÍ. GAR ina ^{arhu} Ululi innamir(ir) (2) mâtu Akala ṭâba ikkal (3) Ana ^{mul} UR. MAḪ kakkabâni ^{pl}-šu (4) . . . . šu-tap-pu-ú (5) . . . du-ku ša ṣis-su (6) . . . SAG. MÍ. GAR (7) . . . UR. GU. LA *Rev.* (1) . . . .ma (2) [ša $^{m\ ilu}$] Nabû-ikiša(ša) mâr Bar-sib ^{ki}. [81-2-4, 107.]

No. 190. *Obv.* (1) Ana ^{mul} SAG. MÍ. GAR ina ^{arhu} Araḫšamna innamir (2) šarru ana šarri zi-ra-a-ti išappar (3) Ana ^{mul} SAG. MÍ. GAR ina mi-šiḫ ^{ilu} PA. BIL. SAG izziz (4) šag-ga-ša-a-ti ina mâti ibašši(ši) (5) ana ^{mul} II ana ^{mul} IN . DUB . AN . NA iṭḫi (6) maḫiru irabbi *Rev.* (1) ^{mul} IN . DUB . AN . NA (2) mi-šiḫ ^{ilu} PA . BIL . SAG (3) ša $^{m\ ilu}$ Nabû-šuma-iškun(un). [83–1–18, 200.]

No. 190A. *Obv.* (1) [Ana ina ^{arḫu} Araḫšamna] ^{mul} SAG . MÍ . GAR innamir(ir) (2) [šarru ana] šarri zi-ra-a-ti išappar(ár) (3) [Ana ^{mul} SAG . MÍ . GAR] ina mi-ši-iḫ (4) [^{mul} PA .] BIL . SAG innamir(ir) (5) . . . lu-u (?)-ti ibaššu ^{pl} *Rev.* (1) [ša ^{m}] Aplâ-a mâr Bar-sib ^{ki}. [K. 987.]

No. 191. *Obv.* (1) Ana ^{mul} SAG . MÍ . GAR ina ^{arḫu} . . . . (2) mâtu | [1]míli-ṣa | . . . (3) Ana ^{mul} SAG . MÍ . GAR ina ḫarran šú-uṭ [Bíl ?] (4) šar Akkadi ^{ki} i-dan-ni-[in] (5) ina mâtâti | na-ki-ri-šu | ina ^{isu} kakki . . . (6) Ana ^{mul} UR . MAḪ kakkabâni ^{pl}-šu . . . . (7) [2]III XX (?) . . . . . (8) [3]^{mul} . . . *Rev.* (1) . . . . (2) Ana ^{mul} . . . . (3) šar Akkadi ^{ki} . . . . (4) ^{mul} SAG MÍ GAR . . . . (5) . . . . [K. 867.]

No. 191A. *Obv.* (1) [Ana] ^{mul} SAG . MÍ . [GAR] ina ḫarran šú-[uṭ Bíli ?] (2) šarru (*sic*) i-dan-nin-ma (3) Ana ^{mul} SAG . MÍ . GAR ina tamarti . . . (4) nuḫšu bar-ru-ú ina mâti . . . . (5) ina tamarti-šu ^{šâru} iltanu *Rev.* (1) Ana ^{mul} SAG . MÍ . GAR . . . . (2) šarru a-ša-ri-du-[tam illak] (*Remainder broken off.*) [K. 1317.]

No. 192. *Obv.* (1) Ana ^{mul} SAG . MÍ . GAR ina lib Sin izziz(iz) (2) ina šatti šiâti šarru imât : atal Sin u Šamši išakan(an) (3) šarru rabû imât (4) Ana ^{mul} SAG . MÍ . GAR ina lib ^{ilu} Sin írub (5) su-un-ḳu ina ^{mâtu} Aḫarrí ^{ki} ibašši(ši) (6) šar Ílama(ma) ^{ki} ina ^{isu} kakki šumḳut(ut) (7) ina ^{mâtu} Subarti ^{ki} bí-ín-šu íbaru *Rev.* (1) Ana ^{mul} SAG . MÍ . GAR ana lib Sin írub(ub) (2) maḫir mâti iṣaḫir(ir) (3) Ana ^{mul} SAG . MÍ . GAR ana ku-tal Sin uṣi (4) nu-kúr-ti ina mâti ibašši(ši). [Bu. 89–4–26, 3.]

No. 193. *Obv.* (1) Ana ^{mul} SAG . MÍ . GAR a-na libbi ^{ilu} Sin írub . . . (2) su-un-ḳu ina ^{mâtu} Aḫarrû ibašši(ši) (3) šar Ílama(ma) ^{ki}

[1] A . ŠI . ŠI . -ṣa, *glossed* mí-li-ṣa. [2] *Glossed* iš . ša . na (?) . . .
[3] MUL, *glossed* ka-[ka-bu].

imât : bí-ín-šu i-ba-ru (4) [Ana] ilu Sin mul UMUN. PA. UD. DU. A i-kil (5) šarru šarrâni pl nakrûti pl ḳat-su ikašad(ád) (6) ûmu XIV kám ilu Sin u ilu Šamšu itti a-ḫa-miš innamru pl (7) sanâḳu ša pî lib-bi mâti iṭâb(ab) (8) ilâni pl mâtu Akkadi ki a-na da-mí-[iḳ-ti] (9) i-ḫa-sa-su *Rev.* (1) bu-lum mâtu Akkadi ki par ga-niš ina ṣíri (2) i-rab-bi-ṣu di-iš íbûri ana ÍN. TÍ. [NA] (3) [di]-iš ÍN. TÍ. NA Ana íbûri uš-ta-bar-[ri] (4) [ḫud] lib-bi ummâni(ni) lib-bi šarri iṭâb(ab) (5) [Ana] Sin u Šamšu šú-ta-tu-ú šar mâti [uzna] (6) ú-rap-pa-aš išid isu kussi-šu [ikân] (7) Ana Sin Šamšu ik-šú-dam-ma itti-šu [ittintu] (8) ḳarnu ḳarnu i-dir kit-ti [ina mâti itamû] (9) mâru itti abî-šu kit-ti i-[ta-mu] (10) ša m Ṭa-bi-ia. [83-1-18, 179.]

No. 194. *Obv.* (1) Ana mul SAG. MÍ. GAR a-na imitti mul Dil-bat (2) i-ti-iḳ mâtu Gu-ti-i (3) ina isu kakku dan-nu ikkasad(ád) (4) Ana mul SAG. MÍ. GAR a-na imitti mul Dil-bat (5) ú da an.... izziz(iz) (6) a-na šatti III kám .... ma.. (*Remainder of obv. and top of rev. broken off.*) *Rev.* (1) ša m Ṭabu-ṣil-[Marduk] (2) mâr m ilu Bíl-upaḫḫir(ir). [K. 1332.]

No. 194A. *Obv.* (1) Ana mul SAG. MÍ. GAR ina imitti [mul Dil-bat i-tiḳ] (2) mâtu Gu-ti-i ina isu kakku [dannu ikkašad] (3) Ana mul Dil-bat ilu UMUN. PA. UD. DU.... (4) i-sid-di :.... (5) bi-ib-lum ub-bal... (6) gab-šu.... [83-1-18, 218.]

No. 195. *Obv.* (1) Ana mul SAG. MÍ. GAR ana pân mul Muš-tabarrû-mûtânu(a-nu) izziz(iz) (2) ší-im iraššî(ši)-ú-ma amílu šumḳut (ut)... ummânu rabû šumḳut(ut) (3) Ana mul SAG. MÍ. GAR u mul Sa-ar-ri... (4) ilu ikkal... zunni pl íli mâti uš-ta-ad-da-nu (5) uš-ta-ad-da-nu šú-ta-du-nu mit-lu-uk (6) Ana mul Muštabarrû-mûtâ-nu(a-nu) Ana mul SAG. MÍ. GAR iṭḫi (7) mi-iḳ-ti dan-nu ina mâti ibašši(ši) (8) Ana mul SAG. MÍ. GAR u mul LU. BAD (9) kakka-bâni pl -šu-nu mit-ḫa-ru (10) limuttim(tim) mâtam(am) išakan(an) *Rev.* (1) Ana mul LU. BAD. DIR u mul Rabû itḫu pl (2) Šumḳutim (tim) bu-lum mul LU. BAD. DIR ilu Muštabarrû-mûtânu(a-nu) (3) mul Rabû mul UMUN. PA. UD. DU. A (4) ilu Muštabarrû-mûtânu(a-nu) ana ilu UMUN. PA. UD. DU iṭaḫḫima (5) Ana mul SAG. MÍ. GAR mul Šanamma(ma) iṭḫi-šu (6) ina šatti šiâti šar Akkadi ki imât-ma îbûr mâti la iššir (7) itti an-ni-ti limutti ša mâtâti pl Ši-i (8) NAM . BUL . BI Šarrù bî-ili li-pu-uš-ma (9) limutti-šu lu-ú-ší-ti-iḳ (10) ša m ilu Nabû-ikiša(ša) mâr Bar-sib ki

[82-5-22, 48.]

No. 195A. *Obv.* (1) [Ana] mul SAG . MÍ . GAR ina AN . UD . . . (2) šattu ina šamí(í) izzaz . . . (3) [mad]-da-giš ûmu(mu) a-ga-a . . (4) . . an-na šu ul . . . (5) ín-na a-di ûmi X kám ša arḫu Kisilimi . . (6) . . ra-a-ti iṣ . . (7) . . ûm ilu ÍN . LIL . . . . . (8) mul Dil-bat lu id (?) a . . *Rev.* (1) . . Dil-bat KUR . . . . . (2) . . pl ? . . . . . (3) mul Dil-bat KUR . . za . . . . (4) lib mâti . . . . (5) mul SAG . MÍ . GAR * ù . . . (6) pl-šu-nu a-na la-ḫa-[miš] . . . (7) ša m ilu Nírgal-íṭir[ir] [K. 907.]

No. 196. *Obv.* (1) Ana mul SAG . [MÍ . GAR] . . . . . ú-ḳar-rib-ma (2) a-šar ilu [Šamšu ul-ta-pa]-a izziz(iz) (3) ba-'-[il zi-mu-šua]-dir (4) nipiḫ-šu ki-[ma nipiḫ ilu Šamši] ga-mir (5) ilâni pl [zinûti itti] mâtu Akkadi ki išallimu pl (6) zunni dah-[du-ti itti] si-id-ru-ti (7) ina mâtu Akkadi ki [ibašši] ší'u u Šamaššammu i-ma-id-ma (8) maḫiru I ḲA ta-a-an a-na I GUR innadin(in) (9) ilâni pl ina šamí(í) ina man-zal-ti-šu-nu izzazu pl (10) parakki pl-šu-nu duḫ-da immaru pl (11) Ana mul SAG . MÍ . GAR ina ší-ir-ti ik-tu-un (12) šarrâni pl nakrûti pl išallimu pl (13) Ana mul SAG . MÍ . GAR šarura naši . . . *Rev.* (1) šarru ša-lim lib-bi mâti iṭâb . . (2) Ana mul SAG . MÍ . GAR ba-'-il (3) šarru . . . tam illak(ak) (4) Ana ilu GAM [šarura naši]išid kussi ikan(an) (5) Ana ilu SAG . MÍ . GAR ina ḫarran šu-uṭ ilu A-nim innamir (6) mílu ibašši-ma íbûr mâti iššir (7) šá m Bu-ul-lu-ṭu [K. 742.]

No. 196A. *Obv.* (*Top wanting.*) (1) . . . . . . (2) . . . . ma íbûr mâti iššir (3) . . . . . [arḫu] Tašrîti innamir(ir) (4) . . . . . . mu iraššu pl (5) [Ana mul SAG . MÍ . GAR ina ší]-ir-ti ik-tu-un (6) . . . DI-mu (7) . . . . mar-ma *Rev.* (1) . . . . . ZI ÍL . LA-ma

[83-1-18, 786.]

No. 197. *Obv.* (1) Ana mul Šarru ana pân Sin itḫi-ma izziz (2) šarru ûmí pl ma-du-ti ibaluṭ(uṭ) (3) mâtu la iššir (4) ša m Apla-a

[K. 723.]

No. 198. *Obv.* (1) [Ana ^{mul}] Šarru ša-ru-ri na-ši (2) [šarru] ga-mí-ru-tam ípuš(uš) (3) . . . . ma it (?)-ti ^{mul} Šarri (4) [iz]-za-az-ma *Rev.* (1) [ša ^{m}] Ištar-šuma-íriš(íš). [K. 3504.]

No. 199. *Obv.* (1) Ittu ša a-na šarri lim-ni-ti a-na mâti dam-ḳi (?) (2) ittu ša a-na mâti dam-ḳa-ti a-na šarri lim-[ni] (3) ina mi-ni-i lu-mur šarru i-ḳab-bi-ma (4) Ana ^{mul} šarru ana pân Sin itḫi-ma izziz ûmí ^{pl} rubi ilabbaru ^{pl} (5) a mat ti ší la (?) ina mâti bilat mâti idamiḳ (6) Ana ^{mul} Šarru ana íli Sin [itḫi-ma] izziz šârru ûmí ^{pl} ma-'-du-tú ibaluṭ(uṭ) (7) . . . limutti (8) . . . . na-du (?) (*Remainder broken.*) *Rev.* (1) ša $^{m\ ilu}$ Nírgal-íṭir[ir].

[K. 4708 + 10298.]

No. 199A. *Obv.* (1) Ana ^{mul} Šarru ṣalmu *mu'ir (KINGAL?) íkalli imât (2) ^{mul} LU . BAD . GUD . UD it-ti ^{mul} šarri izzaz (3) Ana ^{mul} [*erasure*] ḫi-bi . . . (4) ^{mul} [*erasure*] ^{mul} UR . GU . LA izzaz . . . (5) Ana ^{mul} LU . BAD ana ^{mul} Šarru itḫi mâru . . . . (6) ša i-na ali zag . . . . (7) ana abî-šu ḪI . GAR (?) ípuš(uš) *Rev.* (1) mâr (?) šarri ma (?) na . . . . (2) ^{işu} GU . ZA . . . . . (3) ana aš-ri . . u . . . . ka . . . . (4) ú-ka-nu íšrîti ^{pl} ana šarri i-za . . . . (5) ša $^{m\ ilu}$ Nírgal-íṭir(ir). [81–2–4, 136.]

No. 200. *Obv.* (1) Ana kakkabu iṣrur-ma ṣi-ri-ir-šu kima urri na-mir (2) ina ṣa-ra-ri-šu kima nam-maš-ti aḳrabi zibbata šakin (in) (3) ittu ši-i damiḳti ul ša bíl bîti-ma šá mâti ka-la-ša (4) ínuma (ma) bí-ín-nu ina mâti kalâmi ibašši(ši) (5) rag-gu iḫaliḳ kit-tu ibašši(ši) dan-nu i-šar-ri (6) míšrû tap-du bíl bîti šuâtu . . . šarru šuâtu (7) ina kit-ti-šu izzaz(az) taš-mu u šulmu(mu) ina mâti ibašši(ši) (8) an-ni-u šá iš . . . . (9) Ana ^{mul} Rabû ul-tu ti-ib [^{šâru} iltani] (10) a-na ti-ib ^{šâru} Šûti [iṣrur-ma] (11) mi-ši-iḫ-šu kima nam-maš-[ti aḳrabi zibbata šakin?] *Rev.* (1) ša-ḳi-ta ri tu . . . . (2) li-in-ni-di . . . . (3) ^{ilu} IN . LIL ma li . . . . (4) an-ni-u ša pi-i duppi . . . . (5) ki-i $^{m\ ilu}$ Nabû-kudur-uṣur ^{mâtu} Ílama(ma) ^{ki} iḫ-pu-u-ni (6) Ana ^{mul} LU . BAD ina ^{arḫu} Du'ûzi innamir pagrâni ^{pl} ibaššu ^{pl} (7) Ana ^{mul} ÍN . TÍ . NA . MAŠ . ŠIG ina ṣîti-šu mul-lu-uḫ (8) išir íbûri maḫiru ikân (9) an-nu-ti šá ^{ilu} GUD . UD (10) šá $^{m\ ilu}$ Nabû-mu-ší-ṣi. [K. 710.]

No. 201. *Obv.* (1) I kaš-bu muši it-ta-lak (2) ^{mul} Rabû ultu ^{šáru} iltani (3) a-na ^{šáru} šûti (4) iṣ-ṣa-ru-ur (5) i-da-ti-ša a-na (6) ṣi-bu-ti ša šarri (7) ṭa-ba-ti *Rev.* (1) šar Akkadi ^{ki} ši-pìr-šu (2) i-kaš-šad (3) ša ^{m} A-ša-ri-du maḫrû(ú) (4) ardu ša šarri.

[81–2–4, 105.]

No. 201A. *Obv.* (1) [Ana ^{mul}] Rabû ultu ṣît Šamši (2) a-na írib Šamši iṣrur-ma (3) mi-šiḫ-šu ú-mar-ri-ma (4) iškun(un) ummâni nakri ina miḳti-šu (5) šumḳut(ut) *Rev.* (1) [ša $^{m\ ilu}$] Nabû-ḳi-bi.

[K. 933.]

No. 202. *Obv.* (1) [Ana] ^{mul} Rabû ultu ṣît Šamši (2) ana írib Šamši iṣrur-ma irbi (*bi) (3) u mi-šiḫ-šu ú-mar-ri-ma iškun (4) ummâni(ni) nakri ina taḫaṣi šumḳut(ut) (5) Ana kakkabu ša kima nûri (6) : kima dipari (7) ultu ṣît Šamši ana írib Šamši (8) iṣrur-ma irbi(bi) ummân ^{am} nakri (9) ina miḳti-šu šumḳut(ut) *Rev.* (1) II kakkabâni rabûti ^{pl} (2) ina maṣṣarti ḳabliti (3) arki a-ḫa-miš (4) iṣ-ṣar-ru (5) ša ^{m} A-ša-ri-du (6) maḫrû(ú). [83–1–18, 174.]

No. 203. *Obv.* (1) Ana ^{mul} Dil-bat ina ^{arḫu} Nisanni ultu ûmi I ^{kám} (2) adi ûmi XXX ^{kám} ina ṣît Šamši it-bal (3) ú-ru-ba-ti ibaššu ^{pl} (4) Ana Sin tarbaṣu ilmi-ma ^{mul} SIB . ZI . AN . NA (5) ina libbi-šu izziz šar Subarti ^{ki} (6) kiš-šú-ti ipuš(uš) mât-su ina-ḫi-iš *Rev.* (1) $^{[mul]}$ SIB . [ZI . AN . NA ina tarbaṣ] Sin izzaz-ma (2) ^{ilu} . . . . šu (3) ša ^{m} Aḫî ^{pl}-[ša-a ^{am}] Uruk ^{ki}-a-a.

[K. 13087 + 82–5–22, 85.]

No. 204. *Obv.* (1) Ana ^{mul} Dil-bat ina ^{arḫu} Nisanni ultu ûmi I ^{kám} (2) adi ûmi XXX ^{kám} ina ṣît Šamši it-bal (3) ú-ru-ba-a-ti ina mâti ibaššu ^{pl}-A (4) Ana ^{mul} Dil-bat . . . ṣa ut-ta-nak-kar (5) . . . ut-ta kir (?) . . gir-rit ^{am} nakri (6) ṣar-ra-a-ti . . . ḳaš-ra-a-ti (7) . . . . ú ma (?) . . . . (8) . . . . ili-šu ú (?) da (?) . . . . *Rev.* (1) [Ana ^{ilu} Dil-bat] ad-riš uš-tak-ti-ma *ir-*bi (2) šumḳutim(tim) Ílama(ma) ^{ki} ibašši(ši) (3) ša ^{ilu} Nabû-aḫî ^{pl}-[íriba]. [K. 782.]

No. 205. *Obv.* (1) ^{mul} Dil-bat ina ṣît Šamši ir-ti-bi (2) Ana ^{mul} Dil-bat mušḫa irši(ši) la damiḳti (3) šá ûmí ^{pl} ša la ú-šal-li-mu-ma (4) ir-bu-ú (5) Ana ^{mul} Dil-bat ina ^{arḫu} Nisanni (6) ultu ûmi I ^{kám} adi ûmi XXX kám (7) ina ṣît Šamši it-bal (8) ú-ru-ba-a-ti (9) ina mâti ibaššu pl *Rev.* (1) ú-ru-ba-a-ti bi-ka-a-ti (2) limutti šá mâtu Ílama(ma) ki šú-ú (3) šá m ilu [Nabû]-mu-ší-ṣi. [K. 725.]

No. 205A. *Obv.* (1) [Ana] ilu . . . arḫu Nisanni ir-[bi] (2) íbûr mâti ibašši(ši) : . . . . (3) Ana mul A . ÍDIN MUL . MUL ikšud(ud) ilu [Rammânu iraḫiṣ] (4) mul Dil-bat ina lib MUL . MUL [izzaz] (5) [Ana] mul Dil-bat ina ÍN . TÍ . NA . . . . (6) ina íbûri . . . . šu . . . . (*Remains of two lines; remainder of obv. and top of rev. broken.*) *Rev.* (1) . . . . ud ad ni . . . . (2) . . . . í-du ša šarri bíl-ia . . . . (3) . . . . na-tu-ú-a ši (?) . . . . (4) . . . . ana lib a-di-í ki-i í-ru-bu (5) . . . [ṭa ?]-a-bi-ma a-na šarri bíl-ia ul aš-pu-ra (6) . . . . a mâr m ilu Bíl-ú-šal-lim. [K. 1343.]

No. 206. *Obv.* (1) Ana ilu Dil-bat ina írib Šamšu ir-[bi] (2) Ana mul Dil-bat ina [arḫu . . . .] (3) ultu ûmi I kám adi ûmi XXX kám (4) ina írib Šamši it-bal íbûr mâti iššir (5) Ana mul Dil-bat manzaz-za ú-ki-in (6) ûmí pl rubi arkûti pl (7) kit-tum ina mâti ibašši(ši) (8) [Ana] mul Dil-bat ina ḫarran šu-uṭ ilu Í-a (9) . . . . di-ma . . . . (10) . . . . a-na mâtu Aharrî [ki] *Rev.* (1) sa-li-mu iraššî . . . (2) Ana Sin tarbaṣu ilmi-ma MUL . MUL ina libbi-šu izzizu pl (3) ina šatti šiâti sinnišâti pl zakkari pl ullada [pl] (4) Ana II-ma mul ŠÚ . GI ina libbi-šu [izziz] (5) ina šatti šiâti šumḳutim(tim) a-mí-lu-[ti . .] (6) a-na utullâi (?) ṣíni la iṭaḫḫu (7) šá m Ištar-šuma-íriš(iš). [K. 731.]

No. 206A. *Obv.* (1) [Ana] ilu Dil-bat ina arḫu . . . . [ultu ûmi I kám] (2) adi ûmi XXX kám [ina ilu Šamaš-ŠU .]A. (3) it-bal zunni . . . . pl (4) íbûr mâti iššir *Rev.* (1) [šá] m ilu Nabû-mu-ší-ṣi. [K. 1318.]

No. 207. *Obv.* (1) ilu Dil-bat ina írib Šamši ina ḫarran šú-uṭ ilu ÍN . LIL innammar(mar) (2) an-ni-ú pi-ší-ir-šú (3) Ana ilu Dil-bat ina arḫu Simâni innamir(ir) šumḳutim(tim) am nakri (4) Ana ilu Dil-bat ina ḫarran šú-uṭ ilu Bíl innamir(ir) (5) šar Akkadi ki maḫira la iraššî(ši) (6) a-du ûmí pl V VI mul AL . LUL i-kaš-ša-ad (7) an-ni-ú pi-ši-ir-šú *Rev.* (1) [Ana] mul UZA a-na mul AL . LUL itḫi(ḫi) (2) taš-mu-ú u sa-li-mu ina mâti ibašši(ši) (3) ilâni pl ana mâti rîmu iraššu pl iš-šik-ki ri-ḳu-tí (4) i-ma-al-lu u íbûr mâti iššir marṣûti balṭûti (5) ina mâti ibaššu pl sal írâti pl lib-lib-ši-na ú-šak-la-la (6) ilâni pl rabûti pl aš-rat mâti uš-ša-ru bîti pl ilâni pl rabûti pl (7) ú-ta-ad-da-ša : mul UZA ilu Dil-bat (8) šá m Šú-ma-a-a. [K. 121.]

No. 207A. *Obv.* (*Top broken*) (1) Ana ilu Dil-bat ina arḫu Simâni .... (2) Ana ilu Dil-bat ina ÍN . TÍ . [NA] .... (3) ina íbûri ina .... (4) šarrani pl nakrûti pl .... (5) íbûr mâti iššir (6) GAR . ḪI . A DUG . GA [ikkal] *Rev.* (1) taš-mu-ú u salimu(mu) ka-liš išakan(an) (2) ... ina ḫarran šú-[ut] .... innamir(ir) (3) ... tu (?) .... (4) ... ak .... (5) ... ina (?) .... (*Remainder broken off.*) [K. 964.]

No. 207B. *Obv.* (1) [ilu Dil-bat ina] arḫu Simâni innamir(ir) šumḳutim(tim) am nakri (2) [Ana ilu Dil-bat ina ÍN . TÍ . NA ?] ina ṣît Šamši (3) [innamir ?] ..... pa šarrani pl nakrûti pl (4) .... [GAR . ḪI .] A DUG . GA ikkal (5) [tašmû u salimu ka]-liš iššakkan(an) (6) .... innamir(ir) (7) .... ur-rak (8) .... taš-mu-ú *Rev.* (1) .... ši (2) .... pl (3) .... pl íbûr mâti iššir (4) .... ina mâti ibaššu pl ilâni pl rabûti pl (5) ... [uš]-ša-ru bîti pl ilâni pl rabûti pl (6) [utaddaša] mul Dil-bat ana mul AL . LUL iṭaḫḫi-ma (7) .... it-ta-na-an-bi-ṭu (8) .... pl sal damḳâti pl ul-tu Í . KÚR . UD . DU-a (9) ... Igigi ug-ga-nu (10) [ša m ilu] Nírgal-íṭir(ir). [K. 1342.]

No. 208. *Obv.* (1) Ana mul Dil-bat ina írib Šamši irtibi (2) Ana mul Dil-bat ina arḫu Abi ad-riš (3) uš-*tak-*ti-it-ma ir-bi (4) šumkutim(tim) Ílama(ma) ki ibašši(ši) (5) Ana mul Dil-bat ina arḫu Abi ultu ûmi I kám (6) adi ûmi XXX kám ina írib Šamši irbi (7) zunni pl ibaššu pl *Rev.* (1) íbûr mâti iššir (2) ina lib arḫi a-ga-a ina ṣît Šamši (3) ina lib mul UR . GU . LA in-nam-mar (4) ša m ilu Nírgal-íṭir(ir). [81–7–27, 23.]

No. 208A. *Obv.* (1) [Ana mul Dil-bat ina arḫu Abi ultu] ûmi I kám adi ûmi XXX kám (2) [ina írib Šamši irbi zunni] ibaššu pl íbûr mâti iššir (3) [Ana mul Dil-bat ina arḫu Abi ?] ad-riš uš-tak-ti-it-ma ir-bi (4) ... šu ina iṣu kakki išakan(an) (5) ... ú-šad-da-ma (6) ... ma (7) ... ki (8) ... kan-ni (9) ... ḫi *Rev.* (1) ... (2) ... ûmí pl (3) ... ši-i ... (4) ... ni i í-pi ... (5) ...

iṭ-ḫi-ma du . . . (6) . . . ti i ša bi ma . . . (7) . . . ú-rap-pa . . . (8) . . . pu-ut . . . (9) [ša ^{m} Ba-la]-si-i [83–1–18, 300.]

No. 209. *Obv.* (1) Ana ^{mul} [1]SAR . UR [u] ^{mul} [2]SAR . GAZ ša zi-ḳit ^{mul} aḳrabi (2) it-ta-na-an-bi-ṭu ^{isu} kakku ^{mâtu} Akkadi ^{ki} tibû(ú) (3) ^{mu} Dil-bat ina lib ^{mul} PA . BIL . SAG in-na-mar-ma (4) Ana ^{ilu} Ištar [3]agû ^{ilu} Sin ap-rat [4]mu-nik-si-sá (5) ú-ru-ba-a-ti ibaššu ^{pl} (6) ú-ru-ba-a-ti bi-ka-a-ti (7) ^{mul} LU . BAD . GUD . UD ina írib Šamšu . . (8) . . . . ina ^{mul} Dil-bat iz-za-az . . . . *Rev.* (1) . . . . . ^{mul} Dil-bat [3]agû [5]ṣalmu ap-[rat] (2) . . . . [6]ulâda . . . . (3) ^{mul} LU . BAD it-ti ^{mul} . . . . (4) lum-nu šá niši ^{pl} ^{mâtu} . . . . (5) Ana ^{mul} Dil-bat ina ^{arḫu} Kisilimi . . . (6) ḫušaḫḫu ší-am u tibni . . . (7) [ša $^{m\,ilu}$ Nabû]-aḫî ^{pl}-íriba . . . . [81–2–4, 86.]

No. 210. *Obv.* (1) Ana ina ^{arḫu} Kisilimi ultu ûmi I ^{kám} adi ûmi XXX ^{kám} (2) ^{ilu} Dil-bat ina ṣît Šamši it-bal (3) ḫušaḫḫu ší-im u tibni ina mâti ibašši(ši) (4) bíl šarrâni ^{pl} i-ḳab-bi um-ma-a (5) mi-nam-ma arḫi ul . . ti (6) ù damiḳti u limutti taš-[pu]-ra (7) rub šar-ru-ti i-na-ṭi-iš *Rev.* (1) ul iš-šim-mi bíl šarrâni ^{pl} (2) ûmu(mu) ša pa-ni-šu maḫ-ru (3) ri-ša-a liš-si-ma lu-up-ru-us-ma (4) a-na šarri bi-ili-ia lu-uḳ-bi (5) ša ^{m} A-ša-ri-du [80–7–19, 58.]

No. 211. *Obv.* (1) [Ana ^{mul} Dil-bat] ina ^{arḫu} Šabâṭi innamir(ir) (2) [íbûr] mâti iššir (3) ana . . . . ? (4) rîmu u šulmu(mu) ina mâti ibašši(ši) (5) ^{mul} Dil-bat ina lib ^{mul} A-nu-ni-tum izzaz-ma (6) Ana ^{mul} Dil-bat ina lib ^{mul} Dil-gan innamir(ir) (7) zunni ^{pl} ina šamí(í) míli ^{pl} ina [irṣiti] *Rev.* (1) íbûr ^{mâtu} Aḫarrî ^{ki} iššir (2) na-mu-ú šumḳutu ^{pl} KU ^{pl}. . . (3) Ana ^{mul} Dil-bat manzaza(za) [ukin] (4) ûmí ^{pl} rubi arkûti $^{[pl]}$ (5) kit-tu ina mâti ibašši(ši) (6) ša ^{m} Apla-a mâr Bar-sib ^{ki}. . . [K. 758.]

No. 211A. *Obv.* (1) . . . UMUN . PA . UD . DU ík-šú-dam-ma (2) . . . iḳ-rib-ma izziz bi-ib-lum mâti ub-bal (3). . . DU ik-šú-dam-ma ib-ši mílu gab-šu illak (4). . . iṭḫi šar Aḫarrî ^{ki} NAM . KÍL . . . (5) . . . KÚR KÚR KUR ana MAN aḫû aḫî inakkar . . .

[1] ŠÁR . UR, *glossed* ša-ar-ur.
[2] SÁR . GAZ, *glossed* ṣar-gaz.
[3] MIR, *glossed* a-gu-u.
[4] mu-nik-si-sá, *glossed* mu-ni-ik-si-sa.
[5] MI, *glossed* ṣa-al-mu.
[6] Ù . TU *glossed* ú-la-a-[da].

(6) . . . di ^mâtu^ Mí-si ultu (?) pân . . . (7) . . . sa-dir zunni u mîli ^pl^ ra-a . . . (8) . . . í-šu (9) . . . šamû izanun(nun) ^ilu^ TIR . AN . NA. . (10) . . . in ru . . (11) . . . a šar du (*Remainder of obverse and top of reverse broken. Rev.* (1) . . . kak a . . . (2) . . . ni . . . (3) . . . lál du . . . (4) [taš-mu]-ú u Salimu(mu) ina mâti kalâmi . . . (5) . . BAT ^pl^ . . . . . . ^pl^ ina mâti (?) . . . (6) . . . ra-šu Šumkut(ut) ummâni ^pl^ . . (7) . . [ûmu] XXX ^kám^ ḫul pat . . (8) . . . a (?) . . (9) . . . (10) . . . bí-na . . [K. 12176.]

No. 211B. *Obv.* (1) . . . innamir(ir) (2) . . . iššir (3) . . tum du šal lat (4) . . . sa-li-mu ina mâti ibašši(ši) (5) . . . ina lib ^mul^ A-nu-ni-tum (6) . . . . ma *Rev.* (*Destroyed.*) [K. 8407.]

No. 211C. *Obv.* (1) [Ana] ^mul^ Dil-bat ina ^arḫu^ . . . (2) ú-ru-ba-a-tum . . . (3) [Ana] ^mul^ Dil-bat ina lib ^mul^ . . . (4) zunnu ina šamí(í) mîlu . . . (5) [íbûr] ^mâtu^ Aḫarri . . . (*Remainder destroyed.*) [K. 1955.]

No. 211D. *Obv.* (1) Ana ^mul^ Dilbat ina ^arḫu^ . . . . (2) íbûr mâti . . . (3) Ana ^mul^ Dil-bat ina ^arḫu^ . . . (4) nišî ^pl^ ^mâtu^ . . . (*Remainder destroyed.*) [83-1-18, 319.]

No. 211E. *Obv.* (1) Ana ^ilu^ Dil-bat ina ^arḫu^ . . . (2) . . ri(?)ga . . . (3) . . mu ina . . . (4) Ana . . . (*Remainder destroyed.*) [83-1-18, 834.]

No. 211F. *Obv.* (1) . . . ŠÍ u IN . NU (2) . . . ši (3) . . . kit kakkabu du . . . (4) . . . ^mâtu^ Akkadu ti-bu-u (5) . . . [^mul^ PA . BIL . SAG (*Remainder destroyed; traces of one character on reverse.*) [K. 12250.]

No. 212. *Obv.* (1) Ana [1] ^mul^ [2] UZA míš-ḫa [3] im-šuḫ (2) ilâni ^pl^ ana mâti BUL . . . (3) ana mâti [4] rîmu [iraššu] (4) mu-šú an-ni-ú . . . (5) míš-ḫu im-[šuḫ] . . . (6) [Ana] ^mul^ LU . BAD . GUD . UD . . . (7) ultu pân a-ḫi-í-iš . . . (8) í. . . ku du . . . *Rev.* (1) šá ^m ilu^ Nabû-aḫí ^pl^-íriba [83-1-18, 204.]

No. 212A. *Obv.* (*Top wanting.*) (1) A . . . (2) šá . . . *Rev.* (1) iṣ . . . (2) ma-a . . . (3) ^ilu^ Dil-bat ^mul^ . . . (4) an-ni-u [pišir-šu] (5)

[1] MUL, *glossed* MU-UL. [2] UZA, *glossed* U-ZA.
[3] im-šuh, *glossed* im-šú-[uḫ]. [4] rîmu, *glossed* ri-í-mu.

Ana mul UZA . . . (6) taš-mu-ú u DI . . . (7) ilâni pl rîmu ana mâti . . . (8) DIR pl . . . (9) marṣu . . . (10) sal îrâti (?) . . . (11) ilu . . . (*Left-hand edge*) (1) a-na ḫa-ba-li la ta . . . (2) i-lu-um-ma ina ina îli mí-i-ni . . . [K. 13170.]

No. 213. *Obv.* (1) [Ana] mul Aḳrabu (2) ana pân Sin iṭḫi-ma izziz(iz) (3) pâl šarri îrik(ik) (4) am nakru itibba-am-ma (5) šumḳuta (ta)-šu išakan(an) *Rev.* (1) ilu Aššur ilu Šamšu u ilu Marduk (2) iṣu kussi ša ki-na-a-ti (3) a-na da-riš a-na ûmí pl (4) arkûti pl a-na šarri (5) [bîl]-ia id-dan-nu (6) ša m ilu Nabû-iḳ-bi. [82–5–22, 51.]

No. 214. *Obv.* (1) Ana mul Aḳrabu ana pân Sin iṭḫi-ma (2) pal-í šarri arkûti pl (3) am nakru tibû-ma šumḳuta(ta)-šu (4) išakan (an) *Rev.* (1) ša m ilu Bîl-naṣir(ir). [81–2–4, 81.]

No. 214A. *Obv.* (*Top broken*) (1) Ana mul Aḳrabu . . . (2) taš-mu-ú . . . (3) ilu LU . BAD . . . (4) izza-[az] . . . (5) Ana ilu LU . [BAD] . . . *Rev.* (1) u a . . . (2) Ana ilu Sin ûmu XIV . . . (3) in-nam-mar . . . (*Remainder broken off.*) [S. 1327.]

No. 215. *Obv.* (1) ilu GUD . UD ul . . . (2) ilu Sin ilu Šamšu ul . . . . tú (3) ina pân ilu Šamši ir-ti-bi (4) mul Ziḳit-aḳrabi ša ina ḳarni imitti Sin (5) iz-zi-zu a-na ilu Šamši (?) (6) ul iṭaḫḫi mîmma ul i-lap-pat (7) Ana mul Aḳrabi ina tarbaṣ Sin (8) it-ta-ši-iz Ana zunni u mîli *Rev.* (1) itti-šu šarru i-ta-mar (2) ilu Rammanu i-ra-ḫi-iṣ (3) Ana ina arḫu Âiri ûmu XV kám Ana ilu Í-a . . ḳi (4) ša maṣ-ṣarti bar-ir šal-mu-šu (5) ana ta-na-da-a-ti išakan(an) (6) ša m ilu Nabû-šuma iškun(un). [K. 19.]

No. 215A. *Obv.* (1) mul LU . BAD . SAG . UŠ . . . (2) a-na III-šú ina iz-da . . . (3) Ana Šamšu îli-nu ilu [Sin] . . . (4) iz-zi-iz . . . (5) iz-za-az . . . . (6) kit-ti . . . (7) a-ša-an . . . *Rev.* (1) Ana ilu Šamšu . . . (2) šar mâti išid iṣu GU . [ZA] . . . (3) mul LU . BAD . SAG . UŠ . . . (4) damiḳti ša šarri bîl-ia . . . (5) ša m ilu Nabû-ikiša(ša) mâr Bar-[sab ki]. [D.T. 304.]

No. 216. *Obv.* (1) mul LU . BAD . SAG . [UŠ ina] lib (?)-bi (?) . . . (2) ša mul UR . GU . LA it-tan-mar (3) Ana mul UR . GU . LA a-dir (4) III šanâti ^{pl} [UR.] MAḪ. ^{pl} (5) u UR. BAR. RA $^{[pl]}$ . . . u niší díku (6) alkat mâti . . . . su ipparasu *Rev.* (1) Ana ^{mul} LU. BAD ina ^{arḫu} Abi (2) ippuḫa(ḫa) (3) ma'al ḳu-ra-du irappiš (4) ša ^{m} A-ša-ri-du maḫrû(ú). [K. 861.]

No. 216A. *Obv.* (1) . . . ^{ilu} LU. BAD. SAG. UŠ na ḫi (?) . . . (2) . . . GIR. TAB ḳarnâti ^{pl}-ša zu-ú . . . . (3) . . . ZI-ma ina ^{iṣu} kakki šumḳut(ut) (4) . . . * SAG (?). MÍ (?). GAR ša-ru-ri na-ša-a (*Remainder broken off.*) [K. 1347.]

No. 216B. *Obv.* (1) Ana ^{mul} LU. BAD . . . (2) šar kiššutam (tam) . . . (3) Ana Šamšu ina it . . . (*Remainder of obv. and top of rev. broken off.*) *Rev.* (1) . . ^{mul} SIB. ZI. [AN. NA.] . . . . (2) . . ^{mul} LU. BAD. SAG. UŠ . . . (3) i-da-a-ti ša . . . (4) a-na šarri bí-li . . . (5) ša-at . . . (6) ša ^{m} A-ša-ri-du . . . [83–1–18, 313.]

No. 216C. *Obv.* (1) [^{mul} LU.] BAD. GUD. UD (2) it-tan-mar (3) Ana ^{mul} LU. BAD. ina arḫi in-nam-ru (4) mílu ù zunnu (5) [^{mul} LU.] BAD. DIR (6) [nuḫuš] niší ^{pl} *Rev.* (1) ša $^{m\,ilu}$ Nírgal-íṭir(ir). [K. 783.]

No. 217. *Obv.* (1) ^{ilu} GUD. UD ina ṣít Šamši innammar (2) Ana ^{ilu} LU. BAD arḫi innamir (3) zunnu u A. [DAN] (4) Ana ^{ilu} LU. BAD šum-ma[ina] ^{arḫu} Aîri (5) šum-ma ina ^{arḫu} Simâni innamir (6) mílu illak-ma íḳla ugara i-ma-gir (7) Ana ^{ilu} LU. BAD ina ^{šâru} šadi izziz (8) tibut(ut) Subarti ^{ki} (9) ù kaš-ši-i ana mâti *Rev.* (1) si-mí-in dul-li šú-u (2) a-na ^{alu} Ninâ la al-lik (3) ^{am} A. BA ^{pl} a-na (?) ša-*da-ri (4) ina bîti . . . šá id (?) (5) mi-i-nu šá [šarru ? bí ?]-ili . . . (6) ina gab-si ^{alu} Ninâ li-í-pu-uš (7) is-su-ri la ú-ša-ru-ni la í-rab (8) un-ḳu li-di-nu-ni (9) šá $^{m\,ilu}$ Nabû-mu-ší-ṣi.

[82–5–22, 78.]

No. 218. *Obv.* (1) Ana ina ^{arḫu} Aîri ^{ilu} LU. BAD innamir(ir) (2) mílu illak-ma iḳla ugara i-ma-gir (3) Ana $^{mul\,ilu}$ Marduk MUL. MUL ikšud(ud) (4) ^{ilu} Rammânu iraḫiṣ(iṣ) *Rev.* (1) ûmu XIV ^{kám} Sin u Šamšu itti a-ḫa-miš (2) ul in-nam-ma-ru (3) ûmu XV ^{kám} ilu itti ili in-nam-ma-ru (4) šar Subarti ^{ki} maḫira (5) la iraššì(ši) (6) . . i abî-ia ší-ma-a-ku (7) [ša ^{m}] ^{ilu} Bíl-aḫí ^{pl}-íri-ba

[81–2–4, 84.]

No. 218A. *Obv.* (1) Ana ^{mul} LU . BAD . GUD . UD . . . . (2) i-na lib-bi ^{mul} . . . . (3) Ana ^{ilu} LU . BAD a-na ^{mul} . . . (4) ^{ilu} Rammânu [iraḫiṣ] (5) Ana ^{ilu} LU . BAD ina ^{arḫu} Aîri . . (6) lu-ú ina ^{arḫu} Simâni [innamir] (7) mílu illak-ma A . [LIB ugara] (8) i-ma-gir . . *Rev.* (1) ša ^{m} Iraššî(ši)-ilu mâr . . . (2) šarru ú-ra-ši . . . (3) ištín (ín) ^{am} ikkaru ša šarri . . . (4) V arḫâni ^{pl} a . . . (5) dul . . . (6) . . . (7) bí-ili-iá . . . (8) zu (?) man . . ba-u . . .

[82–5–22, 74.]

No. 219. *Obv.* (1) [Ana ^{mul}] LU . BAD ina ^{arḫu} Du'ûzi ippuḫa(ḫa) (2) pâgrâni ^{pl} ibaššu ^{pl} (3) Ana ^{mul} UR . GU . LA ṣalmu (4) lib mâti la iṭâb(ab) (5) bíl šarrâni ^{pl} lu-da-ri (6) ša ^{m} A-ša-ri-du. [82–5–22, 56.]

No. 220. *Obv.* (1) Ana ^{ilu} LU . BAD ina ^{arḫu} Ululi ippuḫ (2) šâ-ḳi-í maḫiri (3) na-pa-aš ^{ilu} Nisaba (4) bíl šarrâni ^{pl} lu-da-ri *Rev.* (1) ša ^{m} A-ša-ri-du (2) ḳa-aṭ-nu. [83–1–18, 178.]

No. 221. *Obv.* (1) ^{mul} LU . BAD . GUD . UD ina ṣît Šamši (2) ina ḳaḳ-ḳar ^{mul} AB . SIN (3) it-tan-mar pi-šir-šu (4) Ana ^{mul} Nunu a-na ^{mul} PAN iṭḫi (5) íbûr mâti iššir bûlu ina ṣíri irappaš(aš) (6) šarru idannin-ma nakrûti ^{pl}-šu LAL . . . šamaššammu u saluppu išširu ^{pl} *Rev.* (1) Ana ^{mul} LU . BAD ina ^{arḫu} Ululi ippuḫa(ḫa) (2) ša-ki-í na-pa-aš ^{ilu} Nisaba (3) Ana ina ^{arḫu} Ululi ^{mul} DAḪ innamir (ir) (4) . . âlu ŠÍ iššir (5) ^{mul} DAḪ ^{ilu} LU . BAD . GUD . UD (6) ša ^{m} A-ša-ri-du mâr ^{m} Dam-ḳa (7) ardu ša šarri. [81–2–4, 132.]

No. 222. *Obv.* (1) Ana ^{mul} LU . BAD ina ^{arhu} Ululi innamir (ir) (2) ša-ḳi-í maḫiri (?) na-pa-aš ni-is-sa-bu (8) Ana ^{mul} UR . MAḪ kakkabâni ^{pl}-šu ul-tap-pu-ú (4) šarru a-šar il-la-ku (5) li-is-su . . (6) Anâ ^{mul} UR . GU . LA a . . . (7) níšî ^{pl} u âḫî $^{[pl]}$ . . . *Rev.* (1) in-nam-da-ru-ma (2) a-lak-ti ^{mâtu} Aḫarrî ^{ki} (3) ša ^{m} Ṭa-bi-ia.

[83–1–18, 181.]

No. 223. *Obv.* (1) Ana ina ^{arḫu} Araḫšamna ^{mul} LU . BAD ippuḫa(ḫa) (2) íbûr mâti iššir (3) Ana ^{mul} Aḳrabi ṣalmu ina lib-bi taš-mu-ú ina mâti ibašši (4) ^{ilu} GUD . UD . ina lib ^{mul} Aḳrabi izzaz-ma (5) Ana ^{mul} Aḳrabu ^{ilu} Iš-ḫa-ra ina la'ab urri-ša (6) irat-ṣa nam-rat zibbat-ṣa í-ṭa-at (7) ḳarnât pl-ṣa nin-mu-ra (8) zunnu u mílu ina mâti i-ḫar-ru-bu *Rev.* (1) aribi itibbû-ma mâta ikkalu (2) šumḳutim(tim) alpi pl u gu-ub-ri (3) . . . ik-kaš-šad (4) . . . Aḳrabu (*Remainder broken.*) [81-2-4, 88.]

No. 223A. *Obv.* (1) Ana Sin tarbaṣu ilmi-ma ilu Muštabarrû-mûtânu(a-nu) ina libbi-[šu izziz] (2) šumḳutim(tim) bu-lim u namaš-ší-í ša [ṣíri] (3) mí-ri-šu la iššir šar-ru iṣaḫir(*ir) (4) Ana kakkabu ina tarbaṣ Sin izziz šarru u ummânu . . . (5) ú-ta-ṣa-ru ilu Muštabarrû-mûtanu(a-nu) mul . . . . (6) Ana Sin tarbaṣu ilmi-ma MUL . MUL ina libbi-šu izziz (7) ina arḫi šuâti sal írâti pl zakkari pl ul-la-da (8) šar kiššuti mât-su inakar-šu-ma(ba ?) i . . (9) MUL . MUL . ilu Muštabarrû-mûtânu(a-nu) (10) ša ilu NI . BAT-a . . . . . *Rev.* (1) MUL . MUL . . . . (2) Ana Sin tarbaṣu ilmi-ma ilu . . . . (3) ina libbi-šu izziz šarru . . . . . (4) Ana ina arḫu kisilimi mul GIR . TAB *ilu* Iš-ḫa-ra (5) ina tamarti-šu ḳarnâti pl-šu ningu-la (6) : nin-bu-ṭa irat-ṣa nam-rat (7) zibbat-ṣa í-ṭa-ti zunnu u mílu (8) NIM pl-ni šumḳutim(tim) alpi pl u gub-[ri] (9) aribi itbu-A̤ išu kakku IL . LA-ma (10) mât nakri ik-kaš-šad (11) ša m ilu Nabû-šuma-iškun(un). (*Left-hand edge*) (1) ša m ilu Nabû-šuma-iškun(*un). [80-7-19, 55.]

No. 224. *Obv.* (1) Ana mul . . . . (2) it-tan-mar (3) Ana mul LU . BAD ina arḫu kisilimi innamir(ir) (4) ḫab-ba-a-ti ina mâti ibaššu pl *Rev.* (1) ša m ilu Nírgal-íṭir(ir). [83-1-18, 208.]

No. 225. *Obv.* (*Top broken*) (1) . . . ana sal damiḳti imalliku pl (2) [zunni] pl ù míli pl ibaššu pl (3) [mul] LU . BAD . GUD . UD ina lib mul SIM . MAḪ izzaz-ma (4) [Ana] mul LU . BAD a-na mul Nâr-Idiḳlat itḫi (5) zunni pl ù míli pl ibaššu . . (6) mul LU . BAD GUD . UD ina ṣît Šamši it-tan-[mar] *Rev.* (*Top broken*) (1) . . atal subarti [ki] . . . (2) Ana Sin ki-i ina arḫu DIR . ŠÍ ûmu I kám [innamir] (3) sanâḳu ša pî lib mâti iṭâb(ab) (4) . . *a-na ina arḫu DIR . ŠÍ *ûmu *I kám Sin in-nam-mar (5) . . . Subarti ki sanâḳu ša pî lib mâti iṭâb (6) [ša m ilu] Nírgal-íṭir(ir). [K. 972.]

No. 226. *Obv.* (1) [mul LU .] BAD . GUD . UD ina írib Šamši (2) itti MUL . MUL it-tan-mar (3) a-na lib-bi mul ŠÚ . GI

(4) iš-ta-naḳ-ḳa-a (5) zunnu u mílu (6) . . $^{mul\ ilu}$ Marduk [ina] riš šatti . . . (7) šattu šiâtu šašurri-šu . . . (8) ša ^{m} Na-di-nu.
[81–2–4, 89.]

No. 227. *Obv.* (1) [Ana ^{ilu} AN . TA .] SUR . RA kakkabâni ^{pl}-šu (2) . . . . a-dir (3) . . . . ana mâti illakam(kâm) (4) . . . Ana ^{ilu} AN . TA . SUR . RA (5) . . . . *mi-ši-iḫ ^{ilu} PA . BIL . SAG (6). . . . GUD . UD ina lib ^{mul} PA . BIL . SAG (7) . . . . izzaz-ma (8) . . . . pâl ûmí ^{pl} arkûti ^{pl} (9) . . . . lu ša-lam šar kiššuti *Rev.* (1) $^{[mul]}$ LU . BAD . GUD . UD ina ṣitaš (2) . . . a-dan-šu ul it-ti-iḳ (3) . . . šu šú pi (4) [lib šarri] bí-ili-ia lu-ṭa-a-bi (5) . . . [a]-na šarri mâr šarri (6) [u] íkalli ^{pl}-u (7) [ša ^{m} Iraššî] (ši)-ilu ardu ša šarri maḫrû(u).
[83–1–18, 230.]

No. 228. *Obv.* (1) ^{mul} GUD . UD ina lib ^{mul} UR . GU . LA (2) it-ti-ti-zi (3) Ana ^{mul} UR . GU . LA ṣalmu (4) lib-bi mâti la iṭâb (5) Ana ^{mul} Šarru ṣalmu (6) mu-'-ir-ru íkalli imât (7) šá $^{m\ ilu}$ Nabû-mu-ší-ṣi.
[K. 704.]

No. 229. *Obv.* (1) . . . [1]í | [2]tappallas . . . (2) [3]šamû(û) | [4]kakkaru | [5]kaš-du-ú . . (3) [6]tib | [7]šâri . . . [8]dup-šum | ibašši (4) [^{mul} LU . BAD .] GUD . UD man-za-as-su . . (5) . . . in-na-mar . . (6) . . . ṣu-ur . . (7) . . . ^{mul} . . . *Rev.* (1) . . . . (2) . . . ti . . . (3) . . . . ^{m} . . .
[81–2–4, 287.]

No. 229A. *Obv.* (1) Ana ^{mul} LU . BAD ina . . . (2) Ana ^{mul} LU . BAD ina du (?) . . . (3) ša-ni-iš bat . . . . (4) Ana ^{mul} LU . BAD ina lib . . . . (5) zunni ^{pl} . . . (6) . . . . *Rev.* (1) ^{mul} . . . . (2) damiḳti ša . . . . (3) ^{ilu} Sin UD . . . . (4) šá . . . . (5) ina ^{arḫu} kisilimi . . . . (6) kan . . . . (7) ^{m} Ṭa-bi-[ia] . . . . (8) ^{m} Za-kir . . .
[80–7–19, 155.]

No. 229B. *Obv.* (1) . . . LU . BAD TÍ (?) . . (2) . . . ina pân mâti ḪA . A (3) . . . tí-šu bûl mâti ḪA . A . (4) . . . SI . DI (*Remainder of obv. and top of rev. wanting.*) *Rev.* (1) . . . . ší (?)

[1] . . . í *glossed* . . . úr.
[2] ŠI . BAR *glossed* tap-pal-la-as.
[3] ANA-ú *glossed* ša-mu-u.
[4] KI *glossed* ḳaḳ-ḳa-ru.
[5] kaš-du-ú *glossed* ka-aš-du-[ú].
[6] ZI *glossed* [ti]-ib.
[7] IM *glossed* ša-a-ri.
[8] dup-šum *glossed* dup-šu.

ḫi (?) . . . (2) . . . mul LU . BAD . SAG . UŠ (3) . . . ana mul LU . BAD . SAG . UŠ iṭaḫḫi ma (4) [ša] m Bu-ul-lu-ṭi. [K. 1375.]

No. 230. *Obv.* (1) Ana mul PAN ina tarbaṣ Sin izziz . . (2) aštûti pl in-na-da-ru-ma (3) ḫu-ub-tum ina mâti ibašši (4) a-na limutti ul i-lap-pat (5) tarbaṣu ša mul AB . SIN (6) a-na zunni u mîli *Rev.* (1) ina ÍN . TÍ . NA i-lap-pat (2) Ana ina arḫu Nisanni ûmu XIII kám (3) PAT . ḪI . A-su ana Sin u ilu Šamši (4) liš-? ilu Sin u ilu Šamšu KA (?) pl šu (5) ša m ilu Nabû-šuma-iškun(un).

[82–5–22, 59.]

No. 231. *Obv.* (1) [Ana] ina arḫu Du'ûzi ilu Muštabarrû-mûtânu(a-nu) innamir(ir) (2) ma'al ḳu-ra-du irappiš(iš) (3) [Ana] ilu LU . BAD . ina šâru iltani izziz(iz) (4) pagrâni pl ibaššu pl tibû(bu) šar Akkadi ki ana mât nakri (5) Ana mul Šanamma(ma) ana mul MAŠ . TAB . BA itḫi(ḫi) (6) šarru imât-ma sal nukurtu ibašši(ši) (7) Ana ilu NI . BAT . . . . (8) . . . . *Rev.* (1) Ana ilu Muštabarrû-mûtânu (a-nu) . . . . (2) ina šatti šiâti šar Ílama [ma ki] (3) bíl šarrâni pl lu-da-ru (4) ša m A-ša-ri-du ḳa-aṭ-nu. [K. 735.]

No. 232. *Obv.* (1) [ilu NI . BAT]-a-nu ina arḫu Du'ûzi it-ta-mar un-nu-ut (2) [Ana ilu NI . BAT-a-nu] ina arḫu Du'ûzi innamir ma'al ḳu-ra-di irappiš (3) . . . . a-na mu-ta-ni ḳa-bi (4) [Ana ilu NI . BAT]-a-nu ina šâru šadi izziz(iz) tibut(ut) Subarti ki (5) ù Kaš-ši-i a-na mâti (6) [Ana ilu] Muštabarrû-mûtânu(a-nu) um-mu-liš ippuḫa-ma šaruri pl-šu iṣrup (7) šar Ílama(ma) ki imât (8) Ana ilu Nírgal ina ribi-šu ina zu-ḫar-u-tú šakin(in) (9) ki-ma kakkabâni pl šamí(í) ma-'-diš um-mul (10) a-na mâtu Akkadi ki rîmu iraššî(ši) (11) id ummâni-ia illak-ma ummân am nakri idâk (12) mâtu (ú) ṣar-ra-mu ikašad(ád) (13) ummâni(ni) am nakri ina pân ummâni(ni)-ia la illaku (14) bûl mâtu Akkadi ki ina ṣíri par-ga-niš irabbiṣu pl (15) šamaššammu sa-luppu išširu pl *Rev.* (1) Ana mul LU . BAD ana mul ilu ZU is-nik imíru sisi pl imâtu pl (2) la is-nik ina muḫ-ḫi la ḳur-bu (3) Ana ilu Muštabarrû-mûtânu(a-nu) ú-ta-na-at-ma damiḳtu ib-il-ma a-ḫi-tú (4) Ana ilu Muštabarrû-mûtânu(a-nu) arkî ilu UMUN . PA . UD . DU illak(ak) šattu šiâtu dam-ḳat (5) šá m Bu-lu-ṭu.

[83–1–18, 198.]

No. 233. *Obv.* (1) Ana ina arhu Ululi ilu Muštabarrû-mûtânu (a-nu) innamir . . (2) íbûr mâti iššir (3) lib-bi mâti iṭâb(ab) (4) Ana mul LU . BAD DIR . . (5) nu-ḫu-uš nišî . . *Rev.* (1) Ana ilu Muš-tabarrû-mûtânu(a-nu) ina ribi . . . (2) ša-ru-ru inaši-ma . . . (3) ša m ilu Nabû-iḳ-bí [699.]

No. 234. *Obv.* (1) [Ana] mul Muštabarrû-mûtânu(a-nu) ana pân Sin iṭḫi-ma izziz(iz) (2) Sin mâta limutta(ta) ušíšib(ib) (3) Ana mul LU . BAD ina ḳarni šumíli Sin izziz šarru kiššutam(tam) ipuš(uš) (4) Ana kakkabu ina pân Sin sumíli izziz šarru kiššutam(tam) ípuš (uš) (5) Ana kakkabu ina arki Sin šumíli izziz šar Akkadi ki (6) kiššutam(tam) ípuš(uš) (7) Ana mul DIL . GAN . ina ḳarni šumíli-šu izziz(iz) ina šatti šiâti (8) mí-riš mâtu Akkadi ki iššir (9) Ana mul DIL . GAN ina maš-ḳa-šu izziz ina šatti šiâti íbûr mâti (10) iššir *Rev.* (1) Ana kakkabu ina ḳarni šumíli Sin izziz mât nakri limutta [immar] (2) Ana kakkabu ina ḳarni šumíli-šu izziz atal * šar Aḫarrî (?) ki (?) (3) GAN . BA mâti šiâti iṣaḫir : ilu Rammânu iraḫiṣ (4) Ana kakkabu ina ḳarni šumíli-šu izziz atal šar MAR išakan (5) Ana ina ḳarni šumíli-šu kakkabu ilu Rammânu ina mât nakri ikkal (6) : atalû išakan : atal šar Aḫarri ki (7) mât-su iṣaḫir(ir) (8) ša m Za-kir. [82-5-22, 46.]

No. 234A. *Obv.* (1) [Ana mul NI .] BAT-a-nu ina . . . (2) iṭâb(ab) in . . . . (3) [Ana mul] Muštabarrû-mûtânu(a-nu) ina lib mul . . . . (4) Šumḳûtim(tim) bûli (5) Ana mul Rab-bu a-na ri (?) . . ut . . . (6) mul Rab-bu mul UR . . . (7) mul Muštabarrû-mûtânu (a-nu) ina lib mul . . . . (8) izzaz-ma *Rev.* (1) Ana mul LU . BAD ina šâru šadi [izziz] (1) tibut(ut) Subarti ki . . (3) Ana mul Mušta-barrû-mûtânu(a-nu) . . (4) . . mul UR . GU . LA izziz . . (5) [ša] m Ba-la-[si-i]. [K. 855.]

No. 235. *Obv.* (1) mul Muštabarrû-mûtânu(a-nu) mul AL . LUL ik-ta-[sad-ma] (2) ina libbi-šu í-ta-rab ma-ṣar-tu at-ta-[ṣar] (3) la in-ni-mid la i-zi-iz šapli-ta il-[lak ?] (4) il-lak ú-ṣu-um-ma ri-í-ḫi a-na a . . (5) ki-ma it-tu-ṣi pi-šir-šu ana šarri bíl-iá a-[sap-ra] (6) is-su-ri mí-mí-í-ni ana šarri bíl-iá i-sap-[ra] (7) ma-a ana mul Šanamma(ma) ana mul AL . LUL iṭḫi rubu . . (8) ki-ma it-tí-mid it-ti-ti-iz šú-u-tú . . . (9) lum-nu šá mâtu Akkadi ki šú-ú (10) is-su-ri mí-mí-í-ni ana šarri bîl-iá i-sap-[ra] (11) ma-a ana ^{ilu} LU . BAD ina ḳabal ti-ib ša-a-ri i . . . *Rev.* (1) šar Subarti ^{ki} ba . . . (2) šú-mu an-ni-u si-li-a-tí šú-u . . (3) šarru bí-ili ina íli libbi-šu la i-šak-[kan] (4) mu-šú an-ni-u ^{ilu} Rammânu pî-šu it-ti-*di (5) Ana ^{arḫu} Abu ^{ilu} Rammânu pî-šu iddi ûmu irûb(ub) šamû izanun(nun) (6) birḳu ib-riḳ mîli ^{pl} ina naḳbi iššapak (7) Ana ina ûmí(mí) la ir-pi ^{ilu} Rammânu is-si (8) da-um-ma-tú : ḫušaḫḫu ina mâti ibašši(ši) (9) šá ^{m} Ak-kul-la-ni.

[K. 747.]

No. 235A. *Obv.* (1) Ana ^{mul} Muštabarrû-mûtânu(a-nu) VII arḫâni ^{pl} ina lib ^{mul} MAŠ . TAB . BA . GAL . GAL (2) . . . it-ta-lak u (?) . . . . ru (3) . . . nu . . . . (*Two lines broken out.*) (6) . . . ku-nu (7) . . . bu-ub (8) . . . ina lib-bi it-ti-iḳ (9) . . . šarru (?) šarru a-ki ša i-li-'-u li-[pu-uš] (10) u . . . . III-šu a-na šarri al-tap-ra . . (11) * um * ma ina (?) pi (?) i (?) dib-bi an-nu-tú ana ḳa-bi-í . . . (12) ardu-ka ša ṭabta-ka i-na-ṣa-ru u i-ra-mu . . (13) lib-ba-a ana muḫ-ḫi-ka i-kab-bab-an-[ni ?] *Rev.* (1) dib(?)-ba . . ù (?) du (?) . . ma pi-is-sa . . . (2) ù ki (?) . . ul-tí(?)-tí(?)-iz ina lib . . . (3) ri-i . . ina maḫ-ru-ti ša i . . . (4) KÚR ul il-li-kam-ma mâtu ul : . . (5) ittu ina lib-bi pi-is-sa-ti . . . (6) Atalû ša Sin ša ina ^{arḫu} Araḫšamna iš-ku-nu . . . (7) ul-tir-ri ù ša ^{mâtu} SU . ZIN mi-nu . . . (8) arki-šu ^{mul} SAG . MÍ . GAR III-šu ana lib Sin i-tí . . . (9) mi-nu-u in-ni-pu-uš-ma ḪUL-šu i-ti-[iḳ] (10) ina tamarti(?)-šu III-šu Sin û ma XVI ^{kám} itti ^{ilu} Šamši it-tan-mar (11) ^{arḫu} Tašrîtu ^{arḫu} Araḫšamna ^{arḫu} Kisilimu Sin ina ta-mar-ti-šu (12) *kal ûmu I ^{kám} ki-ma ša la in-nam-ru ga-mir (*Left-hand edge*) ša $^{m\,ilu}$ Bîl . šuma-iškun(un) ^{am} UŠ . . KU .

[83–1–18, 232.]

No. 236. *Obv.* (1) [^{mul} NI .] BAT-a-nu iḳil ^{mul} AL . LUL (2) i-ru-bu a-na it-tum (3) ul iṣ-ṣab-bat (4) ina lib-bi ul iz-za-zi (5) ul in-ni-im-mi-du (6) *ù ul i-*ka-ši (7) ár-ḫiš uṣ-ṣi *Rev.* (1) ša $^{m\,ilu}$ Bîl-naṣir(ir).

[K. 808.]

No. 236A. *Obv.* (1) Ana ^{mul} AL . [LUL] . . . (2) GIS . PIN mâti ina . . . (3) šur-du-ut mâti . . . (4) ina ḳaḳ-ḳa-ri i . . . (5) sapaḫ(aḫ) Ílama(ma) ^{ki} u . . . (6) Ana ^{mul} Šanamma(ma) ana ^{mul} AL . [LUL] . . . (7) rubu . . . . *Rev.* (1) Ana ^{mul} Muštabarru-mûtânu(a-nu) ana ^{mul} . . . (2) alu . . . . . . (3) ša ^{m} Aḫî ^{pl}-ša-a ^{am} * Uruk-[a-a]. [83–1–18, 233.]

No. 236B. *Obv.* (1) Ana ^{mul} Muštabarrû-mutânu(a-nu) ina ^{ilu} . . . (2) ina šumíl ^{mul} Dil-bat . . . . (3) ub-bu-tu ina ^{mâtu} Akkadi ^{ki} . . . (4) tarbaṣ ^{imiru} sisi ^{pl} . . . *Rev.* (1) Ana ^{mul} UTU . KA . GAB-A ŠI . . . . (2) ta-az-zi-im-ti an-ni . . . (3) (*blank, but for two diagonal wedges*) (4) ^{mul} LU . BAD ^{pl} ina lib-bi ^{mul} (5) izzazu ^{pl} . . . (6) limuttu šú-ú a-na . . . . (7) man-ma la ú-ta . . . (8) ša ^{m} Iraššì (ši)-ilu . . . . [K. 875.]

No. 236C. *Obv.* (? *Top broken*) (1) . . . pa . . . (2) . . . . NI . BAT-a-[nu] . . . . *Rev.* (1) . . . sap la ší í . . . (2) . . . XV ša ^{mul} ŠÚ . . . . (3) . . . za-az . . . . (4) . . . . libbi-šu la í-ru . . . (5) . . . . ka ḳi ri šu . . . (6) . . a . . (7) . . . arḫâni ^{pl} . . . .
[Bu. 91–5–9, 58.]

No. 236D. *Obv.* (1) . . . [1]šumíli ^{ilu} Sin ina (?) . . . . (2) . . . . ^{am} nakra ikkal . . . ra . . . (3) . . . šumíli ^{ilu} Sin . . . (*Remainder of obv. and top of rev. broken off.*) *Rev.* (1) . . . . . (2) . . . . Muštabarrû-mûtânu(a-nu) . . . . (3) . . . irappiš (?) ^{ilu} NI . . . (4) ú-pa . . . (5) [ša ^{m}] ^{ilu} Nabû-aḫî ^{pl}-íriba. [K. 2327.]

No. 236E. *Obv.* (1) [Ana ^{ilu}] Muštabarru-mûtânu(a-nu) ḳak-ḳar ša . . . . (2) . . . i ú-gam-mi-ra it . . . . (3) . . ta lu ki šu un-di-iṭ-ṭu (4) . . a-di V ûmu(mu) am . . . (5) . . . šar . . . . (*Remainder of obv. and top of rev. broken off.*) *Rev.* (1) . . . . (2) [ša] ^{m} Za-kir.
[82–5–22, 67.]

No. 236F. *Obv.* (*Top broken*) (1) * ^{mul} . . . (2) tir (?) . . . (3) Ana ^{mul} . . . (4) tir . . . . tir (?) . . (5) Ana kakkabu *a (?)- dir riu-ḫuš . . . (6) Ana ^{ilu} . . ma ina nipiḫ-ša ud-da-ṣa kíma (?) im . . . (7) Ana ^{mul} Dil-bat (?) ina nipiḫ-ša ÍN . BAT ^{arḫu} Abi ḫi . . . . (8) Ana ^{mul} Muštabarrû-mûtânu(a-nu) ša-ru-ru un . . . (9) a-di II-šu du-un-ḳu ša . . . (10) šarru li (?) -zi (?) tú su ki an ni . . . (*Two lines illegible.*) *Rev.* (1) . . . ul ^{mâtu} Akkadi ^{ki} lum- . . . (?) . . . lum-ma SI . DI GAR (?) an mí ; . . . . (3) . . . mar ^{m} ṣab-ba (?)-a a tú . . . (4) . . . ḫa-a-a ^{m} Di-

[1] GUBU (?), *glossed* šú-mí-li.

lu (?)-ú . . . (5) . . . ^{am} A-ra-su ú . . . . (6) . . . -'- du išdu (?) . . . (7) . . . *gab-*bu . . . . (*Remainder broken off.*) [K. 8704.]

No. 236G. *Obv.* (1) [Ana ^{mul} SAR . UR u ?] ^{mul} ŠAR . GAZ[1] (2) [ša zi ḳit ? ^{mul}] Aḳrabi un-nu-ut (3) - . . . ki ma-aḳ-tú (4) ^{mul} Muštabarrû-mûtânu(a-nu) ina lib ^{mul} PA . BIL . SAG (5) izzaz-ma zi-ḳit ^{mul} Aḳrabi (6) a-na ^{mul} PA . BIL . SAG ḳa-a-bi (7) ^{mul} Muštabarrû-mûtânu(a-nu) ina lib (8) ^{mul} PA . BIL . SAG it-tí-mí-di *Rev.* (1) it-ti-ti-iz (2) i-da-a-ti ina ^{arḫu} Simâni i-sa-ḫu-ur (3) a-na pa *na (?) . . . . . . lak (4) . . . . (*Remainder, except for traces of one character in l.* 5, *destroyed.*) [83-1-18, 236.]

No. 236H. *Obv.* (1) . . . [1]ikšud(ud) (2) bar-ru-ú . . . . (3) . . ^{mul} Muštabarrû-mûtânu(a-nu) ina šap . . . (4) ^{mul} LU . BAD . SAG . UŠ í-[ti]-it-íḳ (5) $^{[mul]}$ UR . BAR . RA ^{mul} Muštabarrû-mûtânu(a-nu) (6) . . . . ^{mul} LU . BAD . SAG . UŠ. (*Remainder of obv. and top of rev. wanting.*) *Rev.* (1) . . . . ilu (?) . . áš (2) . . . . ti-it-iḳ (3) . . . $^{[mul]}$ LU . BAD . SAG . UŠ (4) . . . . íriba.

[82-5-22, 79.]

No. 237. *Obv.* (1) Ana ^{mul} UR . BAR . RA ^{mul} UR . MAḪ . . . (2) úmí(mí) | ru-ḳu-ú-ti | šú . . . (3) a-na n..a-a-ti . . . . (4) ^{mul} UR . BAR . RA ^{mul} [NI . BAT-a-nu] (5) ^{mul} UR . MAḪ ^{mul} . . , . . (6) ^{mul} Muštabarrû-mûtânu(a-nu) ina lib ^{mul} . . . . (7) Ana [1]kakkabu | [2]iṣrur-ma ina lib [3] . . . (8) [4]írub(ub) [5]bartu [6] . . . *Rev.* (1) ša $^{m\,ilu}$ Nabû-aḫî ^{pl}-íriba. [Bu. 91-5-9, 102.]

No. 237A. (*Obverse broken off.*) *Rev.* (1) . . . ma . . . . (2) MI . DAN MI (?) . . . . (3) di . . . (4) . . ^{mul} ŠU . DUN ina UD . DU-šu ana ^{ilu} Šamši . . . . MAR . TU . . . (5) . . . . ^{šâru} šûtu IZ . ḪAR ina ^{arḫu} Ululi UD . . ina pú na . . . (6) . . . ŠU . DUN ina UD . DU-šu ana ^{ilu} Šamši TU . TU . ina (?) šu ša nu ši . -. (7) . . . ši-ma (?) . . . ? sir (?) . . . ik . . [Rm. 2, 254.]

[1] GAZ, *glossed above* GA . AZ.
[1] KUR-ud, *glossed* ik-šú-ud.
[1] MUL, *glossed* ka-ak-ka-bu.
[2] SUR-ma, *glossed* iṣ-ru-ur-ma.
[3] . . . *glossed* mu (?) . . .
[4] TU-ub, *glossed* í-ru-ub.
[5] ḪI . GAR, *glossed* ba-ar-tú.
[6] . . . *glossed* ib-ba (?) . . .

No. 238. *Obv.* (1) Ana ^{mul} [1] ŠUDUN ina [2] aṣi-šu šu . . . (2) . . . ub-bu-ul-ma | da-'-ḫi . . . . (3) . . . . ub-bu-tú il-la-ka (4) . . . ^{mul} LU . BAD . GUD . UD (5) . . . . un-nu-ut (6) . . . í-ṣu- . . *Rev.* (1) . . . [3] ḪA Ana [4] ^{mul} [5] UGA (2) . . . bat [6] nûni ^{pl} | [7] iṣṣuri ^{pl} | ú-diš-šú-u (3) . . ^{mul} LU . BAD . GUD . UD ina lib ^{mul} SÚḪ . TIG . . . (4) in-na-mar-ma (5) ša $^{m\ ilu}$ Nabû-aḫi ^{pl}-íriba. [K. 868.]

No. 239. *Obv.* (1) Ana ^{mul} APIN ana ^{mul} GIR . [TAB iṭḫi] (2) rubu ina zi-ḳit aḳrabi [imât] (3) arki-šu mâru-šu kušsa [isabbat] (4) šubat mât šarri taníḫ mâtu bílu šanumma(ma) . . . (5) ku-dur mâti la kini(i) ^{ilu} Šamšu . . . (6) ^{ilu} Muštabarrû-mûtânu(a-nu) a-na ^{mul} . . . [82-5-22, 54.]

No. 240. *Obv.* (1) Ana MUL . MUL ana ili Sin ibrum-ma izziz(iz) (2) šarru kiššutam(tam) ípuš(uš) mât-su irappiš (3) Ša $^{m\ ilu}$ Nabû-ikiša(ša) mâr Barsab ^{ki} (4) ^{ilu} Bíl u ^{ilu} Nabû ûmí ^{pl} arkûti ^{pl} (5) ù ṭu-ub lib-bi a-na šar mâtâti (6) bí-ili-ia lid-di-nu (7) ina (?) . . šarru za-ku-ta ni-il-ta-kan (8) ín-na a-du-ú it-ti aḫî ^{pl}-í-a (9) ina íkalli ma-sa-ar-ti bît ḳatâ II *Rev.* (1) ip-pu-uš ù mar šip-ra ša ana(?)-ku (?) (2) it-ti-šu-nu šarru ú-ša-aṣ-bi-tan-ni (3) ^{am} ik-ka-ra-a id-du-ku ù ia-a-ši (4) ú-sa-am-mu-'-in-ni um-ma il-ku (5) it-ti-ni a-lik it-ti aḫî ^{pl}-í-iá (6) u šu-lum ip-pu-uš ù ma-aṣ-ṣar-ti (7) ša šarri bí-ili-iá a-nam-ṣar am-mí-ni a-ta (8) . . . . ti ip-pu-uš ^{ilu} Bíl u ^{ilu} Nabû (9) . . . ru-bu šarru di-na-a (10) . . . . um-mi-i-iṣ (?) (11) . . . . ma (?)-at.

[81-2-4, 104.]

No. 241. *Obv.* (1) Ana MUL . MUL ana íli Sin ibrum-ma (2) izziz(iz) šar kiššutam(tam) ípuš(uš) (3) mât-su irappiš(iš) (4) Ana Sin ina tamarti-šu MUL . MUL ina idi-šu (5) izzizu ^{pl} šarru kiššutam(tam) ípuš(uš) (6) mât-su . . . su (7) [Ana] MUL . MUL [ana lib Sin iribu-ma ultu ?] Sin-[ma ?] *Rev.* (1) Ana ^{šâru} iltani UD .[DU ^{pl}] . . . (2) lib ^{mâtu} Akkadi ^{ki} iṭâb(ab) (3) šar Akkadi ^{ki} idannin-ma (4) maḫira la iraššì(ši) (5) Ša $^{m\ ilu}$ Nabû-aḫî ^{pl}-íri-bà mar ^{m} La-a-ba-ši-ili. [K. 902.]

[1] ŠUDUN, *glossed* ŠU . DU . UN. [2] UD . DU-šu, *glossed* a-ṣi-šu.
[3] . . ḪA, *glossed* . . u. [4] MUL, *glossed* MU . UL.
[5] Ú . NAG .[GA . ḪU], *glossed* Ú . GA. [6] *Traces of a gloss.*
[7] ḪU ^{pl}, *glossed* iṣ-ṣu-ri.

No. 242. *Obv.* (1) Ana MUL . MUL Ana lib [Sin írub?] (2) mâtu ana šarri ḪA . A ^{arḫu} . . . . (3) ílama(ma) $^{ki\ am}$ nakru (4) Ana MUL . MUL ana lib Sin írubu [^{pl}-ma] (5) ana ^{šarru} iltani uṣû ^{pl}-ni (6) lib ^{mâtu} Akkadi ^{ki} iṭâb(ab) šar Akkadi $^{[ki]}$ (7) idannin-ma maḫira la irassi(ši) (8) ^{šarru} iltanu illak-ma (9) ul-tu Sin ana lib MUL . MUL *Rev.* (1) i-ru-bu ^{šarru} iltanu illak(ak) (2) maṣṣartu saddurru ^{mâtu} ílama(ma) ^{ki} (3) limuttu ša ^{am} nakri šú-ú (4) Ana MUL . MUL ša ti iḫ (5) iḳla-a-am ina bilti inaši (6) ina šit-ḳul-ti Sin i . . (7) bíl šarrâni ^{pl} lu-ú-da-[ri] (8) ša ^{m} A-ša-ri-[du ḳaṭnu].

[81–2–4, 135.]

No. 243. *Obv.* (1) MUL . MUL a-na UD . BIL . MAL . UD (?) BIL . MAL . . . (2) ^{mul} Dil-bat ina MUL . MUL izzaz . . (3) [Ana] ^{ilu} Ištar agû kaspi ap-rat . . li li . . . . (4) . . . . li-li mílu gab-[šu] . . (5) $^{[mul]}$ Dil-bat ina ^{mul} DU . GAN . NA izzaz [az-ma] (6) . . . . zunni ^{pl} gab-šú-tu ana šarri bí-ili-ia il . . . . (7) . . . . ^{ilu} Rammânu zunnu a-na za-na-[ni] . . (8) . . . ú li-pu-šú ù ŠÚ . IL . LA la . . . (9) . . . . la i-ba-aš-šu-ú it-ti . . . . (10) . . bu . . . *Rev.* (1) . . . ma-ši-'a GAB ^{pl}-ŠU bi (?)-li-ú . . . . (2) a-na ḳu-du-mi-šu lil-lik šum-ma ma . . . . (3) ni-ḳu-ú ina ši-ri-í-ti im-ba-ru li . . . . (4) iḳlu ki-i sar-ra-ḳu-tu-ma a-mu-liš . . . . (5) ki-i zu-un-nu ina ^{mâtu} Akkadi ^{ki} i-tí-ki-ru AN . NA a . . . . (6) ša $^{m\ ilu}$ Bíl-li' mâr ^{m} Í-gi-bi ^{am} Mašmašu.

[K. 761.]

No. 243A. *Obv.* (1) [Ana] MUL . MUL ana lib Sin írubu ^{pl}-ma (2) ana ^{šarru} iltani uṣû ^{pl} (3) lib-bi ^{mâtu} Akkadi ^{ki} i-ṭa-ab (4) šar Akkadi ^{ki} i-dan-nin-ma (5) maḫira la iraššši(ši) *Rev.* (1) ša ^{m} Ṭa-bi-ia.

[K. 1392.]

No. 243B. *Obv.* (1) Ana ina ^{arḫu} . . . . (2) niši ^{pl} . . . (3) Ana Šamšu ina nipiḫ-šu im . . im ḫar šu (4) nu-ḫuš mâtâti *Rev.* (1) Ana ina riš šatti MUL . MUL . (2) ina na-šu ^{mul} Dil-bat izziz (3) ^{am} nakru : mílu íbur ú-mar-rum (4) ša $^{m\ ilu}$ Nírgal-íṭir(ir).

[83–1–18, 172.]

No. 243C. *Obv.* (1) Ana Sin ina tamarti-šu MUL . MUL ina . . . (2) šarru kiššutam(tam) ípuš(uš) mâtu . . (3) Ana MUL . MUL ana íli Sin . . . (4) šarru kiššuta ipuš(uš) (5) Ana MUL . MUL . ina libbi-šu izziz (6) ^{ilu} IMINA . BI mâta . . . *Rev.* (*top broken*)

(1) . . . ûmí(mí)-ma . . . . (2) . . . si mar-ṣa-ku . . . (3) . . . šarru bíl-iá . . . (4) . . . di-ia . . . [81–2–4, 142.]

No. 244. *Obv.* (1) Ana ^{mul} ŠÚ . GI ana íli Sin (2) ibrum-ma izziz ana lib Sin írub (3) šarru ina li-i-ti izzaz(az) (4) i-ša-ab-ma mât-su [urappaš] (5) íli mâti-šu iṭab . . . . (6) kittu u mi-ša-[ru] (7) ina mâti ibašši . . *Rev.* (1) šá ^{m} Ištar-šuma-íriš(iš). [K. 728.]

No. 244A. *Obv.* (1) $^{[mul]}$ ŠÚ . GI kur-kur-ru-šu i-nam-bu-uṭ (2) . . bît bíli-šu barta ípuš(uš) (3) . . . ki NÍR ^{mul} ŠÚ . GI izzaz-ma (4) $^{[ilu]}$ Muštabarrû-mûtânu(a-nu) (5) . . . . $^{[mul]}$ AL . LUL ik-ta-šad *Rev.* (1) [šarru lu]-ú-i-di (2) . . lu la-ti-iḳ (3) a-di uṣ-ṣu-ú (4) [ša] ^{m} Irašši(ši)-ilu ardu ša šarri (5) maḫ-ru-u. [K. 851.]

No. 244B. *Obv.* (*Top broken*) (1) . . . [1] . . . (2) Ana ^{mul} Zi-ba-ni-tum ana pân ^{ilu} Sin . . (3) pâl šarri írik . . . (4) Ana ^{mul} SIB . ZI . AN . NA ana pân . . . (5) . . ^{pl} pâl šarri írik . . . - *Rev.* (1) [Ana] mi-ši-ih Kakkabi ana ^{ilu} Šamši . . . (2) . . šar MAR ^{ki} . . . (3) . . . šamí(í) za . . . (4) . . . SAG . UŠ . . . (*Remainder broken off.*) [K. 1314.]

No. 244C. *Obv.* (1) Ana ^{mul} Zi-ba-ni-tum | . . . . (2) taš-mu-ú sa-li-[mu] . . . . (3) ^{mul} Zi-ba-ni-tum . . . . (4) [2]manzaṣ-ṣa [3]kîni . . . . (5) ina lib ^{mul} AL . LUL . . . (6) Ana ^{mul} LU . BAD ina IM . SI . [DI] . . . (7) [4]tibut(ut) ^{mâtu} Akkadi ^{ki} . . . (8) $^{[mul]}$ LU . SAG . BAD . UŠ ina . . . . *Rev.* (1) [iz]-za-az . . . . (2) [Ana] ^{ilu} Sin u ^{ilu} Ša-maš i . . . . (3) na-an-dur níší [^{pl} u âḫí ^{pl}] (4) . . ûmu XV ^{kám} in-nam-[ma-ru] (5) ta-mar-tú ša ^{mul} LU . BAD . . . . (6) šá šarri bíl-ia šú-u . . . (7) ša $^{m\,ilu}$ Nabû-aḫí ^{pl}-iriba. [81–2–4, 109.]

No. 244D. *Obv.* (1) . . . $^{mul\,am}$ KU . MAL ik-ta-šad (2) . . . un-nu-ut (3) . . . i-dir-tú ŠI . LAL (4) . . . la-aš-šu a-ḫi-ú šú-ú (5) . . . un-nu-tú-ni (6) . . . u-ni i-na-sa-ḫa *Rev.* (1) . . . dir ba-il (2) . . . *ka (?) i-ka-aš-ša-ad (3) . . . šu ru íbûr mâti iššir (4) . . . ma'al ḳu-ra-di irappiš(iš) (5) [ša $^{m\,ilu}$ Nabû]-mu-ší-ṣi. [81–2–4, 380.]

No. 245. *Obv.* (1) Ana ^{mul} KIL . BA ina lib Sin izziz (2) atal Subarti išakan(an) (3) Ana ^{mul} PAN ana íli Sin ibrum-ma (4)

[1] *Traces of four characters.*
[2] KI . GUB . BA-ṣa, *glossed* man-za-as-sa.
[3] GI . NA, *glossed* ki-í-ni.
[4] ZI-ut, *glossed* [ti]-bu-ut.

ạna lib Sin írub ûmí ^{pl} rubi labirûti ^{pl} (5) ^{ilu} Sin ana šatti I ^{kám} írik (6) šarru lu-i-di lu-la-ti-iḳ *Rev.* (1) ma-ṣar-ti ša ra-ma-ni-šu (2) li-iṣ-ṣur ina ûmi *la ṭa-a-bi (3) šarru a-na šu-ú-ḳu la uṣ-ṣa-a (4) *a-di a-dan-šu ša it-ti (5) it-ti-ḳu (6) it-ti ša kakkabi a-di araḫ ûmí ^{pl} (7) ša ^{m} Iraššì(ši)-ilu ardu ša šarri maḫ-ru-ú. [K. 963.]

No. 246. *Obv.* (1) [Ana ^{mul}] ŠÚ . GI Ana íli Sin ibrum ma izziz (2) [šarru ina] li-ti izzazu(zu) (3) [i ?]-šam-ma mât-su urappaš (aš) (4) [Ana ^{mul}] ŠÚ . GI ana íli Sin ibrum-ma izziz (5) . . šar mâti . . . . šarru íli mâti-šu iṭâb-ma (6) [kit]-ti u i-šar-ti (7) [ina] mâti-šu ibašši(ši) *Rev.* (1) [ša] ^{m} Iraššì(ši)-ilu mâr ^{m} Nu-úr-za-nu. [K. 811.]

No. 246A. *Obv.* (1) Ana ^{mul} KAK . [SI . DI] . . . (2) mâtu ḫa-ru-[bi-iš] . . . (3) ^{mul} KAK . SI . [DI] . . . (4) ḫa-ru-bi-iš . . . . (5) [1]ṣít-su . . [2] . (6) ina na-mu-ri-šu . . . (7) šamaššammu i (?) . . . *Rev.* (1) Ana ^{mul} AN . TA . [SUR-ra] . . . (2) [3]kakkabu ša pân . . . . (3) ina arḫi šuâti . . . (4) ^{mul} LU . BAD . *GUD . . . (5) in-na . . . (6) ša ^{m} ^{ilu} . . . [83–1–18, 317.]

No. 246B. *Obv.* (1) Ana [4]^{mul} [5]SIM . MAH . . . . (2) míš-ḫa [imšuḫ ?] (3) [6]tibût(ut) [7]ummâni(ni) . . . (4) mu-šú an-ni-*ú . . . (5) ultu lib ^{mul} . . . . (6) ina [8]ḫarrâni-šu ina . . . *Rev.* (1) lum-nu ša ^{mâtu} . . . (2) ^{ilu} Sin ina pân . . . (3) šá tarbaṣi ina . . . (4) . . ik-ṣur . . . (5) . . lib-bi . . . (6) ša . . . . [Bu. 91–5–9, 34.]

No. 246C. *Obv.* (1) Ana ^{mul} ÍN . MÍ . SAR . [RA] . . . (2) kakkabi-šu ma-'-diš . . . (3) mílu uṣ-ṣa . . . . . (4) . . ^{ilu} LU . BAD . GUD . UD . . . . (*Remainder of obv. and top of rev broken.*) *Rev.* (1) mâru itti . . . . (2) Ana ^{mul} AL . LUL . . . (3) šar Akkadi ^{ki} balaṭa ur-[rak]. [83–1–18, 322.]

No. 246D. (*Obv. and top of rev. broken.*) *Rev.* (1) . . um šú . . . . (2) ínuma(ma) IM . . . . (3) Ana ^{mul} UR . GU . LA ṣalmu lib . . . . (4) Ana kakkabu ṣalmu ^{ilu} LU . . . (5) šá ^{m} Šú-ma-[a-a]. [83–1–18, 298.]

1 UD . DA-su, *glossed* ṣi-is-su.
2 . . ., *glossed* ú (?) . . .
3 MUL . ša ŠI, *glossed* ka-ka-bu ša pa-ni.
4 MUL, *glossed* MU . UL.
5 SIM . MAḪ, *glossed* ši-im-maḫ
6 ZI-ut, *glossed* ti-bu-ut.
7 ṢAB-ni, *glossed* um-ma[ni].
8 KASKAL-šu, *glossed* ḫar-ra-ni-šu.

No. 246E. *Obv.* (*Top broken*) (1) a-na írib Šamši . . . . (2) ummân nakri ina mi . . . . (3) Ana kakkabu im-šú-uḫ im-*šú-[uḫ] . . . (4) iš-kun iš-kun . . . (5) is-sa-pi . . . (6) rubu ina dul . . . (*Remainder broken off*). [K. 6182.]

No. 246F. *Obv.* (1) Ana kakkabu ina pân Sin šuméli izziz (2) šarru kiš-šú-tam ípuš(uš) (3) Ana mul Muštabarrû-mûtânu (a-nu) ana pân Sin iṭḫi-ma izziz(iz) (4) ilu Sin mâta šúl-pu-ut-ti ú-šiš-šib (5) Ana kakkabu ina šumíl ilu Sin izziz(iz) (6) mât nakri šal-pu-ut-ti immar(mar?) *Rev.* (1) ša m ilu Nabû-íriba(ba). [K. 732.]

No. 246G. *Obv.* (1) . . . a-na ilu Sin [1]iṭḫu-ma (2) . . . a-ṣu-u-ni (3) . . . kiš-šu-tam ipuš(uš) (4) . . . a-na ilu Sin i-ṭa-aḫ-ḫu-ma (5) . . . un-ḳi (6) . . . *is-sap-ra (7) . . . . Muštabarrû-mûtanu(a-nu) (8) . . . ti it ú (9) . . . ḳu *Rev.* (1) . . . šá arḫu Simânu (2) . . ta-mar . . (3) . . . GUD . UD ûmu XVI kám (4) . . . Simânu it-ta-mar (5) . . . lib šá *šarri *bíl-ni (6) . . . u-ni (7) . . . *a-dan-niš (8) . . . aḫi pl-íriba. [83-1-18, 297.]

No. 247. *Obv.* (1) Mi-i-nu ra-'-a-mu an-ni-u (2) ša ilu Ištar a-na šarri bíl-ia (3) *ta-ra-'-a-mu-u-ni (4) . . . šá a-dan-niš a-na šarri bíl-iá (5) . . . ra-an-ni (6) . . . a sa tu sa-lim (7) . . . ár-ḫiš ta-at-ta-*mar (8) . . . pal-šu *Rev.* (1) . . . man-za-sa ur-ri-ik (2) [ûmí pl] šarri arkûti pl (3) Ana . . . kakkabu ša-ah-ru-um-ma innamir(ir) (4) šar mâti balaṭa ur-rak (5) šá m Ištar-šuma-íriš. [82-5-22, 55.]

No. 247A. *Obv.* (1) . . . ina lib mul Zi-ba-ni-tum (2) . . . TAB û-zu-us-su (3) . . . ba-ni-tum (4) . . . . GIR . TAB il-lak (5) . . . limutti šú-ú (6) . . . bí-ili-ia al-tap-ra (7) . . . bi (?) u UD ḪUL . IK (8) . . . *tum (?) u ši-ib-ṭu (9) . . . la uṣ-ṣu (10) . . . ša ra-ma-ni-šu (11) . . . u ba-ar-ti li . . (12) . . . ul-tu lib mul . . . (13) . . . uṣ-ṣu . . . *Rev.* (1) . . . maḫ-ru pi-ši . . . (2) . . . *u (?) a-na šarri lu . . . (3) . . . ú lu uš-tik-kak-ma . . . (4) . . . . la . . . . (5) . . . a-na šarri bí-ili-ia lik-ru-[bu] (6) . . . *al-lid-an-ni (7) . . . . ti ina íli iṣu BANŠUR-ia (8) . . . . ul az-zi-iz (9) . . . *ti (?) ki-nu a-na-ku (10) . . . ga-a ú-zu-za-ku-ma (11) . . . [šarru bí]-ili-ia a-nâ za-ri (12) . . . [ardu ša] šarri maḫrû(u). [K. 87-1.]

[1] Tí-ma, *glossed* iṭ-ḫu-ma.

XI. Omens from Clouds.

No. 248. *Obv.* (1) Ana urpatu | [1]sâmu ina šamí(í) (2) [2]ittanaskan [3]šâru tibû *Rev.* (1) ša m ilu Nabû-aḫî-pl íriba.

[K. 748.]

XII. Omens from the Moon's disappearance.

No. 249. *Obv.* (1) . . . ḪI . A ilu Dil-bat minâti pl-šu ibašši (ši) (2) . . . pú tim Gu-ti-i išakan(an) (3) . . ûmu XXVII kam Sin BUL . . (4) Ana ûm bubbuli ina arḫi III-šu . . . (5) atalû išakanma ilâni pl ki (?) . . . . (6) III ûmu(mu) ina šamí(í) . . . . (7) Ana Sin ina arhu ululi ûmu XXX [kam innamir] (8) sapaḫ(aḫ) mâtu . . . . (9) ûmu XXX kam a-*ga-*a . . . . . *Rev.* (1) bíl šarrani pl i-ḳab-bi um-[ma ittu ?] (2) la la-pi-it ûmu XXVII kam Sin it-ta-[mar] (3) ûmu XXVIII kam ûmu XXIX kam ina šamí(í) bu-u-ud (4) ù ûmu XXX kam it-tan-mar (5) im-ma-tim-ma li-in-na-mir (6) ba-ab-ti IV ûmí(mi-i) ina šamí(í) li-b id (7) im-ma-tim-ma IV ûmu(mu) ul i-bid (8) šar mâtâti lu-da-ri (9) ša m A-ša-ri-du.

[K. 768.]

XIII. Omens from Storms.

No. 249. *Obv.* (1) Ana ina arḫu Šabaṭi imbaru iḳ-*tur (2) atal kaš-ši-i (3) ša m ilu Nabû-iḳ-bi (4) mâr kuti ki.

[83-1-18, 188.]

No. 250. *Obv.* (1) [Ana] ina mâti imbaru ibašši(ši) (2) ibûru ina-pu-uš maḫiru kînu (3) [Ana] ina mâti imbaru sa-dir (4) pal mâti kiššutam(tam) ibíl(íl) (5) [Ana ina] arḫu Šabâṭi imbaru iḳ-tur (6) atal kaš-ši-i *Rev.* (1) [ša] m A-ša-ri-du maḫrû(ú) (2) ardu ša šarri.

[Bu. 89-4-26, 18.]

No. 250A. *Obv.* (1) [Ana ina arḫu] Šabâṭi imbaru iḳ-[tur] (2) atal kaš-ši-[i] (3) . . imbaru šú ru . . . . (4) a-na míli kiš-ša-tum . . . .

[1] DIR, *glossed* sa-a-mu.
[2] GAR . GAR . NU, *glossed* it-ta-na-aš-kan.
[3] IM, *glossed* ša-a-ru.

(5) KAN . IK . ši (?) .... *Rev.* (1) Ana imbaru .... (2) a-na zunni .... (3) [ša] m Iraššì(ši)-ilu ardu ša [šarri] (4) pa-nu-[u]. [K. 1310.]

No. 251. *Obv.* (1) Ana ina arḫu Šabâṭi imbaru iḳ-tur (2) atal mâtu kaš-ši-i (3) Ana ina mâti imbaru ibašši(ši) nu-ḫuš niši pl (4) Ana ina mâti imbaru sa-dir pâl mâti kiš-šu-tam ibíl(íl) (5) Ana ina ûm AN . ZU imbaru iḳ-tur la ša-ṭi-ir (6) imbaru damḳu šú-u a-na limutti la uk-ta-la (7) i-na mu-ši an-ni-i-í kak-ka-bu (8) [ina] kakkadi šá mul Aḳrabi *Rev.* (1) ina pân Sin it-ti-ti-iz (2) ittu-šu la i-lap-pa-[at] ... (3) la aš-šu la in-na-sa-[ḫa] (4) šum-ma mul Ṣur-ru mul BIL . TAR šá .... (5) šá mul ..... *iz-za-zu .. (6) ina pân ilu Sin .... ti(?)-ti .... (7) šú-u ittu ka-a-a-ma-nu (8) arḫa (?) lit-ru-ru kakkab šamí(í) gab-bu (9) it-ta-al (?) ku u ina limutti arḫu kisilimi (10) lu la it-ti-iḳ lit-ru-ru. [K. 760.]

No. 251A. *Obv.* (1) [Ana ina arḫu Šabâṭi imbaru] iḳ-tur atal [kaššî] (2) [Ana ina mâti imbaru ibašši] nu-ḫuš niši pl (3) [Ana ina mâti imbaru sadir] pâl mâti kiš-šu-tam i-kaš-šad (4) .... mît (?) ḫar-ra-an-šu ul ka ši (?) .... (5) .... * id-bu-ub di-in-šu ul SI . DI (6) .... ša ú-ší-ib-ru di-in-šu ul ... (7) .... pu-uš ín-ni-id ili (8) .... *it ḫu (?) ud nap-lu-us .... (9) .... mí (?) *Rev.* (*Top broken.*) (1) ... bíl ... (2) .... an alu ... (3 ?) ... iš-lu ... (4 ?) .... ru-u ... (5 ?) ... šu li-iḫ ... (*some lines wanting.*) *End of rev.* (6) .... si (?) ... (7) [ša m] za-kir. [81–2–4, 143.]

No. 252. *Obv.* (1) Ana ina arḫu Addâri imbaru iḳ-tur (2) .. mâtu * ub-bu-tu illak(ak) (3) ilu TIR . AN . NA ul-tu ilu Nabû (4) Ana ilu ÚR KÍL ilu Rammânu la iraḫiṣ(iṣ) (5) Ana ilu TIR . AN . NA íli ali KÍL (6) alu šarru u rubi pl-šu šal-mu *Rev.* (1) ša m Aḫî pl-ša-a am uruk ki-a-a. [K. 1389.]

No. 252A. *Obv.* (1) Ana ina arḫu Addâri IM . MI (*sic*) ibašši ... (2) mâtu * ub-bu-tú illak .. (3) Ana Šamšu ḫarrana-šu KÚR ma Šamšu UD-ma ... (4) šar mât-su RU-di ... (5) Ana íli ma-a-ti i-rab .... (6) ûmí pl ad-ru-ti ina .... (7) ma-'-du ilu Šamšu .... (8) ul ú-šú-uz *Rev.* (1) bíl šarrâni pl II ûmu(mu) .... (2) i-na ali ša pa-ni . . . (3) lu-ši-ib-ši-ma ana ma (?) . . . (4) i-na ṣíri lu-u (?) . . . . . (5) bíl šarrâni ^{pl} lu-da-[a-ri] (6) ša ^{m} A-ša-ri-du . . .

[K. 873.]

No. 252B. *Obv.* (1) Ana ina mâti imbaru ibašši nu-ḫuš niší ^{p} (2) Ana ina mâti imbaru sa-dir pal-í mâti (3) kiš-šu-tam ibíl(íl) (4) Ana ina mâti imbaru ú-sa-dir (5) maḫiru ina-pu-[uš] (6) Ana ina ûmi ir-bi imbaru iḳ-tur (7) ma-ḳat ílama(ma) ^{ki} *Rev.* (1) Ana ina ^{arḫu} Addari imbaru iḳ-tur (2) mâtu ub-bu-*tu illak(ak) (3) ša dan(?) . . . . imbaru (?) (4) ina SAG (?) šú . . di (?) ba (?) ina ^{arḫu} Addâri (5) i-šú-uz (?)-su (?) bît (?) ú ù (6) . . . . . šu imbaru bit (?) ú (7) . . . . (8) ša ^{m} A-ša-ri-du.

[83–1–18, 176.]

No. 252C. *Obv.* (1) . . . . ? ú (?) nu-ḫuš niší ^{pl} (2) . . . nu-ḫuš niší $^{[pl]}$ (3) . . . . nin (?)-šu . . . . . (4) . . . ri (?) . . *Rev.* (*Top broken off*) (1) . . . di UD-mu bal-ṭu . . . (2) . . . í ul i-zak-ku . . (3) . . . ul a-da-mad . . (4) . . . a-na šarri a-ḳab-bi . . (5) [ša $^{m\ ilu}$] Nírgal-iṭir(ir).

[K. 8861.]

No. 252D. *Obv.* (1) Ana ina mâti [imbaru sa]-dir (2) pâl mâti [kiššutam] i-kaš-[šad] (3) Ana imbaru iḳ-tur-*ma im . . . (4) ilâni ^{pl} ana mâti rîmu TUK . . . (5) ma-ṣar-tú šá ^{ilu} Sin . . . . (6) ûmu XXIX ^{kám} IM . DIR [dannat ?] (7) a-na II-í ûmí(mí) | pa . . . (8) šá II ûmí ^{pl} šú . . . *Rev.* (1) ûmu V ^{kám} ûmu VI*^{kám} . . . . (2) is-sa-a-ḫi-í- . . . . (3) li-pu-u-[šu] (4) ša $^{m\ ilu}$ Nabû-aḫí-^{pl} [íriba].

[K. 1326.]

No. 252E. *Obv.* (1) Ana ina mâti imbaru [sadir] (2) pâl šar mâti kiššuta [ibíl] (3) Ana ina ûmí(mí) ir-pi (4) . . ma-ḳa-at *mâti . . . (5) . . ^{arḫu} DIR . ŠÍ . KIN . TAR . . . . (6) mâtu kar-mu-tam . . . . *Rev.* (1) ša ^{m} Ištar-šuma-[íriš].

[K. 1321.]

No. 252F. *Obv.* (1) ša šarru bíl-ni iš-pur-an-na-[ši] (2) [um-ma] ra-aḫ-ṣa-tu-nu-ú (3) . . *riš ra-aḫ-ṣa-a-ni (4) . . . ma-'-du-tu ina lib (5) Ana (?) . . zu-un-ni-i ul ḫi (?) . . . *Rev.* (1) a-na . . . (2) lib SÍ SÍ . . . . (3) ša $^{m\ ilu}$ Marduk-šuma-uṣur u ^{m} Bit (?) . . .

[K. 1460.]

XIV. Omens from Thunder.

No. 253. *Obv.* (1) Ana ina ûm bubbuli [ilu] Rammânu pî-šu iddi (2) îbûru iššir maḫiru kînu (3) Ana ina ûm bubbuli šamû (ú) iznun(nun) (4) îbûra inaši-ma maḫiru kînu (5) bîl šarrâni [pl] luda-ri *Rev.* (1) ša [m] A-ša-ri-du. [S. 1232.]

No. 253A. *Obv.* (1) [Ana ina] ûm bubbuli [ilu] Rammânu pi-*šu *iddi (2) KI. A iššir maḫiru kînu (3) Ana ina ûm bubbuli šamu iznun(nun) (4) îbûra i-na-aš-šam-ma (5) maḫiru kînu *Rev.* (1) ša [m] Apla-a. [K. 1385.]

No. 253B. *Obv.* (1) Ana ina ûm bubbuli [A. AN šamû iznun] (2) îbûra inaši-[ma] (3) maḫiru kînu (4) Ana ina ûm bubbuli [ilu] Rammânu pî-šu iddi(di) (5) KI. A iššir *Rev.* (1) maḫiru kînu (2) ša [m ilu] Bîl-naṣir[ir]. [82-5-22, 1778.]

No. 253C. *Obv.* (1) [Ana] MI sa-am (?) mu (?) . . . . (2) IM irba(ba) . . . . (3) Ana mi ḫi ra . . . . (4) IM. ZI . . . . . (5) Ana ina ûm bubbuli zunnu [iznun] (6) îbûr mâti inaša . . . *Rev.* (1) *KI. [LAM] GI. [NA] *Rev.* (1) *ša [m] Za-kir. [D.T. 53.]

No. 254. *Obv.* (1) Ana ina ûm bubbuli [ilu] [Rammânu pî-šu iddi] (2) RU. DI. IB. TÚ (?) . . . . (3) Ana ina ûm bubbuli šamu-u [iznun] (4) maḫiru kînu RU. DI. IB (?) (5) [ilu] Rammânu ina ḳabal [ilu] Šamši pî-[šu iddi] (6) ri-í-mu ina mâti ibašši(ší) (7) ina ḳabal [ilu] Šamši ša iḳ-bu-u *Rev.* (1) [ilu] Šamšu ina na-pa-ḫi-šu [ilu] Rammânu (2) ina pu-ut [ilu] Šamši na-pa-ḫi iḳ-rib- (?)-šu (3) ina ší-í-ri-*i iḳ-di-bi (4) ša [m] Ba-la-si-[i]. [K. 786.]

No. 255. *Obv.* (1) Ana ina ûm bubbuli [ilu] Rammânu is-si (2) KI. A iššir maḫiru kînu (3) Ana ina ûm *bubbuli zunnu iznun(nun) (4) nu-[ḫuš ?] niši [pl] (5) Ana ina ûmi [la irpi] [ilu] Rammânu pî-šu iddi (6) da-'-um-ma-tú ina mâti ibašši(ši) *Rev.* (1) šá [m] Ištar-šuma-íris(ís). [K. 765.]

No. 256. *Obv.* (1) Ina íli dul-li šá šarri bí-ili (2) iḳ-bu-ú-ni (3) mu-šú an-ni-ú ša ûmi XXII [kám] (4) ina pa-an [mul] Dil-bat (5) ina pa-an ^{mul} KAK . SI . DI (6) A-ni-in-nu ni-ip-pa-aš (7) ^{am} ka-li-í í-pa-šu-ma. *Rev.* (1) Ana ^{ilu} Rammânu ina ḳabal $^{mul\ išu}$ Li-í (2) pî-šu iddi(di) šarru (3) mâtu la šú-a-tum ḳat-su ikašad.

[83-1-18, 209.]

No. 256A. *Obv.* (1) [Ana Sin ûmu I] ^{kám} innamir KA . [GI . NA lib mâti itâb] (2) [Ana ûmu] a-na minâti ^{pl}-šu [írik] (3) pâl ûmí ^{pl} arkûti $^{[pl]}$ (4) an-ni-ú ta-mar-tú šá ûmu I $^{[kam]}$ (5) Ana ^{ilu} Rammânu ina abul Sin pî-šu iddi(di) (6) šumḳutim(tim) ummân Ílama (ma) ^{ki} ina ^{išu} kakki ibašši(ši) (7) GAR . ŠÚ mâti-šu ana mâti ša-ni-ti-im-ma ippaḫḫar(ḫar) (8) an-ni-ú ša ki-i Sin in-na-mar-u-ni (9) ^{ilu} Rammânu pî-šu i-na-du-u-ni *Rev.* (1) šá ^{m} Bu-lu-ṭu.

[K. 787.]

No. 256B. *Obv.* (1) [Ana ina ^{arḫu}] Abi ^{ilu} Rammânu pî-[šu iddi] (2) [úmu ?] i-ru-ub ša-[mu-u ? iznun ?] (3) [íbûr] mâti la iššir . . . (4) Ana ina ûmi la ir-pi . . . IM . . . . . (5) ḫušaḫḫu . . . . . ibašši (6) Ana ina ûmi la ir-pi* birku ib-*ri-[iḳ] (7) ^{ilu} Rammânu RA . . (8) ûmu(mu) la[ir]-pu ^{arḫu} Abu (9) ^{ilu}*Rammânu [RA ?]-iṣ ša iḳ-bu-u-ni . . (10) ^{ilu} . . . iṣ a-na ṣu-ur . . . . *Rev.* (1) Ana mí-ḫi-[í] *šâru Šûti it-[bu-u] (2) Šumḳutim(tim) ^{mâtu} *MAR . TU ^{ki}] (3) [Ana] ^{mul} Muštabarrû-mûtânu (a . .) ina lib ^{mul} AL . [LUL izziz] (4) . . šu úkal . . sit up tú (?) (5) Ša ^{m} Ba-[la-si-i]

[K. 1323 + 1327.]

No. 256C. *Obv.* (1) Ana ina ^{arḫu} Abi ^{ilu} Rammânu pî-[šu iddi] (2) ub-bu-ṭu ina . . . (3) Ana ina ^{arḫu} Abi ^{ilu} Rammânu [pî-šu iddi-ma] (4) ûmu irûb Šamû iznun(nun) birḳu ib-[rik] (5) mí ^{pl} ina naḳbi LAL . . *Rev.* (1) ša ^{m} Arad ^{ilu} [í-a] [K. 853.]

No. 257. (1) Ana ina ^{arḫu} Abi ^{ilu} Rammânu pî-šu iddi-ma (2) ûmu irûb šamu iznun(nun) birḳu ib-riḳ (3) mí ^{pl} ina naḳbi iššapiku ^{pl} (4) Ana ina ûmu la ir-bi ^{ilu} Rammânu is-si (5) da-um-ma-tu . . . ḫušaḫḫu ina mâti.ibbašši (6) ina íli la ṭu-ub šíri an-ni-i (7) šarru bí-ili ultu lib-bi-šu la i-da-bu-ub (8) mur-ṣu šattu šú-ú (9) nišî ^{pl} am-mar mar-ṣu-u-ni (10) gab-bu šul-mu (11) tu-ra-ma šarru bí-ili (12) šá pa-laḫ ilâni ^{pl} šú-tu-u-ni (13 ûmu(mu) ù mu-šu ilâni ^{pl} ú-ṣal-lu-u-ni *Rev.* (1) Kit-tu-ú mí-mí-ni (2) a-na šarri bíl-ia ù zir-šu il-la-ka (3) ì-lu-ut-tu a-šir-tú (4) di-í-i-ḳi i-ba-at-ti (5) šú-ú ki-i an-ni-i ḳa-a-bi (6) rabiš a-ší-ir ûmí ^{pl}-šu arkûti ^{pl} (7) im-da-na-ra-aṣ ûmí ^{pl}-šu arkûti ^{pl} (8) šá $^{m\ ilu}$ Ištar-šuma-íríš(íš).

[81–7–27–, 19.]

No. 258. *Obv.* (1) Ana ina ^{arḫu} Abi ^{ilu} Rammânu pî-šu iddi-ma (2) ûmu irûb šamû iznun ^{ilu} TIR . AN . NA KÍL (3) birḳu ib-ri-ik zunni ina [1]naḳbi iššapiku (4) Ana ina [2]ûmi la irpi ^{ilu} Rammânu is-si (5) da-'-um-ma-tú ina mâti ibašši(ši) (6) ûmu(mu) la ir-pi ^{arḫu} Abu (7) Ana ina ^{arḫu} Abi šamû(ú) iznun(nun) (8) šum-ḳutim(tim) nišî ^{pl} *Rev.* (1) Ana mí-ḫi-í ^{šâru} Aḫarrî itbi (2) šumḳu-tim(tim) ^{mâtu} Aḫarrî ^{ki} (3) Ana ^{ilu} Rammânu II-šu pî-šu iddi(di) (4) mâtu šâ $^{[3]sal}$ nukurta [4]išpur-ka (5) [5]salîma [6]išappar-ka (6) šá $^{m\ ilu}$ Nabû-aḫî-^{pl}-íriba

[S. 1043.]

No. 259. *Obv.* (1) Ana ina ^{arḫu} Tašrîti ^{ilu} Rammânu pî-šu iddi(di) (2) ûmu irûb(ub) šamû iznun(nun) (3) ^{ilu} TIR . AN . NA KÍL (4) birḳu ib-riḳ (5) ilâni ^{pl} ana mâti (6) rîmu iraššu ^{pl} *Rev.* (1) šá ^{am} Rab-dup-šar

[K. 715.]

No. 260. *Obv.* (1) Ana ina ^{arḫu} Tašrîti ^{ilu} Rammânu pî-šu iddi(di) (2) nu-kur-tu ina mâti ibašši(ši) (3) Ana ina ^{arḫu} Tašrîti šamû(û) iznun(nun) (4) šumḳutím(tim) marṣûti ^{pl} (5) u alpi ^{pl} (6) : šumḳutim(tim) ^{am} nakri *Rev.* (1) ša ^{m} Ṭa-bi-ia.

[83–1–18, 180.]

No. 261. *Obv.* (1) [Ana] ina ^{arḫu} Šabâṭi ^{ilu} Rammânu *pî-[šu iddi] (2) tibut(ut) aribi $^{[pl]}$ (3) Ana îna ^{arḫu} Šabâṭi ^{ilu} Rammânu pi-šu [iddi] (4) ina abni šamû izanun . . . (*A few traces on reverse*).

[80–7–19–343.]

No. 262. *Obv.* (1) Ana ina ûm bubbuli ^{ilu} Rammânu pî-šu [iddi] (2) KI . A iššir maḫiru [kînu] (3) Ana ina ûm bubbuli ^{ilu} Rammânu pî-šu iddi . . (4) damiḳti íbûri . . . . (5) Ana ina ^{arḫu} Addâri ^{ilu} Rammânu pî-šu iddi(di) (6) ûmu irûb Šamû iznun birḳu ik-[riḳ] (7) mílu ma-'-du . . . . (8) íbûru . . . *Rev.* (1) šá . . . .

[K. 854.]

[1] IDIM, *glossed* naḳ-ḅi.
[2] UD . NU . ŠU, *glossed* ú-mí la ir-pi.
[3] SAL . KÚR, *glossed* nu-kur-tí.
[4] ḲI . ka, *glossed* iš-pur-ka.
[5] DI-ma, *glossed* sa-li-i-mu.
[6] ḲI-ka, *glossed* i-šap-par-ka.

No. 262A. *Obv.* (1) . . . A . AN ^{ilu} (?) . . . (2) Šamí(í) ana íli . . . (3) . . . . arkûti ^{pl} u ṭu-ub . . . (4) . . . *IM KA-šu RU alu . . . (5) . . . rubu niší ^{pl} mâti . . . (6) ša . . .

[83–1–18, 718.]

No. 262B. *Obv.* (1) . . . ZI . A (2) . . . MAR . TU ^{ki} (3) . . . TAR ^{pl} (4) . . . . ḫu (?) UD . ŠU-am (5) . . . tibut(ut) ^{šâru} Šutu (6) . . . im mir (7) . . . IM II (8) . . . IM . IV (9) . . . *Rev.* (1) . . . *GI . NA (2) . . . (3) . . . SAR (4) . . . . (5) . . . u Sin (6) . . . MIŠ

[K. 12555.]

No. 262C. *Obv.* (1) . . . sad-dir-ma (2) . . . . íbûr mâti SI . DI (3) . . . . ṣu (4) . . . iṣ (5) . . . alu u . . . (*Remainder of obverse and top of reverse broken.*) *Rev.* (1) . . . (2) . . . kak (?) ir (3) . . . šarru (4) . . .

[K. 1593.]

XV. Omens from Earthquakes.

No. 262D. *Obv.* (1) Ana irṣitim(tim) ina kâl ûmi [inuš] (2) sapaḫ mâti (3) Ana ú-sad-dir-ma i-[nu-uš] (4) ti-ib ^{am} [nakri] *Rev.* (1) ša ^{am} Ša-pi-ku mâr . . .

[81–2–4, 344.]

No. 263. *Obv.* (1) [Ana irṣitim] tim ina ka-la (2) ûmi(mi) i-nu-uš (3) [sapaḫ] mâti (4) Ana sa-dir-ma í-nu-uš (5) ti-ib nakri *Rev.* (1) ša $^{m\,ilu}$ Nabû-iḳ-bi (2) mâr kûti ^{ki}.

[K. 1380.]

No. 264. *Obv.* (1) Ina íli ri-i-bi ša šarri [bí-ili] (2) iš-pur-an-ni an-ni-u [pi-šir-šu] (3) Ana irṣitim(tim) ú-sa-dir-ma [inuš] (4) ti-ib [nakri] (5) Ana irṣitim(tim) ina muši inuš(uš) na-[zaḳ mâti] (6) ina íli ša ûmi V (?) ^{kám} i . . . (7) il-lik-an-ni mušu šá . . . . (8) i-ru-ub . . . . (9) ina muḫ-ḫi irṣitum(tum) ú-sa-[dir] (10) at-ta-as-[ḫa] *Rev.* (1) Ana ina ^{arḫu} Nisanni irṣitu irûb . . . (2) rubu mât-šu ibbalkat-[su] (3) lu-u la ^{arḫu} Addâri ú-šar-ri a . . . (4) a-kan-ni an-ni-u pišir-[šu] (5) ina íli šá ^{arḫu} Addâri ^{arḫu} Nisanni arki . . . (6) i-ru-ub-u-ni ina muḫ-ḫi ú-sa-*dir . . . (7) i-nu-uš zi . . . (8) lu-u arḫu ina bir-tu-šu-nu ip-tu . . . (9) a-kan-ni ^{arḫu} Nisannu ṭâbu-ma a-na na-sa . . . (10) ša ^{m} Ištar-šuma-íriš(íš) (*Left-hand edge*) (1) Lim-mu ^{m} La-ba-si (2) ^{am} Rab ka-a-ri.

[83–1–18, 287.]

No. 265. *Obv.* (1) Ana ina arḫu Nisanni irṣitu i-ru-ub (2) šarru mât-su ibbalkat-su . . (3) Ana irṣitim(tim) ina muši i-nu . . . (4) na-zaḳ mâti miḳtí(í) mâti *Rev.* (1) Ša m Apla-[a]. [82-5-22, 61.]

No. 265A. *Obv.* (1) Ana ûmu XIV kám Sin u Šamšu itti a-ḫa-miš innamru . . (2) sanâḳu ša pî lib-bi mâti iṭâb(ab) (3) ilâni pl mâtu Akkadi ki ana damiḳtim(tim) i-ḫas-sa-[su] (4) ḫu-ud lib-bi ummâni (ni) lib-bi šarri iṭâb . . (5) bûl mâtu Akkadi ki par-ga-niš ina [ṣíri irabbiṣ] (6) Ana Sin Šamša ikšuda-ma it-tin-tu-ú ḳarnu [ḳarnu idir] (7) ina mâti kit-ti ibašši . . (8) mâru itti abî-šu kit-ti [itamu] *Rev.* (1) Ana irṣitim(tim) ina ka-la [ûmi irûb] (2) sapaḫ(aḫ) [niši] (3) Ana irṣitim(tim) ina arḫu Du'uzi i-nu-[uš] (4) rubu ina mât nakri . . (5) i-rab- . . . (6) ša m Ša-pi-ku . . [K. 790.]

No. 265B. *Obv.* (1) Ana ri-i-bu . . . (2) šarru itti . . . (3) Ana ki ina arḫu Du'uzi . . . (4) : ina bît . . . . (5) Ana ki ina MI . . . (6) : RU . . . . (7) . . . . *Rev.* (*Top broken*) (1) . . . (2) ilu . . . (3) . . . . (4) damiḳti (5) i . . . [K. 12281.]

No. 265C. *Obv.* (1) [Ana ribu] ina arḫu Tašrîti i-ru-ub (2) [íbûr mâti SI .] DI šal nukrâti pl ibaššu pl (3) . . . i-ru-ub šal nakurti ina mâti . . (4) . . . . i-nu-uš . . . . (5) . . . ša ûmi XI kám . . . . (6) . . ŠI A . . . . (7) . . . . mí bît bar (?) . . . . (8) . . . ta si (?) . . . *Rev.* (1) . . . ia i-ba-aš-ši (2) . . . lu-uḳ-bi (?) (3) . . . ša iṣ . . . (4) . . . a . . . (5) . . . ia liš . . . (6) . . . di II-šu a-na . . . . (7) . . . gi a-šap-pa-*ra . . . (8) [ša] m Ri-mu-* tu . . [82-5-22, 68.]

No. 266. *Obv.* (1) Ana Sin ûmu I kám innamir (2) sanâḳu ša pî lib mâti iṭâb(ab) (3) Ana ûmu a-na minâti pl-šu í-ri-ik (4) pâl ûmí pl arkûti pl (5) muša an-ni-ú (6) ri-i-bu ir-tu-bu (7) Ana ina arḫu Ṭíbîti ri-i-bu irub(ub) (8) šarru ina al nakri-šu uššab(ab) *Rev.* (1) Ana ina arḫu Ṭíbîti irṣitu irub(ub) (2) íkal rubi šumḳut-ma kar-mu-tam illak(ak) (3) Ana ina muši irṣitu i-ru-ub (4) na-zaḳ mâti . . . miḳtí(í) mâti (5) ša am Rab-A . BA. [K. 779.]

No. 266A. *Obv.* (1) [Ana ina arḫu Šabâṭi] ri-i-bu i-ru-ub (2) [širû] bilat-sa inaši . . . išaḳal (LAL . DA) (3) [gir-rit] nakri ibaššu pl (4)... i-ru-ub ina ikalli rubu nakru KU-ab (5)... šu *i-gal-* lil (6).... MI i-nu-uš na-zaḳ mâti (7)... miḳtí(í) mâti *Rev.* (1)... ri-i-bu ana na-bal-kat-ti (2).. an uš ša Zi-ib nakri ši-i (3) ... ÍN. NUN imitti u šumíli a-šar (4)... kir-bu li-í-tu (5)... kúr(?) *ib-*ba-aš-ši (6)... mâr Bar-sib ki. [K. 813.]

No. 266B. *Obv.* (*Top broken.*) (1)... kima... (2)... li-i ... (3)... UR. GU. LA DU... (4)... šu i-nu-uš (5)... šarri arkûti pl (6)... šú(?) UD ilu ÍN. LIL ib-il-ma (7)... Akkadi ki i-na-ḫi-iš lib-ša ibaluṭ(uṭ) (8)... šar Akkadi ki DAN. GA-ma mí-li-ṣa (?).. (9) [ša m ilu habû]-mu-ší-ṣi. [83-1-18, 310.]

No. 267. *Obv.* (1) Ana šamû(ú) is-su-ma irṣitim(tim)... (2) ilâni pl mâti... (3) kibrat irba(ba) ša.... (4) alâni pl sal nukurti ... (5) marṣûti pl mâti šumḳutu pl...... (6) Ana šamû(ú) is-su-ma irṣitim(tim)... (7) ilu ÍN. LIL ka-mar mâti... (8) Ana šamû(ú) is-su-ma irṣitim(tim) sa... (9) mí-riš mâti i-ma-ad-di šu du bu uk .... (10) Ana ilu Í-ri-iš-KI. GAL ik-kil-la-ša kima ur... tak (11) irṣitim(tim) mâta inadi(di) (12) Ana ina arḫu Šabâṭi ri-i-bu i-ru-ub širû bilat-ṣa (13) išaḳal gir-rit am nakri ibaššu pl (14) Ana ina arḫu Šabâṭi irṣitu i-ru-ub (15) ina ikalli rubu šanumma(ma) uššab(ab). *Rev.* (1) Ana irṣitu ina muši i-nu-uš (2) na-zaḳ mâti... [miḳtí mâti] (3) Ana šamû(ú) is (?)-su.... (4) Ana šamû.... (5).... (6) ina mâti ilu.... (7) lu-u ilu SAG. MÍ. GAR lu-u ilu Dil-bat .... (8) ki-ma i-tab-bu-lu la.... (9) šum-ma ilu Rammânu pí-šu [iddi] (10) šum-ma AN ḫu-ú-du... (11) šum-ma ri-i-bu.... (12) an-ni-ú ina lib-bi šú-ú... (13) bi-it ilu Dil-bat it-bal-u-ni ù ilu Šamšu (?) (14) ḳaḳ-ḳu-ru bi-it ri-ik... (15) ša m Ištar-šuma-[íriš]. [K. 124.]

No. 267A. *Obv.* (1) Ana šamí(í) DIR ma-ḫi-iṣ duḫdu ina mâti ibašši(ši) (2) m Ṣil-la-a ina ḳatâ II m Šakin-šumi il-tap-ra (3) um-ma ana mi-tu-tu a-na-ad-di-ka (4) um-ma mi-nam-ma ta-ḳab-bi um-ma (5) m Ṣil-la-a nikasi-ia it-ta-ši (6) um-ma m Mun-na-bit-tum am mu-kin-ni-ka (7) u ilu Bíl (?)... am Bíl-di-ni-iá am mu-kin-nu (8) mi-nu-ú ina lib nikasi-iá ma-la *Rev.* (1) iš-šu-ú ki-i la-mí-du-ú (2) mim-(sal)-ma ma-la ina pa-an šarri ad-bu-bu (3) u i-ba-aš-ši ša a-na šarri la aḳ-bu-ú (4) gab-bu it-ta-ši ḳatâ II-a ina bît abí-iá (5) ul-tí-li

g

u ka-a-a-ma-nu ni-ík-la-a-tum (6) ú-nak-ka-la ana íli ^am^ ša-ti-iá (7) i-dib-bu-ub šarru bílu la ú-maš-šir-an-ni (8) ša ^m^ Za-kir.

[80-7-19, 19.]

XVI. Omens from Eclipses.

No. 268. *Obv.* (1) Dib-bi ša atalî ina pi-ia a-na šarri bí-ili-iá ul ú-ší-íš-mu (2) a-du-ú la al-ṭa-ru ku ú mu a-na šarri bí-ili-iá al-tap-ra (3) ša atalî limutti-šu a-na adi arḫi adi ûmu(mu) adi ma-aṣ-ṣar-tum adi ur-ri-tum (4) a-šar ú-šàr-ru ú . . ù a-šar ^ilu^ Sin atalû-šu i-šaḫ-ḫa-ṭu-ma i-na-*as-su-ku (5) limutti-šu an-nu-tum i-maḫ-ḫa-ru ^arḫu^ Simânu ^mâtu^ Aḫarrû ^ki^ ù (6) pu-ru-us-su a-na uri ^ki^ na-din limutti ša ûmi XIV ^kám^ ša ḳa-bu-ú (7) ûmu XIV ^kam mâtu^ Ílama(ma) ^ki^ ur-ri-tum a-šar ú-ší-ir-ru-ú ul ni-i-du (8) *mi-ni-tú atalî-šu a-na íli ^šâru^ šûti u ^šâru^ Aḫarrî il-ta- ḫa-aṭ (9) limutti ana ^mâtu^ Ílama(ma) ^ki^ u ^mâtu^ Aḫarri ^ki^ ul-tu ^šâru^ šadi u ^šâru^ iltani (10) ki (?) im-mir damiḳti ša su-bar-tum ^ki^ u Akkadi ^ki^ i-ḳab-bi-šu ša i-ri-mu (11) it-tum ša ma-ta-a-ti gab-[bi]-i (?) imitti ^ilu^ Sin Akkadi ^ki^ šumíli ^ilu^ Sin (12) ^mâtu^ Ílama(ma) ^ki^ í-la-a-ti ^ilu^ [Sin Aḫarrû] ^ki^ šap-la-a-ti ^ilu^ Sin ^mâtu^ Subartu ^ki^ (13) aš-šu ma-aṣ-ṣar-tum ša . . . . . . ú-ṣa-a . . . . . (14) gab-bi-šu ša i-ri-mu . . . . . . (15) u man-ma ka-la-mu la . . . . (16) ^mâtu^ Šìr-ra-pu i-káb . . . . . (17) nišî ^pl^ ma-a-ti la i-šim . . . . . (18) ^am^ Rab-a-ši-pa a-ki ša i-li (?) . . . . *Rev.* (1) ù ina rabûti ^pl^ ša ^mâtu^ ka-al-du lu-u ^mâtu^ *A-*ra-mu (?) *ana mâti . . . . (2) íštín(ín) rubu šarru lu-ší-ín-ni la-kip-ti-šu lu-pi-it-tu-šu *an-*nu . . . . (3) it-tum i-maḫ-ḫa-ru-ma lib-bi šarru bí-ili-iá i-ṭa-ab ina atalî . . . (4) ^mul^ SAG . MÍ . GAR izziz(iz) a-na šarri šu-lum ku-mi-šu kab-tu í-du-ú . . . . (5) ina íli šú-mu a-ga-a šarru ma-ʿ-du lu-ú ra-ḫu-uṣ a-di man-nu šú-lum (6) a-na šarri i-ḳab-bu-ú ki-i šarru i-kip-pi šar ilâni ^pl^ ša šamí(í) u irṣitim(tim) (7) šú-lum a-na šarri bí-ili-iá il-tap-ra man-di-í-ma šarru i-ḳab-bi um-ma (8) šar ilâni ^pl^-ma šú-lum il-tap-ra ša ^mâtu^ Šìr-ra-pu ù ša ru-bi-í (9) am-mí-ni-i taš-pu-ra a-na-ku-um-ma šarru í-li dul-li-šu lu-ú (10) í-ti-iḳ-ma í-li dul-li-šu lu-ú-ša-kin-ma lib-bi šarri bí-ili-iá li-ṭib (11) ^ilu^ Bíl u ^ilu^ Nabû ma-ta-a-ti gab-bi a-na pu-uḫ Šarri bí-ili-iá lid-di-nu (12) šarru ṭí-í-mu il-tak-na-an-ni um-ma maṣṣarta-a ú-ṣur u mimma(ma) ša ti-bi-ú (13) ḳi-ba-a ín-na mimma(ma) ša ina pa-ni-iá ba-nu-ú ù ša-lam ina íli šarri bí-ili-iá (14) ṭa-a-bu a-na šarri al-tap-ra II-šu III-šu ma . . . . . pa-*an šarri (?)

(15) lil-su-ma šarru a-na lib dib-bi li-*ru-*ub . . . šarru lu ni is su (?) (16) ša dib-bi ša kit-tum a-na šarri bí-ili-iá aš-pur *Left-hand edge* (1) ša-^{m} Mun-na-bi-tí. [K. 2085.]

No. 269. *Obv.* (1) . . . ^{šâru} Aḫarrû ḪU . BI . A i-ta-ḳil ḫušaḫḫa šar Aḫarrî (2) . . ú-kal . . (3) . . . DIR-ma ^{šâru} šûtu ra-kib aribi itabbu . . . (4) . . ^{arḫu} Aîri ûmu XXVIII ^{kám} Šamšu kupuru šarru ûmí ^{pl}-šu arkûti ^{pl} (5) . . mâtu maḫiru nap-ša ikkal (6) . . ^{arḫu} Aîri Šamšu kupuru iškun nap-ša ikkal ûmí ^{pl} šarri arkûti ^{pl} (7) Ana Šamšu ina nipiḫ-šu kima azkari-ma kima Sin agû a-pir (8) šar mâti nakri-šu ikašad(ád) mâtu limutta-ša ḳaṭ-lim-ma damiḳta immar(mar) (9) Ana ina ^{arḫu} Aîri ûmu XXIX $^{kám\ ilu}$ Šamšu atalû iškun ina ^{šâru} iltani ušarri-ma (10) ina ^{šâru} šûti ikân ḳarnu šumíli-šu *id-da-at (11) ḳarnu imitti-šu írkat(at) ilâni ^{pl} kibrat irba(ba) LÚ ^{pl} (12) *LU'. GAL ina pî *ili iḳabbi tibut(ut) šarri IM ZI (?) (13) . . TÍ ana šatti V ^{kám} ? ir bartu ina ^{mâtu} Akkadi ^{ki} ibašši(ši) *Rev.* (1) . . . mâru abî-šu idâk aḫu aḫî-šu idâk rubî ^{pl} imtaraṣu ^{pl} . . (2) . . . ^{pl} ûmí ^{pl} ina ^{mâtu} Akkadi ^{ki} ibašši šarru šuâtu LIK . KU in-na-bal (3) nakru alu zag-mu iṣabbat(bat) šarru šuâtu imât mâru ana ašabi ina bit ^{ilu} ÍN . LIL (4) ^{nam} pagrâni ^{pl} ûmu I ^{kám} ibaššû ^{pl} : šar Aḫarrî ^{ki} (5) íli . . . . . a-ḫa-miš itaḫḫu ^{pl} (6) ina írib Šamšu a . . . . *aṣ mat ti išakan(an) (7) ina ṣît Šamši . . . in-na-ḳa-ru (8) . . . MIŠ i . . . a alu SIS . TI . ilu buša-šu UD . DU (9) šar (?) Ílama (?) . . . . šar Subarti ^{ki} imât šar Aḫarrî imât (10) ilâni ^{pl} zi-*nu . . . ana mâti SI ^{pl}-nim-ma (11) . . . an mat in (12) . . . ṣa-a-ti ana ^{mâtu} Ílama(ma) ^{ki} (13) [ša ^{m} Iraššî]-ilu ardu ša šarri maḫrû(u) [K. 815.]

No. 270. *Obv.* (1) . . . . lum nakrûti ^{pl} (?) (2) . . . míli ^{pl} ina naḳbi ibaššu ^{pl} (3) . . . atal maṣṣarti barariti . . . . . atal šar Akkadi ^{ki} šarru rabû imât (4) [Ana] atalû iškun-ma ^{šâru} iltanu illik ilâni ^{pl} ana mâti rîmi iraššu ^{pl} (5) Ana Sin ad-riš uṣi a-di-ru iš-ti išakan(an) (6) Ana Sin ad-riš ṣitu-šú u id-ru (?) šaḫluḳti mâti kalami (7) Ana Sin ad-riš uṣi-ma kima ṭí-im šamí(í) iškun šarru mâtâti (8) ina abikti ú-šam-kat : ilâni ^{pl} mâtâti ina abikti ú-šam-ḳa-tu (9) Ana Sin ina ^{arḫu} Simâni a-dir ^{ilu} Rammanu arki šatti íbûr mâti iraḫiṣ(iṣ) (10) Ana ina ^{arḫu} Simâni Atal maṣṣarti barariti iškun tibut(ut) nuni u aribi (11) Ana ina ^{arḫu} Simâni ûmu XIV ^{kám} atalû iškun šarru ga-mi-ru ša šatti îraššî imât-ma (12) mâru-šu ša ana šarrûti la zak-ru kussa iṣabat-ma ^{sal} nukrâti ^{pl} ibaššu ^{pl} (13) Ana ina ^{arḫu} Simâni ultu ûmi I ^{kám} adi ûmi XXX ^{kám} atalû iškun atal šar Akkadi ^{ki} (14) . . . DAN kiš-ša-ti ibašši-ma ibûr mâti ^{ilu} Rammânu iraḫiṣ(iṣ) ummânu rabû (?) (15) [. . .] ummânu imḳut(ut) ínuma(ma) ana šulmu(mu) šarru âlu u niši-šu ipuš-ma išallim (16) [la šur]-ri-í bu-bul-ti : ina šatti šiâti ibašši(ši) *Rev.* (1) . . . ^{kám} atalû iškun-ma ilu ina kupuri-šu (2) . . . BA adi maṣarti ḳabliti taḳ-tú (3) . . . ^{šâru} iltanu-ina ḳatâ ^{II}-ka írib(rib) (4) . . . ma u šar Uri ^{ki} purussu innadan Uru ^{ki} (5) hušaḫḫa immar pagrâni ^{pl} i-man-du Šar Uri ^{ki} mâru-šu (6) i-ḫab-bil-šu-ma mâru ḫa-bil abi-šu ^{ilu} šamšu ikašad-su-ma (7) ina KI . ḪUL abi-šu ımât mâr šarri ša ana šarrûti la zak-ru (8) kussa iṣabat(bat) (9) Ana atal maṣṣarti barariti a-na pagrâni ^{pl} (10) Ana ûmu na'ru maššarti barariti a-na arḫi III ^{kám} ûmi X ^{kám} (11) ^{arḫu} Simânu ^{mâtu} Aḫarrû ûmu XIV ^{kám} ^{mâtu} Ílama maṣṣartu bararitu ^{mâtu} Akkadu ^{ki} (12) . . . ana šarri šulmu(mu) (13) . . . . . du. [K. 955.]

No. 271. *Obv.* (1) [Ana ina] ^{arḫu} Simâni ûmu XIV ^{kám} atalû iškun-ma ilu ina kupuri ID . IM III ſli-ta kupuru-ma (2) . . ID . IM IV šapli-ta iz-ku IM . IÍ maṣṣartu bararitú itbi-ma (3) . . maṣṣartu ḳabliti tak-tú kupuri-šu innamir-ma IM II ina ḳata ^{II}-ka írib(rib) (4) ina lib Uri ^{ki} u šar Uri ^{ki} purussu innadin šar Uri ^{ki} ḫušaḫḫa im-mar (5) . . pagrâni ^{pl} i-man-du šar Uri ^{ki} mâru-šu i-ḫab-bíl-šu-ma (6) . . mâru ḫa-bíl abí-šu ^{ilu} Šamšu ikašad-su-ma ina KI . ḪUL abí-šu ^{ilu} imât (7) . . mâr šarri ša a-na šarruti la zak-ru ^{isu} Kušsa iṣabat(bat) (8) [Ana] kakkabu ina šaplit ^{mul} PA . BIL . SAG a-dir purus mut-ta-bal u Babili (9) Atal maššarti Šadurri ana murṣi ibašši-ma ûmu na'ri maṣṣarti šadurri ana arḫi X (?) ^{kám} (10) maṣ-ṣartu šadurru ^{mâtu} Ílama ^{ki} ûmu XIV ^{kám} ^{mâtu} Ílama ^{ki} ^{arḫu} Simânu ^{mâtu} MAR IM II ^{mâtu} Akkadu ^{ki} (11) ina ^{arḫu} Simâni ûmu V ^{kám} ^{ilu} SAG . MÍ . GAR ina lib . . . . a-šar ^{ilu} Šamši ul-ta-pa-a izziz(iz) (12) ina ba-il zi-mu-šu DIR . . . . mâtu (?) itti mâti . . šulmí(mí) (13) [zunnı] ^{pl} daḫ-du-tú míli ^{pl} sad-ru-ti a-[na ^{mâtu} Ak-kadi ^{ki}] (14) [maḫiru] I ḲA $^{\text{ta-a-an}}$ a-na I GUR $^{\text{ta-a-an}}$ innadin(in) . . . (15) parakki ^{pl} -šu-nu daḫ-du immaru ^{pl} : ^{arḫu} Simânu ^{ilu} SAG . MÍ . GAR ba-il in . . . . (16) Ana ^{ilu} SAG . MÍ . GAR šarura [na]-ši šarru ša-lim lib mâti iṭâb(ab) . . . *Rev.* (1) atal maṣṣarti šaddurri . . .'šum-ma mitḫariš innamir(ir) pagrâni ^{pl} ibaššu ^{pl} rubu imât

(2) . . atal maṣṣarti šadurri iškun-ma maššarta íg-mur ṣâru iltanu illik marṣûti balṭuti ina mâtu Akkadi ki ibaššu (3) . . atalû ina IM I ušarri-ma IM II izziz šumḳutim(tim) Ílama(ma) ki Gu-ti- ki Ana Akkadi ki la iṭaḫḫi (4) Ana atalû ina IM I ušarri-ma ma IM II immir(ir) Šumḳutim(tim) Ílama(ma) ki Ana Akkadi ki la iṭaḫḫi (5) Ana atalû iškun-ma IM II izziz ilâni pl Ana mâti rîmu iraššu pl (6) Ana Sin ina arḫu Simâni a-dir arki šatti ilu Rammânu iraḫiṣ(iṣ) (7) Ana Sin ina arḫu Simâni atalû iškun mílu ibašši-ma bi-ib-lu mí pl mâti ub-bal (8) Ana ina arḫu Simâni atal maṣṣarti šadurri iškun íš-rit mâti šumḳutu pl ilu Šamšu i-maḫ-ḫa-ra (9) Ana ina arḫu Simâni ûmu XIV kám atalû iškun šarru ga-mí-ru šá šatti iraššì u imât-ma (10) mâru-šu ša a-na šarrûti zak-ru iṣu Kussa iṣabat-ma nu-kúr-tu ibašši : pagrâni pl ibaššu pl 11 Ana ina arḫu Simani ultu ûmi I kám adi ûmi XXX kám Atalû iškun atai šarri Akkadi ki (12) mílu kiššati ibašši-ma íbûr mâti ilu Rammânu iraḫiṣ(iṣ) ummânu rabú šumḳut(ut) (13) Šum-ma ana Šulmí(mi) šar âli u niši-šu ípuš-ma išallimu(mu) la šur-ri-í bu-bul-ti ibašši (14) Ana ina arḫu Simâni ina la mi-na-ti-šu atalû iškun šar kiššati imât-ma ilu Rammânu iraḫiṣ(iṣ) (15) mílu illakam(kám) íbûr mâti ilu Rammânu ina-šar a-lik pân ummâni(ni) šumḳut(ut) *Left-hand edge.* (1) [Ana ilu SAG . MÍ . GAR] ší-ir-ti ik-tu-un (2) šarrâní pl nakrûti pl išallimu [pl] (3) ša m ilu . . . .

[K. 750.]

No. 271A. *Obv.* (1) [ilu] Sin ina arḫu Ululi ûmu XV kám (2) . . . ilu Ša-maš in-na-mar (3) [atalû] | ú-ší-taḳ (*Remainder much broken.*) *Rev.* (*Top broken.*) (1) . . . ultu ilu Ša-maš in . . . (2) . . . ú-ší-taḳ la i-ša-kan (3) ša m ilu Nabû-aḫî pl-íriba (4) ûmu XIII kám

[K. 839.]

No. 272. *Obv.* (1) Ana ina arḫu Araḫšamni ilu Rammânu pi-šu iddi(di)-ma . . . . (2) ilu TIR . AN . NA KÍL birḳu . . . . (3) bíl šarrâni pl la i-ḳab-bi um-ma . . . . (4) tal-la-ka la taš-pu-ra . . . . (5) a-na am SAG. pl ki-i ad-di-nu u . . . . (6) am kap-tu í-du-ú ša iḳ-bu-ú ul (?) . . . . . . a-na muḫ-ḫi man-ma ša- nam-ma (7) Ana ilu SAR . UR u ilu SAR . GAZ ša mul Zi-ḳit mul Aḳrabi it-tan-na-an-bi-ṭu (8) iṣu kakki pl mâtu Akkadi ki itabbu pl (9) Zi-ḳit mul Aḳrabi bílu rabû mul PA . BIL . SAG (10) mul Dil-bat ina lib mul PA . BIL . SAG izzaz-ma (11) Ana ilu Nírgâl ina lib mul Aḳrabi izziz(iz)

^{am} nakru dan-nu mâta inaši(ši) ^{ilu} ÍN . LIL ^{ilu} kakki ^{pl}-šu (12) Ana ^{am} nakri inadin(in) ummân ^{am} nakri mi-ṣu ummani(ni) ^{pl}-tim [1] idâk (13) Ana ^{mul} Aḳrabu a-dir šarrâni ^{pl} ša mâti kalâmi ^{am} (?) nakri išakanu ^{pl} . . . šarrâni ^{pl} ša mâti kalâmi iš (?)-tan-na-an (14) Ana ^{mul} Aḳrabu i-ṭa-tu iškun uk-ku-la niší ^{pl} i-lam-mi-na ^{ilu} Muštabarrû-mûtânu(a-nu) ina libbi-šu izzaz-ma (15) [Ana] ^{mul} Zi-ba-ni-tum a-dir šattu III ^{kám} aribi itabbu-ma íbûr mâti ikkalu . . . aribi mâti ikkalu (16) . . íbûra im-di-i ikkal šattu III ^{kám} iṣ . . ka (17) ^{mul} Muštabarrû-mûtânu(a-nu) ina lib ^{mul} Aḳrabi izzaz-ma an-nu-ú pi-ši-ir-šu *Rev.* (1) Ana ^{mul} APIN ana ^{mul} Aḳrabu iṭḫi rubu ina zi-ḳit ^{mul} Aḳrabi imât . . . ina íkalli-šu (2) iṣṣabat(bat) . . . šu DIL . TÍ la iṣabat(bat)-ma ší . . ni . . bíl man-ma ip (?) ? ki ma mâtu la (?) kînu (3) i . . . . ilâni ^{pl} rabûti ^{pl} ana mâti : ^{ilu} muštabarrû-mûtânu (a-nu) ina lib ^{mul} . . . . . ma (4) Ana ^{mul} SAG . MÍ . GAR ik-šad-am-ma ^{mul} Šarru ítiḳ(iḳ)-ma ib-ni-šu arka-nu ^{mul} Šarru (5) ša ^{mul} SAG . MÍ . GAR ítiḳ-šu-ma ib-nu-šu [2] ikaššada-ma ^{mul} SAG . MÍ . GAR ítiḳ(iḳ)-ma ana ri-bi-šu il-lak (6) ur-nun-tu ibašši-ma a-a-ab itibbi-ma DIL . TÍ iṣabat(bat) šaniš(iš) mâtu ina-an-ziḳ (7) idâti ^{pl} ma-la il-li-ka-ni ša ^{mâtu} Akkadi ^{ki} ù ^{am} rubi ^{pl}-šu lim-na (8) mim (sal-ma ina lib lum-ni lim-na ana šarri bí-ili-iá ul iṭaḫḫi(ḫi) atal ^{ilu} Sin u ^{ilu} Šamši ša ina ^{arḫu} Simâni išakan(an) (9) idâti ^{pl} an-na-tu ša lumnu(nu) ša ^{mâtu} Akkadi ^{ki} ù šarrâni ^{pl} ^{mâtu} Aḫarri ^{ki} ša ^{mâtu} Akkadi ^{ki} (10) lim-na ù a-du-ú ina ^{arḫu} kisilimi a-ga-a atalû iš-sak-kan arḫu (?) lib (?) arḫu (?) KI MÍ (11) ù ^{mul} SAG . MÍ . GAR ina atali-ša izzaz(az) ana šarri bí-ili-ia šul-mu (12) an-nu-ú mim(sal)-m a ša $^{m\,ilu}$ Bíl-ú-ší-zib a-na šarri bí-ili-šu i-šap-pa-ru šarru li-pu-šu (13) ù pu-ú-tu šarri bí-ili-ia na-ša-ku ^{am} rubi ^{pl} ša ^{mâtu} Akkadi ^{ki} ša šarri a-bu-ka (14) iš-ku-nu TIN . TIR ^{ki} iḫ-tí-pu-ú ù bu-ší-í ša TIN . TIR ^{ki} it-ta-šu-ú (15) a-na muḫ-ḫi idâti ^{pl} an-na-tu ša lum-nu il-li-ka-ni í-mu-ḳa ša šarri (16) lil-lik-ma ina íkalli ^{am} . . ḳatâ (?) ṣab-bit-šu-nu-tu ù ša-nu-ti-ma (17) a-na šú-mi-šu-nu liš-kun ki-i šarru ḫa-an-ṭiš la i-pu-ú (?)-šu ^{am} nakru (?) . . (18) il-la-kám-ma ú-ša-an-ni-šu-nu-tu . . . (19) za-ka-ku . . . [K. 8713.]

No. 272A. *Obv.* (1) Ana atal maṣṣarti sadurri ÍN immir(ir) uš-ta-ni-iḫ . . . . (2) . . atal maṣṣarti sadurri iškun-ma maṣṣarta ig-

[1] *glossed* ma-at-tu. [2] KUR-ma, *glossed* i-káš-ša-dam-ma.

mur u IM . DIR (?) . . . (3) GIG . AN TIL . LA ina ^{mâtu} Akkadi ^{ki} . . . (4) Ana atalû ina ^{išâru} sadi ušarri-ma u ^{šâru} iltani illik šattu III . . . (5) [Ana] atalû ina ^{šâru} šadi ušarri-ma ana ^{šâru} MAR i-lik atalû . . . . (6) Ana Sin atalû iškun-ma ^{šâru} iltani illik(ik) ilâni ^{pl} ana . . . . (7) Ana Sin atalû iškun-ma ga-du šípâ ^{II} ^{pl}-šu-nu LUḪ . MIŠ ir-bi *ti . . . (8) Ana Sin a-dir-ma ki-ma ṭi-im šamí(í) šakin(in) šarru mâtâti ina abikti [ušamḳat] (9) : ilâni ^{pl} mâtâti ina abikti ú-šam-[ḳa-tu] (10) Ana ina ^{arḫu} Tašrîti Sin a-dir šum-ḳutim(tim) ummâni rabî tibut nakri imât-ma tibut(ut) aribi ibašši (ši) . . (11) Ana ina ^{arḫu} Tašriti Sin atalû iškun(un) ana šarri bartu šumḳutim(tim) ummâni(ni) . . . (12) . . . Tašrîti ûmu XXI ^{kám} atalû iškun-ma kupuru-šu-ma TU šarru a-gi-i ka-mu-su . . . (13) . . atal maṣṣarti sadurri la iškun(un) ra-kab : NÍR . ŠÚM . GA mu (?) *lu . . . . (14) . . . . ultu ûmi I ^{kám} adi ûmi XXX ^{kám} atalû iškun (un) RU . . . . (15) . . . . niši ^{pl}-šu ḳat ikašad(ád) ínuma(ma ?) ana DI . . . . . (16) . . . . míli ^{pl} . . . . (17) . . . . atalû iškun-ma . . . . *Rev.* (*Top broken.*) (1) . . . ri (?) . . . (2) *ú lu . . . . (3) . . . maṣ-ṣartu sadurru Ílama (4) . . . . sit . . ru šá mâti . . . . (5) . . . da . . . (6) . . . maṣṣartu sadurru . . . . (7) . . . . ? ga maṣṣartu sadurru (8) šá ^{m} Ak-kul-la-[nu]. [K. 1406.]

No. 272B. *Obv.* (1) Ina ^{arḫu} Addâri ûmu XIV ^{kám} atal Sin išakan(an) (2) Ana ina ^{arḫu} Addâri ûmu XIV ^{kám} atal maṣṣarti barariti (3) atalû iškun-ma purussu-šu a-na šar KI . SAR . RA (4) Uri ^{ki} ù Aḫarrî ^{ki} i-nam-din (5) ina atal Sin ^{mul} SAG . MÍ . GAR u ^{mul} Dil-bat (?) . . . . ^{pl} (6) Ana ina ^{arḫu} Addâri atal Sin iškun šar Ílama (ma) ^{ki} . . . . (7) Ana ina ^{arḫu} Addâri atal maṣṣarti [barariti] . . . *Rev.* (1) Ana ina ^{arḫu} Addari ultu ûmi I ^{kám} *adi [ûmi XXX ^{kam}] . . . (2) pal šarri labiru ^{sal} nukurtu . . . . (3) šum-ma ana šulum šar âli u niši ^{pl}-šu ipus-ma DI . . . (4) ina pan šatti mílu illak-ma A . MAḪ ^{pl} TAR ^{pl} (5) kima ^{ilu} Sin atalû iš-tak-nu šarru liš-pur-ma (6) a-na pu-ḫi šarri A . MAḪ ^{pl} i-na ^{mâtu} Akkadi ^{ki} (7) . . mu ši lu-bat-ti-ik man-ma (8) [ul ?] i-šim-mi (9) ša ^{m} ^{ilu} Nírgal-íṭir(ir). [K. 702.]

No. 272C. *Obv.* (1) . . Sin ina ^{arḫu} Addâri ûmu XXX (?) ^{kám} innammar atalû išakan(an) (2) . . . . . . arḫu zunna ú-kal (3) . . . . ŠI-ma (4) . . . . . ^{arḫu} Addâri maṣṣartu (5) . . . . a-na *šú-*tu-ḳu KI ru-ub (6) . . . . ḳab-bi um-ma (7) . . . . *a-*mat *la pa-ri-is-tum tašpur (8) . . . . ^{arḫu} Kisilimu a-di íli ín-na (9) . . . . *ip *pa dir ma Sin u kakkabâni ^{pl} . . *Rev.* (1) . . . . . pad-ru-ma (2) . . . . *ul KI ru-ub a-na (3) . . . . KI ru-ub (4) Ana IM . . . . *ma il-li-ku (5) . . . . *al-tak-nu nišî ^{pl} bît-ṣa (6) . . . . la-a SAL ^{pl} ana ^{sal} Dam-ḳa-a (7) . . . . šu it-ta-din um-ma ki-rib (?) (8) . . . . . ina pa-ni-ki lim-ḫa-ṣa (9) . . . . . ú-ṣal-li it-ta-din (10) . . . . . . ut ka li-pu-šu (11) ša ^{m} Za-kir. [K. 8391.]

No. 273. *Obv.* (1) ûmu XIV ^{kám} Atal ^{ilu} Sin i-šak-kan (2) limutti ša ^{mâtu} Ílama(ma) ^{ki} (3) u ^{mâtu} Aḫarri ^{ki} (4) damiḳti ša šarri bí-ili-ia lib-bi sa šarri bí-ili-ia (6) lu-ú-ṭa-a-bi (7) ul-tu ^{mul} Dil-bat (8) in-nam-mar *Rev.* (1) a-na šarri bí-ili-ia (2) aḳ-ta-bi (3) um-ma atalû iš-šak-kan (4) ša ^{m} Iraššî(ši)-ilu (5) ardu ša [šarri pa]-nu-ú. [S. 231.]

No. 274. *Obv.* (1) A-na Šarri mâtâti bí-ili-ia ardu-ka $^{\text{m ilu}}$ Bíl-ú-ṣur (?) (2) ^{ilu} Bíl ^{ilu} Nabû u ^{ilu} Šamšu a-na šarri bí-ili-iá lik-ru-ú-bu (3) Atalû iš-ša-kin-ma ina ^{alu} BAL-Í la in-na-mir (4) Atalû šuâtu i-tí-ti-iḳ ^{alu} BAL alu ša šarri (5) ina lib-bi aš-bu ín-na urpâti ^{pl} ka-la (?)-a-ma (6) ki-i atalû iš-ku-nu ù la iš-ku-nu (7) ul ni-di bíl šarrâni ^{pl} a-na BAL. BAT ^{KI} a-na ala ka-la-ma (8) a-*na TIN. TIR ^{KI} a-na ÍN-LIL ^{KI} a-na Uruk ^{ki} (9) ù Bar-sib ^{ki} liš pur man di-í-ma (10) ina lib-bi alâni ^{pl} an-nu-ti i-ta-mar . . (11) ka-a-a-ma-ni-ti šarru liš-mí *Rev.* (1) idâti (?) ^{pl} ma (?) . . it-tu ša atalî (2) ina lìb-bi ^{arḫu} Addâri u ina ^{arḫu} Nisanni it-tal-ka . . (3) gab-bi a-na šarri bí-ili-ia al-tap-ra ù . . (4) NAM. BUL. BI ša atalî . . i-tí-ip-šu mi-nu-ú (5) ḫi-ṭu a-na í-pi-šu ṭa-a-bi šarru la ú maš-[šir-an-ni] (6) ilâni ^{pl} rabûti ^{pl} ša ina ali ša šarru bí-ili-iá aš-bu šamû(ú) (7) ú-ṣal-lil-ú-ma atalû la ú-kal-*li-mu (8) um-ma šarru lu-ú-i-di ki-i atalî a-ga-a (9) la ina íli šarri bí-ili-iá ù mâti-šu sú-ú šarru lu-u-*ḫa-di (10) Ana ina ^{arḫu} Nisanni ^{ilu} Rammânu pi-šu iddi(di) (11) ŠÍ. TAR. NU. iṣaḫir (ir) [K. 772.]

No. 274A. *Obv.* (1) Atalû it-ti-iḳ la išakan(an) (2) ki-i šarru i-ḳab-bu-ú um-ma (3) *mi-nu-ú i-da-tu ta-mur (4) [ilâni] ^{pl} a-ḫa-miš la innammaru ^{pl} (5) . . . . a-na mu-ši (6) . . . . . ma *Rev.* (1) . . . . it-ti-iḳ (2) . . . . ^{ilu} Šamšu in-nam-mar (3) ša ^{m} Mun-na-bi-tu [K. 921.]

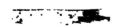

No. 274B. *Obv.* (1) . . . *i ^{alu} Ḫarrânu ina ûmí(mí) an-ni i (2) . . . ma-a ûmu XXIX $^{\text{kám ilu}}$ Ša-maš (3) . . . i-sa-kan-ma-a ûmu (mu) an-ni . . (4) . . . . nu-ka-a-la (5) . . . an-ni-u nu-tar-ra . . (6) . . . . ri (?) . . . . (*perhaps two lines broken*) (9) . . . . u ana man-ni (?) . . . . *Rev.* (1) . . ^{am} Mar-šip-ri šá ina íli $^{\text{m ilu}}$ Marduk . . . . (2) il-lik-u-ni it-tal-ka iḳ-di-bi (3) ma-a ^{ilu} Šamšu la-a ní-mu-ur-ma-a urpata šú-u (4) šú-nu la í-mu-ru a-ni-nu la ni-í-mur-ma (5) . . ma-a-šu la-a nu-tar-ra. [K. 810.]

No. 274C. *Obv.* (1) A-na šarri bí-ili-ia ardu-ka ^{m} A-ša-[ri-du] (2) ḳa-aṭ-nu Sin atalû ul i-[šakan] (3) lib-bi ša šar mâtâti bí-ili-iá lu-ú-[ṭâbi] (4) ^{ilu} Bíl u ^{ilu} Nabû šanâti (?) ^{pl} ša ana a lu . . . (5) bíl-iá li-ki (?)-ši mim(sal)-ma ma . . . (6) id-di . . na-ši a-na man-ni . . . (7) lu-uḳ-bi šarru . . . (8) lid-di-nu-nu . . . (9) . . *šarru . . . (*Rev. blank*). [83–1–18, 210.]

No. 274D. (*Obv. remains of seven lines badly mutilated*) *Rev.* (1) . . . iṣ (?) . . (2) IM . KUR . RA . . . . . u . . (3) šul-mu a-*na . . . . (4) AN . MI šá . . . . (5) šá ^{mâtu} Subarti ^{ki} . . . A . AN u A . DAN . . . . (6) šá ^{m} Šú-ma-a-[a]. [K. 8960.]

No. 274E. *Obv.* (1) ^{ilu} Sin | ina ^{arḫu} Du'uzi ûmu(mu) ú-šal-[lam] (2) ûmu XIV ^{kám} ultu ^{ilu} Ša-maš in-*na-*mar . . (3) [1] atalû | ú-ší-taḳ | la i-ša-[kan] *Rev.* (1) . . . íriba. [K. 865.]

No. 274F. *Obv.* (1) . . . *šarri bí-ili-ia al-tap-ra (2) . . . atalû išakan(an) ín-na (3) [la i]-tí-it-tí-iḳ išakan(an) (4) i-na ša-ka-an atalî an-ni-i (5) a-na šarri bí-ili-ia šul-mu (6) ^{arḫu} Airu ^{mâtu} Ílama(ma) ^{ki} ûmu XIV ^{kám} (7) ^{mâtu} Ílama(ma) ^{ki}; maṣṣartu UD . ṢAL . *LI . . . . *Rev.* (1) ^{arḫu} . . . (2) ša ^{mâtu} *Ílama . . . . (3) ad-riš . . . . *kaš-bi-ma (4) Ana [^{ilu} Dil ?]bat it-bal . . . Aḫarrû ^{ki} (5) . . Aḫarrû ^{ki} it-ti Ílama ^{ki} la pi-it (6) . . Aḫarrû ^{ki} pal šu ḳa ti (7) ša ^{m} Na-di-nu. [K. 1384.]

No. 274G. *Obv.* (1) . . . . ša ^{ilu} Ša-maš (2) . . . ûmu XXIX ^{kám} (3) . . . ta-ṣar (4) ir-ti-i-bi (5) . . . us-si-it-iḳ (6) . . . ^{arḫu} kisilimu (7) . . . ú-tar-ra *Rev.* (1) [ša $^{\text{m ilu}}$] Nabû-aḫî ^{pl}-íriba. [83–1–18, 320.]

[1] AN . MI *glossed* a-ta-lu-u.

No. 274H. *Obv.* (1) . . . XV ^kám^ (2) . . . ša-maš in-na-mar (3) . . ú-ší-taḳ (4) . . . sak-kan *Rev.* (1) šá ^m^ . . . . ^pl^ íriba. [K. 984.]

No. 274I. *Obv.* (1) [Ana Sin ûmu I ^kám^] innamir (2) [sanâḳu ša pí] lib mâti iṭâb (3) [Ana ûmu ana mi]-na-ti-šu [GID]-DA (4) [pâl ûmí] GID . [DA] ^pl^ (5) . . . . arḫi (6) . . . . ú-šal-lam-ma *Rev.* (1) . . . ÍN . NUN ša ^ilu^ Sin (2) . . . . ri . . . . šu (3) . . . . ú-*ší-*taḳ (4) . . . [i]-šak-kan (5) [ša ^m^ Ba]-la-si-i [83–1–18 207.]

No. 274K. *Obv.* (*Top broken.*) (1) . . . [ÍN .] NUN šimítan ušarri-ma nu . . . . (2) . . . . šar Akkadi šarru . . . (3) . . . . IM . SI . DI ušarri-ma . . . . (4) . . . . šumḳutim(tim) Akkadi ^ki^ ana . . . . (5) . . [AN .] *MI ina IM . SI . DI ušarri-ma . . . . (6) . . . . . ^ilu^ Rammânu ri-iḫ-[ṣi] (7) . . . [IM .] SI . DI ušarri-ma *IM . . . . (8) . . . ri-ir . . . (9) . . . pa (?) . . . (*Remainder lost.*) [K. 12004 + 12006.]

No. 274L. *Obv.* (*Top broken.*) (1) . . . . MU III ^kám^ . . . . (2) . . . . SI . DI ^ilu^ Rammânu ŠÍ . TAR . NU (3) . . . ša ḳa ^mâtu^ ZÍ-am-ma (4) . . . šu (?) ḪA . A-ma (5) . . . . gur (6) . . . . *Subarti ^ki^ (*Remainder lost.*) *Rev.* (*End of one line*) . . . . ra [K. 12369.]

No. 274M. (*Obv.*) (1) . . . pagrâni ^pl^ ina mâti SAG . UŠ (2) . . . . mati ibaššu ^pl^ (3) . . . . ÍN . UD . SAL . LI (4) . . . ra-šu a-na lib a (?) . . . (*Remainder broken off.*) [80–7–19, 364.]

No. 274N. *Obv.* (1) . . . . MI (2) . . . . na-mir (3) . . . . mâtu ú-šal-pa-tu (4) . . ḳabli kat mu (5) . . . nim-mi-du (6) . . . ibašši(ši) *Rev.* (1) . . . . ut at ti du (?) ti (2) . . . ma-ki iraššu ^pl^ (3) . . . . *tu ra-kib (4) . . . . mât-su im-bar-' (5) . . . . MI iškun (un) (*Remainder lost.*) [K. 12013.]

No. 274O. *Obv.* (*Top broken.*) (1) . . . . a . . . . (2) šum . . . kima GAR ^pl^ šarri . . . . . (3) . . . šú lib (?) a-di ^ilu^ Šamši la i . . . . (4) . . a . . si ut tu ku *mu . . . (5) . . . šarri bíl-ia as-sa-[ap-ra] (6) . . . . AN . MI ú-ší-[taḳ] (*Remainder lost.*) *Rev.* (*Top broken.*) (1) ša ^m^ Ba-la-si-[i] [K. 1333.]

No. 274P. *Obv.* (1) Ú-nu-ut ša atali . . . (2) li-in-tu-ḫu-ma lu šad rak (?) . . . (3) la aš-ša ÍN - NUN la tal . . . (4) ša m ilu Bíl-naṣir . . . [82–5–22, 69.]

No. 274Q. *Obv.* (1) Mu-*ši *ša ûmi XIII maṣṣaru ia-'-nu (2) mâr šarri li-it-til (3) [muši] ša ûmi XIV kám maṣṣarti ia-'-nu (4) *mâr *šarri li-it-til (5) mu-[ši ša] ûmi XV kám maṣṣartu ia-'-nu (6) *mâr *šarri li-it-til (7) mu ši ša ûmi XVI kám maṣṣartu rab-ti (8) *atal ilu Sin ša . . . . MI šú-a-*ti (9) . . . . Sin . . . . . ma (*Reverse, some six lines, with remains of characters.*) *Rev.* (7) [ša m] ilu Nírgal-iṭir(ir) [Rm. 197.]

XVII. Omens from Akulutum.

No. 275. *Obv.* (1) Ana ina arḫu Simâni a-[ku-lu-tum] . . . . (2) sal nukurtu ina [mâti ibašši ?] (3) Ana a-ku-lu-tum . . . . . (4) ûmu(mu) . . . (5) Ana a-ku-lu-tum ina . . . . (6) mâtu i . . . . *Rev.* (1) ša am. [Rm. 211.]

XVIII. Omens from Births.

No. 276. *Obv.* (1) Ínuma IZ . BU zikaru u sinništu [iššakkin ?] (2) íš-tú sal íllu AN . BA . . . (3) šá mâti i-bí-lum (4) mâtu šarri kar-tú illak . . (5) Ínuma IZ . BU zikaru u sinništu iššakkin-ma . . . la irši (6) mâr íkalli mâta ú-ma-ar (7) : šarru i-bar (*Rev. blank.*) [K. 766.]

No. 277. *Obv.* (1) Ínuma IZ . BU VIII šípî pl-šu (2) II zibbâti pl-šu (3) rubu šar-ru-ti (4) kiš-šu-ti i-ṣa-bat (5) am ma-ḫi-ṣu šu-ú (6) m Ud-da-nu šum-šu (7) i-ḳab-ba-a um-ma sal šaḫita-a (8) ki-i tu-li-du *Rev.* (1) VIII šípî pl u II zibbâti pl-šu (2) um-ma i-na ṭabti an-di-di-il-šu (3) ù i-na bîti al-ta-kan (4) ša m ilu Nírgal iṭir(ir). [K. 749.]

XIX. Miscellaneous Fragments.

No. 277A. *Rev.* (*a*) mul . . . . (*b*) ša m ša-pi-[ku]. [K. 6184, b.]

No. 277B. *Obv.* (1) Ana mul .... (2) mâru .... (3) ḪI. GAR ana .... (4) mâru .... (5) bîtâti pl .... (6) ... ka ... (7) Í. KUR (?) ... (8) Ana mul LU .... (9) Ana mul PA (?) .... (10) mí-ri .... (11) mul (?) ... *Rev.* (1) Ana mul Ú .... (2) ilu LU. BAD .... (3) it-ti ..... (4) ḪUL-šu a .... (5) ittu ..... (6) a-di arḫi .... (7) ša m Iraššì [ši-ilu]. [K. 1594.]

No. 277C. *Obv.* (1) .... nam-ru (2) ... ba-aš-ši (3) .... *sa-li-mu ir-šu-ú (4) .... lu-mur (5) ... pa ri ma tú (?) (6) .... -'-nu (7) ... i (8) ... (9) ... it-ti-iḳ *Rev.* (1) ... šú (2) .... ú (3) .... di (4) ... ta-šu-ú-šu (5) .... ḫi (?) ul in-nam-ru (6) .... ilâni (?) pl-šu iš-šú-ú (7) ... da ab u ru (?) (8) .... in-nam-ma-ru. [K. 1557.]

No. 277D. *Obv.* (1) Ina arḫu Šabâṭi ûmu .... (2) ina íkalli .... (3) MU. AN. NA ga (?) ... (4) šar-ra bu (?) .... (5) ina arḫu Addâri ûmu III .... (6) a-na a-ki .... (7) ù ilu Nabû (?) .... (8) ina lib .... *Rev.* (1) šarru liš-pur (?) .... (2) ûmu III kám .... (3) iṣu kakku a-na .... (4) u ilu Nabû (?) .... (5) .. ḫi alpu .... (6) ša m ..... [K. 1336.]

No. 277E. *Obv.* (1) .... ana pân Sin iṭḫi-ma izziz(iz) (2) .... ummâni (?) pl (3) ... tim šu isakan(an) (4) .... a mâr m Kudurri. [K. 1328.]

No. 277F. *Obv.* (1) .... MUL DU (2) .... iš-tí-niš išakan (an) (3) .... ru it-ti-mí-du (4) .... ad-da-nu (5) .... miš ša tí (6) .... mâti ibašši (*five lines with fragmentary characters*) *Rev.* (1) ... BAT-a-nu iṭ-ṭi-ḫu-u (2) .... pi-[ší]-ir-šu (3) .... mâti ši-i (4) .... ú-ḫi-in ? ? (5) ... tal-li-kan-ni zi-it-ti-ni (6) .... ší-ti-iḳ (7) .... a i-ba-aš-ši (8) .... a-na šarri ú-šaḫ-kam (9) .... ûmu (mu) (10) .... lu-šaḫ-ki-im (11) [ša m Ba-la]-si-i. [K. 1301.]

No. 277G. *Obv.* (1) ... í-ri tarbaṣu ilmi (2) ... [ilu] Rammânu ìraḫiṣ(iṣ) (3) .... SI. DI (4) .... ru (5) .... ba bat (6) ... bu-u (7) .... kúr *Rev.* (1) ... bu u ... (2) .... mâtu i- ... (3) .... arḫu Simânu .... [K. 1535.]

No. 277H. *Obv.* (1) . . . . raš tí (?) (2) . . . GIR . TAB . . . . (3) . . . SI (?) . . . (4) . . . mâtu . . . (5) . . . gi . . . (6) . . . ti pal (?) . . (7) . . ana (8) . . . lib mul . . . *Rev.* (1) . . . mi (?) mu (?) nu (?) . . . (2) mí (3) . . . . mul GIR . TAB DU (4) . . . . tum ina šuḳi (5) . . . . inadi(di) (6) . . . pa-nu ša-ṭir (7) . . . mfli pl ibaššu pl (8) . . . ûmu XIII kám ša arḫi a-ga-a (9) . . . . uṣ (?)-ṣu (10) . . . u (11) . . . ku šú a . . . . [K. 1300.]

No. 277I. *Obv.* (1) Ana . . . (2) . . . (3) . . . im (4) . . . tum (5) . . . NI . BAT-a-nu (6) . . . bu-lim (7) . . . šú (8) NU . SI . DI pl : mâtu MAR ki . . . . *Rev.* (1) . . . pl ina tarbaṣ Sin izzizu pl (2) . . . pl GID . . . (3) . . . kúr . . . [K. 967.]

No. 277K. *Obv.* (1) Ana ilu Nírgal pl it-ti . . . (2) . . . UTU . KA . GAB-a ilu Nírgal ša . . . (3) . . . bi (?) Ílama(ma) ki . . . . (4) . . . . iḫ mat . . . (5) . . . ilu Nírgal . . . (6) . . . . lal TUR *SAL . . . (7) . . . ba di . . . (8) . . . tab zi (?) . . . *Rev.* (*broken*) (1) . . . mi (?) an (?) . . u . . . . (2) . . arḫu Kisilimi imbaru . . . (3) . . iš (?) na an í-ri-ia . . . (4) ša m ilu Nírgal-íṭir(ir) [K. 1302.]

No. 277L. *Obv.* (*Top broken*) (1) . . . . išakan(an) (2) ittu ṣít Šamšu (3) šá mâtu Ílama(ma) ki (4) ša m Ištar-šuma-íríš . . [K. 966]

No. 277M. *Obv.* (1) . . UD ŠU A šar Akkadi ki . . *Remainder broken* *Rev.* (1) . . . ŠI-ir (2) . . . NU IK-ši (3) . . . írib Šamši (4) . . . damiḳti ša mâtu Akkadí ki (5) . . . a mâr Bar-Sib ki [K. 1236.]

No. 277N. *Obv.* (1) . . . ina su ša šarri . . . (2) . . . ti lib-bi . . . (3) . . . man ni ma la ina (4) . . . šarru . . . (5) . . ? ? tu . . (*Remainder broken*) *Rev.* (1) ša m ilu Bíl . . . [K. 13012.]

No. 277O. *Obv.* (1) . . . alu (2) . . . ma-ḫi-*iṣ (3) . . . uššab(ab) (4) . . . iraššu pl (5) ša m Apla (?)-a . . . [81–2–4, 140.]

No. 277P. *Obv.* (*Top broken*) (1) . . . ina ṣít Šamši it ti (?) ri (?) . . *Rev.* (1) ilu TIR . AN . Na it-tab-ḫa (?) (2) . . . arḫu (?) KAN ultu ilu Šamšu (3) . . . na mar [81–7–27, 215.]

No. 277Q. (*a*) . . . im ù . . . (*b*) . . . tamarti-šu ŠI . ŠI tum . . . (*c*) . . . ti išdu tak-rib . . (*d*) . . . mâtât . . . (*e*) . . . ir . . . (*Reverse, traces of three lines.*) [82–3–23, 112].

No. 277R. *Obv.* (1) Ana ûmu XXVIII kám II + BAR kas[bu] . . . . . . (2) ina IM . MAR . TU ki . . . . (3) is-si-niš í-tí-ri (?) . . . . (4) II ŠÚ . SI a-na IM . . . . (5) is-sa-kan IM . KUR . RA . . . . (6) IM . SI . DI it-ta . . . (7) Ana UD ID IM . MAR . TU ú . . . . (8) Ana UD ID IM . TAR . BA ú . . . . (9) Ana UD a-dir-ma IM . SI . DI . . . (10) Ana ina arḫu Nisanni ûmu XXVIII kám . . . . (11) ki mu šu TUR SAL šarri . . . . (12) ina mâti šiâti . . . . . . (13) mâtu ir-ru . . . *Rev.* (1) ina mâti ša . . . (2) Ana ina arḫu Nisanni AN . MI . . . . (3) Ana šarri šulmu(mu) . . . . (4) Ana ultu ûmi I kám adi ûmi XXX kám . . . . (5) Ana ina arḫu Nisanni ûmu XXIX kám an . . . (6) RU-ti ílama(ma) . . . . (7) šar ílama(ma) . . . (8) lu-u ûmu XXVIII [kám] lu-u XXIX . . . (9) šá . . . . [82–5–22, 87.]

No. 277S. *Obv.* (1) . . šu í-tu-ú šarru . . . (2) . . . il-lap . . . (3) . . ? šar mâti . . . (4) . . . i . . . *Rev.* (*Top broken*) (1) . . . bat . . . (2) . . . UD ina pi-i . . . (3) . . . ra šarri li (?) . . . (4) [ša m ilu Nírgal]-iṭir(ir). [83–1–18, 301.]

No. 277T. *Obv.* (1) . . . a . . . (2) . . . tí-ib-ba . . . (3) . . . LAL-šu ḫi-il-lu (4) . . . ilu šu ma (5) . . . Sin mul GIR . TAB (6) . . . ki KI . LAM *iṣaḫir (7) . . . i-za-za *Rev.* (1) . . [ni ?]-mí-il-šu i-ma-ad-*di (2) . . . šá SAG DU mul GIR . TAB (3) . . . šu a-na ṣi-ḫi-ir ma-ḫi-ri (4) . . . bar a-na šarri bíl-ia (5) . . . BAD . GUD . UD ma-a íbûru damḳu (6) . . . * ilu Rammânu iraḫiṣ . . . (7) . . . uṣ (?) . . . [83–1–18, 309.]

No. 277U. *Rev.* (*a*) . . . ul-tú ša . . . (*b*) íbûru ṣi-iḫ-ru . . . (*c*) arḫu ŠÍ . SA íbûru . . . . (*d*) arḫu Simânu . . . . [83–1–18, 318.]

No. 277V. (*a*) . . . nab-ṭi-í Sin u Šamši . . . (*b*) . . . ša du-ú ša-ḳu ki ia . . . (*c*) . . . ru a-na šarri . . . (*d*) . . . *ra-a (?) [83–1–18, 774.]

No. 277W. *Obv.* (*a*) ûmu IV kám . . . (*b*) a-na an-nu . . . (*c*) gan (?) gu . . . . (*d*) ana sal . . . . (*e*) ša ûmi IV kám . . . . (*f*) ana Sin u . . . . *Rev.* (1) Ana ilu . . . . [83–1–18, 884.]

No. 277x. *Obv.* (*ll.* 1–5 *almost illegible*) (6) . . šarri bí-ili-ia . . . . . . *Rev.* (1) . . . arḫu (?) ŠÍ a-ga[a] . . . (2) . . ilu ul il-lak . . . (3) ša m ilu Bíl-ú-šal-[lam] . . . . [K. 6149.]

No. 277y. (*a*) . . . GU . ZA ša ki-na . . . (*b*) . . . ti ri . . . (*c*) . . . da . . . (*d*) . . . *riš a-*na . . . (*e*) na . . . na *šarri . . . [83–1–18, 883.]

No. 277z. *Obv.* (1) Ana ilu . . . (2) pal . . . (3) kúr zi . . . (4) Ana MUL ana . . . (5) am MAR . TU KI . . . . (6) . . . . . . *Rev.* (1) ša m . . . (2) ûmu XIV kám . . . (3) ûmu XV kám . . . (4) ilâni pl . . . (5) mâti . . . . [Bu. 91–5–9, 29.]

No. 277aa. *Obv.* (1) Ana . . . (2) Ana MUL . . . (3) šar Akkadi . . . (4) ša m ilu nabu-aḫî . . . [83–1–18, 303.]

No. 277ab. *Obv.* (1) . . ta ḫi is-sa-kin (2) . . . ina pan ilu PA . BIL . SAG DU-az-ma (3) . . . mul GIR . TAB DU-iz (4) . . . tum ina mâti IK-ši (5) . . . mul PA . BIL . SAG (*Remainder lost*) *Rev.* (1) . . . KU-ab (2) . . . it tú ší-mu-u (3) . . . ina (?) i-tap-pa-lu. [80–7–19, 355.]

No. 277ac. *Obv.* (*a*) ina íli | išdu (?) ḫarrani ina . . . (*b*) it-tu-bil ina arḫu . . . [S. 508.]

No. 277ad. *Obv.* (1) . . . tab ûmu XV kám (2) . . . UD UD . DU . A pl lik-ki (3) . . . mi (?) lik-ru-ub (4) . . . ni nu UD DU (5) . . . u (?) tak ši-i (6) . . . ši *Rev.* (1) . . . ilu Šamšu (2) . . . ilu Šamšu šarru kak-kar (3) . . . lik (?) (4) [ša m ilu] Nabu-šuma-iškun (un) [Bu. 89–4–26, 19.]

No. 277ae. *Obv.* (1) [Ana šarrî bíl-ia ardu-ka ? ilu] *Bíl-ú-ší-zib (2) . . . lik-ru-bu (3) . . . Sin itḫi(ḫi) (4) . . . šarru ina li-it-ti DU-ak (5) . . . mât-su irappíš(íš) (6) . . uk-tap-pad (7) . . . . mur (8) . . . (9) . . . tum (*Remainder of obv. and top of rev. broken*) *Rev.* (1) . . uz-zu (2) . . ú-maš-ša-ram . . (3) . . ma ana ilu Sin um-ma (4) . . . ša m Nadina(na)-aḫi bíl-ḫi-ṭu (5) . . . bi ù a-na šarri ina muḫ-ḫi-šu (6) . . . i-mur-šam-ma man-ma (7) . . . na-an-ni pa-ni-šu a-na (8) . . . su šarri la it-ta-šu-u (9) . . . il-lak (10) . . . šu it-ta . . . (11) . . . su *pu-*ut iš . . . (12) . . . a-na m Ṣíl-la-a (13) . . . lu-ú-bil (?) [K. 13191.]

VOCABULARY.

---

*An asterisk * indicates that every occurrence of the word is quoted.*

---

a, *ia*, my.
u, and.
**aibu*, enemy, 49, 3: 272, *r.* 6:
**uiltu*, despatch, 168B, *r.* 4: 188, *r.* 4:
**ianu*, '(there is) not,' 67, *r.* 1: 85A, *r.* 10: 274Q, 1, 3, 5:
Aîru, month Iyyar.
**iâši*, me, 240, *r.* 3:
Abu, month Ab.
abu, father, 90, 4, 11: 124, 2: 134, 2: 136, 8: 154, *r.* 2: 174, 3: 180, 3:
**am A.BA*, magician, 109, *r.* 4, 6: 217, *r.* 3:
**abâku*, bring, I, 1, *ps.* ibbaka, 90, *r.* 17: *pc.* libuk, 124, *r.* 9: libukam, 124, *r.* 11: lîbukniš-šumma, 183, *r.* 7: libukunu, 124, *r.* 3:
**abiktu*, defeat, 94, *r.* 7: 270, 8: 272A, 8:
**abkallu*, governor, 170, 4.
ibîlu, bring I, 1, *ps.* ubbal 194A, 5: 211A, 2: ubbala, 70, 6: ubbalu, 59, 6: *pt.* ubil, 85, 2: III, 1, lušíbi[la], 34, *r.* 10:
**biltu*, weight, 199, 5: 242, *r.* 5:
abullu, city gate, 156, 3: 157A, 3: pl. 157D, 5:
**abnu*, stone, hail, 20, 5: 261, 4:
**ubanu*, a measure of length, 88, 8:
ibûru, crops, 10, 6: 11, 6: 12, 6: 26, 4: 35, 2:
aburriš, securely, 10, *r.* 1: 11A, 5: 12, 6: 24A, 2: 32, 2: 41, 3: 42, 3: 43, 2:
ubbutu, blasting, 91, 3: 236B, 3: 252A, 2:
agû, crown, (*esp.*) full moon, 7, 5: 9, 4: 10, 5: 17, 1: 26, 3: 41, 1: 269, 7: 272B, 12:
agâ, that, 90, *r.* 7: 272, *r.* 10:
agannu, that, 124, *r.* 3: 264, *r.* 4, 9: f. pl. 82, *r.* 6:
**ugaru*, meadows, 217, 6: 218, 2:
adi, up to, as far as.
**adu*, ago, 207, 6:
adû now, yet, 145, *r.* 6:
**adu*, agreement, 70, *r.* 7: 90, *r.* 17: 205A, *r.* 4:
**idu*, side, forces, 22, 7: 241, 4:
idû, to know, I, 1, idi, 124, *r.* 4: *nidi*, 274, 7: *nîdu*, 268, 7: *lu-idi*, 85, *r.* 5: 90E, 2, 3: 245, 6:
**idû*, unique, 86, 4: 268, *r.* 4:
uddatu, light, 82, 7: 133, *r.* 5: 142, 8: 181, 3: 236F, 6:

*ídîdu, be sharp, I, 1, inf.
[ídi]du, 34, 8 : ídidu, 36, r. 1 :
36A, 2 : pm. iddit, 69, 6 : iddat,
269, 10 : idda, 29, 2 : 32, 4 :
34, 3 : 35, 8 : 38, 3 : II, 1,
udduda 26, r. 1 : 34, 5 : 35, 6 :
36, 4 : 37, 2 : 44, 5 : udu . .
31, 6 :
    idlutu, power, 115E, 3 :
    udina (particle), 112, r 5 :
    adannu, time, 245, r. 4 : (adv.,
31, r. 7 : 76, r. 4 :
    Addâru, month Adar.
    adâru, be dark, I, 1, DIR pl
29, r. 5 : idir, 124, 1, 12 : 127,
1 : DIR, 69, 5 : dir-at (?) 43,
5, r. 1 :
    adru, dark, 32, r. 4 : (adv.)
204, r. 1 : 270, 6 :
    adiru, darkening, 270, 5 :
*ídišu, alone, 67, 5 :
*ídišu, be new, II, 2 : utaddaša,
207, r. 7 :
*udîššu, 238, 2 :
    ittu, sign, ITI, 16, r. 2 : ittum,
108, 6 : ittu, 57, 6 : 74, r. 2 :
itti, 57, r. 4 : idât, 31, r. 8 :
84, 4 : idâti 55, r. 1 :
    izu, stand, I, 1 : ízi, 153, 7 :
I, 2, ittitzi, 96, 3 : 106, 7 :
180, 8 : 228, 2 : ittitiz, 235, 8 :
236G, r. 1 : 251, r. 1 :
*IZ. BU., young one, 276, 1,
5 : 277, 1 :
*izîzu, be angry, I, 1, ŠUR
29, r. 4, iz-ziz, 183, 3 :
*azkaru, crescent, 269, 7 : pl.
86, 1 : 86A, 2.
    uznu, ear, 125, r. 4 : 135A, 6 :
145, 6 : PI II, 132, r. 3 : PI pl
57, 2 : IZ. KU. PI., 155A, r. 2 :
    aḫú, unpropitious, aḫiu, 94, r.
8 : f. BAR-tum, 62, 3 : aḫitum,
78, 3 : aḫitu, 77, 3 :

aḫu, brother, 52, r. 6 : 115 F, r.
4 : pl. 240, 8 : (adv.) aḫiš, 70, 7 :
aḫamiš, 15, 6 : 46, 5 : 52, 3 :
157D, 2 :
*aḫâzu, seize, III, 1, ušaḫaz,
91, r. 4 :
*aḫâru, delay, I, 1, iḫḫiramma,
82, 1 : iḫḫirama, 88, 1 : iḫ . .,
89, 4 :
    Aḫarrú, west.
*îṭu, be dark, I, 1. pm. íṭat,
223, 6 : íṭati, 223A, r. 7 :
    aki, how, 90, r. 13 : 112, r.
4, 7 :
*akka', how ? 155, r. 2 :
    ukkú, want, 37, r. 4 : 47, 7 :
    akâlu, eat, I, 1. KU, 25, 2 :
28, 5 : 47A, 2 : ikkal, 69A, 3 :
91, r. 2 :
*akalu, food, 85A, r. 6 : 189, 2 :
*akulutum,   ? 275, 1, 3,
5 :
    ikîlu, darken, I, 1, ikil, 193, 4 :
I, 2, itakil, 269, 1 :
*ikkillu, mourning, 267, 10.
    ikallu, palace, 55, 7 : 82, r. 2 :
*ikîru, I, 2, itíkiru, 243, r. 5 :
*ikkaru,   115F, r. 3 : 218A
r. 3 : 240, r. 3 :
    ul, not.
    íli, over.
    ílû, go up, II, 2 : ultíli, 267A,
r. 5 :
    ílinu, upper, 136U, 3 :
    ílitu, upper, íli-ta, 271, 1 : í-la-
a-ti (top), 268, 12 : íli-ta-nu, 176,
3 :
    ilu, god.
    âlu, city.
*íllu, pure, 276, 2 :
*alla, (particle) 124, r. 7 :
*alâdu, bear, I, 1, Ù. TU [pl],
97, 4 : Ù. TU, 100, 6 : ullada,
98, r. 3 : 112A, 6 : tulidu, 277, 8 :

*talittu, offspring, 103, 11 :

alâku, go, I, 1, ps. DU-ak, 7, 6 : DU . BU, 32, 3 : DU-kám, 60, r. 3 : illak, 23, 4 : 139, 9 : illaka, 66, r. 5 : tallaka, 22, r. 4 : illaku, 112, 8 : illakuni, 70, r. 1, 7 : NI.NI (?) 104, 2 : DU pl 82, r. 4 : DU-ku, 29, 3 : pt. DU-ik, 20, 5 : ilik, 272C, 5 : illikanni, 264, 7 : allik, 217, r. 2 : illuku, 109, 3 : pc. lillik, 8, r. 6 : inf. alaku, 139, r. 1 : alaki, 84, 1 :

I, 2 : ittalak, 201, 1 : ittalka, 274, r. 2 : tattalka, 181, r. 1 : ittalku, 55, r. 2 :

* ilku, edict, 240, r. 4 :

alaktu, traffic, A . DU ., 82, 6 : 94, r. 4 : alakti, 24, 5 : 120, 3 : pl. 143, r. 1 :

Ululu, month Elul.

*alpu, ox, 151, r. 8 : pl. 101, 8 : 103, 11 : 105, 5 :

*ilippu, ship, 159, r. 2 (?).

*iluttu, calf (?), 257, r. 3 :

ultu, from.

iltanu, north.

ima = ašar, 'where,' 29, 3, 4 : 31, 7 :

*amtu, handmaid, 183, r. 5 :

*amatu, word, 52, r. 3 : 272C, 7 :

ûmu, day.

*UD-mu-us-sa, 'daily, 84, 5 : UD-mu-us-su, 73, r. 1 :

umâ, now, 31, r. 6 : 112, r. 4 :

umma, thus, 73, r. 4 :

*ammiu, that, 152, r. 1 : 34, 9 :

imbaru, storm, 111, r. 1, 2, 4 : 243, r. 3 :

*imîdu, stand, IV, 1, innimid, 235, 3 : innimída, 68, r. 3 : innimmidu, 236, 5 : IV, 2. ittímid, 235, 8 : ittímidi, 236G, 8 :

*imdu, standing (of crops), im-di-i, 272, 16 :

*A . MAḪ, pl 'great waters,' 272C, r. 4, 6 :

*imîlu, II, 1, grow indistinct (?), ummul, 232, 9 :

*ummuliš, dimly (?), 232, 6 :

amîlutu, human beings, 86, r. 4 :

*umamu, beasts, ú-ma-am, 182, 4 :

ummânu, troops, people, 91, 2 : pl. 28, r. 5 : 35, 8 :

imittu, right, 30, 5 : 41, 5 : 43, r 1 : i-mit-ti, 43, 6 : 70, 9 : 145, r. 4 :

*imuḳu, army, 22, 5 : 272, r. 15 :

amâru, see I, 1, ŠI-mar 31, 5 : 123, 6 : nimaruni, 70, r. 7 : ímura, 272, r. 15 : amur, 155, r. 3 : amurûni, 188, 10 : nimur, 76, r. 2 : ni-í-mur, 21, 7 : 274B, r. 4 : limur, 18, r. 6 :

I, 2 : itamru, 144D, 2 : nitamar, 76, r. 3 : 170, r. 6 :

IV, 1, ps. ŠI 17, 3 : 144, 7 : 151, 3 : ŠI-mar, 124, 3 : innamar, 43, r. 9 : 45, r. 2 : 62, r. 2 : 86, 6 : innammar, 69, r. 6 : 85, r. 4 : 145, 8 : innamaru, 22B, 6 : 45, 5 : 126, 4 : ŠI pl 15, 6 : ŠI-ru 82, 4 : pt. ŠI 4, 1 : 7, 1 : 9, 1 : 13, 1 : 17, r. 1 : 29, 1 : 63, 1 : 68, 1 : 77, 1 : 151, 11 : 172, 1 : ŠI . LAL I, 1 : 16, 1 : 21, 1 : 23, 1 : 24, 1 : 25, 1 : 47, 1 : 61, 1 : ŠI-ir, 2, 1 : 3, 1 : 12, 1 : 14, 1 : 15, 1 : 18, 1 : 19, 1 : 20, 1 : 26, 1 : 30, 1 : 59, 1 : 60, 3 : 184, 1 : innamir, 22A, 1 : 43, r. 3 : innamru, 22B,

5 : innamıruni, 180, 7 : ŠI pl 46, 5 : 52, 2 : 120, 1 : 125, 1 : 127, 4 : 128, 6 : 144, 1 : 155, 3 : ŠI LAL pl 123, 1 : 135, 2 : linnamir, 249, r. 5 :

IV, 2 : ittanmar, 48, 5 : ittammarma, 22A, r. 5 : ittanmaru, 136B, r. 3 : 151, 6 :

tamartu, appearance, ŠI. LAL, 7, 5 : 10, 5 : 11, 6 : tamartu, 244B, r, 5 : tamarti, 22A, 4, r. 4 : 89, 1 : (? 36, A, 3 :). *pl.* tamarâti, 82, r. 6 :

****ammar***, whoever, 257, 9 :

****amašu***, II, 2, go, uttamiš, 68, r. 1 : 70, r. 3 :

ina, in.

****înu***, eye, 124, r. 6 :

ana, to, for : (= înuma).

annu, this, *pl.* annuti.

inna, now, 73, r. 3 : 85A, r. 3 : 90, r, 11 :

intu, princess, 94, r. 3 : 108, 2 : 143, 8 :

****inbu***, fruit, 23A, 6 : 123, 7 :

****undiṭṭu***, 236E, 3 :

anaku, I.

aninu, we, 62, 4 : aninnu, 256, 6 :

****unninu***, prayer, 162, r. 3 :

****unḳu***, ring, sealed document, 152, r. 8 : 217, r. 8 :

****inîšu***, II, 1, ravage, unnaš, 29, 5 : 34, 6 : 35, 7 : 36, 6 : 48, 2 :

inîtu, become dim, I, 2 : ittintu (*see index*), ittîni . . 133, r. 1 : ittintum, 138A, 4 ; II, 1 : unnut, 60, 1 : 167, r. 10 : 181, r. 5 : 232, 1 : 236G, 2 : 238, 5 : 244D, 2 : unnutuni, 244C, 5 : unut, 274P, 1 :

*II, 2 : utanatma, 232, r. 3 :

****asu***, physician, 18, v. 5 :

isiru, enclose, II, 2, utasar, 82, 3 : 92, 3 : 94, 4 : 95, 2 : utassar, 93, 3 : 101, 6 :

****usurtu***, halo, IZ. ḪAR, 112, 4, 6 : 237A, 5 : usurtu, 91, 4 :

issi, with, is-sa-a-a-ḫi-í . . , 252D, r. 2 :

issuri, when, 21, r. 1 : 217, r. 7 : 235, 6, 10 :

****ipû***, III, 2, shine, ultapâ, 185, 4 : 271, 11 : ultappû, 222, 3 : šutappû, 189, 4 :

apâru, put on, I, 1, *ps.* ippir, 43, 4 : *pm.* apir, 7, 5 : 9, 4 : 10, 5 : 18, 5 : 26, 3 : 34, 1 : 41, 1 : 43, 1 : aprat, 209, 4 : 243, 3 :

ipîšu, make, I, 1, ippuš, 86, r. 8 : 240, r. 1 : KAK-uš, 38, 8 : KAK, 94, r. 7 : nippaš, 256, 6 : ípašuma, 256, 7 : ni-í-pu-šu, 34, r. 4 : *pc.* lipuš, 82, r. 9 : li-í-puuš, 217, r. 6 : lipušu, 272, r. 12 : li-pu-u-šú, 96, 4 : *inf.* ípišu, 274, r. 5 :

I, 2, itipšu, 274, r. 4 :

aṣû, go forth, I, 1, uṣṣi, 236, 7 : uṣṣû, 33, r. 4 : 70, r. 6 : uṣa, 21A, 4 : uṣumma, 235, 4 : UD. DU pl-ni 242, 5 : *pm.* aṣi, 182, 5 : *inf.* aṣûšu, 155, r. 3 : aṣí, 33, 5 :

I, 2, ittaṣâ, 155, r. 4 : ittuṣi, 235, 5 :

****ṣâtu***, exit, ṣâsu, 55, 7 :

ṣîtu, exit, 140, 8 : *ṣit Šamši*, sunrise.

****iṣu***, half, 155, r. 4 :

iṣu, tree, wood.

****aṣâru***, enclose, *I, 1, íṣiruni, 152, r. 9 : liṣiru, 152, r. 7 : II, 2, utaṣaru, 105, r. 4 :

****iṣṣuru***, bird, 238, r. 2 :

iḳlu, field, 85A, r. 7 : iḳlâ, 124, r. 4 : iḳlâm, 242, r. 5 :

****aḳâru***, be valuable, I, 1, iḳḳir, 88, 4 :

**akrabu*, scorpion, 200, 2 : 239, 2.

íratu, pregnant, pl. 98, 2 :

**urru*, light, 116, 3 : 200, 1 :

**urritum*, point of light, 268, 3 :

írîbu, enter, I, 1, *ps.* írab, 217, *r.* 7 : *pt.* írubu, 205A, *r.* 4 : 236, 2 :

I, 2 : *ps.* ítarab, 103, 2 : 175, 7 : 235, 2 : *pt.* itírub, 90, *r.* 15 :

III, 1. lušíribûni, 152, *r.* 3 :

III, 2, ultíribu, 22, 9 :

írib Šamši, sunset.

irbu, four, ir-bi, 88, 8 : irba, 269, 11 :

**aribu*, locust, 223, *r.* 1 : 261, 2 : 269, 3 :

urubatu, desolation, *pl.* 203, 3 : 204, 3 : 205, *r.* 1 : 209, 6 :

ardu, slave, 15, *r.* 1, 2 : 26, *r.* 5 : *pl.* 22, 10 :

arâdu, go down, I, 1, *ps.* urradu, 187, 2 : *inf.* arad, 27, *r.* 3 : 48, 7 : 128A, *r.* 1 : *pt.* (?) . . *ridu*, 184, *r.* 3 :

arḫu, month, *arhussu*, monthly, 82, 10 : 134, 7 :

**arḫiš*, quickly, 70, *r.* 5 : 235, 7 : 247, 7 :

arâku, belong, I, 1, *pt.* GID . DA, 1, 4 : 2, 3 : 3, 3 : 16, 3 : 41, 5, *r.* 3 : GID . DA-ik, 10, 3 : 12, 3 : 20, 3 : GID, 17, 4 : írik, 7, 3 : *inf.* arak, 151, 5 : araku, 15, *r.* 5 : GID . DA, 16, *r.* 3 :

II, 1, *ps.* urrak, 90, 7 : 111, 4 : *pt.* urrik, 247, *r.* 1 : *inf.* urruku, 15, *r.* 6 :

arku, long, GID . DA ^{pl}, 1, 5 : 2, 4 : 3, 4 : 10, 4 : 18, 4 : 30, *r.* 4 : 35, *r.* 7 : GID ^{pl}, 7, 4 : 17, 5 :

arki, after.

**arkanu*, back part, 272, *r.* 4 :

**urnuntu*, war, 272, *r.* 6.

**arasu*, 236F, *r.* 5 :

**irpu*, cloudy, ŠU . ŠU . RU, 87, 3, 5, 6 : irpi, 47A, *r.* 1 : 87, 5, 6 : 235, *r.* 7 : irbi, 252B, 6 :

urpatu, cloud, DÍR ^{pl}, 35, 4 : IM . DIR, 76, *r.* 1 : IM . DIR ^{pl} (*gl.* urpâti), 98, 2 : 139, 6 :

**irtu*, breast, 223, 6 : 223A, *r.* 6 :

AŠ . A . AN, corn, 181, *r.* 2 :

**išu*, be, I, 1, la aššu, 21, *r.* 4 : 89, *r.* 5 : laašša, 274P, 3 :

**aššu*, now, so, 108, 7 :

ašabu, dwell, I, 1, *ps.* KU-ab, 10, *r.* 1 : 12, 6 : KU, 32, 2 : uššab, 42, 3 : išabma, 244, 4 : išamma, 246, 3 : KU ^{pl} : *pm.* ašbaku, 183, *r.* 6 : ašbu, 274, 5, *r.* 6.

III, 1 : ušiššib, 246E, *r.* 4 :

šubtu, seat.

išdu, foundation.

**išdiḫu*, 144B, 7 :

**ašlu*, 159, *r.* 2 :

**iššikku*, *pl.* 207, *r.* 3 :

išîru, prosper, I, 1 : SI . DI, 10, 6 : 11, 6 : 12, 6 : 26, 4 : 41, 2 : SI . DI . ^{pl} 88, *r.* 5 : iššir, 49, 2 : 103, *r.* 1 : ašir, 257, *r.* 6 :

II, 1, uššaru, 207, *r.* 6 :

**išartu*, justice, 246, 6 :

**mišaru*, justice, 49, *r.* 3 :

**miširtu*, justice, 121, 4 :

ašar, where.

**aširtu*, sanctuary, ašrat, 207, *r.* 6 :

ašaridutu, pre-eminence.

**iširtu*, temple, 199A, *r.* 4 : 271, *r.* 8 :

ištínu, one, I-ín, 218, *r.* 3 : 268, *r.* 2 :

**ištu*, trouble, 137, *r.* 4 : 276, 2 : pl. 186, *r.* 3 : 187, 8, *r.* 5 :

*ištu, 270, r. 6:

*ata, now, 240, r. 7:

itti, with.

*atû, III, 2, be invisible, šu-tatû (see index, under moon and sun). uštatâ, 147, r. 7: 148, r. 4:

*atta, thou, 170, r. 3:

*utukku, demon, 163, 7:

atalû, eclipse.

*ittimali, yesterday, 55, 6:

atmû, speech, 127, r. 1: 128, 2:

*atinnu, 181, r. 5:

itiḳu, pass. I, 1, ps. ittiḳ, 251, r. 10: 227, r. 2: lu-la-ti-iḳ, 243A, r. 2: 245, 6: pt. LU-iḳ, 29, r. 2: 272, r. 4: ítiḳ, 187, 1: 194, 2: lu-ítiḳ, 103, r. 3: I, 2, itítiḳ, 274, 4: itíttiḳ, 274F, 3:
III, 2, ps. ušittiḳ, 64A, r. 3: pt. ušítaḳ, 271B, 3, r. 2:

*mitiḳu, journey, 151, r. 6:

*ba'âdu (separate), I, 1, ibid., 249, r. 6: libid, 249, r. 6:

*ba'âlu, grow bright, I, 1, ps. ibail, 172, r. 5: iba'il, 186, 7: pt. ib-il, 232, r. 3: 266B, 6: pm. bail, 84, r. 3: 244D, r. 1: ba'il, 167: r. 7, 186, 5: inf. ba'il, 185, 5: 196, 3, r. 2: ba-il, 271, 11: I, 2, ibtail, 30, r. 1: ibta'il, 69, r. 3:

*bâbu, gate, esp. opening in a halo, 179, 2:

*bâru, capture, I, 1, i-bar, 276, 7:

bibbu, planet, LU . BAD pl 112, r. 7:

*bubutu, hunger, 85A, r. 6: 73, r. 2:

bubbulu, Moon's disappearance (see index).

*biblu, 194A, 5: 211A, 2: 271, 7:

*bubultu, produce, 270, 16: 271, r. 13:

*babtu, uncovered space, 249, r. 6:

*bikitu, weeping, pl. 205, r. 1: 209, 6:

bîlu, rule, I, 1, ÍN-il, 29, 3: ibíl, 26, r. 3: 38, 5: ? i-bí-lum, 276, 3: (or i-til-lum).

bîlu, lord.

*bil damí, murderer, 90, r. 11: bíl-dini, 267A, 7:

*bilutu, lordship, 85A, 8:

bûlu, cattle, 86, r. 5: 88, r. 4: 98, 6: 101A, 3: 103, r. 4: 105, r. 2: pl. 129, 5:

*balû, finish, wear out, I, 1, balat, 123, r. 2:

balâṭu, live, I, 1, ibaluṭ(uṭ), 35, r. 2: 31, 4:

balaṭu, life, ba-[la]-ṭi 85A, 7: ba-la-ṭu, 111, 4: ba-la.., 105, r. 6: TIN, 90, 7: TIL . LA, 93, 6:

balṭu, alive, pl. 207, r. 4:

*balkatu, revolt, IV, 1, 264, r. 2: 265, 2:

*banû, build, I, 1, banû, 268, r. 13:

*banû, make shine, I, 1, ibni, 272, r. 4: ibnu, 272, r. 5:

*binnu, 200, 4:

*barû, revolt, I, 1, ḪI . GAR, 192, 7: ibaru, 193, 3:

*bartu, revolt, ḪI . GAR, 43, 7 (gl. bar-ti): 168, 5, 181, 3: 237, 8: 244A, 2: 269, 13: 272A, 11: ba-ar-ti, 247A, 11:

*barû, III, 2: satiate, uštabarri, 187, r. 1: uštabarru, 186, r. 6: 193, r. 3 (?)

*barrû, 191A, 4:

**birtu*, fortress, *pl.* 27, *r.* 2 : 48, 6 : 130A, *r.* 1 : 136R, *r.* 3 :
**birtu*, between, 264, *r.* 8 :
**barâmu*, be coloured, I, 1, TAR, 175, 4 : 244, 2 : 245, 3 : 246, 1, 4 :
**barâḳu*, lighten, I, 1, ibriḳ, 235, *r.* 6 : 256B, 6 : 256C, 4 : 257, 2 :
birḳu, lightning, 235, *r.* 6 :
**bariru*, evening, bar-ir, 215, *r.* 4 :
**bararitu*, evening, 271, 2 : 272B, 2 :
bašû, be, I, 1, *ps.* IK . . 25, 6 : IK-ši : IK, 88, *r.* 4 : ibaši, 21, *r.* 2 : ibašši, IK pl-a, 95, *r.* 2 : *inf.* bašû, 22, 8 :
*I, 2, ittabši, 22A, 5 :
*III, 1, lušibšima, 252A, *r.* 3 :
*IV, 1, ibbašši, 145, 2 : ibbaššû, 162, *r.* 3 :
**bušu*, property, 256A, 7 : 269, *r.* 8 : 272, *r.* 14 :
bîtu, house.
**bit tamartí*, 39, 7 :
**bit ḳatâ* II, 240, 9 :
**bit*, 89, *r.* 10 : 267, *r.* 1 : 267, B, 14 :
**batû*, cut in pieces ? I, 1, ibatti, 257, *r.* 4 :
**bûtu*, interval, 89, *r.* 8 : 152, *r.* 6 :
**batâḳu*, burst forth, II, 1, lubattiḳ, 272B, *r.* 7 :
gabbu, all.
**gubru*, man, gu-ub-ri, 223, *r.* 2 :
**gabšu*, plentiful, 170, 2 : 217, *r.* 6 :
**gadu*, 272A, 7 :
**gamâru*, complete, I, 1, *pt.* igmur, 271, *r.* 2 : 272A, 2 : *pm.* gamir, 185, 6 : 196, 4 :
II, 1, lugammíru, 270, 12.

gamiru, complete, 270, 12 : 271, *r.* 9 :
gamirutu, completion, 38, 7 :
*GAN . BA, plenty ? (in No. 69 *napša* seems to be a gloss to GAN . BA) 34, 3 : 69, 4 : 88, 5 :
*GUR, a measure, 185, 1 : 196, 8 : 271, 13.
**gurru*, 88, *r.* 4 : 185, 11 : 196, 8 : 271, 13 :
*GAR . ḪI . A, 207A, 6 :
**girritu*, expedition, 204, 5 :
**da'âmu*, be dark, I, 1, du-'-ú-mat, 82, 7 :
da'ummatu, darkness, 235, *r.* 8 : 255, 6 : 257, 5 :
Du'ûzu, month Tammuz.
**da'aḫu*, da-'-ḫi, 238, 2.
**dabâbu*, speak, I, 1, *ps.* idibbub, 267A, 7 : idabub, 57, 5 : 257, 7 : *pt.* adbubu, 267, *r.* 2.
**dibbu*, word, 88, 7 : 137, 5 : 268, 1 :
duḫdu, plenty, 64, 2 : 65, 5 : 66, 2 :
**daḫdutu*, plenty, 185, 8 : 271, 12 :
dâku, kill, I, 1, *ps.* GAZ, 63, 3 : 269, *r.* 1 : *pt.* idduku, 240, *r.* 3 : *pc.* liduk, 146A, *r.* 4 : *pm.* dîku, 175, 6 : di-í-i-ḳi, 257, *r.* 4 :
**dullu*, service, 82, *r.* 8 : 268, *r.* 10 :
**dalḫatu*, trouble, 186, *r.* 3 : 187, 9 :
**duluḫḫu*, disturbance, 112, 5 :
**dalâlu*, be thin, I, 1, idlul, 111, 8 : 117, 7 : 144A, *r.* 6 :
damḳu, lucky, 8, *r.* 2 : da-an-ḳu, 89, edge 1 : f. 16, *r.* 2 : 126, 9 : *pl.* 123, *r.* 5 :
dimḳu, 56, 3 (?) ; 140, *r.* 5 :
**dunḳu*, propitious, 103, 10 : 139, 5 :

***dânu*, judge, I, 1, *imp.*, dinâ, 240, *r.* 9 :
**dînu*, judgment, 251A, 5, 6 :
danânu, be great, I, 1, *ps.* DAN. GA, 37, 3 : idannin, 82, *r.* 5 : 145, *r.* 3 : *pm.* dan[nat], 76, *r.* 1 :
II, 1, udan[nin], 269, 2 :
dannu, strong, 90, 10 :
**duppu*, tablet, *pl.* 160, 7 :
**dupšarru*, scribe, amêl Rab-dupšar, 160, *r.* 5 :
**diparu*, torch, 202, 6 :
**dupšum*, 229, 3.
**DIR . ŠÍ*, intercalary Adar, 225, *r.* 4 : DIR . ŠÍ . KIN . TAR, 371, *r.* 5 :
**DIR*, be dark, I, 1, *pm.* (?) di-rat, 43, 5, *r.* 1 :
dâru, be longlasting, I, 1, *pc.* ludari, 22B, *r.* 3 : 136D, *r.* 5 : *pm.* darat (= 'consecutive'). 70, 7 :
dariš, long, 15, *r.* 8 : 19, *r.* 6 : 20, *r.* 4 :
**diš*, 186, *r.* 5 (bis) : 187, 10, *r.* 1 : 193, *r.* 2, 3 :
**dišpu*, honey, 89, edge 3 :
zibbatu, tail, 200, 2 : 223, 6 : *du.* 277, 2, *r.* 1 :
**zagmu*, 28, *r.* 4 : 199A, 6 : 269, *r.* 3 :
**zuharutu*, 232, 8 :
**zakû*, be clear, I, 1, *ps.* izakkâ, 186, *r.* 3 : 187, 9 : *pt.* izku, 271, 2 : *pm.* zakaku, 272, *r.* 19 :
**zakuta*, purity, 240, 7 :
zakkaru, male, UŠ pl 94, *r.* 4 : zak-ka . . 98, *r.* 3 :
**zakaru*, call, I, 1, *pm.* zakru, 270, 13, *r.* 7 : 271, 6, *r.* 10 :
**zallummû*, brilliance, 183, 1 :
**zalpu*, unrighteousness, 181, 1 :
**zimu*, brightness, 185, 5 : 271, 11 :
**zinu*, angry, 82, 8 : *pl.* 185, 7 :
zanânu, rain, I, 1 : SUR-nun, 60, 3 : izanun, 84, 9 : izzanun, 139, *r.* 3 :
zunnu, rain, A . AN, 37, 4 : *pl.* 70, 10 : zu-un-nu, 98, 2 : 139, *r.* 3 : zu-un-ni-i, 252F, 5.
**zîku*, wind, 103, *r.* 3 :
**zakapu*, overcome, I, 1, tazakip, 69, 7 :
**ziktu*, sting, 95, *r.* 4 : 141, *r.* 1 : 209, 1 : 236G, 5 : 239, 2 : 272, *r.* 1 :
**ziru*, seed, 257, *r.* 2 :
**zaru*, 247A, *r.* 11.
**zirtu*, *pl.* 190, 2 : 190A, 2 : *ḪU . BI . A*, 269, 1 :
**ḫabâlu*, destroy, I, 1, *p.* iḫabbil, 270, *r.* 6 : 271, 4 : *pm.* ḫabil, 270, *r.* 6 : 271, 5 :
**ḫabalu*, 212A, edge 1.
**ḫablu*, destructive, 163, 7 :
**ḫabâtu*, spoil, I, 1, liḫbuti, 22, *r.* 2 :
I, 2, iḫtabtuni, 22, 7 :
IV, 1, iḫḫabbatanimma, 168, 4 :
**ḫabbatu*, robber, 88, *r.* 2 : 103, 7 : 224, 4 :
**ḫubtu*, spoil, 115E, 4 : 230, 3 :
**ḫubbutu*, spoil, 22, 6, 9 : 118, 7 : 153, *r.* 5 :
**ḫadû*, rejoice, I, 1, luḫa[di], 33, *r.* 3 : luḫâ[di], 50, *r.* 7 :
**ḫadû*, joy, 48, *r.* 3 :
ḫudu, joy, 46, *r.* 3 :
**ḫidutu*, joy, 19, *r.* 4 :
**ḫaṭu*, III, 2, ultaḫṭuni, 158, *r.* 4.
**ḫiṭṭu*, sin, 88, 10 : ḫitu, 274, *r.* 5 :
**ḫakâmu*, III, 1, inform, ušaḫkam, 68, *r.* 5 :
*amêl ḪAL, magician, 18, *r.* 3 : 186, *r.* 9 : 187, *r.* 3 :

*ḫalâpu, be obscure, I, 1 : iḫallup, 43, r. 3 : _inf._ ḫalapu, 43, r. 4 :
*_ḫalâḳu_, perish, I, 1, _ps._ ḪA . A, 181, 1 : iḫalliḳ, 103, 10 :
I, 2, taḫtiliḳ, 183, r. 6 :
šaḫluḳtu, destruction, 88, r. 4 : 114, 7 :
*_ḫanṭiš_, swiftly, 48, r. 2 : 272, r. 17 :
*_ḫannû_, that, 112, r. 7 :
ḫasâsu, intend, understand, I, 1, _ps._ iḫassasu, 46, r. 2 : 133, 4 : iḫasasu, 117, 6 : iḫassu, 144A, 3 : _pm._ ḫassuma, 268, r. 15, _pm._ luḫasi[s], 164, r. 8 : lûḫasis, 160, r. 3 :
*_ḫasisu_, variant for _uznu_, 144D, r. 2 :
*_ḫipû_, spoil, I, 1, iḫpûni, 200, r. 5 :
I, 2, iḫtípû, 272, r. 14 :
*_ḫarâbu_, be dry, I, 1, iḫarrubu, 57, 6 : 223, 8 :
*_ḫarbiš_, fiercely, 59, 5 : 70, 5 :
*_ḫarubiš_, 246A, 2, 4 :
*_ḫarrânu_, road.
*_ḫuraṣu_, gold, 22, r. 3 : 85A, r. 1 :
ḫušaḫḫu, famine.
ṭâbu, be good, I, 1, _ps._ DUG . GA, 3, 2 : 7, 2 : 14, 3 : DUG-ab, 1, 3 : 2, 2 : DUG, 27, 1 : 29, 1 : iṭâb, 12, 2 : iṭabi, 19, 2 : 22A, 3 : _pc._ liṭib, 268, r. 10 : luṭâbi, 33, r. 2 : 50, r. 6 : 85, r. 7 :
*II, 1, luṭibka, 187, r. 10 :
ṭâbu, good, 90, 13 : _f._ 120, 3 : _pl._ 112, 8 : _f. pl._ 201, 7 :
ṭûbu, goodness, 15, r. 4, 5 : 19, r. 3 : 19A, r. 4 :
*_ṭabtu_, salt, 235A, 12 : 277, r. 2 :
Ṭibîtu, month Tebet.
ṭiḫû, approach, I, 1, _ps._ iṭaḫḫi, 89, r. 5 : 112, r. 6 : _pt._ TÍ-ḫi : itḫi, 88, 9 :
*III ^{II}, 2, uštaḫḫâ, 94, r. 3 : 108, 3 : uštaḫâ, 143, 8 :
IV, 1 (?), iṭṭiḫi 112, r. 3 :
*_ṭîmu_, command, III, 2, nusaṭimuni, 109, r. 2.
*_ṭîmu_, command, 34, 9 : 48, r. 2 : 268, r. 12 :
ṭimu, 270, 7 :
_kî_, for, kî pî, 'according to,' 22, 10.
_-ka_, thy.
kaîmanu, constant, SAG . UŠ, 9, 4 : ka-a-a-ma-nu, 34, r. 6 : 251, r. 7 : 267A, r. 5 : ka-a-a-ma-ni-ti, 274, 11 :
kibratu, region, 269, 11.
*_kabtu_, heavy, 86, r. 7 : 268 r. 4 : 272, 6 :
*_KI . ḪUL_, pain, 270, r. 7 271, 5 :
kakku, weapon.
kakkabu, star, 251, 7 : _pl_ 56, 6 :
*_kal_, all, 262D, 1 : kala, 200, 3 : 263, 1 : _f._ 123, 7 : _adv._ 136L, 6 : 207A, r. 1 :
*_kâlu_, bring, II, 1, ukal, 98, 2 (_gl._ ukala) : ukallu, 111, 7 : nukâla, 274B, 4 :
II, 2 : uktala, 251, 6 :
*^{am} _kalu_, magician, 256, 7 :
*_kalbu_, dog, 269, r. 2 :
*_kalâlu_, complete, III, 1, ušaklala, 207, r. 5 :
kalâmu, all, KAL . A . BI, 190, 3 : kalâma, 274, 5 (?), r. 7 : kalamu, 268, 15 :
*_kalâmu_, II, 1, shew, ukallimu, 274, r. 7 :
kima, like.

**kûmu*, 268, 2, *r*. 4 :

**kamasu*, I, 1, kamusu, 272A, 12 :

**kamar*, 267, 7 :

kânu, be firm, I, 1, *ps*. ikan, 42, 5 : 127, *r*. 1 : 136C, 7 : ikana, 126, 1 : ikanu, 82A, 2, 7 : *pm*. kini, 24, 5 : kinu, 136, 5 :

*I, 2, iktun, 185, 1 : 186, 1 : 196, 11 : 271, edge 1 :

*II, 1, *ps*. ukanu, 199, *r*. 4 : *pt*. ukin, 206, 5 : *pm*. kunna, 25, *r*. 4 : *inf*. kunnu, 15, *r*. 7 : *part* mukinnu, 267A, 6, 7 :

*II, 2, uktinnu, 90, *r*. 11 :

kînu, firm.

kittu, truth, justice.

**kinunu*, censer, 151, *r*. 10 :

**kinatu*, servants, 90, *r*. 13 : 170, *r*. 7 :

kussu, throne.

Kisilimu, month Kislew.

**kasâsu*, divide, IV, 1, muniksisa, 209, 4 :

**kaspu*, silver, 22, *r*. 3 : 90, *r*. 18 :

*kâpu, bend, I, 1, *pm*. kipat, 69, 6 : *ps*. ikippi, 268, *r*. 6 :

**kapâdu*, II, 2, uktappad, 277AE, 6 :

**kupuru*, covering, 269, 4, 6 : 270, *r*. 1 : 271, 1, 3 :

kuṣṣu, cold, 62, 7 : 84, *r*. 4 :

**kaṣâru*, I, 1, be uninterrupted (of halos), *pm*. kaṣir, 95, 3 : kaṣru, 96, 5 : *pt*. ikṣur, 112, 3, 6 : II, 2, uktaṣara, 98, 3 : 124, 10 : 180, *r*. 2 : uktaṣṣara, 115A, *r*. 3 : 115D, *r*. 3 :

**kiṣru*, 28, 2 (?) : 160, *r*. 6 :

**karû*, be short, I, 1, *pt*. ikri, 41, 6 : ikru, 30, 6 :

*kiru, *garden*, 123, 7 :

**kirbu*, 82, *r*. 8 :

**kurkurru*, circle, 243A, 1 :

**karmutu*, ruin, 252E, 6 : 266, *r*. 2 :

**karanu*, wine, 123, 8 (?).

**kurusissu*, worm (?), 98, 4 :

**kartu*, want (?), 164, *r*. 3 : 276, 4 :

**kâšu*, cease (?), I, 1, ikaši, 236, 6 :

**kašbu*, two hours, 94, 8 : 155, *r*. 8 : 201, 1 :

kašâdu, conquer, reach, I, 1, *pt*. KUR-ud, 88, 5 : ikšud, 88, 9 : ikšudamma, 124, 1 : ikšadamma, 272, *r*. 4 : *ps*. KUR-ád, 41, *r*. 1 : ikaššad, 30, 7 : 31, 8 : 207, 6 : ikaššadu, 44, *r*. 10 : *pm*. kašdû, 229, 2 :

I, 2, iktašad, 235, 1 : 243A, 5 :

IV, 1, ikkaššad, 105, 7 : 223, *r*. 3 :

kiššatu, might, 73, 3 :

kiššutu, might, 56, 5 : 60, *r*. 3 : 85A, 8 :

**kutallu*, back, 192, *r*. 3 :

**katâtu*, III, 2, grow dim (?), uštaktitma, 208, 3 : 208A, 3 : uštaktima, 204, *r*. 1 :

la, not.

lû, or, lû-lû 82, 5, *r*. 7–8 : 166, 6 : lu-lu, 169, 1 :

*li'u, tablet, 152, *r*. 1, 4 : 160, 6 : 181A, *r*. 3 :

**la'abu*, flame, 223, 5 :

libbu, heart.

**liblibbu*, offspring, 207, *r*. 5 :

**labânu*, make bricks, I, 1, libin, 73, *r*. 4.

**libittu*, brick, 73, *r*. 3, 4 :

**labâru*, be old, II, 1, *ps*. BAD-bar, 127, *r*. 3 : ulabbar, 129, 10 : ulabar, 1360, 9 :

**labiru*, old, *pl*. 245, 4 :

**labâšu*, clothe, IV, 1, illabiš, 151, *r.* 9:
lamû, surround, I. 1, *pt.* KIL, 85, 5: KIL-mi, 90, 8: NIGIN, 49, *r.* 1: ilmíšu, 141, *r.* 2: ilmû, 85, *r.* 1: *ps.* NIGIN-mi, 49, 6: *inf.* lamu, 89, *r.* 7.
I, 2, ilti(mí), 141, *r.* 3: iltami, 153, *r.* 1:
**limmu*, eponymy, 264, edge 1:
* *lamânu*, be evil, I, 1, *ps.* ilammina) 272, 14: *pm.* limna, 272, *r.* 7, 8, 10:
**limnitu*, evil, 199, 1:
lumnu, evil.
limuttu, evil.
**lapâtu*, turn, I, 1, *ps.* ilapat, 95, 4. ilappat, 215, 6: 230, 4, *r.* 1: 251, *r.* 2: talapat, 108, 6: *pm.* lapit, 249, *r.* 2:
I, 2: ilta[pat], 33, 6:
II, 1, ulappat, 172, *r.* 3, 6:
**šalputtu*, evil, 246E, *r.* 6:
**šulputtu*, evil, 246E, *r.* 4:
laķû, take, I, 1, *ps.* TIL-ķi, 120, 5: iliķķi, 59, 4: 66, *r* 1:
lišânu, tongue, ÍMÍ, 62, 3: 76, 3. lišânu, 76, 3: lišânu, 76, 3:
lîtu, valiance, 104, 6: 244, 3: 246, 2:
-ma, and.
mâ, thus.
**ma'âdu*, be many, I, 1, *ps.* imaid, 185, 10: 196, 7: imandi, 60, 2: imaddi, 267, 9: imandu, 152, *r.* 5: 271, 4:
**ma'adu*, much, 18, *r.* 4: 22A, *r.* 1: 56, 3: 117, *r.* 1: *pl.* 34, *r.* 3: 197, 2: 199, 6: *f. pl.* 19, *r.* 7: *adv.* 33, *r.* 3: 181. *r.* 4:
**ma'alu*, bed, 216, *r.* 3: 231, 2: 232, 2: 244C, *r.* 4:
**ma'âru*, direct, I, 1, *pm.*, ma'ar, 22A, *r.* 2:
II, 1, umâr, 276, 6:
mu'irru, ruler, 199A, 1: 228, 6:
* *magâru*, benefit, I, 1, imagar, 217, 6: 218, 2: 218A, 8.
III, 1, lušamgur, 70, *r.* 6:
**maddagiš*, 195A, 3:
muḫḫu, presence.
**miḫû*, storm, 258, *r.* 1:
maḫâṣu, strike, I, 1, *ps.* imaḫ-ḫaṣ, 23, 6: 39, *r.* 2: 47A, 6: *pc.* limhaṣa 272C, *r.* 5: *pm.* mahiṣ, 267A, 1:
*IV, 1, immaḫḫaṣ, 151, *r.* 8:
^am^ *maḫiṣu*, 277, 5:
taḫaṣu, battle, 181, 2:
**maḫâru*, I, 1 (face), be hostile, pray = *ps.* imaḫḫara, 271, *r.* 8: amaḫḫar, 73, *r.* 2: imaḫḫaru, 186, *r.* 8: 268, 5: *pm.* maḫru, 187, *r.* 3:
I, 2, *ps.* imdaḫḫaru, 99, *r.* 5: imdahhar-ú-ma, 103, *r.* 7: *pm.* mitḫara, 26, 6: 44, 7: mitḫaru, 195, 9:
IV, 2, ittammíḫir, 57, *r.* 4 (?): 180, 6:
IV, 3, issanaḫḫar, 88, 4: 103, *r.* 11:
maḫrû, former, ŠI-u, 26, *r.* 6: 33, *r.* 7: 59, *r.* 5: 60, *r.* 4: 65, *r.* 2: 66, *r.* 6: 85, *r.* 8: 96B, *r.* 3: ŠI-ú, 27, *r.* 7: 32, *r.* 6: 87, *r.* 3: maḫrí, 151A, 7: *f.* 70, *r.* 5: 159, *r.* 3.
miḫritu, 86, *r.* 2:
maḫiru (1) rival, GAB. RI, 82, *r.* 5: maḫiru, 36A, 5: 88, 12:
(2) market-tariff, KI. LAM, 20, *r.* 1:
**mitḫariš*, reciprocally, 39, 4:
**muk*, 57, 2: 111, 7 (?)
mîlu, flood.

**mala*, all, 22, 8, *r.* 4: 267A, 8, *r.* 2: 272, *r.* 7:

**malû*, be full, I, 1, imallu, 207, *r.* 4:

**malâḫu*, II, 1, mulluḫ, 200, *r.* 7:

malâku, counsel, I, 1, *ps.* 45, 4: 82, 3:

*I, 2, *pm.* mitluk, 195, 5:

milku, counsel, 45, 4: 82, 3:

**mîlammu*, brilliance, 145, 1:

**mîliṣu* (?) 191, 2:

mammu, anyone, 85A, *r.* 8; 60, 2:

**mimmu*, anything, 85A, *r.* 5, 7: 215, 6, *r.* 4: 267A, *r.* 21, 272, *r.* 8:

**mîmîni* (indefinite interrog. particle), 21, *r.* 2: 57, 4: 89, 11: 235, 6, 10: 257, *r.* 1:

mînu, what, 76, *r.* 6: 124, *r*, 2, 5: 210, 5: ammíni, 170, *r.* 7: 240, *r.* 7: 268, *r.* 9:

**mannu*, who, 124, *r.* 5:

manû, count, I, 1, *ps.* imnû, 22, 5: *pc.* limnû, 22, *r.* 2:

minatu, number, 1, 4: 2, 3: 5, 3: 11, 3: 82, *r.* 2: 119, 4:

**minitu*, part (?) 268, 8:

**mandîma*, anything, 90, *r.* 2: 268, *r.* 7: 274, 9:

**manma*, any one, 236B, *r.* 7:

**masû*, clean, II, 1, umassi, 181, *r.* 6.

**masartu*, siege, attack (?) ma-sa-ar-ti, 240, 9:

maḳâtu, smite, I, 1, *pm.* maḳtu, III, 1, ušamkat, 270, 9: ušam-ḳatu, 270, 9: 272A, 9: *inf.* RU-ut, 44, *r.* b: 49, 2: RU-ta, 119, 7: 213, 5: RU-tim, 86, *r.* 4: 94, 6:

**marû*, II, 1, spoil, umarri, 201A, 3: 202, 3: umarrum, 243B, *r.* 3:

mâru, son, 10, *r.* 3: 11, *r.* 3: 124, *r.* 10.

mâr-šipri, messenger, 66, *r.* 4:

**marâṣu*, be sick, I, 1, *pm.* marṣaku, 158, *r.* 5: 243C, *r.* 2: maruṣ, 18, *r.* 4: murṣat (?) 81K, 7: marṣûni, 257, 9:

I, 2, GIG [pl] 269, *r.* 1:

I, 3, imdanaraṣ, 257, *r.* 7:

marṣu, sick, *pl.*, 181B, 4:

**murṣu*, sickness, 69A, 5: 81G, 3: 257, 8: 271, 9:

**mirišu*, planting, 88, *r.* 5: 99, *r.* 1: 101, 2: 234, 8: 267, 9:

mušu, night, 21A, 3: 52, 4: 94, 1:

**mašâḫu*, I, 1, imšuḫ, 91, *r.* 1: 164, *r.* 2:

mišḫu, 91, *r.* 1: 164, *r.* 1: 190, 3, *r.* 2: mišḫu mašaḫu = grow brilliant.

mašmašu, magician.

**mašâru*, leave, II, 1, *pt.* umaš-širanni, 73, 4, *r.* 5: 158, *r.* 6: 267A, *r.* 7: umašširu, 90, *r.* 14: *ps.* .. maš (?) šaršu, 136B, *r.* 4:

**mišru*, plenty, 200, 6:

mâtu, land.

mâtu, die, I, 1. *ps.* amati, 73, *r.* 6; 158, *r.* 7: BAD, 84, *r.* 8: BAD [pl], 82, 6:

**mati*–immatimma, 249, *r.* 5, 7:

**matâḫu*, I, 1, *pm.* matiḫ, 76, *r.* 4: *pc.* lintuḫu, 274P, 2:

IV, 3: ittantaḫa, 84, 6: 188, *r.* 2:

**mutânu*, plague, 232, 3:

**mitutu*, death, 267A, 3:

**na'alu*, put, *esp.* preserve, an-didilšu, 277, *r.* 2:

**nâru*, river, corona, 90, 8: 91, 5: 112A, 3: 118, 1: 153, *r.* 6:

**na'ru*, bright, 270, *r* 10: 271, 9:

NU . BAD-tu, festival, 55, *r*. 1 :

nabâṭu, be brilliant, IV, 1, inambuṭ, 244A, 1 :

IV, 3, ittananbiṭu, 86, 6 : ittannanbiṭu, 272, 7 : *pm.* ninbuṭa, 223A, *r*. 6 :

**nabṭu*, brilliance, 277V, a.

**nibṭu*, brilliance, 86, 3 :

**nabâlu*, destroy, IV, 1, innabal, 269, *r*. 2 :

**nagâlu*, IV, 1, ningula, 223A, *r*. 5 :

nadû, place, I, 1, *pm.* nadi, 70, 9 : RU, 137, *r*. 3 : *ps.* inandu, 188, 7 : inadûni, 256A, 9 : anaddika, 267A, 3 : *pt.* RU, 253, 1 :

I, 2 : ittidi, 235, *r*. 4 :

**nidu*, parhelion, 29, *r*. 4 : 68, 7 : 70, 9 : 137, *r*. 3 : 182, 1, 3, 5, *r*. 1 : 183, 3 :

nadânu, give, I, 1, *ps.* inamdin, 182R, 2 : 272B, 4 : SÍ-in, 185, 11 : *pm.* nadin, 268, 6, *pt.* iddannu, 20, *r*. 6 : addinu, 272, 5 : *pc.* liddinu, 183, *r*. 7 : lidinu, 217, *r*. 8 : *inf.* nadanu, 90, *r*. 1 : nadan, 143A, *r*. 7 :

I, 2, ittadin, 272C, *r*. 4, 6 :

III, 2, uštaddanu, 195, 4, 5 : šutadunu, 195, 5 :

nadâru, rage, IV, 1, innadaru, 153, *r*. 4 : innandaru, 88, *r*. 2 : 103, 7 : innamdaru, 143, *r*. 1 : *inf.* nandur, 140, 2 : 153, 2 :

nazâzu, stand, I, 1, *ps.* DU, 86, *r*. 9 : DU-az, 27, *r*. 6 : izzaz, 39, *r*. 4 : izzazûni, 70, *r*. 8 : *pt.* DU-iz, 49, *r*. 2 : DU-zi, 29, *r*. 1 : izzizu, 103, *r*. 8 : azziz, 247A, *r*. 8 : *by-forms*, izuz, 170, 6 : uzuzaku, 247A, *r*. 10 : uzussu, 247A, 2 : ittašiz, 215, 8 :

manzazu, station, 27, *r*. 6 : 37, *r*. 3 : 87A, *r*. 3 : 91, *r*. 4 : 247, *r*. 1 :

**manzaltu*, station, 185, 12 :

**nazâku*, IV, 2 : ittazkinni, 73, *r*. 3 :

nazâḳu, injure, I, 1, *inf.* nazaḳ, 265, 4 : 266, *r*. 4 : 267, *r*. 2 :

IV, 1, inanzik, 272, *r*. 6 :

**niziḳtu*, harm, 59, 6 : 70, 6 :

nâḫu, rest, I, 1, *pm.* RU-iḫ, 56, 2 : niḫ, 142, *r*. 2 :

*III, 2, uštaniḫ, 272A, 1 :

**nîḫu*, restful, *f.* 26, 7 : 29, *r*. 3 : 44, 8 : 183, 7 : 187, 2, *r*. 2 :

**naḫâšu*, be abundant, I, 1, *ps.* inaḫiš, 187, 6 : 266B, 7 : KAN-aš (?), 37, 3 :

nuḫšu, plenty, 20, 6 : 31, 5 : 35, 3 : 233, 5 :

**naṭâšu*, leave, IV, 1, inaṭiš, 210, 7 :

**nakâlu*, be cunning, II, 1, unakkala, 267A, *r*. 6 :

**niklâtum*, cunning, 267A, *r*. 5.

**nikasu*, property, 267A, 5, 8 :

**nakapu*, overcome, I, 1, inakap (kip), 82, 8.

II, 1, unakkap, 32, 5 : 44, 6 : unakap, 26, *r*. 4 : 46, 3 :

**nakâru*, be hostile, I, 1, KÚR-ir, 86, *r*. 4 :

II, 2, uttanakkar, 204, 4 :

nakru, foe, 28, *r*. 4 : 357 : 61, 3 :

nakurtu, hostility, 82, *r*. 2 : 260, 2 :

**namû*, ruin, 165, 6 : 211, *r*. 2 :

**NAM . BUL . BI*, 82, *r*. 7 : 88, 10 : 96, 4 : 195, *r*. 8 : 274, *r*. 4 :

namâru, be bright, I, 1, *pm.* namir, 200, 1 : namrat, 223, 6 : *pt.* ṢAB-ir, 31, 3, 4 : *ps.* inammira, 187, 8 :

*IV, 1, ninmura, 223, 7 : nanmur, 59, 5 : 70, 5 :
namru, bright, 28, 3 : *pl.* 35, *r* 4 :
**namuru*, brightness, 246A, 6 :
nammašu, beast, 94, 6.
**nammaštu*, beast, 101A, 3 (?) : 105, 2 (?) : 200, 2, 10 :
nunu, fish, 270, 11 :
**nissabu*, cereals, 222, 2 : ilu Nisaba, 220, 3 : 221, *r.* 2 :
*nasâḫu, determine, I, 1, anassaḫa, 188, *r.* 4 : inasaḫa, 244D, 6 :
I, 2, attasḫa, 88, 9 : 264, 10 :
IV, 1, innasaḫa, 112, *r.* 4 : 251, *r.* 3 :
**nasiku*, chief, 90, *r.* 8, 9, *f.* 90, *r.* 9 :
Nisannu, month Nisan.
napâḫu, culminate, I, 1, *pt.* KUR-ḫa, 29, *r.* 4 : KUR, 123, *r.* 4 : *inf.* napaḫi, 254, *r.* 1, 2 :
**nipḫu*, zenith, 68, 7 : 103, *r.* 9 : 181, 7 : 185, 6 : 269, 7 :
**napâlu*, IV, 1, become apparent, [in]-nap-pa-lu, 186, *r.* 10 :
IV, 2, itanappal, 187, *r.* 4 :
**napašu*, be plentiful, I, 1, *pt.* inapuš, 111, *r.* 5 : 250, 2 : 252B, 5 : *inf.* napaš, 220, 3 : 221, *r.* 2 : 222, 2 :
**napšu*, abundance, 91, *r.* 2 : 269, 5, 6 :
**naṣu*, naṣ, 109, *r.* 8 :
**naṣâru*, guard, I, 1, *ps.* anamṣar, 240, *r.* 7 : *pt.* iṣṣarru, 202, *r.* 1 : *pc.* liṣṣur, 33, *r.* 6 : 245, *r.* 2 : *imp.* uṣur, 73, 3 : 268, *r.* 12 :
I, 2, atta[ṣar], 235, 2 : nitaṣar, 21, 6 : 76, *r.* 1, 3 :
maṣartu, watch, 33, *r.* 5 : 52, 5 : 85, 7, *r.* 3 : 108, 7 : *pl.* 27, *r.* 3 : 48, 7 : 147, *r.* 2 :

**niḳu*, niḳû, 243, *r.* 3 :
naḳbu, channel, 112, *r.* 1 : 235, *r.* 6 :
naḳâru, destroy, I, 1, inaḳar, 156, 3 : 157, 5 : 157B, 5 : 157D, 5 : inaḳḳar, 164, 4 :
IV, 1, innaḳaru, 269, *r.* 7 :
**niru*, yoke, 49, 2 :
našû, bring, raise, I, 1, *pm.* naši, 38, 6 : našâ, 216A, 4 : našaku, 272, *r.* 13 : našaka, 52, *r.* 1 : *ps.* inaššu . . 90, *r.* 19 : inaššâ, 164, 3 : inašâ, 157D, 4 : ÍL . LA pl, 111, 6 : *pt.* iššû, 267A, *r.* 1 : *pc.* lišši, 151, *r.* 5 : 210, *r.* 3 : *inf.* niš, 155B, *r.* 3, 7 :
*I, 2, ittaši, 267A, 5, *r.* 4 : ittanši, 146, *r.* 3 : ittašû, 158, *r.* 5 : 272, *r.* 14 :
**našu*, 243B, *r.* 2 :
**nâšu*, quake, I, 1, inuš, 263, 2, 4 : 264, *r.* 7 : 265A, *r.* 3 : 265C, 4 : 266A, 6 : 266B, 4 : 267, *r.* 1 : inu . . 265, 3 : BUL-uš, 264, 5 :
nišu, people.
nišu, lion, UR . A pl, 82, 6 : UR . MAḪ pl, 94, *r.* 4 :
**natâlu*, sleep, I, 1, littil, 274Q, 2, 4, 6 :
**sâ'u*, overcome, I, 1, isi', 119, 6 :
**sadâru*, I, 1, isdiruni, 31, *r.* 9 :
**sadâru*, prevail, I, 1, *pm.* sadir, 111, *r.* 2 : 141, *r.* 6 : 250, 3 : 251, 4 : 252B, 2 : 252D, 1 : 263, 4 : sadrat, 123, 4 :
II, 1, usadir, 111, *r.* 4 : 252B, 4 : 264, 3, 9, *r.* 6 : usaddir, 262D, 3 :
**sadru*, copious, *pl.* 271, 12 :
**sidru*, copious, *pl.* 185, 8 : 196, 6 :
**saḫâru*, go round, I, 1, isâḫur,

236G, *r.* 2 : IV, 1, issuḫur, 70, *r.* 2 :
**sili'tu*, weakness, 235, *r.* 2 :
**sililitu* = Sebat, 49, 1, 4 :
salimu, goodwill, 27, *r.* 4 : 99, 9 : 100, 4 :
saluppu, dates, 29, 7 : 88, *r.* 5 :
**sâmu*, be dark, I, 1, isimu, 123, *r.* 4 :
**sâmu*, dark, 37, 4 : 248, 1 :
**simnu*, 217, *r.* 1 :
Simanu, month Siwan.
simanu, calculated time, 82, 1 : 88, 1 :
sanâku, draw near, I, 1, *pt.*, isnik, 232, *r.* 1, 2 : *inf.* sanâku, *passim.*
*II, 1, usanaku, 26, *r.* 4 : 44, 6 :
**sunku*, famine, 103, *r.* 5 : 192, 5 : 193, 2 :
sinništu, woman.
**sisu*, horse, *pl.* 232, *r.* 1 :
sapâḫu, destroy, I, 1, *inf.* BIR-aḫ, 32, *r.* 2 : BIR, 72, 2 : sapaḫ, 138, 5 :
**supuru*, fold, halo of 46° : 117, 1, 7 :
**sarâru*, I, 1, isarir, 89, *r.* 12 :
**sittu*, rest, remainder, 48, *r.* 1 :
pû, mouth.
pagru, corpse, *pl.* 146, *r.* 5 : 163, 5 :
**tapdu*, destruction, 200, 6 :
**puḫu*, presence, 268, *r.* 11 : 272B, *r.* 6 :
**paḫâru*, collect, IV, 1, 256A, 7 :
**paṭâru*, be interrupted (of halos), I, 1, *pt.* ipṭuru, 117, *r.* 2 : *inf.* paṭar, 27, *r.* 2 : 48, 6 : 130A, *r.* 1 :
palû, reign.
pâlu, be dark, I, 1, *pm.* pil, 37, 2 : pilu, 37, 4 :
**palâḫu*, fear, I, 1, *pm.* palḫaku, 34, *r.* 8 : *inf.* palaḫ, 257, 12 :
**naplusu*, see, IV, 1, tappallas, 229, 1 :
panû, face, former, *f.* panitu, *lapan*, before.
**paššuru*, dish, 247A, *r.* 7 :
**pakâdu*, command, I, 1, *pc.* lipkidu, 152, *r.* 8 :
parâgu, shine (?), I, 1, parig, 86, 4 :
parganiš, securely, par-ga-niš, 125, 8 : pár-ga-niš, 129, 6 : par-ga-ni-iš, 136, o, 6.
**parakku*, shrine, *pl.* 157, 5 : 271, 14 :
**parâsu*, decide, I, 1, iprus, 179, 2 (*gl.*) : luprus, 210, *r.* 3 : *part*, *f.* paristum, 52, *r.* 3 : 272C, 7 :
**purussu*, decision, 268, 6 : 271, 7 : 272B, 3 :
**pâšu*, pass off, I, 2, iptušu, 55, *r.* 3 :
**pašâru*, interpret, IV, 1, ippaššir, 833 : IV, 2 : ittapšar, 170, *r.* 1 :
pišru, interpretation, 89, *r.* 9 : 111, 2 : 144D, 3 : *rab pi-[šir ?]*, 158, *r.* 1, 5 :
**pûtu*, direction, 254, *r.* 2 : 272, *r.* 13 :
**patû*, leave an interval, I, 1, *ps.* ipatti, 88, *r.* 10 : 112, *r.* 6 : I, 2, *pm.* pa-a-tí, 88, 9 :
**patû*, open, I, 1, lipittu-šu, 268, *r.* 2 : ipittuni, 152, *r.* 8 : I, 2, aptítí, 89, *r.* 11 : iptíti, 112, *r.* 12 :
pitû, clear, open, 155, *r.* 7 :
**PAT . ḪI . A*, 230, *r.* 3 :
ṣabâtu, seize, I, 1, *ps.* i-iṣ-ba-tu-ú, 90, *r.* 17 : iṣbatuš (*gl.*),

137, *r.* 4 : iṣabat, 277, 4 : LU-bat, 163, 7 : 272, *r.* 6 :
II, 1, ṣabbit (?), 272, *r.* 16 :
III, 1, ušaṣbitanni, 240, *r.* 2 : ušaṣ-?-tu, 115, 7 :
IV, 1, iṣṣabat, 236, 3 : iṣṣabtanni, 90, edge 2 :
***ṣibutu*, desire, 201, 6 :
ṣaḫâru, be small, I, 1, TUR, 88, 5 : TUR-ir, 103, 5 :
***ṣalû*, pray, II, 1, uṣalli, 272C, *r.* 6 : uṣallû, 124, *r.* 7 : uṣallûni, 257, 13 :
***ṣulû*, prayer, 162, *r.* 4 :
***ṣalâlu*, obscure, II, 1, uṣallil, 274, *r.* 7 :
ṣalmu, dark, 98, 1 : 124, 10 :
***ṣalmu*, image, 170, *r.* 2 :
ṣapâru, point, I, 1, ṣaparu, 34, 8 : 36, *r.* 1 :
ṣîru, field, 94, 6 :
***ṣiru*, snake, 146A, *r.* 4 :
***ṣarramu*, audacious, 232, 12 :
ṣararu, shine, I, 1, *pt.* SUR, 28, *r.* 2 : iṣrur, 89, *r.* 6 : *inf.* ṣarari-šu, 200, 2 : IV, 1, iṣṣarur, 201, 4 :
***ṣirru*, brilliance, 200, 1 :
***ṣarratu*, sedition, 204, 6 :
***ḲA*, a measure, 185, 11 : 196, 8 : 271, 13 :
***ḳû* (?), vegetables, 181, *r.* 3 :
ḳâ'u, wait for, II, 1, uḳi, 140, 1 :
ḳabû, speak, I, 1, *ps.* aḳabbi, 252C, *r.* 4 : taḳabbi, 267A, 4, iḳabbi, 21, *r.* 1 : 34, *r.* 9 : iḳabbû, 90, *r.* 11 : iḳabû . . 76, *r.* 7 : *pt.* aḳbû, 180, *r.* 2 : aḳbu, 181, *r.* 4 : iḳbâ, 124, *r.* 2 : iḳbû, 254, 7 : iḳbûni, 43, *r.* 2 : 256, 2 : *pc.* luḳbi, 22B, *r.* 2 : 210, *r.* 4 : 274C, 7 : liḳbi, 18, *r.* 5 : liḳbû, 15, *r.* 9 : *pm.* ḳabi, 232, 3 : ḳâbi, 236G, 6 : ḳabû, 268, 6 : *imp.* ḳibâ, 268, *r.* 13 :
I, 2, aḳtabi, 273, *r.* 2 : iḳdibi, 183A, 6 : 254, *r.* 3 :
***ḳabâlu*, fight, I, 1, iḳabbal, 174, 6 :
ḳablu, middle, 94, *r.* 1 : 235, 11 : 254, 5, 7 :
ḳablitu, middle, 202, *r.* 2 : 271, 3 :
***ḳaṭâlu* (?), kill (?), ḳat-lim-ma, 269, 8 :
***ḳaṭnu*, less, 136D, *r.* 6 : 220, *r.* 2 : 274C, 2 :
***ḳudumu*, 243, *r.* 2 :
***ḳalû*, [išu] ḳa-lu-a-tí, 89, *r.* 10 :
***ḳallu*, magician, 85A, *r.* 9 : 134, *r.* 7 :
***niḳilpû*, go, IV, 1, *inf.* niḳilpû, 139, *r.* 1 : iḳilippu (*gl.* to DIR-pu), 139, 8 :
***ḳapâšu*, weigh down (?), II, 2, uḳdappašamma, 86, *r.* 7 :
***ḳaṣaru*, be joined, uninterrupted (of halos), I, 1, *pm.* kaṣir, 95, 3 : kaṣru, 96, 5 : *pt.* ikṣur, 112, 3, 6 :
II, 2, uḳtaṣara, 98, 3 : uḳtaṣṣara, 115D, *r.* 3 :
***ḳaḳḳaru*, ground, 221, 2 : 236A, 4 : 236E, 1 :
***ḳaḳḳuru*, ground, 267, *r.* 14 :
***ḳarû*, call, I, 2, iḳdiri, 55, 8 :
***ḳarâbu*, approach, I, 1, *ps.* iḳarrib, 112, *r.* 5 : *pt.* iḳrub, 67, 6 : iḳrib, 112, *r.* 11 : *pc.* liḳrûbu, 90, 2 : 274 2 : *pm.* ḳurbu, 232, *r.* 2 :
I, 2, iḳdírib, 112, *r.* 5 : 176, *r.* 3 : 188, *r.* 3 :
II, 1, uḳarrib, 185, 3 : 196, 1 :
iḳribu, prayer, 186, *r.* 8 :
***ḳuradu*, warrior, 216, *r.* 3 : 231, 2 : 232, 2 : 244C, 4 :

karnu, horn, 30, 5 : 36, *r.* 1 : 43, 6 :

**kašratu*, conspiracy, 204, 6 :

katû, hand.

kâtâru, burst, I, 1, iktur, 249A, 1 : 250, 5 : 250A, 1 : 251, 1, 5 :

**ra'âbu*, be angry, I, 1, tar'ubu, 170, *r.* 4 :

**ru'ubtu*, anger, 170, *r.* 4 :

**râbu*, quake, I, 1, *pt.* irub, 264, 8 : 265, 1 : 265C, 1, 3 : 266, *r.* 3 : 266A, 1, 4 : 267, 12, 14 : ŠU-ub, 266, 7, *r.* 1 : ŠU, 264, *r.* 1 : irubûni, 264, *r.* 6 : *pm.* rub, 272C, 5, *r.* 2, 3 :

I, 2, irtubu, 266, 6 :

**rîbu*, earthquake, 264, 1 : 265B, 1 : 266, 6, 7 : 266A, 1 : 267, 12, *r.* 11 :

rabû, be great, I, 1, *ps.* irabbi, 90, *r.* 12 : *pt.* GAL, 30, 8 : *inf.* rabû, 117, 9 :

rabû, great, *pl.* 56, *r.* 1 : **adv.* MA.GAL 30, 8, *r.* 1 : 69, *r.* 3 : **officials* Rab-A.BA, 74, *r.* 5 : 109, *r.* 9 : 266, *r.* 5 : Rab-ašipa, 268, 18 : Rab-dupšar, 81, *r.* 1 : 259, *r.* 1 : Rab-kâri, 264, edge, 2 : Rab-SAG, 90, *r.* 10, 12, 14 : Rab Kisir pl 90, *r.* 16 :

rubû, prince, 37, 3 : *pl.* 268, *r.* 8 : 272, *r.* 7 :

rabû, disappear, be invisible, I, 2, *ps.* irabbi, 88, 3 : *pt.* irbi, 140, 1 : 204, *r.* 1 : BUL, 208, 1, 6, irbû 205, 4 : irbûni, 21, *r.* 3 : *inf.* (?) rûbi, 109, 3 :

I, 2, irtibi, 21, 8, 205, 1 :

**rîbu*, disappearance, 272, *r.* 5 :

rabâṣu, lie down, I, 1, *ps.* NÁ-iṣ, 127, *r.* 4 : irabbiṣ, 129, 6 : irabbiṣu, 134, *r.* 6 : irabiṣu 124, 9 :

tarbaṣu, halo of 22°, 49, 6 :

**raggu*, violence, 200, 5 :

rigmu, clamour, 59, 2 : 65, 3 : 68, 4 : 88, 6 :

**rîḫu*, breeze, 235, 4 :

rahâṣu, inundate, I, 1, *ps.* RA 69, 7 : RA-iṣ, 24, 1 : irahiṣ 215, *r.* 2 : *pc.* lû-rahuṣ, 268, *r.* 5 : *pm.* raḫṣâni, 252F, 3 : raḫṣatunû (*interrog.* -ú) 252F, 2 :

rihṣu, inundation, 90, 8 : 112, *r.* 11 :

**riḫtu*, rest, 139, 5 : 178, *r.* 1 :

**rakâbu*, ride, I, 1, *pm.*, rakib, 49, 1 : 269, 3 :

**narkabtu*, chariot, 49, 1 :

rîmu, mercy, 130, 3 :

**râmu*, favour, I, 1, irimu, 268, 10, 14 : tara'amuni, 247, 3 :

II, 1, turama, 257, 11 :

**ra'amu*, favour, 247, 1 :

**ramânu*, self, ramnišu, 33, *r.* 5 : ramanišu, 245, *r.* 1 :

rapâšu, be wide, I, 1. DAGAL-iš, 117, 1 : DAGAL, 232, 2 : DAGAL pl 184, 7 :

II, 1, DAGAL-aš, 117, *r.* 4 : DAGAL-áš, 135A, 6 : urappaš, 126, 5 :

**raṣâṣu* (?) I, 1, iriṣiṣi, 89, edge, 2 :

rukû, distant, *f.* 60, *r.* 2 : 66, *r.* 3 : 77, 5. *m. pl.* 85A, 7 :

**rîku*, empty, *pl.* 207, *r.* 3 :

**rikku*, spice, *pl.* 89, edge 3 :

rašû, have, I, 1, DUK-ši, 24, 6 : irašši, 88, 12 : DUK-ši-ú-ma, 195, 2 : iraššû, 162, *r.* 6 :

rišu, head, 16, 5, *r.* 1 : 55, 2 : 210, *r.* 3 :

rištu, joy, *pl.* 19, *r.* 4 : 19A, *r.* 5 :

ša, relative pronoun.

ša, poss. fem. pronoun.

i

šu, poss. masc. pron., with interrog-ú, 21, *r.* 2 : *pl.* šunu.
šu "times," 52, *r.* 1 :
šû, he, *pl.* šunu.
šî, she.
šuâtu, this.
*ší'u, corn, 88, 4 : 185, 10 : 209, *r.* 6 :
**ší'u*, pursue, I, 2, šutûni, 257, 12 :
**ša'âlu*, ask, I, 2, *pc.* lišal, 89, edge 4 : 90, *r.* 12 :
**tašlitu*, prayer, 187, *r.* 3 :
**šiâru*, morning, 68, *r.* 4 :
**šibṭu*, 247A, 8 :
šabâṭu, month Sebat.
**šaggaštu*, destruction, *pl.* 190, 4 :
**šadû*, I, 1, išiddi, 194A, 4 :
II, 1, ušaddama, 208A, 5 :
**šidu*, 159, *r.* 4 :
**šadâdu*, draw near, I, 2, niltadad, 170, *r.* 5 :
**šadâḫu* = *alâku* I, 1, šadaḫišu, 83, 1 :
šadurru, morning, watch, 242, *r.* 2 :
**šaḫitu*, sow, 277, 7 :
šaḫâṭu, draw, off, I, 2, iltaḫaṭ, 268, 9 :
**šaḫâru*, go round, I, 1, šaḫrumma, 247, *r.* 3 :
šuṭ, in *ḫarran šuṭ Ani*, *etc.* 183, 1 :
**šâṭu*, despise, I, 1, išaṭu, 82, *r.* 7 :
**šaṭâru*, write, I, 1, *ps.* alṭaru, 268, 2 : *pt.* išṭuruni, 152, *r.* 2 : *pm.* šaṭir, 251, 5 : 277H, 6 : *inf.* šaṭari, 217, *r.* 3 :
**šakâku*, III, 2, luštikkak, 247A, *r.* 3 :
šakânu, place, I, 1, *ps.* GAR-an, 30, 9 : išakan 129, 9 : išakkan, 273, 1 : išakkamma, 181, *r.* 5 : *pm.* GAR-nu, 26, *r.* 2 : šaknu, 34, *r.* 6 : GAR pl 82, 9 : GAR-in, 145, *r.* 1 : *pt.* iškun, 246E, 4 : iškunu, 272, *r.* 14, *pc.* liškun, 272, *r.* 7 : lû-šakin, 268, *r.* 10 :
I, 2, *ps.* altaknu, 272C, *r.* 5 : ištaknu, 272B, *r.* 5 : iltaknanni, 268, *r.* 12 : niltakan, 240, 7 :
II, 1, ušakan, 188, *r.* 5 :
IV, 1, *ps.* iššakkan, 52, *r.* 2 : iššakin, 274, 3 :
IV, 3, ittanaškan (gl.), 248, 2 :
šalṭaniš, triumphantly, 82, *r.* 4 : 89, 9 : 166, 5 : 167, 4 : 168B, 10 :
šalâmu, prosper. I, 1, *pt.* išallim, 151, *r.* 6 : *ps.* DI pl 35, *r.* 5 : 39, 4 : *pm.* šalim, 49, *r.* 2 : šalmu, 123, 6 : *inf.* šalamu, 25, *r.* 2 : 87A, *r.* 2 :
II, 1, ušallam, 5, 3 : 8, 6 : 11, 3 : ušalama, 42, 4 : ušallimu, 205, 3 : *ptc.* mušallim, 159, *r.* 4 :
**šalmu*, health, 90, *r.* 12 : 148, *r.* 2 (?) :
šulmu, peace, 39, *r.* 1, 128, 3 : 240, *r.* 6 :
**šulummu*, peace, 170, *r.* 6 :
šalšu, three, 21, 5 : 145, *r.* 7 :
šamû, heaven.
**šamû*, hear, I, 1, *ps.* išimmi, 272B, *r.* 8 : išimmu, 48, *r.* 3 : 162, *r.* 5 : išimmû, 186, *r.* 9, *pm.* šímaku, 90, *r.* 7 : šímâku, 218, *r.* 6 : šímû, 187, *r.* 3 : *pc.* lišmí, 90, *r.* 12 : 274, 11 :
I, 2, iltímí, 90, *r.* 8 :
II, 2, usammu'inni, 240, *r.* 4 :
III, 1, ušíšmu, 268, 1 :
IV, 1, iššimmi, 22B, 7 : 210, *r.* 1 :

tašmû, obedience, 25, 5 : 27, *r.* 3 : 48, 8 :
**šumu*, name, 235, *r.* 2 : 268, *r.* 5 : 272, *r.* 17 : 277, 6 :
šumma, if, 57, 4 : 84, *r.* 3, 4 : 217, 4, 5 :
šumîlu, left, 29, 6 : 30, 6 : 41, 6 : 145, *r.* 4, 5, 6, 7 :
**šamnu*, oil, *pl.* 89, edge, 3.
**šamaru*, rage, I, 1, *pm.* šamru, 146, *r.* 5 :
šamaššammu, sesame, 28, 5 : 100, *r.* 2 : 185, 10 :
**šanû*, II, 1, change, *ps.* ušanni, 272, *r.* 18 : *pc.* lušínni, 268, *r.* 2 :
šanû, two, 21, 5 : 70, 7 : *pl.* 272, *r.* 16 : *f.* 188, *r.* 4 : 256A, 7 : *adv.* 88, 6 : 272, *r.* 6 :
šattu, year, 16, 5, *r.* 1 : 19, *r.* 3 : 150, *r.* 3 : *pl.* 19A, *r.* 7 : 22, *r.* 9 : 31, 6 :
šanânu, I, 2. ištannan (?) 272, 13 :
šasu, speak, I, 1, issi, 235, *r.* 7 : issu, 267, 1, 6, 8 :
šîpu, foot, 82, *r.* 3 : *du*, 56A, 3 :
**šapâlu*, be low, I, 1, šapil, 77, 4 :
III, 1, ušappil, 66, *r.* 2 :
III, 2, uštappil, 60, *r.* 1 : 66, 6 :
**šupalu*, lower part, 90, *r.* 14 :
**šupiltu*, submission, 66, *r.* 3 :
šupultu, submission, 60, *r.* 2 : 77, 5 :
šaplitu, lower part, 235, 3 : 271, 2 : *pl.* 268, 12 : šaplitanu, 176, 3 : 177, 2 :
**šapâku*, pour, I, 1, DUB-ik, 139, *r.* 2 :
**šapiktu*, pouring (*f. part.*), 139, *r.* 4 :
šapâru, send, I, 1, *ps.* ašappara, 265C, *r.* 7 : [iš]-parûni, 19, *r.* 3 : [i]-šapparuni, 57, 7 : išapparu, 272, *r.* 12 : ḲI, 82, *r.* 2 : 258, 5 : *pt.* išpu[ra], 34, 10 : išpur-anni, 55, 5 : tašpur, 272C, 7 : ašpura, 108, 8 : ašpur, 57, 1 : ḲI, 258, 4 : *pc.* lišpur, 272B, *r.* 5 : lišpuraššumma, 124, *r.* 8 :
I, 2, iltapra, 19, 7 : altapra, 52, *r.* 4 : 151A, 8 : isapra, 16, *r.* 5 : assapra, 89, *r.* 9 : 188, *r.* 1 :
**šipru*, mission, 201, *r.* 1 :
**šaḳu*, be high, I, 1, *ps.* iša-ḳamma, 91, *r.* 5 : išaḳḳama, 94, 8 : *pm.* šaḳu, 59, 3 : šaḳî, 20: *r.* 1 : 220, 2 : 221, *r.* 2, 222, 2 :
I, 3, ištanaḳḳâ, 226, 4 :
**mašḳu*, top, 234, 9 :
**suḳu*, street, 245, *r.* 3 :
šaḳâlu, balance, I, 2, šitkulu, 127, *r.* 1 : 128, 1 : 136, 5 (?) : šitḳulu, 127, 7 : 131, 1 : 135A, 7 : 139, 1 : šitḳullu, 136F, 4 : 136G, *r.* 4 : 136M, *r.* 1 : 137, 5 : šitḳulum, 136B, *r.* 5 : šitḳulim, 136I, *r.* 4 :
**šitḳultu*, balancing, 242, *r.* 6 :
šâru, wind, 235, 11 : *pl.* 112, 8 :
**širu*, morning, 170, *r.* 1 : 178, 3 : 181, 6 :
**širtu*, morning, 23, 7 (?) : 185 : 1 : 186, 1 : 196, 11 : 271, edge 1 : *pl.* 243, *r.* 3 :
šîru, flesh, 15, *r.* 5 : 19, *r.* 4 : 19A, *r.* 4 :
šarû, begin, I, 1, išarri, 200, 5 :
II, 1, uširri, 264, *r.* 3 : uširrû, 268, 4, 7 : ušarûni, 217, *r.* 7 · šurru (= *growth*), 88, *r.* 7 · šurrí, 270, 16 :

**mîšrû*, growth, 200, 6:

šurubbû, cold, 59, 1: 60, 5: 61, 2: 62, 6, 7: 68, 3: 84, *r.* 6:

**šurdutu*, 236A, 3:

**šurinnu*, willow (?), 182, *r.* 2:

šarru, king.

**šarrutu*, kingdom, 22, 8: 187, *r.* 8:

**šaruru*, brilliance, 33, *r.* 1: 38, 6: 167, *r.* 8, 10: 181, 4: 185, *r.* 1: 216A, 4: 271, 15:

**šušanu*, 158, *r.* 2:

šašurru, crops, 184, 2: 226, 7:

šûtu, south.

ŠÍ . TAR . NU, corn (?), 274, *r.* 11:

tibû, come, I, 1, ZI, 28, 4: 105, 5: 137, *r.* 1: tibû, 211F, 4: tíbí, 82, 2: *cf.* 88, 2: tib, 235, 11.

tibutu, invasion, 91, 2: 99, *r.* 6:

**tabâlu*, diaappear, I, 1, *ps.* itabbal, 85, 4: itabbulu, 267, *r.* 8: *pt.* itbal, 85, 1, *r.* 2: 203, 2: 204, 2: itbaluni, 267, *r.* 13:

tibnu, straw, 209, *r.* 6: 210, 3:

tazzimtu, √nazâmu, 236B, *r.* 2:

tamû, speak, I, 1, itamí, 100, 3: 127, 2: itami, 56, 4: 90, 4: itama, 135, *r.* 2: itamamma, 83, 2: itammí, 138A, 6: itamû, 90, 3: 99, 7:

tanattu (√na'âdu), 271, 3:

taḳtu (√ḳatû), end.

**tarû*, turn, II, 1, utarra, 53, 3, 4: 62, *r.* 5: nutarra, 274B, 5, *r.* 5: uttirirra, 70, 7: utirra (?), 62, *r.* 5:

tarâku, rend asunder, I, 1, *inf.* taraku, 27, *r.* 5: 87A, *r.* 1: taraki, 25, *r.* 1:

II, 1, turruka, 25, 3: 27, *r.* 1: 87A, 6:

INDEX.

Ab=Akkad, 17, *r*. 4.

Ab-sin (Virgo), 221, 2: in moon's halo, 153, *r*. 1.

Achilles Tatius, XIII.

Aelian, XIII.

Aharrû, XV, XXIX, omens for, sent, 272, *r*. 9.

Ahisâ of Erech, writer of, 13, 125, 203, 236A, 252. Mentioned 124, *r*. 8.

A-idin (Spica), 95, 5: in halo, 153, *r*. 1, 7: reaches Mulmul, 112, *r*. 9: 205A, 3:

Akkad, XV, XXIX, omens for, sent, 272, *r*. 7, 9, 13: tablets, 152, *r*. 4.

Akkullanu. writer of, 34, 36, 87A, 89, 138A, 144?, 144B, 166, 235, 272A.

Akulutum, 275, 3, 5: in Siwan, 275, 1.

Allul (Cancer, XXXV), 21A, 4: 236A, 1: 244C, 5: 246C, *r*. 2: dark, 163, 6: in Moon's halo, 90, 6, 9: 93, 5: 105, *r*. 5: 110, 1: 111, 1, 3: 112, 1: 112A, 1: 112B, 1: 113, 4: 114, 4: 114A, 1: in halo of, 46°, 117, 3:

Anna, brilliant, 165, 5:

Anu-agû (*Anna-mir*), in Moon's halo, 49, *r*. 1: 104, *r*. 10: 106, 2:

Anunit, 211B, 5:

Apin=Mars.

Aplâ, of Borsippa, writer of, 46, 79A, 86A, 120, 132, 190A, 197, 211, 253A, 265.

Arad-Gula, 90, *r*. 6:

Arad-Ia, writer of, 72, 100, 256C:

Aramu (?), 268, *r*. 1:

Aratus, XXVI.

Asaridu, greater, writer of, 27, 29, 32, 87, 170, 172, 201, 202, 216, 250: son of Damka, 187, 221.

Asaridu, writer of, 22B, 48, 64A, ? 81F, 116A, 133, 210, 216B, 219, 252B. The less, writer of, 136D, 220, 231, 242, 249, 252A, 253, 274C.

Assur city, 86, 5: astronomical station, 274, 3, 4, 7:

Assur-sar-a-ni, writer of, 16, 175.

Assyria, 124, *r*. 4:

Babylon, 271, 7: 272, *r*. 14: astronomical station, 274, 8:

Balasî, writer of, 8, 55, 68, 88, 91, 119, 136Q, 138, 140, 171, 218A, 234A, 254, 256B, 274K, 274Q.

Bamaî, writer of, 81B, 99?, 102, 127, 156, 161, 185.

bed of warriors wide, 244D, *r*. 4, explained by 'plague.'

Berossus, XIV.

Bil-ahi-iriba, writer of, 218.

Bil-ipus, mentioned, 18, *r.* 3:

Bil-li', son of Igibi the magician, writer of, 24, 83, 115F, 183, 243.

Bil-nasir, writer of, 18, 52, 155B, 157C, 214, 236, 253B, 274R.

Bil-riminû-ukarrad-Marduk, 170, 5.

Bil-suma-iskun, writer of, 24A, 134.

Bil-usur (?), writer of, 274.

Bil-usallim, writer of, 277X.

Bil-usizib, 90, 1 (?); 272, *r.* 12: 277AE, 1:

binnu, in the land, 200, 4:

Borsippa, astronomical station, 274, 9. See Nabû-ikisa and Sapiku.

Bullutu, writer of, 1, 3, 4, 76, 77, 114, 131, 196, 229B, 232, 256A.

clouds, 155, *r.* 2: dark cloud omen, 248, 1:

comet, reaches path of Sun, 88, 5:

Dah, 221, *r.* 3 = Mercury 221, *r.* 5:

Damkû, 272C, *r.* 3:

dated tablets, 136B, *r.* 9: 264, edge 1: 271A, *r.* 4.

day, proper length, XXXIII, 1, 4: 2, 3: 3, 3: 4, 2: 5, 1: 6, 3: 6A, 4: 7, 3: 8, 3: 10, 3: 11, 1: 11A, 7: 12, 3: 15, 3: 16, 3; 17, 4: 18, 3: 19, 3: 19A, 3: 20, 3: 21, 3: 21A, 1: 22, 2: 22B, 3: 28, 2: 30, *r.* 3: 31, *r.* 1: 31, *r.* 3 (pl.): 35, *r.* 6: 36, 1: 41, *r.* 3: 44, 3: 45, 6: 135, *r.* 3: 183, *r.* 3: 256A, 2: 274K, 3: completed, XXI, 5, 3: 8, 5: 17, 6: 30, *r.* 5: 35, *r.* 8: 36, 3: 41, *r.* 2: 42, 4: 45, *r.* 1: 51, 1: 52, 1: 52A, *r.* 2: 53, 1: 54, 1: 55, 1: 62, *r.* 3, 7: 88, *r.* 12: 140, *r.* 1: 144B, *r.* 1: 160, 4: 171, 6: 274D, 1: which are not completed, 205, 3: *utarra*, 53, 3, 4, 5 (?): *utirra*, 62, *r.* 5: *utirirra*, 70, 7: *day of Bel*, 152, *r.* 2: 160, *r.* 5: 195A, 7: 266B, 6: *scribe of*, 160, *r.* 5. *cloudless day* = Ab 258, 6: 14*th day* = Elam, 268, 7: 271, 9: 274F, 6: 15*th day* = Aharrû, 156, *r.* 2: 160B, *r.* 2: 16*th day* = Subarti, 89, 2:

Dilbat city, astronomical station, see Nabû-ahî-iddina.

Dilgan = *Ab-sin* = Virgo, XLI; 88, *r.* 8: in Moon's halo, 88, *r.* 6: on left horn of Moon, 234, 7: at its height, 234, 9.

Dilgan-after-which-is-Mulmul in halo, 101, 7: = *ku-mal*, XL, 101, *r.* 3:

Earthquake, 272D, 5, *r.* 2, 3: enquired about by king, 264, 1: all day, 262D, 1: 263, 1: in night, 264, 5: 265, 3: 267, *r.* 1: prevails, 262D, 3: 264, 3: 263, 4: *in Nisan*, 264, *r.* 1, 5: 265, 1: *in Sebat*, 267, 12, 14: *in Adar*, 264, *r.* 3, 5:

east = Subarti (and Guti?) 277A, *r.* 12:

eclipse, 52, 4: explained by 'disturbance,' 112, 5: predicted, 30, 9: 181, 4: of king of Akkad, 270, 4, 14: of king of Aharrû, 234, *r.* 2, 4, 6: of Elam, 30, *r.* 6: 85, 6: of Kašši, 249A, 2:

88, 8: bright (ba'il), 172, *r.* 5: brilliant, 146, 3: 236F, 8?: goes forward, 68, *r.* 1: 70, *r.* 2: dim, 232, *r.* 3: culminates, 232, 6: in East, 232, 4: in Tammuz, 231, 1: 232, 2: Elul, 233, 1:
— *Sanamma* with *Sagmigar*, 195, *r.* 5: *Allul*, 235, 7: 236A, 6: *Inmîsarra*, 184, 6: *Gemini*, 84, *r.* 7: 231, 5:

Lula, 103, *r.* 9:

Urbarra = Mars, 236H, 5: [237, 4:] in Urmaḫ, 237, 1: Lubad-dir, 146, *r.* 4, 5: 216C, 5: 233, 4: = Mars, 146, *r.* 6: 195, *r.* 2: with *Rabû*, 195, *r.* 1:

Sudun, 238, 1: with Sun, 237A, 6: = Mars, in halo, 107, *r.* 1:

Apin (= Mars) with Sun, 103, *r.* 4: Scorpio, 239, 1: 272, *r.* 1:

Mulmul = *Mustabarrû-mûtânu*, 223A, 9: see under Mulmul.

Mastabba-galgal (= Gemini), 231, 5: in halo, 114, 1:

Mazzaloth, XXVII, 185, 12:

Mercury Lubad-gudud or *gudud*, 22A, *r.* 3: 36A, *r.* 1: 55, 4: 105, 8: 212, 6: 215, 1: 216C, 1: 238, 4: 246C, 4: 277T, *r.* 5: with Moon, 39. *r.* 3: 151, *r.* 3: *Mulmul* at sunset, thence rises to *Sugi*, 226, 1: Venus (?) 209, 7: *Kumal* 44, *r.* 6. *Suh-tig*, 238, *r.* 3: *Pabilsag*, 227, 6: *Urgula* (Leo), 228, 1: *Gudanna* (Taurus), 184, *r.* 2: goes down from Taurus to Sugi, 184, *r.* 2: in . . . 210A, 1: in Virgo, 221, 1: in month 216C, 3: Nisan, 184, 3: Siwan, 246F, *r.* 3: its position, 229, 4: at sunrise, 217, 1: 225, 6: sunset, 146, *r.* 1: mul *Dah* = Mercury, 221, *r.* 5:

Meteor (*Antasurra*), 246A, *r.* 1: 227, 1, 4:

Monstrosity, 277, 1 ff.:

Moon, Appearance on 1st day, 1, 1: 2, 1: 3, 1: 4, 1: 5, 4: 6, 1: 6A, 1: 7, 1: 8, 1: 9, 1 10, 1: 11, 4: 11A, 1: 12, 1: 13, 1: 14, 1: 15, 1: 16, 1: 17, 3, *r.* 1: 18, 1: 19, 1: 19A, 1: 20, 1: 21, 1: 22, 1: 22A, 1: 22B, 1: 26, 1: 27, 1: 28, 1: 29, 1: 30, 1: 31, 1: 33, 1: 35, 1: 36A, *r.* 3: 37, *r.* 1: 38, 1: 39, 1: 40, 1: 41, *r.* 5: 42, 5, 7: 43, *r.* 6: 44, 1: 45, 1: 46A, 1: 46B, 2: 47, 1: 56, 1: 56A, 1: 183. *r.* 2, 4: 256A, 1: 274K, 1:

Of *Nisan*, 44, 3: *Tammuz*, 23, 1: *Kislew*, 48, 1: intercalary month, 225, *r.* 2, 4:

On the 12*th*, 119, *r.* 1: 13*th*, 84, 3: 14*th*, 144B, *r.* 7: 151, 11: 155, 8: 16*th*, 88, 11: 89, 1: 166, *r.* 2: 169, *r.* 3; 27*th*, 249, 3: 28*th*, 57, 1: 58, 1, 3: 29*th*, 24, 3: 30*th* (of?), 25, 1: 46B, *r.* 1, 3: 59, 1: 61, 1: 62, 5: 65, 1: 66, 3: 68, 3: 70, 3: 71, 3: 72, 3: 74, 1: 81B, 2:

On the 30*th of Nisan*, 62, 1: 115D, *r.* 5: *Iyyar*, 63, 1: 64, 1: 64A, 1: 64B, 1: 162, 4, 5: *Siwan*, 65, 4: 66, 1: 67, 1: 68, 1: 69, 1: 69A, 1: 87A, 3: *Tammuz*, 32, *r.* 1: *Ab*, 70A, 1: 71, 1: 72, 1: 73, 1: 86, 6, 7: *Elul*,

209, r. 1: bright, 205, 2: high (?), 174A, r. 1: with Jupiter (Umunpauddu), 194A, 3: with Mars, 109, 3: in Gu-anna, 243, 5: in Mulmul, 205A, 4: 243, 2: in Pabilsag, 209, 3: 272, 10: in Dilgan, 211, 6: in Anunit, 211, 5: in Urgula at sunrise, 208, r. 2: in . . . . 211C, 3: 211E, 1: faces Scorpio, 112, 7: Irat-Akrabi ('breast of Scorpio'), 112, r. 3: before ———, 256, 4: faces Allul, 208, r. 6: reaches Allul, 207, 6: before Sibzianna, 86, r. 3, 9: eclipse away from Venus, 273, 7:

Uza, 212A, 5: hright, 212, 1: faces Allul, 207, r. 1:

Watch, none kept on 13th, 14th, 15th day, 274S, 1, 3, 5: none kept for Moon, 155B, 6: long watch on 16th, 274S, 7: watch for Moon on 29th, 252D, 5: morning watch = Elam, 242, r. 2: 271, 9.

Wind, South at Moon's appearance, 137, r. 1: 141, r. 5: at Moon's disappearance, 179, 4: storm of south wind, 256B, r. 1: North wind at Moon's appearance, 68, 5: halo and north wind, 111, 5: storm of west wind, 258, r. 1:

Zaddin (?), son of Hurbi (?), 116A, r. 1:

Zakir, writer of, 25, 28, 108, 114A, 122, 181, 183B, 229A (with Tabia?), 234, 236E, 251A, 253C, 272C.

Zibanit, Libra, 244C, 3: 247A, 1, 3: before Moon, 244B, 2: dark, 272, 15:

Zikit-Akrabi (Sting of Scopio) = Great lord Pabilsag, 272, 9: means Pabilsag, 236G, 5: on right horn of Moon, 215, 4:

Note:—The following tablets have traces of the sender's name left: 6, 19A, 23, 23A, 36A, 42, 44, 45, 46B, 47A, 50, 53, 56, 56A, 57, 64B, 69A, 70A, 81A, 81E, 81G, 81H, 81I, 85A, 90, 96A, 103, 104, 105, 112, 115, 115A, 115B, 116, 116B, 118A, 123A, 130A, 136, 136A, 136C, 136G, 136K, 136N, 136R, 136S, 136U, 142, 142C, 151A, 155A, 157A, 158, 160A, 160B, 167, 180, 183A, 184, 188, 191, 205A, 207A, 211A, 211B, 211C, 211D, 211E, 212A, 214A, 216A, 223, 229, 236C, 236F, 236G, 236H, 237A, 239, 243D, 244A, 246A, 246B, 246C, 261, 262, 262A, 262B, 262C, 265B, 266A, 271, 272, 274, 274A, 274E, 274I, 274L, 274M, 274O, 274P, 275, 277Y, 277AB, 277AC.

Never signed:—9, 40, 124, 129, 135A, 136B, 136I, 152, 165, 176, 192, 251, 276.

LISTS.

K. 19, 215 : 86, 91 : 92, 127 : 119, 182 : 120A, 94 : 121, 207 : 124, 267 : 172, 46 : 178, 117 : 188, 183 : 692, 75 : 693, 58 : 694, 166 : 695, 169 : 696, 7 : 697, 128 : 698, 126 : 699, 233 : 700, 134 : 701, 14 : 702, 272C : 703, 119 : 704, 228 : 705, 43 : 706, 140 : 710, 200 : 711, 99 : 712, 88 : 713, 80 : 714, 132 : 715, 259 : 718, 161 : 719, 174 : 721, 130 : 722, 78 : 723, 197 : 725, 205 : 727, 165 : 728, 244 : 729, 37 : 730, 135 : 731, 206 : 732, 246F : 733, 168 : 734, 83 : 735, 231 : 736, 139 : 737, 133 : 739, 97 : 740, 106 : 741, 30 : 742, 196 : 744, 10 : 745, 177 : 747, 235 : 748, 248 : 749, 277 : 750, 271 : 752, 85 : 753, 22B : 754, 15 : 755, 158A, : 756, 11 : 758, 211 : 759, 184 : 760, 251 : 761, 243 : 763, 123, 765, 255 : 766, 276 : 767, 136E : 768, 249 : 769, 82 : 770, 25 : 772, 274 : 773, 1360 : 774, 68 : 775, 16 : 776, 63 : 779, 266 : 780, 178 : 781, 180 : 782, 204 : 783, 216C : 784, 8 : 785, 95 : 786, 254 : 787, 256A : 788, 31 : 789, 136M : 790, 265A : 791, 41 : 793, 153 : 794, 121 : 795, 138 : 799, 137 : 801, 118 : 803, 17 : 804, 40 : 805, 164 : 806, 187 : 807, 148 : 808, 236 : 809, 66 : 810, 274B : 811, 246 : 813, 266A : 815, 269 : 839, 271A : 840, 13 : 842, 146A : 843, 165A : 850, 147 : 851, 244A : 853, 256C : 854, 262 : 855, 234A : 856, 22A : 861, 216 : 864, 98 : 865, 274E : 866, 157 : 867, 191 : 868, 238 : 869, 136N : 870, 188 : 871, 185 : 873, 252A : 874, 27 : 875, 236B : 876, 136L : 877, 84 : 878, 130A : 900, 5 : 901, 81K : 902, 241 : 904, 46A : 907, 195A : 921, 274A : 933, 201A : 955, 270 : 960, *see note to* 1 : 963, 245 : 964, 207A : 966, 277L : 967, 277I : 972, 225 : 973, 151A : 984, 274H : 987, 190A : 994, 160A : 1007, 87A : 1236, 277M : 1300, 277H : 1301, 277F : 1302, 277K : 1304, 89 : 1305, 115C : 1306, 144A : 1307, 81H : 1308, 11A : 1309, 181A : 1310, 250A : 1311, 115B : 1312, 136D : 1314, 244B : 1316, 181B : 1317, 191A : 1318, 206A : 1320, 70A : 1321, 252E : 1322, 136T : 1323, 256B : 1324, 136C : 1326, 252D : 1327, 256B : 1328, 277E : 1329, 144E : 1330, 174A : 1331, 115E : 1332, 194 : 1333, 274O : 1334, 114 : 1335, 55 : 1336, 277D : 1338, 116A : 1339, 136K : 1340, 64A : 1341, 56 : 1342, 207B : 1443, 205A : 1344, 47A : 1346, 96B : 1347, 216A : 1369, 157B : 1373, 143 : 1375,

229B: 1380, 263: 1383, 72: 1384, 274F: 1385, 253A: 1388, 6: 1389, 252: 1392, 243A: 1393, 52: 1394, 187A: 1395, 59: 1398, 38: 1399, 24: 1405, 100: 1406, 272A: 1407, 79A: 1412, 141: 1460, 252F: 1508, 141: 1535, 277G: 1557, 277C: 1592, 116: 1593, 262C: 1594, 277B: 1606, 85A: 1921, 113: 1927, 64B: 1955, 211C: 2085, 268: 2327, 236D: 3488, 113: 3504, 198: 4708, 199: 5723, 56A: 6077, 114A: 6078, 155A: 6149, 277X: 6182, 246E: 6184B, 277A: 8391, 272C: 8393, 144D: 8407, 211B: 8432, 57: 8704, 236F: 8711, 247A: 8713, 272: 8861, 252C: 8960, 274D: 10298, 199: 11046, 136Q: 12004 + 12006, 274K: 12013, 274N: 12017, 157C: 12176, 211A: 12250, 211F: 12281, 265B: 12283, 23A: 12367, 24A: 12369, 274L: 12388, 32: 12469, 36A: 12555, 262B: 13012, 277N: 13087, 203: 13101, 32: 13170, 212A: 13175, 24A: 13191, 277AE: 14150, 167A:

S. 86, 29: 231, 273: 366, 167: 375, 103: 508, 277AC: 694, 115: 885, 136U: 1027, 171: 1043, 258: 1062, 39: 1073, 42: 1179, 136F: 1232, 253: 1327, 214A: 1664, 6A: 1974, 62:

D.T. 53, 253C: 148, 129: 249, 81E: 304, 215A:

Rm. 191, 146: 193, *see* 270A: 194, 86: 195, 157D: 196, 162: 197, 274Q: 198, 19: 200, 159: 201, 181: 203, 74: 204, 131: 207, 175: 208, 144B: 209, 183A: 211, 275: 212, 136P:

Rm. 2, 254, 237A: 345, 136S:

79-7-8, 100, 172. **80-7-19,** 19, 267A: 54, 61: 55, 223A: 56, 81: 57, 93: 58, 210: 59, 28: 61, 160: 62, 81F: 63, 44: 65, 23: 66, 81C: 154, 19A: 155, 229A: 176, 69A: 197, 81D: 335, 55: 343, 261: 355, 277AB: 364, 274M: 371, 167. **81-2-4,** 79, 70: 80, 176: 81, 214: 82, 120: 83, 101: 84, 218: 85, 12: 86, 209: 88, 223: 89, 226: 102, 151: 103, 35: 104, 240: 105, 201: 106, 173: 107, 189: 108, 136: 109, 244C: 132, 221: 133, 1: 134, 2: 135, 242: 136, 199A: 138, 52A: 140, 277O: 141, 112B: 142, 243C: 143, 251A: 144, 109: 145, 104: 273, 136H: 287, 229: 321, 46B: 344, 262D: 380, 244D: 483, 136A: 504, 118A. **81-7-27,** 19, 257: 23, 208: 58, 210: 215, 277P. **82-3-23,** 112, 277Q. **82-5-22,** 46, 234: 48, 195: 49, 69: 50, 65: 51, 213: 52, 96: 53, 60: 54, 239: 55, 247: 56, 219: 57, 186: 58, 125: 59, 230: 60, 9: 61, 265: 63, 170: 64, 142: 65, 105: 66, 53: 67, 236E: 68, 265C: 69, 274P: 72, 80A: 74, 218A: 78, 217: 79, 236H: 83, 4: 84, 96A: 85, 203: 87, 277R: 89, 124: 1778, 253B. **83-1-18,** 47, 90: 48, 155: 171, 154: 172, 243B: 173, 79: 174, 202: 175, 48: 176, 252B: 177, 87: 178, 220: 179, 193: 180, 260: 181, 222, 182, 71: 183, 76: 184, 77: 185, 3: 186, 150: 187, 49: 188,

249A : 189, 54 : 190, 51 : 191, 138A : 194, 67 : 195, 18 : 196, 183B : 197, 112 : 198, 232 : 200, 190 : 202, 22 : 203, 45 : 204, 212 : 205, 34 : 207, 274I : 208, 224 : 209, 256 : 210, 274C : 212, 50 : 214, 115A : 216, 47 : 218, 194A : 219, 20 : 220, 160B : 221, 92 : 222, 111 : 223, 152 : 224, 21 : 225, 158 : 227, 179 : 228, 144 : 229, 136G : 230, 227 : 232, 235A : 233, 236A : 236, 236G : 240, 136I : 241, 112A, 242, 26 : 243, 33 : 244, 163 : 245, 145 : 246, 102 : 248, 122 : 286, 136B : 287, 264 : 290, 101A : 292, 157A : 296, 155B : 297, 246G : 298, 246D : 299, 64 : 300, 208A : 301, 277S : 302, 149 : 303, 277AA : 305, 22 : 309, 277T : 310, 266B : 311, 96C : 312, 86A : 313. 216B : 314, 81G : 316, 144A : 317, 246A : 318, 277U : 319, 211D : 320, 274G : 322, 246C : 694, 272A : 718, 262A : 774, 277V : 775, 115F : 780, 143 : 786, 196A : 834, 211E : 870, 144C : 881, 116B : 883, 277Y : 884, 277W : 885, 81I. **Bu. 89-4-26,** 3, 192 : 8, 108 : 11, 73 : 18, 250 : 37, 81B : 61, 123A : 159, 36 : 166, 107. **Bu. 91-5-9,** 7, 115D : 8, 156 : 9, 110 : 14, 21 : 19, 277AD : 28, 136R : 29, 277Z : 34, 246B : 38, 81A : 58, 236C : 102, 237 : 161, 135A.

A COMPLETE LIST OF

BOOKS & PERIODICALS,

PUBLISHED AND SOLD BY

LUZAC and Co.,

Publishers to the India Office, the Asiatic Society of Bengal, the University of Chicago, etc.

(With Index)

1740

LONDON:
LUZAC & Co.
46, GREAT RUSSELL STREET (Opposite the British Museum).
1898.

Asiatic Society of Bengal, Journal of. Messrs Luzac and Co are the sole agents for Great Britain and America of the Asiatic Society of Bengal and can supply the continuation of the Journal at 3*s.* each No., of the Proceedings at 1*s.* each No. As they keep a large stock of the Journal and Proceedings, they can also supply any single No. at the published price.

Assab'iniyya. — A philosophical Poem in Arabic by Mūsā B. Tūbi. Together with the Hebrew Version and Commentary styled Bāttē Hannefeš by Solomon Immānuēl Dapiera. Edited and translated by HARTWIG HIRSCHFELD. 8vo. pp. 61. 2*s.* 6*d.* net.

Assyrian and Babylonian Letters. 4 vols. See: Harper.

Aston (W. G.) — A Grammar of the Japanese Written Language. Second Edition, enlarged and improved. Roy. 8vo. Cloth. pp. 306. (Published 28*s.*) Reduced-Price, 18*s.*

Aston (W. G.) — A Short Grammar of the Japanese Spoken Language. Fourth Edition. Crown 8vo. Cloth. pp. 212. (Published 12*s.*) Reduced-Price, 7*s.* 6*d.*

Babylonian and Oriental Record. (The) — A Monthly Magazine of the Antiquities of the East. Edited by Prof. TERRIEN DE LACOUPERIE. Vol. I—VI. (Vol. VII in progress). Published monthly. Single Numbers, 1*s.* 6*d.* each.

Babylonian Magic and Sorcery. See: King.

Bāna's Kadambari. Translated, with Occasional Omissions, with a full Abstract of the Continuation of the Romance by the Author's Son Bhushanabhatta, by C. M. RIDDING. 8vo. Cloth. pp. XXIV, 232. 10*s.*

Bāna's Harsa Carita. An Historical Work, translated from the Sanskrit, by E. B. Cowell and F. W. Thomas. 8vo. Cloth. pp. XIV, 284. 10*s.*

Bezold (Ch.) — Oriental Diplomacy: being the transliterated Text of the Cuneiform Despatches between the King of Egypt and Western Asia in the XVth. century before Christ, discovered at Tell el Amarna, and now preserved in the British Museum. With full Vocabulary, grammatical Notes, &c., by CHARLES BEZOLD. Post 8vo. Cloth. pp. XLIV, 124. 18*s.* net.

"For the Assyriologist the book is a servicable and handy supplement to the British Museum volume on the Tell El-Amarna tablets. The author is specially skilled in the art of cataloguing and dictionary making and it is needless to say that he has done his work well". — *The Academy.*

"Die in dem Hauptwerke (The Tell el Amarna Tablets in the British Museum with autotype Facsimiles, etc.) vermisstte Transcription des Keilschrifttextes der Tafeln, sowie ein sehr ausführliches, mituntur die Vollständigkeit einer Concordanz erreichendes Vocabulary bietet die Oriental Diplomacy von C. Bezold, das eben deshalb gewissermassen als Schlüssel zu dem Publicationswerke betrachtet werden kann." — *Liter. Centralblatt.*

„Wichtig und sehr nützlich vor allem wegen der Einleitung und des Wörterverzeichnisses ... Transkription und kurze Inhaltsangabe der Briefe sehr zweckmässig .... eine anerkennenswerthe Leistung."
Deutsche Litteraturzeitung.

Biblia. — A Monthly Magazine, devoted to Biblical Archaeology and Oriental Research. Vol. I—X. (Vol. XI in progress). Published monthly. Annual Subscription, 5*s.*

Biblical World (The) — Continuing the Old and New Testament Student. Edited by WILLIAM R. HARPER. New Series. Vol. I—X. (Vol. XI and XII in progress). Published monthly. Annual Subscription, 10*s.* 6*d.*

"The Biblical World makes a faithful record and helpful critic of present Biblical Work, as well as an efficient practical and positive independent force in stimulating and instructing the student, preacher and teacher"

Bibliographical List of Books on Africa and the East. Published in England. 2 Vols. Vol. I. Containing the Books published between the Meetings of the Eighth Oriental Congress at Stockholm, in 1889, and the Ninth Congress in London in 1892. Vol. II. Containing the Books published between the Meetings of the Ninth Oriental Congress in London, in 1892, and the Tenth Oriental Congress at Geneva, in 1894. Systematically arranged, with Preface and Author's Index, by C. G. Luzac. 12mo. each Vol. 1*s*.

Bibliotheca Indica. — Messrs Luzac & Co. are agents for the sale of this important series and keep most of the numbers in stock.

Blackden (M. W.) and G. W. Frazer. — Collection of Hieratic Graffiti, from the Alabaster Quarry of Hat-Nub, situated near Tell El Amarna. Found December 28th. 1891, copied September, 1892. Obl. pp. 10. 10*s*.

Buddhaghosuppatti; or, Historical Romance of the Rise and Career of Buddaghosa. Edited and translated by JAMES GRAY, Professor of Pali. Rangoon College. Two Parts in one. Demy 8vo. Cloth. pp. VIII, 75 and 36. 6*s*.

Budge (E. A. Wallis) — The Laughable Stories collected by Bar-Hebraeus. The Syriac Text with an English Translation, by E. A. WALLIS BUDGE, Litt. D., F. S. A., Keeper of the Department of Egyptian and Assyrian Antiquities, British Museum. 8vo. Cloth. 21*s*. net. [Luzac's Semitic Texts and Translation Series, Vol. I].

"Dr. BUDGE's book will be welcome as a handy reading book for advanced students of Syriac, but in the mean time the stories will be an addition to the literature of gnomes and proverbs, of which so many are found in India, and in Persian, Hebrew and Arabic, although not yet published. We are happy to say that Dr. BUDGE's new book is well edited and translated as far as we can judge". — *Athenæum.*

"The worthy Syrian Bishops idea of humour may excite admiration when we hear that he collected his quips in the grey dawn of the middle ages". — *Pall Mall Gazette.*

"Man sieht, das Buch ist in mehr als einer Hinsicht interessant, und wir sind Budge für die Herausgabe aufrichtig dankbar. — *Lit. Centralb.*

"Sous le titre de *Récits amusants*, le célèbre polygraphe syrien Barhébraeus a réuni une collection de sept cent vingt-sept contes, divisés en vingt chapitres et renfermant des aphorismes, des anecdotes et des fables d'animaux ayant un caractère soit moral, soit simplement récréatif. Le livre nous était connu par quelques spécimens publiés précédement. M. BUDGE, qui a déja rendu tant de services aux lettres syriaques, vient d'éditer l'ouvrage entier avec une traduction anglaise..... En tous cas, M. B. a eu raison de ne pas faire un choix et de donner l'ouvrage en son entier.... Les aphorismes, écrits dans un style concis et avec, une pointe dont la finesse n'est pas toujours sensible, présentent des difficultés de traduction dont M. B. a généralement triomphé." — *Revue Critique.*

"È questo un libro singolare, appartemente ad un genere assai scarso nella letteratura siriaca, quantunque così ricca, cioè a quello dell'amena letteratura. Bar Ebreo scrisse questo libro nella vecchiaia, o forse allora mise insieme e ordinò estr atti che avea prese nelle lunghe letture da lui fatte, di tanto opere e cosi svariate.... I cultori degli studi siriaci saranno assai grati al Dr. Budge per questo suo novello contributo; l'edizione per carte e per tipi è veramente bellissima." — *La Cultura.*

Budge, see Luzac's Semitic Text and Translation Series. Vols. I, III, V and VII.

Cappeller (Carl) — A Sanskrit-English Dictionary. Based upon the St. Petersburg Lexicons. Royal 8vo. Cloth. pp. VIII, 672 [Published £ 1. 1*s*]. Reduced to 10*s*. 6*d*.

"Linguistic and other students should hail with satisfaction the publication of a cheap and handy Sanskrit-English Dictionary, such as is now to be found in the new English edition of Prof. CAPPELLER's Sanskrit-German 'Wörterbuch,' recently published by Messrs. Luzac. The book is well adapted to the use of beginners, as it specially deals with the text usually read in commencing Sanskrit; but it will be of use also to philological students — or such as have mastered the Nāgari character — as it includes most Vedic words, a great desideratum in many earlier dictionaries, especially such as were founded on native sources. The basis of the present work is, on the contrary, the great lexicon of Boethlingk and Roth with the addition of compound forms likely to be of service to beginners." — *Athenæum.*

"The English edition of Prof. CAPPELLER's Sanskrit Dictionary is some thing more than a mere translation of the German edition. It includes the vocabulary of several additional texts; many compounds have been inserted which are not given in the Petersburg lexicons; and some improvements have been made in the arrangement. The errors enumerated by the reviewer of the *Academy* have for the most part been corrected, though a few still remain. .... The book is certainly the cheapest, and, for a beginner, in some respects the best, of existing Sanskrit-English dictionaries." — *Academy.*

"Professor CAPPELLER furnishes the Student of Sanskrit, if not with a complete Lexicon, — for that he tells us, was not his object, — still with a handy and yet very full vocabulary of all the words occurring in the texts which are generally studied in that language. His plan is to avoid all unnecessary complications, to give each word in such a manner as to show its formation, if it is not itself a stem. It is not merely an English version of the author's Sanskrit-German Dictionary, nor merely an enlarged edition of the same; it is a new work, with a distinct plan and object of its own. We can recommend it to the Sanskrit student as a sufficient dictionary for all practical purposes, which will enable him to dispense with larger and more costly and complicated Lexicons till he has acquired a considerable proficiency in this difficult and scientific language." — *Asiatic Quarterly Review.*

Ceylon. A Tale of Old..... See: Sinnatamby.

Chakrabarti (J. Ch.) — The Native States of India. 8vo. Cloth. pp. XIV, 274. With Map. 5*s*. net.

Cool (W.) — With the Dutch in the East. An Outline of the Military Operations in Lombock, 1894, Giving also a Popular Account of the Native Characteristics, Architecture, Methods of Irrigations, Agricultural Pursuits, Folklore, Religious Customs and a History of the Introduction of Islamism and Hinduism into the Island. By Capt. W. COOL (Dutch Engineer), Knight of the Order of Orange Nassau; decorated for important War Services in the Dutch Indies; Professor at the High School of War, the Hague. Translated from the Dutch by E. J. Taylor. Illustrated by G. B. HOOYER. Late Lieut. Col. of the Dutch Indian Army; Knight of the Military Order of William; decorated for important War Services in the Dutch Indies. Roy. 8vo. Cloth. 21*s*.

"There are, it is to be feared, but few books published in this country from which English readers can obtain information as to the doings of the Dutch in their Eastern colonies. — For this reason we are glad that Capt. Cool's account of the Lombock expedition has been translated." — *Athenæum.*

"The book contains an interesting account of the Balinese and Sassak customs, and throws some light on the introduction of the Mahomedan and Hindu religions into Lombock ... The translation by Miss E. J. Taylor is satisfactory, and some of the illustrations are excellent." — *The Times.*

"Lombock forms a small link in the long chain of volcanic lands ... To folklorists and students of primitive religions it has always presented many attractive features ... They will be much interested in the local traditions recorded in the volume before us. Miss Taylor's version deserves a word of recognition, and the general equipment of the book is creditable to the Amsterdam press. There is a good index." — *Academy.*

"The author not only describes the military operations, but gives a full history of Lombock and its people. Much curious information as to a land very much out of the way and little known to English readers is given. In addition the account of the actual warfare is full of incident. The book is freely illustrated." — *Yorkshire Daily Post.*

"This is a work which will no doubt attract considerable attention, both in the West and throughout the East. Miss Taylor has acquitted herself as a translator with rare ability and taste, and the comprehensive and excellent way in which the work is illustrated adds an additional charm to what is at once the most entertaining and most attractive chapter of Netherlands Indian history." — *European Mail.*

"Besides containing a great deal of information concerning this hitherto very slightly known island and its inhabitants, Captain Cool's volume is profusely and excellently illustrated... Miss Taylor's translation of it is fluent and thoroughly readable." — *Glasgow Herald.*

Cowell, E. B., See: Bāna's Harsa Carita.

Cowper (B. H.) Principles of Syriac Grammar. Translated and abridged from the work of Dr. HOFFMANN. 8vo. Cloth. pp. 184. *7s. 6d.*

Cust (R. N.) — The Gospel Message or Essays, Addresses, Suggestions and Warnings of the different aspects of Christian Missions to Non Christian Races and peoples. 8vo. pp. 494. Paper *6s. 6d.* Cloth. *7s. 6d.*

"....There are few objects of controversy in missionary matters which are not very fully discussed by Dr. CUST, and if we not infrequently differ from him we gladly thank him for copious information and the benefits of his long experience". — *Guardian.*

"It is a big book. it ranges over a very wide field, and it is never dull or dry". — *Expository Times.*

"The scheme is so comprehensive as to include almost every detail of the missionary enterprise. Every essay is stamped, of course with the personality of its author, whose views are expressed with characteristic force and clearness". — *The Record.*

Cust (R. N.) — Essay on the Common Features which appear in all Forms of Religious belief. Post 8vo. Cloth. pp. XXIV, 194. *5s.*

"Dr. CUST has put his very considerable knowledge to excellent purposes in this modest little publication. He seems most at home with the faiths of the East, but even the most elementary of savage creeds have not escaped him". — *Pall Mall Gazette.*

Cust (R. N.) — Essay on Religious Conceptions. Post 8vo. Cloth. pp. V, 148. *5s.*

Cust (R. N.) — Linguistic and Oriental Essays. Fourth Series. From 1861 to 1895. 8vo. pp. XXV, 634. Paper Covers. 16*s.*, Cloth. 17*s.* 6*d.*

Dawlatshah's Lives of the Persian Poets. Edited by EDWARD G. BROWNE, Lecturer in Persian in the University of Cambridge. Vol. 1. Tadhkiratu'sh Sh'arā. 8vo. Cloth. 18*s.* net.

Edkins (Joseph) — China's Place in Philology. An Attempt to show that the Languages of Europe and Asia have a common Origin. Demy 8vo. Cloth. pp. XXIII, 403. (Published 10*s.* 6*d.*) 7*s.* 6*d.*

Edkins (Joseph) — Introduction to the Study of the Chinese Characters. Royal 8vo. Boards. pp. XIX, 211, 101. (Published 18*s.*) 12*s.* 6*d.*

Edkins (Joseph) — Nirvana of the Northern Buddhists. 8vo. pp. 21. Reprint. 6*d.*

Edkins (Joseph) — Chinese Architecture. Contents. — 1. Classical Style. — 2. Post-Confucian Style. — 3. Buddhist Style. — 4. Modern Style. 8vo. pp. 36. 1*s.*

Edkins (Joseph) — Chinese Currency. Roy. 8vo. pp. 29. 1*s.*

Edkins (Joseph) — Ancient Symbolism among the Chinese. Cr. 8vo. pp. 26. 6*d.*

Efes Damîm. — A Series of Conversations at Jerusalem between a Patriarch of the Greek Church and a Chief Rabbi of the Jews, concerning the Malicious Charge against the Jews of using Christian Blood. By J. B. LEVINSOHN. Translated from the Hebrew by Dr. L. LOEWE. Roy. 8vo. Cloth. pp. XVI, 208. (Published 8*s.*) Reduced Price 2*s.* 6*d.*

Eitel (E. J.) — Europe in China. The History of Hongkong. From the Beginning to the year 1882. 8vo. Cloth. pp. VII, 575. With Index. 15*s.* net.

"His work rises considerably above the level commonly attained by colonial histories written from a colonial point of view". — *Times.*

"His painstaking volume is really a detailed history of the colony and of the adminstration of successive governors from 1841 down to the present day". — *Daily Telegraph.*

"This is an interesting book. The subject is full of matter, and Dr. EITEL has, as a rule, treated it successfully. — *Athenæum.*

"....The student will find Dr. EITEL's book a very storehouse of information....has told it with a mastery of fact that vouches for his industry and perseverance". — *Saturday Review.*

Gladstone (Right Hon. W. E.) — Archaic Greece and the East. 8vo. pp. 32. 1*s.*

Gribble (J. D. B.) — A History of the Deccan. With numerous Illustrations, Plates, Portraits, Maps and Plans. Vol. I. Roy. 8vo. Cloth. 21*s.*

„In a style easy and pleasant the author tells the story of the Mohammedan occupation of the Deccan ....the general style of the book and the admirable photographs and drawings with which it is enriched leave nothing to be desired". — *Athenæum.*

"Mr. J. D. B. GRIBBLE has accomplished a difficult task. He has constructed from original materials a continuous narrative of one of the most confused periods of Indian history. He has also presented it with a lucidity of style which will go far to render it acceptable to the reading public....The book is illustrated by a number of interesting reproductions of scenery and architecture in Southern India. These and the maps, plans, and clear genealogical tables reflect credit both upon the author and the publisher". — *Times.*

"Mr. GRIBBLE has brought great industry and knowledge of the country to this compilation....The work is of some historical importance". — *Saturday Review.*

Gray (James). See Buddhaghosuppatti.

Gray (James). See Jinalankara.

Guide to the Dutch East Indies. By Dr. J. F. van BEMMELEN and G. B. HOOYER. Trans. from the Dutch by the Rev. B. J. BERRINGTON B.A., with 16 Plates, 13 Maps and Plans, and a copious index. Sm. 8vo. pp. 202. 1*s.* 6*d.*

"For any one going in that direction this remarkably complete little work is indispensable". — *Pall Mall Gazette.*

"The guide book omits nothing needed by the traveller. It describes the necessary outfit, customs afloat and ashore, mode of living, how to dress, how often to bathe, who to tip, and how much". — *The Shipping World.*

Guirandon (F. G. de) — Manuel de la langue foule, parlée dans la Sénégambie et le Soudan. Grammaire textes, vocabulaire. 8vo. Cloth. pp. 144. 6*s.*

Halcombe (Charles J. H.) — The Mystic Flowery Land. A Personal Narrative. By CHARLES J. H. HALCOMBE. Late of Imperial Customs. China, 8vo. Cloth. gilt. pp. 226. 16*s.*

"This valuable and handsome volume contains thirty long chapters, a frontispiece of the Author and his wife — the latter in her Oriental costume — numerous fine reproductions from photographs, and several beautiful coloured pictures representing many scenes and phases of Chinese life, etchings and comprehensive notes by the Author.

"His pages are full of incident and his narrative often vivid and vigorous". — *Times.*

"The illustrations are good and numerous. Many are facsimiles of coloured Chinese drawings showing various industrial occupations: others are photogravures representing buildings and scenery". — *Morning Post.*

"Handsomely attired in red, yellow and gold, with Chinese characters to give further appropriateness to the outer garb, is this volume of freely illustrated personal experience in China.... Mr. HALCOMBE gives a graphic description of places and peoples, with their manners and customs". — *Liverpool Courier.*

"The illustrations are all good, and the Chinese pictures reproduced in colours interesting. We have not seen any of them before". — *Westminster Review.*

Hansei Zasshi. Monthly. Vol. I—XII. (Vol. XIII in progress). Annual subscription. 6*s.*

Hardy (R. Spence) — The Legends and theories of the Buddhists. Compared with History and Science. 8vo. Cloth. pp. 244. 7*s.* 6*d.*

Harîri. — The Assemblies of al Harîri. Translated from the Arabic with an Introduction and notes, Historical and Grammatical, by TH. CHENERY and F. STEINGASS. With Preface and Index, by F. F. ARBUTHNOT, 2 Vols. 8vo. Cloth. pp. X, 540 and XI, 395. £ 1.10*s.*

Harper (Robert Francis) — Assyrian and Babylonian Letters, belonging to the K. Collection of the British Museum. By ROBERT FRANCIS HARPER, of the University of Chicago. Vols. I to IV. Post 8vo. Cloth. Price of each Vol. £ 1. 5*s.* net.

"The Assyriologist, will welcome them with gratitude, for they offer him a mass of new material which has been carefully copied and well printed, and which cannot fail to yield important results." — *Athenæum.*

"The book is well printed, and it is a pleasure to read the texts given in it, with their large type and ample margin." — *Academy.*

Hebraica. — A Quarterly Journal in the Interests of Semitic Study. Edited by WILLIAM R. HARPER and the Staff of the Semitic Department of the University of Chicago. Vol. I—XI. Published quarterly. Annual Subscription. 14*s.*

See American Journal of Semitic Languages, etc.

India. (The Native States of). See: Chakrabarti.

India. (The Armenians in). See: Seth.

Indian Antiquary (The) — A Journal of Oriental Research in Archaeology, Epigraphy, etc. etc. Edited by R. C. TEMPLE. Vol. I—XXVI. (Vol. XXVII in progress). Annual Subscription, £ 1. 16*s.*

Indian Terms. (A Glossary of). See: Temple.

Indian Wisdom. See: Monier-Williams.

Jastrow's Dictionary of the Targumim, the Talmud Babli and Yerushalmi, and the Midrashic Literature. Compiled by M. JASTROW, Ph. D. Parts I to IX. 4to. pp. 480. 5*s.* each Part.

"This is the only Talmudic dictionary in English, and all students should subscribe to it. The merits of this work are now too well known to need repetition." — *Jewish Chronicle.*

Jinalankara or **"Embellishments of Buddha",** by Buddharakkhita. Edited with Introduction, Notes and Translation, by JAMES GRAY. Two Parts in one. Demy 8vo. Cloth. 6*s.*

"The commendable care with which the volume has been prepared for the use of students is evident throughout its pages. — *Athenæum.*

Johnson (Capt. F. N). — The Seven Poems etc. See: Muallakat.

Johnston (C.) Useful Sanskrit Nouns and Verbs. In English Letters. Compiled by CHARLES JOHNSTON,

Bengal Civil Service, Dublin University Sanskrit Prizeman, India Civil Service Sanskrit Prizeman. Small 4to. Boards. pp. 30. 2*s.* 6*d.*

Johnston (C.) — The Awakening to the Self. Translated from the Sanskrit of Shankara the Master. Oblong 8vo. Paper covers. 2*s.*

Journal of the Buddhist Text Society of India. Edited by Sarat Candra Das, C. J. E. Vols. I to IV. 8vo. Calcutta, 1893—1897. £ 1. 10*s.*

Messrs. Luzac & Co. are the English agents for the above and can supply the Continuation. Subscription. 10*s.* each Vol.

Judson (A.) — English-Burmese Dictionary. Fourth Edition. Royal 8vo. Half bound. pp. 1752. £ 1. 12*s.*

Judson (A.) — Burmese-English Dictionary. Revised and enlarged by ROBERT C. STEVENSON. Royal 8vo. Paper covers. pp. 1192.

Kathâkoça. See Tawney.

King (Leonard W.) — Babylonian Magic and Sorcery. Being "The Prayers of the Lifting of the Hand". The Cuneiform Texts of a Group of Babylonian and Assyrian Incantations and magical Formulae, edited with Transliterations, Translations, and full Vocabulary from Tablets of the Kuyunjik Collection preserved in the British Museum. By LEONARD W. KING, M. A., Assistant in the Department of Egyptian and Assyrian Antiquities, British Museum. Roy. 8vo. Cloth. 18*s.* net.

"We cannot pretend to form an adequate judgment of the merits of Mr. KING's work, but it is manifestly conceived and executed in a very scholarly spirit." — *Times.*

"Mr. KING's book, will, we believe be of great use to all students of Mesopotamian religions, and it marks an era in Assyriological studies in England.... A word of special praise is due to Mr. KING for the excellence of his autograph plates of text." — *Athenæum.*

"The work will be found a valuable addition to our knowledge of Babylonian history, and to the study of comparative philology."
Morning Post.

King, L. W. See: Luzac's Semitic Text and Translation Series, Vols. II, IV and VI.

Kittel (Rev. F.) — A Kannada-English Dictionary. By Rev. F. KITTEL, B. G. E. M. Royal 8vo. Half-Bound. pp. L. 1725. £ 1. 12*s.*

Korean Repository. Vols. I to III. Annual Subscription 15*s.* Post free.

Land (J. P. N.) — The Principles of Hebrew Grammar. By J. P. N. LAND, Professor of Logic and Metaphysics in the University of Leyden. Translated from the Dutch by REGINALD LANE POOLE, Balliol College, Oxford. Demy 8vo. Cloth. pp. XX, 219 (Published 7*s.* 6*d.*) Reduced price 5*s.*

Lives of the Persian Poets Series. See Dawlatshah.

Loewe (L.) — A Dictionary of the Circassian Language. In two Parts. English—Circassian—Turkish, and Circassian—English—Turkish. 8vo. Cloth. (Published 21*s.*) Reduced price 6*s.*

Loewe (L.) Efes Damim. See: Efes.

Luzac's Oriental List. — Containing Notes and News on, and a Bibliographical List of all new Publications on Africa and the East. Published Monthly. Annual Subscription, 3*s.* Vols. I to VIII (1890—1897) are still to be had (with Index, half-bound), at £ 2. 15*s.*

Vols. I to IV are nearly out of print and can only be sold in the set. Vols V to VIII are still to be had at 5*s.* each vol.

"It deserves the support of Oriental students. Besides the catalogue of new books published in England, on the Continent, in the East, and in America, it gives, under the heading of "Notes and News" details about important Oriental works, which are both more full and more careful than anything of the sort to be found elsewhere." — *Academy.*

"A bibliographical monthly publication which should be better known." *The Record.*

Luzac's Semitic Text and Translation Series. Vol. I: See: Budge.

Vol. II. The Letters and Despatches of Hammurabi king of Babylon about B. C. 2250, to Sin-idinnam, King of Larsa, together with other royal and official correspondence of the same period: the Cuneiform texts edited with an Introduction and short descriptions by L. W. King, M. A.

This volume will contain about 100 letters relating to a variety of official subjects, and their contents are of great importance for the study of the history of Babylonia, Elam and the neighbouring districts about the time of the patriarch Abraham. These letters reveal the system by which Hammurabi maintained his rule in the remote provinces of his newly acquired empire, and contain some of the orders and directions which he issued for the movements of troops, for the building of canals and waterways, for the food-supply of his capital, and for the regulation of legal tribunals. The letters of Hammurabi are the oldest Babylonian despatches extant. — *Ready in June.*

Vol. III. The History of the Blessed Lady Mary the Virgin, and the History of the Image of Christ, which the men of Tiberias made to mock at; the Syriac text edited, with an English translation, by E. A. WALLIS BUDGE, Litt. D., D. Lit., etc. — *Ready in October.*

This Life of the Virgin is the fullest known to exist in Syriac, and varies in many important particulars from the versions of which fragments have already been published. The Life has been copied from an ancient Nestorian MS., to the text of which have been added all the variants found in the XVIth century MS. in the possession of the Royal Asiatic Society of Great Britain.

Vol. IV. The Letters and Despatches of Hammurabi together with other official and private correspondence of the same period, by L. W. KING, M. A.

This volume will contain a number of transliterations and translations of the texts of the 100 letters and despatches which are printed in volume 2; to these will be added indexes of proper names etc. and a List of Characters. An attempt will be made to give a description of the circumstances under which these letters were written, and short notes on points of grammar, history, etc. will be added. — *In the Press.*

Vol. V. The History of Rabban Hormizd by Mâr Simon, the disciple of Mâr Yôzâdhâḳ; the Syriac text edited, with an English translation by E. A. WALLIS BUDGE, Litt. D., D. Lit., etc.

The text describes the life of this famous Nestorian anchorite, the building of his monastery, and the struggle which went on in the VIIth century between the rival sects of Jacobites and Nestorians in Mesopotamia. This prose version of the life of Rabban Hormizd is, probably, the source from which the metrical versions were drawn; and it is of great importance for the study of the second great development of monasticism in Mesopotamia. — *In the Press.*

Vol. VI. Babylonian Private Letters written during the period of the First Dynasty of Babylon; the Cuneiform texts edited with Introduction and short descriptions by L. W. KING, M. A.

This volume will contain about 200 letters of a private nature which reveal the social condition of the country and incidentally throw much light upon the civilization of the period. From grammatical and lexicographical points of view these texts are of considerable importance, for they afford numerous examples of unusual words and forms of expression. — *In the Press.*

Vol. VII. The Life of Rabban Bar-Idtâ by John his disciple; The Syrac text edited, with an English translation, by E. A. WALLIS BUDGE, Litt. D., D. Lit., etc.

Bar-Idtâ was the founder of a famous rule and monastery in Mesopotamia in the VIIth century, and the author of a verv valuable work on monastic history which is quoted with respect by Thomas. Bishop of Margâ. He was a contemporary of Babhai of Mount Izlâ, and of Jacob of Bêth Abbê.

Volumes 5, 6, and 7 will, it is hoped be ready early next year.

Macnaghten (Sir W. Hay) — Principle of Hindu and Mohammedan Law. Republished from the Principles and Precedences of the same. Edited by the late H. H. WILSON. 8vo. Cloth. pp. 240. 6*s*.

Margoliouth (D. S.) — Arabic Papyri of the Bodleian Library reproduced by the Collotype Process. With Transcription and Translation. Text in 4to. pp. 7 and 2 Facsimiles in large folio. 5*s*.

Margoliouth (D. S.) — Chrestomathia Baidawiana. The Commentary of El-Baidâwi on Sura III. Translated and explained for the Use of Students of Arabic. By D. S. MARGOLIOUTH, M. A., Laudian Professor of Arabic in the University of Oxford, etc. etc. Post 8vo. Cloth. 12*s*.

"The book is as scholarly as it is useful. Of particular importance are the numerous grammatical annotations which give the beginner an insight into the method of the Arabic national grammarians, and which form an excellent preparatory study for the perusal of these works in the original..... The introduction and the remarks in particular show how well Mr. MARGOLIOUTH has mastered the immense literatures of Moslim Tradition, Grammar and Kalaım.... The perusal of the book affords pleasure from beginning to end." — *Journal Royal Asiatic Society.*

Mirkhond. — The Rauzat-us-Safa; or, Garden of Purity. Translated from the Original Persian by E. REHATSEK; edited by F. F. ARBUTHNOT. Vols. I to V. 10*s*. each Vol.

Vols. 1 and 2 contain: The Histories of Prophets, Kings and Khalifs.
Vols. 3 and 4 contain: The life of Muhammad the Apostle of Allah.
Vol. 5 contains: The Lives of Abû Bakr, O'mar, O'thmân, and Ali', the four immediate successors of Muhammad the Apostle.

Monier-Williams (Sir Monier) — Indian Wisdom; or Examples of the religious, philosophical, and ethical Doctrines of the Hindus, with a brief History of the chief Departments of Sanskrit Literature, and some account of the past and present Condition of India, moral and intellectual. By Sir MONIER MONIER-WILLIAMS, K. C. I. E., M. A., Hon. D. C. L., Oxford. Fourth Edition, enlarged and improved. Post 8vo. Cloth. pp. 575. £ 1. 1*s*.

"His book .... still remains indispensable for the growing public, which seeks to learn the outline of Indian literature and thought in a simple and readable form. We are glad to welcome the fourth edition of this eminently readable book." — *Daily Chronicle.*

"The learned professor's thorough mastery of his subject enables him to deal effectively with his difficult task. .... He omits nothing that enters the scope of his work: he is choice in his selections and accurate in his comments, and the result is a work as instructive and sound as it is pleasant to read." — *Asiatic Quarterly Review.*

"For all students of the philosophy of religion, as well as for all especially interested in Indian literature and thought, the work is one of very great value." — *Glasgow Herald.*

"It is a fine volume and contains valuable additions by the author .... this edition will be more than ever prized by students of Indian lore." *Scotsman.*

Muallakat. — The Seven Poems suspended in the Temple at Mecca. Translated from the Arabic. By Capt. F. E. JOHNSON. With an Introduction by Shaikh Taizullabhai. 8vo. pp. XXIV, 238. 7*s*. 6*d*.

"This handy volume decidedly supplies a great want for those who make a serious study of Arabic .... The grammatical, historical, geographical and other notes comments and explanations are ample and thorough". — *Imperial and Asiatic Quarterly Review.*

Müller (F. Max) — Address delivered at the Opening of the Ninth International Congress of Orientalists, held in London, Sept. 5, 1892, 8vo. pp. 66. 1*s*. 6*d*.

Mystic Flowery Land. See: Halcombe.

Oriental Translation Fund (New), See: Mírkhond, Tawney, Bana, and Harîri.

Oudemans Jzn. (A. C.) — The Great Sea-Serpent. An historical and critical Treatise. With the Reports of 187 Appearances (including those of the Appendix), the Suppositions and Suggestions of scientific and non-scientific Persons, and the Author's Conclusions. With 82 Illustrations. Royal 8vo. Cloth. pp. XV, 592. £ 1. 5*s*. net.

"The volume is extremely interesting". *Athenaeum.*

Reis Sidi Ali. The Travels and Adventures of the Turkish Admiral. In India, Afghanistan, Central Asia and Persia 1553—1556. Translated from the Turkish into English with notes. By H. VAMBERY. — *In the Press.*

Ridding (C. M.) — See: Bana's Kadambari.

Rosen (F.) — A Modern Persian Colloquial Grammar, containing a short Grammar, Dialogues and Extracts from Nasir Eddin Shah's Diaries, Tales, etc. and a Vocabulary. Cr. 8vo. Cloth. pp. XIV, 400. 10*s*. *6d*,

"Dr. ROSEN'S learned work will be useful to all who have occasion to go to Persia, Baluchistan, and Afghanistan. The Vocabulary will be a boon to students, especially as it is in the same volume with the grammar and the dialogues." — *Publ. Circular.*

"Very useful to students." — *Westminster Review.*

"Excellent Guide to the acquisition of Persian." — *Asiatic Quarterly Review.*

Rosthorn (A. de) — On the Tea Cultivation in Western Ssüch'uan and the Tea Trade with Tibet via Tachienlu. 8vo. pp. 40. With Sketch Map. 2*s*. net.

Ruben (Paul) — Critical Remarks upon some Passages of the Old Testament, by PAUL RUBEN, Ph. D. 4to. Cloth. pp. II. 24, 14. 3*s*. *6d.*

"It may suffice to congratulate ourselves that a scholar of vigorous mind and accurate philological training is devoting his leisure to a subject worthy of attention .... Very many of the notes are in a high degree stimulating and suggestive. The get up of the book is excellent". *Academy.*

"Dr. RUBEN shows much originality, a wide knowledge of authorities, and a true grasp of critical principles". — *Jewish Chronicle.*

Sacred Books of the Old Testament. — A critical Edition of the Hebrew Text, Printed in Colours, with Notes. Prepared by eminent Biblical Scholars of Europe and America. Under the editorial direction of PAUL HAUPT, Professor in the John Hopkins Univ. Baltimore. **Edition de Luxe,** in 120 numbered Copies only. 4to. Subscription price for the complete Work (20 Parts), £ 20.

Prospectuses sent on application. The following Parts have already been issued:

Part 1: **Book of Genesis,** by C. J. Ball. pp. 120. London. 1896. £ 2.
Part 3: **Leviticus,** by Prof. S. R. Driver. pp. 32. 1894. 16*s*.
Part 6: **Joshua,** by Prof. W. H. Bennet. pp. 32. 1895. £ 1.
Part 8: **Samuel,** by Prof. K. Budde. pp. 100. 1894. £ 1. 10*s*.
Part 11: **Jeremiah,** by Prof. C. H. Cornill. pp. 80. 1895. £ 1.
Part 14: **Psalms,** by J. Wellhausen, pp. 96. 1895. £ 1. 10*s*.
Part 18: **Book of Daniel,** by A. Kamphausen, 4to. pp. 44. 1896. £ 1.
Part 20: **Chronicles,** by R. Kittel. pp. 82. 1895. £ 1. 10*s*.

A valuable "Edition de Luxe" in 120 numbered copies only, and which may be described as the most splendidly got up Hebrew work in existence.

Each single part is numbered and signed by the editor with his own hand. The single parts will be issued in highly elegant covers. After the conclusion of the work a handsome binding cover will be supplied.

Sankaranarayana (P.) — English-Telugu Dictionary, by P. SANKARANARAYNA M. A., M. R. A. S., Tutor to their Highnesses the Princes of Cochin. 8vo. Cloth. pp. 61, 756, 10*s*. 6*d*.

Sanskrit Phonetics. A Manual of. See: Uhlenbeck.

Sanskrit Nouns and Verbs. See: Johnston.

Sayce (A. H.) — Address to the Assyrian Section of the Ninth International Congress of Orientalists. 8vo. pp. 32. 1*s*.

Sauerwein (G.) — A Pocket Dictionary of the English and Turkish Languages. Small 8vo. Cloth. limp. pp. 298. 3*s*. 6*d*.

Scholia on passages of the Old Testament. By MAX JACOB Bishop of Edessa. Now first edited in the original Syriac with an English translation and notes by G. PHILLIP. DD. 8vo. Paper Covers. 5*s.*

Seth (Mesrovb J.) — History of the Armenians in India. From the earliest Times to the present Day. 8vo. Cloth. pp. XXIV, 199. 7*s.* 6*d.* net.

"The subject is invested with peculiar interest at the present time by recent events in Asia Minor .... his unpretending little work is a valuable reportory of original information never before accessible in print and scarcely even known to exist." — *Times.*

"The book is happily distinguished among the number of books recently issued concerning Armenia in that it deals strictly with fact..... The volume deserves the attention of every one interested in the history of India and of the hardly treated race which seems to flourish better there than in its own country." — *Scotsman.*

"Sinnatamby". Letchimey. A Tale of Old Ceylon. 8vo. pp. III, 54. With Photogr. Plates and Illustrations. *In the Press.*

Stein (M. A.) — Catalogue of the Sanskrit MSS. in the Raghunata Temple Library of His Highness the Maharaja of Jammu and Kashmir. 4to. Cloth. pp. 423. 12*s.*

Steele's (R.) The Discovery of Secrets, attributed to Geber from the MS Arabic text. 8vo. 1*s.*

Stoffel (C.) Studies in English, Written and Spoken. For the Use of continental Students. With Index. First Series. Roy. 8vo. Cloth. pp. XII, 332. 7*s.* 6*d.*

Suhrillekha (The); or **"Friendly Letter;"** written by Lung Shu (Nàgàrjuna), and addressed to King Sadvaha. Translated from the Chinese Edition of I-Tsing, by the late Rev. SAMUEL BEAL, with the Chinese Text. 8vo. pp. XIII, 51. 5*s.*

Swami Vivekananda's Addresses. **See: Vivekananda.**

Tawney (C. H.) — The Kathákoça; or **Treasury of Stories.** Translated from Sanskrit Manuscripts. With Appendix, containing Notes, by Prof. ERNST LEUMANN. 8vo. Cloth. pp. XXIII, 260. 10*s.*

Temple (G.) — A Glossary of Indian Terms relating to Religion, Customs, Government, Land, and other Terms and Words in Common Use. To which is added a Glossary of Terms used in District Work in the N. W. Provinces and Oudh., and also of those applied to Labourers. With an Appendix giving Computation of Time and Money, and Weights and Measures, in British India, and Forms of Address. Roy. 8vo. Cloth. pp. IV, 332. *7s. 6d.*

"The book is moderate in price and clear in print." — *Athenæum.*

"The book is handy, well printed and well got up and no student of Indian subjects should be without it." — *Asiatic Quarterly Review.*

"Students of Oriental travel may find something servicable in its pages; and those who are engaged in trade in the East Indies might occasionally turn to the volume, with profit, if it were on the office shelf." — *The Nation.*

Temple (Major R. C.) — **Notes on Antiquities in Ramannadesa.** (The Talaing Country of Burma.) 4to. pp. 40. With 24 Plates and a Map. *18s.*

Thomas, F. W., See: Bāna, Harsa Carita.

Tiele (C. P.) — **Western Asia,** according to the Most Recent Discoveries. Rectorial Address on the Occasion of the 318th Anniversary of the Leyden University, 8th February, 1893. Translated by ELIZABETH J. TAYLOR. Small 8vo. Bound. pp. 36. *2s. 6d.*

"An authoritative summary of the results of recent Oriental research and discovery." — *The Times.*

"The address presents a graphic picture of the political situation in Western Asia in the fifteenth and fourteenth centuries B. C."
Morning Post.

"The professor's grasp of his subject is very evident, and his deductions from the materials commented on worthy of all attention."
Imperial and Asiatic Quarterly Review.

T'oung Pao. — **Archives pour servir à l'étude de l'histoire,** des langues, de la géographie et de l'ethnographie de l'Asie orientale. (Chine, Japon, Corée, Indo-Chine, Asie Centrale et Malaise.) Rédigées par MM. G. SCHLEGEL et H. CORDIER. Vol. I—VIII. Vol. IX in progress). Annual Subscription. £ 1

Transactions of the Ninth International Congress of Orientalists. London, 5th to 12th September, 1892.) Edited by E. DELMAR MORGAN. 2 Vols. Roy. 8vo. Cloth. £ 1. 15 *s.*

Vol. I. contains: Indian and Aryan Sections. £ 1. 1*s.*

Vol. II. contains: Semitic, Egypt and Africa, Geographical, Archaic Greece and the East, Persia and Turkey, China, Central Asia and the Far East, Australasia, Anthropology and Mythology Sections. £ 1. 1*s.*

Uhlenbeck. (C. C.). A Manual of Sanskrit Phonetics. In comparison with the Indogermanic mother-language, for students of Germanic and classical philology. 8vo. pp. 115. 6*s.*

Ummagga Yataka. See: Yatawara.

Usha. — The Dawn. A Vedic Periodical, edited by Pandit Satya Vrata Samasrami. 8vo. Published monthly. Annual subscription. £ 1. 1*s.*

Valmiki. — The Ramayan of Valmiki. Translated into English Verse, by R. T. H. GRIFFITH, M. A., C. I. E. Complete in one Volume. 8vo. Cloth. pp. IX, 576. 7*s.* 6*d.*

Vambery, see: Reis Sidi Ali.

Vivekânanda (Swami). — Lectures delivered in London. Nos. 1—12. 6*d.* each.

Vivekânanda (Swami). — Madras Lectures. 8vo. 1*s.* 6*d.*

Vizianagram Sanskrit Series. — Under the Superintendence of ARTHUR VENIS, M.A., Oxon, Principal, Sanskrit College, Benares. Different Prices.

West (Sir Raymond) — Higher Education in India: Its Position and Claims. 8vo. pp. 61. 1892. 1*s.*

Wildeboer (G.) — The Origin of the Canon of of the Old Testament. An historico-critical Enquiry. Translated by WISNER BAÇON. Edited with

Preface by Prof. GEORGE F. MOORE. Royal 8vo. Cloth. pp. XII, 182. 7*s*. 6*d*.

"We will only add that we cordially echo the professor's hope that his book may not only be read by professed students but that it may come also into the hands of such as have already left the University." *Guardian.*

"The method adopted is that of historical investigation: the student is thus enabled to see how the results of critical inquiry have been obtained .... he accompanies a guide who is familiar with the way which leads to them." — *Academy.*

"The first thing to notice is the translation. This is how a book ought to be translated .... The book must be used, not read merely ... it is independent, painstaking, farseeing." — *Expository Times.*

Winckler (H.) — The Tell-El-Amarna Letters. Transliteration, English Translation, Vocabulary, etc. Roy. 8vo. Cloth. pp. XLII, 416, and Registers 50 pages. £ 1. 1*s*. net.

The same. In Paper Covers. £ 1.

With the Dutch in the East. See: Cool.

Wright (W.) — The Book of Jonah in four Semitic versions. Chaldee, Syriac, Aethiopic and Arabic. With corresponding glossaries. 8vo. Cloth. pp. 148. 4*s*.

Wynkoop (J. D.) — Manual of Hebrew Syntax. Translated from the Dutch by C. VAN DEN BIESEN. 8vo. Cloth. pp. XXII, 152 and Index. 2*s*. 6*d*. net.

"It is a book, which every Hebrew student should possess, ... we recommend it for general usefulness, and thank Dr. van den Biesen for giving it to the English reader." — *Jewish World.*

"It is one of those books which will become indispensable to the English student who will desire to become acquainted with the construction of Hebrew syntax .... this takes a high rank and will undoubtedly become a general text book on the subject in many colleges and universities." *American Hebrew News.*

Wynkoop (J. D.) — Hebrew Grammar. Translated from the Dutch by C. VAN DEN BIESEN. 8vo. Cloth. 2*s*. 6*d*. net.

Yatawara (J. B.) — The Ummaga Yataka, translated into English. *In the Press.*

FOREIGN AND ORIENTAL BOOKS.

Messrs. LUZAC & Co. having Agents in all the principal Towns of the Continent, America and the East, are able to supply any Books not in stock at the shortest notice and at the most reasonable terms.

Subscriptions taken for all Foreign, American and Oriental Periodicals.

LIST OF
INDIAN GOVERNMENT PUBLICATIONS.

Messrs. LUZAC & Co. are Official Agents for the sale ot the Indian Government Publications.

Acts of the several Governments in India. Different dates and prices.
Aden Gazetteer. By Captain F. M. Hunter. 1877. 5*s*.
Adi Granth. By E. Trumpp. 1877. £ 1.
Agriculture, Report on Indian. By J. A. Voelcker, Ph. D. 1893. 3*s*. 6*d*.
Annals of the Calcutta Botanic Gardens:

I. Monograph on Ficus. Part 1. 1887. £ 1 5*s*.
„ „ Part 2. 1888. £ 2.
„ „ Appendix. 1889. 10*s*. 6*d*.
II. Species of Artocarpus, &c. 1889. £ 1 12*s* 6*d*.
III. Species of Pedicularis, &c. 1891. £ 3 10*s*.
IV. Anonaceæ of British India. 1893. £ 3 10*s*.
V., Part 1. A Century of Orchids. Memoir of W. Roxburgh. 1895. £ 3 3*s*. coloured, £ 1 12*s*. 6*d*. uncoloured.
V., Part 2. A Century of New and Rare Indian Plants. 1896. £ 1 12*s*. 6*d*.
VI., Part 1. Turgescence of Motor Organs of Leaves. Parasitic species of Choanephora. 1895. £ 1 10*s*.
VII. Bambuseæ of British India. 1896. £ 2.

Anwar-i-Soheli. By Colonel H. S. Jarrett. 1880. 15*s*.
Archæological Survey of India. (New Series):

IX. South Indian Inscriptions. By E. Hultzsch, Ph.D. Vol. I. 1890. 4*s*.
X. „ „ „ „ Vol. II, Part. 1. 1891. 3*s*. 6*d*.

South Indian Inscriptions. By E. Hultzsch, Ph.D. Vol. II, Part 2. 1892. 3*s.* 6*d.*

South Indian Inscriptions. By E. Hultzsch, Ph.D. Vol. II, Part 3. 1895. 5*s.* 6*d.*

XI. Sharqî Architecture of Jaunpur. By A. Führer, Ph.D. 1889. £ 1 1*s.* 6*d.*

XII. Monumental Antiquities in the North-West Provinces. By A. Führer, Ph.D. 1891. 13*s.* 6*d.*

XV. South Indian Buddhist Antiquities. By A. Rea. 1894. 12*s.* 6*d.*

XVII. Architectural, &c. Remains in Coorg. By A. Rea. 1894. 2*s.*

XVIII. The Moghul Architecture of Fatehpur Sikrî. By E. W. Smith. Part 1. 1894. £ 1 5*s.*

The Moghul Architecture of Fatehpur Sikri By E. W. Smith. Part 2. 1896. 17*s.* 6*d.*

XXI. Châlukyan Architecture. By A. Rea. 1896. £ 1 2*s.*

XXIII. Muhammadan Architecture in Gujarat. By J. Burgess, C.I.E., LL.D. 1896. £ 1.

Army List, The Indian. Quarterly. 4*s.*

Art Ware, Photographs of Madras and Burmese. 1886. £ 1 15*s.*

Arzis: Bengali, Canarese, Hindi, Mahratta, Malayalam, Tamil, Telugu, and Urdu. 7*s.* 6*d.* each.

Translations of the above (except Hindi). 7*s.* 6*d.* each.

Beer Casks, Destruction of, by a Boring Beetle. By W. F. H. Blandford. 1893. 6*d.*

Bibliographical Index of Indian Philosophical Systems. By F. Hall. 1859. 9*s.*

Bihar Peasant Life. By G. A. Grierson, Ph.D., C.I.E. 1885. 6*s.* 6*d.*

Bihari Language, Seven Grammars of. By G. A. Grierson, Ph.D. C.I.E. (8 parts). 1883—87. £ 1.

Bihari, The Satsaiya of. Edited by G. A. Grierson, Ph.D., C.I.E. 1896. 7*s.* 6*d.*

Bombay Gazetteer, Edited by J. M. Campbell, LL.D., C.I.E.:

I. (Not yet published). — II. Surat and Broach. 1877. 5*s.* 6*d.* — III. Kaira and Panch Mahals. 1879. 2*s.* 6*d.* — IV. Ahmedabad. 1879. 3*s.* — V. Cutch, Palanpur, and Mahi Kantha. 1880. 4*s.* — VI. Rewa Kantha, Narukot, Cambay, and Surat States. 1880. 3*s.* — VII. Baroda. 1883. 5*s.* — VIII. Kathiawar. 1884. 6*s.* 6*d.* — IX. (Not yet published). — X. Ratnagiri and Savantvadi. 1880. 5*s.* — XI. Kolaba and Janjira. 1883. 5*s.* — XII. Khandesh. 1880. 6*s.* — XIII. Thana. (2 parts). 1882. 8*s.* — XIV. Thana: places of interest. 1882. 5*s.* — XV. Kanara. (2 parts). 1883. 7*s.* 6*d.* — XVI. Nasik. 1883. 6*s.* 6*d.* — XVII. Ahmadnagar. 1884. 7*s.* — XVIII. Poona. (3 parts). 1885. 15 *s.* 6*d.* — XIX. Satara. 1885. 6*s.* 6*d.* — XX. Sholapur. 1884. 5*s.* — XXI. Belgaum. 1884. 6*s.* — XXII. Dharwar. 1884. 7*s.* 6*d.* — XXIII. Bijapur. 1884. 6*s.* 6*d.* — XXIV. Kolhapur. 1886. 5*s.* — XXV. Botany of the Presidency. 1886. 4*s.* 6*d.* — XXVI. Materials for a Statistical of Bombay Town and Island, Parts I., II., and III. 1893—94. 5*s.* each.

British Burma Gazetteer. Edited by H. R. Spearman. (2 vols.) 1879—80. £ 1 13*s.* 6*d.*

Buddha Gaya; the Hermitage of Sakya Muni. By Rajendralal Mitra. 1878. £ 3.

Burmese, Tables for the Transliteration of, into English. 1896. 1*s.*

Catalogue of the India Office Library, Vol. I (with Index). 1888. 10*s*. 6*d*.
" " " (Supplement). 1895. 5*s*.
" of the Arabic MSS. in the India Office Library. By O. Loth. 1877. 15*s*.
" of the Mandalay MSS. in the India Office Library. By V. Fausböll. 1897. 2 *s*.
" of the Pali MSS. in the India Office Library. By H. Oldenberg. 1882. 5*s*.
" of the Sanskrit MSS. in the India Officc Library. By Dr. J. Eggeling. (Parts I to V). 1887—96. 10*s*. 6*d*. each.
" of Sanskrit MSS., Bikanir. By Rajendralal Mitra. 1880. 3*s*.
" " " Tanjore. By A. C. Burnell. 1880. £ 1 11*s*. 6*d*.
" of MSS. in Oudh. By A. Sprenger 1854. 15*s*.

Chestnuts, Papers on Spanish. With Introduction by Sir George Birdwood, K. C. I., C. S. I. 1892. 1*s*.

Cholera, What can the State do to prevent is? By Dr. J. M. Cunningham. 1884. 3*s*.

Coorg Gazetteer. 1884. 5*s*.

Corpus Inscriptionum Indicarum:
I. Inscriptions of Asoka. By Major-General Sir A. Cunningham, K. C. I. E., C. S. I. 1877. 9*s*. 6*d*.
II. (Not yet published.)
III. Inscriptions of the early Gupta King. By J. F. Fleet, C. I. E. 1889. £ 1 13*s*. 6*d*. with plates. £ 1 without plates.

Covenanted Civil Servants, Manual of Rules applicable to. Second edition. 1891. 2*s*. 6*d*.

Dictionary of Indian Economic Products. By Dr. Geo Watt, C. I. E. (6 vols. in 9). 1889—93. £ 3 3*s*.
Ditto, Index to. 1896. 3*s*.

Durga puja. By Pratapa Chandra Ghosha. 1871. 6*s*.

English-Sanskrit Dictionary. By Sir M. Monier-Williams, K. C. I. E. 1851. £ 1 10*s*.

Fibres. Report on Indian. By C. F. Cross, E. J. Bevan, &c. 1887. 5*s*.

Finance and Revenue Accounts of the Government of India. Annual volumes. 2*s*. 6*d*. each.

Forest Working Plans. By W. E. D'Arcy. (Second edition). 1892. 1*s*. 6*d*.

Fort St. George Diary and Consultation Books: 1681 (Selection) 1893. 3*s*. 6*d*. — 1682. 1894. 4*s*. — 1683. 1894. 5*s*. 6*d*. — 1684. 1895. 5*s*. 6*d*. — 1685. 1895. 7*s*.

Geological Survey Department Publications.

Glossary of Indian Terms. By H. H. Wilson. 1855. £ 1 10*s*.

Hastings, Warren, Selections from the Records of the Foreign Department relating to the Administration of. Edited by G. W. Forrest, B. A. (3 vols.) 1890. 16*s*.
" " The Administration of. (A reprint of the Introduction to the foregoing.) By G. W. Forrest, B. A. 1892. 5*s*. 6*d*.

India Office Marine Records, List of. 1896. 5*s*.

Kachin Language, Handbook of the. By H. F. Hertz. 1895. 1*s*.

Lansdowne, Lord, The Administration of. By G. W. Forrest, B. A. 1894. 2*s*. 6*d*.
Lepcha Grammar. By Colonel G. P. Mainwaring. 1876. 3*s*.
Lighthouse Construction and Illumination, Report on. By F. W. Ashpitel. 1895. £ 1 9*s*. 6*d*.

Madras District Manuals (revised issues:)
South Canara (2 vols.) 1894. 4*s*.
North Arcot (2 vols.) 1895. 6*s*.
Malabar Manual. By W. Logan. (3 vols.) 1891. £ 1 2*s*. 6*d*.
Manava-Kalpa-Sutra. By Th. Goldstücker. 1861. £ 3.
Manual of Hydraulics. By Captain H. D. Love, R. E. 1890. 5*s*.
Marathi Dictionary. By J. T. Molesworth. 1857. 16*s*.
Marathi Grammar. By the Rev. Ganpatrao R. Navalkar. (Third edition.) 1894. 10*s*. 6*d*.
Meteorological Department Publications.
Muntakhabat-i-Urdu. (Second edition.) 1887. 1*s*. 10*d*.
Mutiny, the Indian, Selections from the Records of the Military Department relating to. Edited by G. W. Forrest, B. A. Vol. I. 1893. 12*s*. 6*d*.

North-East Frontier of Bengal, Relations of the Government with the Hill Tribes of the. By Sir Alexander Mackenzie, K. C. S. I. 1884. 6*s*. 6*d*.
North-West Provinces Gazetteer:
I. Bundelkhand, 1874. 8*s*. 6*d*. — II. Meerut Part. I. 1875. 6*s*. 6*d*. — III. Meerut, Part. II. 1876. 8*s*. 6*d*. — IV. Agra, Part. I. 1876. 8*s*. 6*d*. — V. Rohilkhand. 1879. 8*s*. 6*d*. — VI. Cawnpore, Gorakhpur and Basti. 1881. 9*s*. — VII. Farukhabad and Agra. 1884. 8*s*. — VIII. Muttra, Allahabad and Fatehpur. 1884. 10*s*. — IX. Shahjahanpur, Moradabad aud Rampur Native State. 1883. 8*s*. — X. Himalayan Districts, Part. I. 1882. 13*s*. — XI. Himalayan Districts, Part. II. 1884. 12*s*. 6*d*. — XII. Himalayan Districts Part. III. 1886. 12*s*. — XIII. Azamgarh, Ghazipur and Ballia 1883. 8*s*. — XIV. Benares, Mirzapur and Jaunpur. 1884. 10*s*.

Oudh Gazetteer. (3 vols.) 1877—78. £ 1.

Paintings, &c. in the India Office, Descriptive Catalogue of. By W. Forster. 1893. 1*s*.
Prakrita Prakasa. By E. B. Cowell. 1854. 9*s*.
Prem Sagar. By E. B. Eastwick. 1851. 15*s*.

Rajputana Gazetteer. (3 vols.) 1879—80. 15*s*.
Rigveda Sanhita. Vols. IV to VI. By Professor Max Müller. 1862—74. £ 2 12*s*. 6*d*. per volume.
Index to ditto. £ 2 5*s*.
Rigveda Translations. By H. H. Wilson. Vols I, III and IV. 1850—66. 13*s*. 6*d*. per volume.
Vols. V and VI. 1888. 18*s*. per volume.

Sanskritt MSS. in S. India, First and Second Reports on. By Dr. Hultzsch. 1895—96. 1*s*. 8*d*. each.
Scientific Memoirs by Medical Officers of the Indian Army:
Part I. 1885. 2*s*. 6*d*. — Part II. 1887. 2*s*. 6*d*. — Part III. 1888.

4*s.* — Part IV. 1889. 2*s.* 6*d.* — Part V. 1890. 4*s.* — Part VI. 1891. 4*s.* — Part VII. 1892. 4*s.* — Part VIII. 1893. 4*s.* — Part IX. 1895. 4*s.*

Selections from the Records of the Burmese Hluttaw. 1889. 6*s.*

Sikkim Gazetteer. By H. H. Risley, C. I. E., and others. 1894. 12*s.* 6*d.*

Specimens of Languages in India. By Sir G. Campbell, K. C. S. I. 1874. £ 1. 16*s.*

Survey Department Publications.

Surveys 1875—90, Memoir on the Indian. By C. E. D. Black. 1891. 7*s.* 6*d.*

Tamil Papers. By Andrew Robertson. 1890. 4*s.*

Technical Art Series of Illustrations of Indian Architectural Decorative Work for the use of Art Schools and Craftsmen:

1886—87. (6 plates.) 2*s.* — 1888—89. (18 plates.) 6*s.* — 1890. (12 plates.) 4*s.* — 1891. (18 plates.) 6*s.* — 1892. (13 plates.) 4*s.* 6*d.* — 1893. (12 plates) 4*s.* — 1894. (14 plates.) 5*s.* — 1895. (12 plates.) 4*s.* — 1896. (15 plates.) 4*s.*

Telegu Reader. By C. P. Brown. (2 vols.) 1852. 14*s.*

Textile Manufactures and Costumes of the People of India. By Dr. Forbes. Watson. 1866. £ 1. 1*s.*

Tibetan-English Dictionary. By H. A. Jaeschke. 1881. £ 1.

Timber, Mensuration of. By P. J. Carter. 1893. 1*s.*

Tobacco. Cultivation and Preparation of; in India. By Dr. Forbes Watson. 1871. 5*s.*

Tombs or Monuments in Bengal, Inscriptions on. Edited by C. R. Wilson, M.A. 1896. 3*s.* 6*d.*

Vikramarka, Tales of. By Ravipati Gurumurti. 1850. 1*s.*

Yield tables of the Scotch Pine. By W. Schlich, Ph. D. 1889. 1*s.*

N.B. In addition to the above, a large number of departmental reports, &c., are on sale at the various Government presses in India. These publications are not kept in stock at the India Office; but should copies of them be required, they will be furnished (on payment), as far as possible, from the supply received for official purposes.

In all cases applications for publications must be made through the official agents.

INDEX OF PRIVATE NAMES.

LUZAC'S ORIENTAL LIST.

NOTICE TO OUR READERS.

With this number we enter upon the eighth year of the publication of our «Oriental List." Four years ago in the first number of our fourth volume we thanked our readers for the generous support we had received from various quarters, including some flattering notices in our contemporaries referring to the value of our «List", and we now tender our thanks to an extended circle of readers. Within recent years the number of works on oriental subjects has increased enormously, and our «List" was started with the object of furnishing a record of such works which should be published at regular intervals. Our aim has therefore been to give each month a complete list of oriental books published in England, on the Continent, in the East and in America, while under the heading «Notes and News" we have endeavoured to give a faithful account of the progress made during the month in the various branches of oriental learning, literature and archaeology. The encouragement we have continuously received from the beginning of the undertaking emboldens us to believe that the «List" has really supplied a want on the part of those who from taste or profession are interested in the languages, literatures and antiquities of the East, and we therefore venture to appeal to our readers who are in the habit of consulting our «List" when making out their orders to send them to us direct.

LONDON, Jan. '98. LUZAC & Co.

PRINTED BY E. J. BRILL, LEYDEN (HOLLAND).

Lightning Source UK Ltd.
Milton Keynes UK
UKHW020620080419
340664UK00005B/664/P